Biological Psychology

TENTH EDITION

James Kalat

Prepared by

Elaine Hull
Florida State University

Juan Dominguez
The University of Texas at Austin

CENGAGE
Learning

Australia • Brazil • Japan • Korea • Mexico • Singapore • Spain • United Kingdom • United States

ISBN-13: 978-0-495-80916-6
ISBN-10: 0-495-80916-0

Wadsworth
10 Davis Drive
Belmont, CA 94002-3098
USA

Cengage Learning is a leading provider of customized learning solutions with office locations around the globe, including Singapore, the United Kingdom, Australia, Mexico, Brazil, and Japan. Locate your local office at: **www.cengage.com/international**

Cengage Learning products are represented in Canada by Nelson Education, Ltd.

To learn more about Cengage Learning, visit **www.cengage.com/phychology**

Purchase any of our products at your local college store or at our preferred online store **www.ichapters.com**

Printed in the United States of America
1 2 3 4 5 6 7 12 11 10 09

Table of Contents

CHAPTER 1

The Major Issues

Introduction

Biological psychology is the study of the physiological, evolutionary, and developmental explanations of behavior and experience. Bird song provides an example of the four types of explanation. Increased testosterone levels during mating season cause a brain area that is important for singing to increase in size, providing a physiological mechanism for singing. Ontogenetic explanations focus both on the genes that prepare for a behavior and on experience during a sensitive period, when a bird must hear the appropriate song. Evolutionary explanations discuss the selection of traits in terms of their adaptive value to the organism. Similar behavior patterns in two different species suggests that those species evolved from a common ancestor. Functional explanations describe the advantages conferred by each trait. For example, a male bird's song attracts a female and deters competition from other males.

Human behavior is also subject to biological explanation. There are a number of theories about the relationship of the mind to the brain. According to the dualist position, the mind and the brain exist independently, but somehow interact. However, that "somehow" causes a problem. Monism holds that there is only one kind of substance, though various theorists differ as to whether that substance is mental, physical, or some combination of the two. The materialist position (a form of monism) holds that everything that exists is material (physical). Mentalism suggests that only the mind really exists. The identity position (another form of monism) proposes that mental processes are the same thing as brain activity but are described in different terms.

David Chalmers proposed that there are "easy problems" concerning the specific application of the term consciousness to wakefulness vs. sleep, or to the focusing of attention, for example. However, the "hard problem" is how *any* kind of brain activity is associated with consciousness. One approach is to determine what brain activity is necessary and sufficient for consciousness. A major difficulty in studying consciousness is that it is not directly observable. This has led some to a solipsist position: I alone am conscious. However, while few people doubt that other people are conscious, they do question whether other animals, plants, or inanimate objects, including robots, are conscious. Neuroscience cannot resolve the issues of the essence and functional significance of the mind or of its relationship to the brain, but it can contribute relevant data.

Genes are the units of heredity; they maintain their structural identity from one generation to another. DNA (deoxyribonucleic acid, the substance of genes) serves as a template for the synthesis of messenger RNA (ribonucleic acid), which in turn provides a template for the production of structural proteins and enzymes. Chromosomes and the genes they contain come in pairs, one from each parent. An individual with identical genes of a given pair is said to be homozygous for that gene; an individual with an unmatched pair of genes is heterozygous for that gene. Genes may be dominant or recessive; dominant genes have strong effects in either homozygous or heterozygous individuals, whereas recessive genes have effects only in the homozygous condition. Sex-linked genes are usually found on the X chromosome; any characteristic produced by a recessive X-linked gene will be observed primarily in males, who do not have a second X chromosome to overrule the recessive gene. Sex-limited genes are found on autosomal chromosomes, and are therefore equally present in both sexes; however, their expression is activated by sex hormones that are more abundant in one sex than the other.

Heritability describes the extent to which variations in a characteristic are due to genetic, as opposed to environmental, variations. It is determined either by comparing the resemblance between monozygotic (identical) twins with that between dizygotic (fraternal) twins or by comparing the resemblance of adopted children to their adoptive vs. biological parents. New biochemical methods can provide evidence that certain genes are more common among people with a particular disorder, such as depression. Genetic influences on behavior may be either relatively direct, via control of brain chemicals, or indirect, by affecting height, attractiveness, or physical activity, for example. Furthermore, certain environmental conditions, such as malnutrition or severe stress, early in development can attach a methyl group to a gene and inactivate it. Heritability may be overestimated if members of a population live in similar environments, if genetic and prenatal influences are confounded, and if the effects of a trait are magnified by their influence on the social environment. Even traits with high heritability in "standard" conditions may be influenced by environmental interventions. For example, phenylketonuria (PKU) results from a recessive gene that prevents metabolism of the amino acid phenylalanine. The resulting high levels of phenylalanine lead to brain malformations and mental retardation. However, a diet low in phenylalanine can greatly reduce the abnormalities, although the diet is difficult to follow.

Evolution is a change over generations in the frequencies of various genes in a population. Genes that confer a reproductive advantage will become more prevalent in later generations. Neither use nor disuse of a given structure or behavior can cause an evolutionary increase or decrease in that feature, contrary to the theory of Lamarckian evolution. Furthermore, humans have not stopped evolving; medical treatments and welfare programs may increase survival, but may not enhance an individual's reproductive success. Evolution does not necessarily imply improvement, since previous success does not guarantee future success in a changing world. Evolution is based on the benefit for genes, not for individuals or species. Genes for altruistic behavior, for example, may be favored by reciprocal altruism or by kin selection. Evolutionary psychology seeks functional explanations for the evolution of social behaviors. However, these explanations are often speculative. Furthermore, even if genes do predispose us towards certain behavior patterns, we still have flexibility in acting on those predispositions.

The issue of animal experimentation has become controversial. The usefulness of animal research rests both on the similarity across species of many biological functions and on the difficulty or impossibility of conducting such research on humans. In addition, we are interested in animals, both for their own sake and for the light they can shed on human evolution. Some animal rights activists, the "abolitionists," believe that all animals have the same rights as humans and should never be used by humans for any purpose. "Minimalists" believe that some animal research is necessary, but that it should be minimized. Valuable clinical treatments of human disorders have been gleaned from animal experiments. However, even though experimenters attempt to minimize pain, and even though animal care committees (which include veterinarians and community members as well as scientists) oversee the research, a certain amount of distress accompanies much animal experimentation. In this case, as in many other ethical issues, it is difficult to resolve the competing values.

Learning Objectives

Module 1.1 The Mind-Brain Relationship
1. Be able to describe four kinds of biological explanations of behavior and give an example of each.
2. Understand the two major positions concerning the relationship between the brain and conscious experience.
3. Know which kinds of problems are thought to be "hard" or "easy."
4. Be able to describe the professionals who conduct neuroscience research and who provide clinical treatment for brain disorders.

Module 1.2 The Genetics of Behavior
1. Understand the concept of Mendelian genetics.
2. Be able to describe the relationship between DNA, RNA, and proteins.
3. Understand the concepts of dominant and recessive genes and of sex-linked and sex-limited genes.
4. Understand the concept of heritability and reasons why it can be overestimated.
5. Be able to discuss natural selection and the goals and criticisms of evolutionary psychology.

Module 1.3 The Use of Animals in Research
1. Understand the reasons for animal research.
2. Be able to discuss the ethical debate concerning the use of animals in research.
3. Be able to describe the regulatory committees that oversee animal research.

Key Terms and Concepts

Module 1.1 The Mind-Brain Relationship
1. Biological explanations of behavior
   No need for organism to understand function of behavior
   Physiological explanation
       Relates a behavior to activity of the brain and other organs
       Testosterone and bird song: increase in size of a brain area
   Ontogenetic explanation

Describes the development of a structure or behavior

Song development: requires both genes and hearing song during early sensitive period

Evolutionary explanation

Examines a structure or behavior in terms of evolutionary history

Common ancestor

Functional explanation

Describes why a structure or behavior evolved as it did

Genetic drift within isolated community

Appearance and behavior as camouflage

Male sings to attract mate and defend territory

2. The brain and conscious experience

Dualism: mind and body—different kinds of substance; exist independently but interact

Rene Descartes

Pineal gland

Conflict: law of conservation of matter and energy

Monism: only one kind of existence

Materialism

Mentalism

Identity

Mental and brain processes described in different terms

Mind is brain activity

Function of consciousness?

Solipsism: I alone exist.

Problem of other minds

David Chalmers

Easy problems: difference between wakefulness and sleep; mechanisms that focus attention

Hard problem: how any brain activity is associated with consciousness

Problem of other minds

Other mammals? Insects? Rocks?

Just-fertilized egg?

Computers? Robots?

Humans: programmed by genes and past experiences

3. Career opportunities

Research fields

Require Ph.D. in psychology, biology, neuroscience, or related field

Therapy fields

Clinical, counseling, or school psychologist

Medical fields

Neurologist

Social worker

Clinical psychologist

Allied medical fields

Physical therapist

4. In closing: Your Brain and Your Experience

Module 1.2 The Genetics of Behavior

1. Mendelian genetics
    - Genes: units of heredity that maintain structural identity from one generation to another
        - Chromosomes
        - Deoxyribonucleic acid (DNA)
            - Template for ribonucleic acid (RNA)
        - Translation of RNA
            - Structural proteins or enzymes
        - Homozygous vs. heterozygous
        - Dominant vs. recessive
            - Recessive gene: effects only in homozygous condition
                - Ability to taste phenylthiocarbamide (PTC)
    - Sex-linked and sex-limited genes
        - Sex-linked: genes on sex chromosomes
        - Autosomal genes
        - X and Y chromosomes
            - Y chromosome: genes for only 27 proteins
                - Some sites influence genes on other chromosomes
            - X chromosome: genes for 1500 proteins
            - Most sex-linked genes on X chromosome
                - Recessive gene for red-green color vision deficiency
        - Sex-limited genes: genes activated by sex hormones

2. Heredity and environment
    - Individual differences: due to differences in heredity or environment?
        - Monozygotic ("from one egg," "identical") twins
        - Dizygotic ("from two eggs," "fraternal") twins
        - Adopted children: resemblance to biological parents → high heritability
    - New biochemical methods
        - Specific genes associated with a disorder
        - Significant heritability of most behaviors
    - Possible complications
        - Overestimating heritability
            - Biological mother also provides prenatal environment
            - Early experience → attachment of methyl group to a gene → inactivation of gene → passed on to next generation
        - Multiplier effect: environment magnifies early tendencies
    - Environmental modification
        - Phenylketonuria (PKU)
        - Inability to metabolize phenylalanine
        - Brain malformations, mental retardation, irritability
        - Modified by low phenylalanine diet
        - "Heritable" not equal to "unmodifiable"
        - Diet difficult to follow
    - How genes affect behavior
        - Increasing production of a protein
        - Indirect effects

3. The evolution of behavior
    Evolution: change over generations in frequencies of various genes in a population
        Evolutionary tree
        Genes associated with reproductive success
            Artificial selection
        Natural selection
    Common misunderstandings about evolution
        Does use or disuse cause evolutionary change in that feature?
            Lamarckian evolution
        Have humans stopped evolving?
        Does evolution mean improvement?
            Fitness: number of copies of genes that endure in later generations
            Current genes evolved because they were fit for previous generations
        Does evolution benefit individual or species?
            Neither: genes
    Evolutionary psychology
        Functional explanations
        Altruistic behavior
        Group selection
        Reciprocal altruism
        Kin selection
  In closing: Genes and behavior
        Flexibility in acting on predispositions

Module 1.3 The Use of Animals in Research
1. Reasons for animal research
    Similar mechanisms of behavior and ease of studying animals
    Curiosity about animals
    Clues to human evolution
    Can't experiment on humans
2. The ethical debate
    Animal research → useful discoveries
    Degrees of opposition
    Minimalists vs. abolitionists
      Possible compromise
        Three Rs:
            Reduction in animal numbers
            Replacement with computer models or other substitutes
            Refinement by reducing pain and discomfort
    Institutional Animal Care and Use Committees
    National laws and professional organization guidelines
  In closing: Humans and animals
        Difficulty of resolving moral issues

Short-Answer Questions

Module 1.1 The Mind-Brain Relationship

1. *Biological explanations of behavior*

   a. What should we infer about an animal's or human's understanding of his or her behavior?

   b. What are the four major types of explanation of behavior sought by biological psychologists?

   c. What is the effect of testosterone on the brain of male songbirds?

   d. What is an ontogenetic explanation?

   e. What is an evolutionary explanation?

   f. What are the two functions of the male bird's song?

   g. What is genetic drift, and under what circumstances does it occur?

2. *The brain and conscious experience*

   a. What are the two major positions regarding the mind-brain relationship? List the main variants of these major positions. Give a strength and a weakness of each of these positions.

   b. According to David Chalmers, what kinds of issues do "easy problems" deal with?

   c. What is the main "hard problem"?

   d. What is the problem of other minds? How does solipsism deal with that problem?

   e. How do non-solipsists deal with the problem of other minds in humans? In animals, rocks, or computers?

   f. Describe the main issues studied by neuroscientists, and specifically, behavioral neuroscientists.

   g. What is a neuropsychologist? Where do they usually work?

   h. What does a psychophysiologist study?

   i. What issues do neurochemists investigate?

   j. Compare the main issues studied by comparative psychologists with those studied by evolutionary psychologists.

   k. Distinguish among neurologists, neurosurgeons, and psychiatrists.

Module 1.2 Nature and Nurture

1. *The genetics of behavior*

   a. Briefly, what is a gene?

   b. What is the relationship between DNA and RNA? Between one type of RNA and protein molecules?

c. What are two major functions of protein molecules?

d. What does it mean for an individual to be homozygous for a particular gene? Heterozygous?

e. What is a dominant gene? When can the effects of a recessive gene be seen?

f. On which chromosome are almost all sex-linked genes?

g. What is a sex-limited gene? On which chromosomes may it occur? Why are its effects usually limited to one sex?

h. How is heritability of a trait determined?

i. What three factors may lead to overestimation of heritability? What is the multiplier effect?

j. What is phenylketonuria (PKU)? How can its effects be modified?

k. What are some of the ways in which genes may influence behavior?

2. *The evolution of behavior*

a. What is evolution?

b. What is artificial selection?

c. Does the use or disuse of a structure or behavior cause an evolutionary increase or decrease in that feature? What is Lamarckian evolution?

d. Have humans stopped evolving?

e. Does evolution always imply improvement? Why or why not?

f. How can a gene that promotes altruistic behavior be maintained in evolution, if it places its possessor in danger?

g. What kinds of issues do evolutionary psychologists seek to explain? What is a criticism of this approach?

Module 1.3 The Use of Animals in Research

1. *Reasons for animal research*

a. What are four reasons biological psychologists study nonhuman animals?

2. *The ethical debate*

a. Compare the positions of the "minimalists" and the "abolitionists" with regard to the conduct of animal research.

b. What is the role of Laboratory Animal Care Committees? What groups are represented in their membership?

True/False Questions

1. Physiological explanations describe the development of a structure or behavior.

   TRUE or FALSE   *ontogenetic*

2. The observation that a male bird sings to attract a mate and defend his territory is a functional explanation.

   TRUE or FALSE

3. Rene Descartes believed that the pineal gland was the site at which mind and brain interact.

   TRUE or FALSE

4. According to David Chalmers, the hard problem is to discern the mechanisms that focus attention.

   TRUE or FALSE

5. DNA is the template for RNA.

   TRUE or FALSE

6. A sex-limited gene is one whose expression depends on the presence of sex hormones, which are more abundant in one sex or the other.

   TRUE or FALSE

7. An autosomal gene is one located on the X or Y chromosome.

   TRUE or FALSE

8. Heritability may be overestimated in studies of biological children of low-IQ, criminal, or mentally ill parents, even if they were adopted at an early age, because the parents provided not only their genes but also their prenatal environment.

   TRUE or FALSE

9. The mental retardation caused by PKU can be completely ameliorated by providing a low-phenylalanine diet for the first 10-12 years of life.

   TRUE or FALSE

10. A gene can affect behavior directly by increasing or decreasing the production of a structural protein or an enzyme or indirectly by influencing height, weight, or activity level.

    TRUE or FALSE

11. Humans have stopped evolving, thanks to our fabulous medical system and social support network.

    TRUE or FALSE

12. The ethical treatment of animals depends solely on the good will and morals of individual researchers.

    TRUE or FALSE

Fill In The Blanks

1. The observation that testosterone increases the size of a brain area that controls singing is a(n) _physiol_ explanation.

2. The observation that bird song requires both genes and hearing song during the early sensitive period is a(n) _ontogenetic_ explanation.

3. The observation that the tendency of humans to have "goose bumps" in frightening situations is related to the erection of hairs in our hairier ancestors, which made them look larger, is a(n) _evolutionary_ explanation.

4. The spread of a gene within a small isolated community is called _genetic drift_.

5. Rene Descartes was a(n) _dualist_, who believed that mind and body interact at the _pineal gland_.

6. Three types of monism are _materialism_, _mentalism_, and _identity_.

7. The search for neural mechanisms that distinguish waking and sleep is a pursuit of a(n) _easy_ problem.

8. The belief that "I alone exist" is referred to as _solipsism_.

9. The units of heredity that maintain structural identity from one generation to another are _genes_.

10. The function of _DNA_ is to serve as a template for one type of RNA, which in turn is translated into _proteins_ or _enzymes_.

11. An individual who has an identical pair of genes on the two matched chromosomes is said to be _homozygous_ for that gene.

12. The inability to metabolize phenylalanine is called _PKU_.

13. The proposal that use or disuse can cause evolutionary change in a feature is called _Lamarckian_.

14. The field of study that seeks functional explanations for how behavior evolved is called _evolutionary_.

15. People who believe that no animal should ever be used by humans for any purpose are called _abolitionist_.

16. People who believe that animal research is useful, but that it should be closely regulated, are called _minimalist_.

17. Institutional Animal Care and Use Committees that oversee the use of animals in research include _vets_, _community_, and _scientists_ as members.

Matching Items

1. ___h___ Dualist
2. ___j___ Type of monism
3. ___g___ Easy problem
4. ___i___ Hard problem
5. ___k___ Template for protein synthesis
6. ___a___ Dizogotic twin
7. ___f___ Monozygotic twin
8. ___d___ Sex-limited gene
9. ___b___ Sex-linked gene
10. ___c___ PKU
11. ___e___ Lamarckian evolution

a. Fraternal twin
b. Gene on X chromosome that is expressed mostly in males
c. Inability to metabolize phenylalanine
d. Autosomal gene that depends on sex hormone for expression
e. Belief in evolutionary change caused by use or disuse
f. Identical twin
g. Difference between waking and sleeping
h. Rene Descartes
i. How any brain activity is associated with consciousness
j. Materialism
k. RNA

Multiple-Choice Questions

1. Which of the following is not a major category of biological explanation?
   a. physiological explanations
   b. ontogenetic explanations
   c. evolutionary explanations
   d. mental explanations

2. Most adult male songbirds
   a. sing throughout the year and throughout wide territories.
   b. sing when testosterone levels are high enough to increase the size and activity of a brain area that is critical for singing.
   c. sing because they are consciously aware that their songs will attract females and deter male competitors.
   d. sing the correct song, even if they have never heard the song.

3. The dualist position
   a. is problematic because it does not fit with our commonsense notion of the mind.
   b. proposes that the mind is the same thing as brain activity.
   c. cannot explain how, if the mind is not a type of matter or energy, it could possibly alter the electrical and chemical activities of the brain.
   d. proposes that mind is just an illusion.

4. The view that everything that exists is physical, and that mental events either don't exist or can be explained in purely physical terms, is characteristic of which position?
   a. materialism
   b. dualism
   c. mentalism
   d. functionalism

5. David Chalmers proposed that the "hard problem" concerning consciousness
   a. is how neural mechanisms differentiate between wakefulness and sleep and allow us to focus our attention.
   b. is why and how *any* kind of brain activity is associated with consciousness.
   c. really consists of an enormous number of easy problems.
   d. is impossible to answer, under any circumstances.

6. A solipsist
   a. assumes that other people, animals, and computers are conscious because they look and/or act much like I do.
   b. assumes that other people are conscious, but animals and computers are not.
   c. assumes that I alone exist, or I alone am conscious.
   d. is frequently a member of an organization called Solipsists United.

7. The order of bases on DNA
   a. determines the order of bases on RNA, which in turn determines the order of amino acids in proteins.
   b. directly determines the order of amino acids in proteins, which in turn determines the order of bases in RNA.
   c. is less important for genetic function than is the total number of particular bases.
   d. is more important for determining the shapes of carbohydrates and fats than of proteins.

8. An individual with a pair of identical genes at a given site on a pair of chromosomes
   a. is homozygous for that gene.
   b. is heterozygous for that gene.
   c. must have phenylketonuria.
   d. must not have the ability to taste phenylthiocarbamide.

9. Sex-linked genes are usually
   a. genes on autosomal chromosomes that are expressed only under hormonal conditions that are usually found only in one sex.
   b. genes on autosomal chromosomes that are expressed in both sexes.
   c. genes on the X chromosome, which cannot be overridden by a second X chromosome in males.
   d. genes that govern the development of the genitalia.

10. Heritability can be overestimated
    a. if populations are studied in extremely varied environmental conditions.
    b. because a democratic society treats all individuals similarly.
    c. because parents provide their offspring both genes and prenatal environment.
    d. all of the above

11. Phenylketonuria (PKU)
    a. is a heritable condition.
    b. results from inability to metabolize phenylalanine, which results in high levels of that amino acid, which in turn results in brain damage and mental retardation.
    c. effects can be minimized by a low phenylalanine diet throughout the affected individual's life.
    d. all of the above

12. The survival of genes for altruistic behavior
    a. can be explained by either reciprocal altruism or kin selection.
    b. can be explained by the fact that altruism to strangers is not in fact harmful to the individual.
    c. can be explained by both a and b
    d. cannot be explained at all and is likely to die out in later generations.

13. Animal research
    a. yields no useful discoveries.
    b. is regulated by Institutional Animal Care and Use Committees, which are composed of veterinarians, community representatives, and scientists.
    c. depends entirely on the wisdom and good intentions of individual researchers for maintaining good care of the animals.
    d. all of the above

14. "Abolitionist" animal advocates
    a. agree that some animal research is acceptable if an important goal can be achieved with minimal suffering.
    b. maintain that use of primates in experimentation should be abolished, but that "lower" animals may be used.
    c. maintain that all animal experimentation, as well as any other use of animals, should be totally eliminated.
    d. are also called "minimalists."

Solutions

True/False Questions

1.	F	4.	F	7.	F	10.	T
2.	T	5.	T	8.	T	11.	F
3.	T	6.	T	9.	F	12.	F

Fill In The Blanks

1. physiological
2. ontogenetic
3. evolutionary
4. genetic drift
5. dualist; pineal gland
6. materialism; mentalism; identity.
7. easy
8. solipsism
9. genes
10. DNA; structural proteins; enzymes
11. homozygous
12. phenylketonuria (PKU)
13. Lamarckian evolution
14. evolutionary psychology
15. abolitionists
16. minimalists
17. veterinarians; community members; scientists

Matching Items

1.	h	4.	i	7.	f	10.	c
2.	j	5.	k	8.	d	11.	e
3.	g	6.	a	9.	b		

Multiple Choice Questions

1.	d	5.	b	9.	c	13.	b
2.	b	6.	c	10.	c	14.	c
3.	c	7.	a	11.	d		
4.	a	8.	a	12.	a		

CHAPTER 2

Nerve Cells and Nerve Impulses

Introduction

Neurons, like all animal cells, are bounded by a fatty membrane, which restricts the flow of chemicals into and out of the cell. Animal cells also contain structures, such as a nucleus, ribosomes, mitochondria, and an endoplasmic reticulum, that are important for various genetic, synthetic, and metabolic functions. A neuron is composed of (1) dendrites, which receive stimulation from other cells; (2) the soma or cell body, which contains the genetic and metabolic machinery and also conducts stimulation to the axon; and (3) the axon, which carries the nerve impulse to other neurons, frequently across long distances. Sensory neurons are highly sensitive to specific external stimuli; motor neurons stimulate muscles and glands; and local neurons have either no axon or a very short one and can convey information only to adjacent neurons. One can infer a great deal about a neuron's function from its shape. For example, a neuron that integrates input from many sources has many branching dendrites. The nervous system also contains many support cells called glia, which help synchronize the activity of axons, remove waste, build myelin sheaths, and guide neurons during development and during regeneration of peripheral axons.

A blood-brain barrier prevents many substances, including most viruses and bacteria and most forms of nutrition, from entering the brain. In most parts of the brain, glucose is the only nutrient that can cross the barrier in significant amounts. Therefore, the brain is highly dependent on glucose and on thiamine (vitamin B_1), which is needed to metabolize glucose. Whereas fat-soluble molecules and small-uncharged molecules can cross the barrier freely, glucose, amino acids, purines, choline, a few vitamins, iron, and certain hormones require active transport. The barrier depends on tight junctions between endothelial cells lining the capillaries.

The ability of a neuron to respond quickly to stimulation depends on the resting potential. A metabolically active sodium-potassium pump establishes concentration gradients by transporting sodium (Na^+) ions out of the cell and potassium (K^+) ions into the cell. There is a resultant negative charge inside the cell, because three sodium ions are pumped out for every two potassium ions pumped in. Selective permeability of the membrane increases this potential by allowing potassium ions to flow out, down their concentration gradient; the loss of the positive potassium ions leaves the inside of the neuron even more negative. The relative impermeability of sodium results in minimal inflow of positive ions to offset the potassium outflow. The concentration and electrical gradients exert opposing influences on potassium. The electrical gradient (the negative charge inside the cell) attracts more potassium inside the cell than would be there if the concentration gradient were the only influence. Sodium ions, however, are attracted to the inside by both the electrical and concentration gradients. Therefore, when the sodium channels are opened, there is considerable impetus for sodium to flow into the cell.

A neuron may receive input that either hyperpolarizes it (makes the inside more negative) or depolarizes it (makes the inside less negative). If the membrane is depolarized to a threshold level, it briefly loses its ability to exclude sodium ions, and these ions rush in through voltage-gated sodium channels. They cause the inside of the neuron to become positive, at which point the membrane quickly becomes impermeable to sodium again. However, as the neuron becomes more depolarized, voltage-gated potassium channels open, resulting in even greater permeability than usual to potassium, which is repelled out of the neuron by both the positive electrical gradient and its own concentration gradient. The exit of the positively charged potassium ions returns the neuron approximately to its previous resting potential. This rapid exchange of ions is called the action potential. All action potentials of a given axon are approximately equal in size, shape, and velocity, regardless of the size of the depolarization that gave rise to them. This principle is called the all-or-none law. Immediately after an action potential, a neuron is resistant to re-excitation, because sodium channels are closing and are resistant to reopening. During the 1 millisecond absolute refractory period, no stimulus can initiate a new impulse; during the subsequent relative refractory period of about 2-4 milliseconds, slight hyperpolarization resulting from potassium outflow makes it difficult, but possible, to produce an action potential. Greater variation in the types of protein channels present on mammalian axons brings about greater differences in the dimension of their action potentials, when compared to the previously studied squid axon.

Once an action potential occurs, entering sodium ions spread to adjacent portions of membrane, thereby depolarizing these areas to their threshold and allowing sodium to rush in there. Thus the action potential is regenerated at each succeeding area of the axon until it reaches the end. The regenerative flow of ions across the membrane is slower than electrical conduction within the axon. In some axons, 1-mm-long segments of myelin (a fatty insulating substance) are wrapped around the axon, with short uncovered segments (nodes of Ranvier) in between. The action potential is conducted passively with some decrement under the myelin sheath. There is still sufficient potential to depolarize the next node of Ranvier to its threshold, and the action potential is regenerated at full strength at each node. The impulse appears to "jump" from node to node. This mode of transmission is called saltatory conduction and is much faster than transmission without myelin. It forces the action potential to use the faster electrical conduction within the axon for a longer distance before engaging in the slower regenerative flow across the membrane. Very small local neurons use only graded potentials, not action potentials, because they transmit information over very short distances.

Learning Objectives

Module 2.1 The Cells of the Nervous System
1. Know the main structures of neurons and the structural differences among neurons.
2. Know the main types of glia and their functions.
3. Be able to describe the advantages and disadvantages of the blood-brain barrier.

Module 2.2 The Nerve Impulse
1. Understand why the neuron uses considerable energy to produce a resting potential.
2. Understand the competing forces of the electrical and concentration gradients on potassium ions and how this competition produces the resting potential.
3. Be able to describe the function and the molecular basis of the action potential.

4. Understand how an action potential is conducted down an axon and how myelin sheaths contribute to this process.
5. Know how local interneurons transmit information without benefit of action potentials.

Key Terms and Concepts

Module 2.1 The Cells of the Nervous System

1. Anatomy of neurons and glia
   Santiago Ramon y Cajal, a pioneer of neuroscience
   The structures of an animal cell
       Membrane
           Two layers of fat molecules
           Protein channels
       Nucleus
       Mitochondrion
       Ribosomes
       Endoplasmic reticulum
   The structure of a neuron
       Motor neuron
       Sensory neuron
       Dendrites
           Synaptic receptors
           Dendritic spines
       Cell body or soma
           Nucleus, ribosomes, mitochondria
       Axon
           Myelin sheath, node of Ranvier
           Presynaptic terminal, end bulb, or bouton
           Afferent
           Efferent
       Interneuron, intrinsic neuron
   Variations among neurons
       Purkinje cell of cerebellum
       Cells in retina
   Glia (neuroglia)
       Astrocytes
           Encircle several presynaptic terminals
           Take up, store, and transfer chemicals
           Help synchronize activity of axons
           Remove waste
           Help control blood flow
               Increase blood flow to areas experiencing heightened activity
       Microglia
           Remove waste, viruses, fungi
       Oligodendrocytes (brain and spinal cord) and Schwann cells (periphery)
           Form myelin sheaths

Surround and insulate vertebrate axons
   Radial glia (type of astrocyte): guide migrating neurons, growing axons and dendrites during development
    Following development, most differentiate into neurons

2. The blood-brain barrier
  Why we need a blood-brain barrier
   Virus-infected non-neural cells: targeted for destruction
   Virus-infected cells in nervous system: virus particles remain
   Area postrema: monitors blood chemicals that cannot enter other brain areas
  How the blood-brain barrier works
   Endothelial cells of capillaries
   Small uncharged molecules cross freely
   Fat-soluble molecules
   Active transport system
    Moves some chemicals from blood to brain
     Glucose
     Amino acids
     Purines, choline, and iron
     Certain vitamins and hormones
  Alzheimer's disease impairs blood-brain barrier
  Prevents many medications from entering brain

3. The nourishment of vertebrate neurons
  Dependence on glucose and oxygen
   Due to blood-brain barrier
   Ketones
   Liver: converts carbohydrates, amino acids, and glycerol into glucose
  Requirement for thiamine (vitamin B_1)
   Deficiency leads to Korsakoff's syndrome

4. In closing: Neurons
  Importance of communication among neurons

Module 2.2 The Nerve Impulse
1. The resting potential of the neuron
  Electrical gradient: difference in electrical charge between inside and outside of cell
  Phospholipid membrane with embedded proteins
  Polarization
  Resting potential
   Negatively charged proteins inside
   Microelectrode
  Forces acting on sodium and potassium ions
   Selective permeability
   Ion channels
   Sodium-potassium pump
    Moves three sodium ions out for every two potassium ions in

True/False Questions

1. Physiological explanations describe the development of a structure or behavior.

   TRUE or FALSE   *ontogenetic*

2. The observation that a male bird sings to attract a mate and defend his territory is a functional explanation.

   TRUE or FALSE

3. Rene Descartes believed that the pineal gland was the site at which mind and brain interact.

   TRUE or FALSE

4. According to David Chalmers, the hard problem is to discern the mechanisms that focus attention.

   TRUE or FALSE

5. DNA is the template for RNA.

   TRUE or FALSE

6. A sex-limited gene is one whose expression depends on the presence of sex hormones, which are more abundant in one sex or the other.

   TRUE or FALSE

7. An autosomal gene is one located on the X or Y chromosome.

   TRUE or FALSE

8. Heritability may be overestimated in studies of biological children of low-IQ, criminal, or mentally ill parents, even if they were adopted at an early age, because the parents provided not only their genes but also their prenatal environment.

   TRUE or FALSE

9. The mental retardation caused by PKU can be completely ameliorated by providing a low-phenylalanine diet for the first 10-12 years of life.

   TRUE or FALSE

10. A gene can affect behavior directly by increasing or decreasing the production of a structural protein or an enzyme or indirectly by influencing height, weight, or activity level.

    TRUE or FALSE

11. Humans have stopped evolving, thanks to our fabulous medical system and social support network.

    TRUE or FALSE

12. The ethical treatment of animals depends solely on the good will and morals of individual researchers.

    TRUE or FALSE

Fill In The Blanks

1. The observation that testosterone increases the size of a brain area that controls singing is a(n) _physiol_ explanation.

2. The observation that bird song requires both genes and hearing song during the early sensitive period is a(n) _ontogenetic_ explanation.

3. The observation that the tendency of humans to have "goose bumps" in frightening situations is related to the erection of hairs in our hairier ancestors, which made them look larger, is a(n) _evolutionary_ explanation.

4. The spread of a gene within a small isolated community is called _genetic drift_.

5. Rene Descartes was a(n) _dualist_, who believed that mind and body interact at the _pineal gland_.

6. Three types of monism are _materialism_, _mentalism_, and _identity_.

7. The search for neural mechanisms that distinguish waking and sleep is a pursuit of a(n) _easy_ problem.

8. The belief that "I alone exist" is referred to as _solipsism_.

9. The units of heredity that maintain structural identity from one generation to another are _genes_.

10. The function of _DNA_ is to serve as a template for one type of RNA, which in turn is translated into _proteins_ or _enzymes_.

11. An individual who has an identical pair of genes on the two matched chromosomes is said to be _homozygous_ for that gene.

12. The inability to metabolize phenylalanine is called _PKU_.

13. The proposal that use or disuse can cause evolutionary change in a feature is called _Lamarckian_.

14. The field of study that seeks functional explanations for how behavior evolved is called _evolutionary_.

15. People who believe that no animal should ever be used by humans for any purpose are called _abolitionist_.

16. People who believe that animal research is useful, but that it should be closely regulated, are called _minimalist_.

17. Institutional Animal Care and Use Committees that oversee the use of animals in research include _vets_, _community_, and _scientists_ as members.

Active transport
Sodium stays out; some potassium leaks out
Concentration gradient
More sodium outside
More potassium inside
Why a resting potential? Strong, fast response
Hyperpolarization, depolarization
Threshold of excitation
Action potential
Subthreshold stimulation small response
Stimulation beyond threshold of excitation leads to action potential

2. The molecular basis of the action potential
Voltage-gated channels
Sodium inflow: depolarization
Potassium outflow: temporary hyperpolarization
Drug effects
Scorpion venom: opens sodium channels and closes potassium channels
Local anesthetic: blocks sodium channels
The all-or-none law
Intensity of stimulus does not influence amplitude and velocity of action potential
Action potentials vary between neurons
The refractory period
Absolute refractory period
Relative refractory period

3. Propagation of the action potential
Axon hillock
Successive depolarization of adjacent areas
Diameter of the axon influences flow of ions
Regenerative ion flow slower than current spread in axon

4. The myelin sheath and saltatory conduction
Myelinated axons
Nodes of Ranvier
Saltatory conduction
Increases speed by increasing distance current spreads within axon
Conserves energy by decreasing sites of sodium inflow
Multiple sclerosis

5. Local neurons
Graded potentials
Depolarization
Hyperpolarization
Horizontal cell in retina
Astrocytes: exchange chemicals with neighboring neurons
Small neurons and big misconceptions

Large neurons easier to study
Small cells functionally important

6. In closing: Neural messages
Communication based on multiple on/off messages

Short-Answer Questions

Module 2.1 The Cells of the Nervous System

1. *Neurons and glia*

    a. What did Ramon y Cajal demonstrate?

    b. List the major structures of animal cells and give the main function of each.

    c. What are the main subdivisions of the neuron and the function of each?

    d. List several anatomical distinctions between dendrites and axons.

    e. What is the myelin sheath?

    f. What is the function of the presynaptic terminal or end bulb?

    g. Describe the structural and functional differences among sensory, motor, and local neurons.

    h. What do the terms afferent and efferent mean? Can an axon be both afferent and efferent? Explain.

    i. What is an intrinsic neuron?

    j. How do glia cells differ from neurons?

    k. What are four functions of glia?

    l. What are two functions of astrocytes?

    m. What two kinds of glia form myelin sheaths?

    n. What is the function of radial glia? What related function do Schwann cells perform?

2. *The blood-brain barrier*

    a. Why do we need a blood-brain barrier? Why don't we have a similar barrier around other body organs?

    b. What happens if a virus does enter the nervous system?

    c. Describe the arrangement of the endothelial cells that form the blood-brain barrier.

    d. What types of chemicals can cross the blood-brain barrier freely?

    e. How does the area postrema differ from most other brain areas? What is its major function.

    f. What is the role of the active transport system? What types of chemicals are transported in this way?

    g. How does Alzheimer's disease affect the blood brain barrier?

    h. What prevents some medications from entering the brain?

3. *The nourishment of vertebrate neurons*

   a.   What is the major fuel of neurons?

   b.   Why can't most parts of the adult brain use fuels other than glucose?

   c.   Why is a shortage of glucose usually not a problem?

   d.   Why is a diet low in thiamine a problem? What is Korsakoff's syndrome?

Module 2.2 The Nerve Impulse

1. *The resting potential*

   a.   What is the composition of the membrane covering the neuron? Describe its structure.

   b.   How is the electrical potential across the membrane measured?

   c.   What is meant by selective permeability of the membrane? Which chemicals can cross the membrane and which ones cannot? How do a few biologically important ions cross?

   d.   What is the sodium-potassium pump? How does its exchange of sodium and potassium ions lead directly to an electrical potential across the membrane?

   e.   How does the selective permeability of the membrane increase the electrical potential?

   f.   Describe the competing forces acting on potassium ions. Why don't all the potassium ions surrounding a neuron migrate inside the cell to cancel the negative charge there?

   g.   What is the advantage of expending energy during the "resting" state to establish concentration gradients for sodium and potassium?

2. *The action potential*

   a.   What happens to the electrical potential of a cell if a negative charge is applied? What is this change called?

   b.   What happens to the potential if a brief, small positive current is applied? What is this change called?

   c.   What happens to the potential if a threshold depolarization is applied?

   d.   What does the term "voltage-gated sodium channels" mean?

   e.   What causes the initial rapid increase in positivity of the action potential?

   f.   What accounts for the ensuing repolarization? Why does the neuron hyperpolarize slightly, rather than stopping at the previous resting potential?

   g.   What effect does scorpion venom have on the membrane?

   h.   What is the effect of local anesthetic drugs like Novocain and Xylocaine?

   i.   What is the all-or-none law? How may a neuron signal "greater than"?

   j.   What is the absolute refractory period? What causes it?

   k.   What is the relative refractory period? What causes it?

3. *Propagation of the action potential*

   a.   How does an action potential propagate down an axon?

   b.   How does diameter of axon influence flow of ions?

4. *The myelin sheath and saltatory conduction*

   a.   What is the major advantage of the myelin sheath, and how is this advantage conferred?

   b.   What is a node of Ranvier? What would happen if the axon were wrapped with one long expanse of myelin, without any nodes of Ranvier?

   c.   What is meant by saltatory conduction?

5. *Signaling without action potentials*

   a.   In what ways is transmission by local neurons different from the usual conduction by axons? Why is this local transmission restricted to very short distances?

True/False Questions

1. Ramon y Cajal demonstrated that neurons are continuous with one another, providing a basis for our sense of unified beings.

   TRUE or FALSE

2. The membrane of a cell consists of a bilayer of protein molecules, through which only electrically charged ions and molecules can pass.

   TRUE or FALSE

3. Neurons that are afferent to one structure can also be efferent from another structure.

   TRUE or FALSE

4. Dendrites carry information from one neuron to another, releasing neurotransmitters from their end bulbs (boutons).

   TRUE or FALSE

5. Dendritic spines increase the surface area available for synapses.

   TRUE or FALSE

6. Intrinsic neurons typically have long axons that convey action potentials from one brain area to another.

   TRUE or FALSE

7. Astrocytes are glia that wrap around the terminals of several axons and, by taking up and then releasing chemicals released by axons, may help to synchronize the activity of those axons.

   TRUE or FALSE

8. The major function of the blood-brain barrier is to keep the blood from spilling into the brain.

   TRUE or FALSE

9. The brain depends heavily on glucose, because the blood-brain barrier keeps out most other nutrients.

TRUE or FALSE

10. The neuron expends considerable energy to produce a resting potential, based on unequal distributions of ions across the membrane, so that a small stimulus that opens ion channels can produce a large, rapid flow of ions.

TRUE or FALSE

11. The sodium-potassium pump extrudes 3 sodium ions for every 2 potassium ions that it brings in.

TRUE or FALSE

12. The dimensions of action potentials in mammalian axons are identical to those measured in squid.

TRUE or FALSE

13. Hyperpolarization decreases the charge across the membrane.

TRUE or FALSE

14. The absolute refractory period ensures that an action potential is conducted in both directions from a given site on the axon.

TRUE or FALSE

15. Saltatory conduction increases the speed of conduction of an action potential down an axon.

TRUE or FALSE

16. A node of Ranvier is the site of release of neurotransmitter from an axon terminal.

TRUE or FALSE

Fill In The Blanks

1. Some structures common to all cells are the _____, _____, _____, and the _____.

2. _____ carry information from other neurons toward the soma.

3. _____ are fatty coverings that force the action potential to use faster electrical conduction within an axon for a longer distance before engaging in slower regenerative flow of ions across the membrane.

4. An _____ axon carries information toward a structure.

5. _____ and _____ form myelin sheaths.

6. _____ absorb, store, and release chemicals released from axons.

7. _____ guide neuron migration during early development.

8. Brain areas experiencing increased activity also experience _____ blood flow.

9. The _____prevents most viruses, bacteria, harmful chemicals, and many nutrients from gaining access to the brain.

10. The cell membrane is composed of a double layer of _____, with embedded proteins.

11. There is an excess of sodium ions _____ the neuron, and an excess of potassium ions _____ the neuron.

12. The neuron expends energy to produce a resting potential in order to ensure a _____ and _____ response to a stimulus.

13. A _____ is an increase in the voltage across the membrane; it _____ the likelihood of an action potential.

14. In many neurons an action potential begins at the _____.

15. The _____law states that the intensity of a stimulus does not influence the amplitude or velocity of an action potential.

16. A _____ of _____ is a break between myelin sheaths.

17. _____ conductio refers to the jumping of the action potential from node to node.

18. Local neurons are able to s al to adjacent neurons without the aid of _____.

Matching Items

1. _____ Dendrite
2. _____ Soma
3. _____ Axon
4. _____ Efferent axon
5. _____ Afferent axon
6. _____ Myelin sheath
7. _____ Astrocytes
8. _____ Oligodendrocytes
9. _____ Radial glia
10. _____ Sodium
11. _____ Potassium
12. _____ Action potential
13. _____ Resting potential
14. _____ Regenerative ion flow

a. Carries action potentials away from soma
b. Fatty covering on an axon
c. Glia that produce myelin sheaths
d. Receiver of neural input to a neuron
e. Carries information toward a neural structure
f. Location of nucleus, ribosomes, endoplasmic reticulum
g. Ion actively transported out of the cell
h. Carries information away from a neural structure
i. Generated by sodium/potassium pump
j. Glia that absorb, store, and release chemicals
k. Slower than electrical conduction within axon
l. Rapid inflow of sodium and slower outflow of potassium
m. Glia that guide neural migration during development
n. Ion actively transported into the cell

Multiple-Choice Questions

1. The membrane of a cell consists primarily of
   a. two layers of protein molecules.
   b. two layers of fat molecules.
   c. two layers of carbohydrate molecules.
   d. one layer of fat molecules adjacent to a layer of protein molecules.

2. Which of the following is the site of protein synthesis in cells?
   a. ribosomes
   b. endoplasmic reticulum
   c. nucleus
   d. mitochondria

3. Which of the following is the site of chemical reactions that produce energy for the cell?
   a. ribosomes
   b. endoplasmic reticulum
   c. nucleus
   d. mitochondria

4. Which part of the cell consists of a network of thin tubes that transport newly synthesized proteins to other locations?
   a. ribosomes
   b. endoplasmic reticulum
   c. nucleus
   d. mitochondria

5. Which part of the cell contains the chromosomes?
   a. ribosomes
   b. endoplasmic reticulum
   c. nucleus
   d. mitochondria

6. Which part of the neuron is specialized to receive information from other neurons?
   a. dendrites
   b. soma
   c. axon
   d. end bulbs

7. Dendritic spines
   a. are structures inside the dendrite that give it rigidity.
   b. are the sites of all synapses on a neuron.
   c. increase the surface area available for synapses.
   d. are long outgrowths that stretch for several millimeters.

8. Sensory neurons
   a. are afferent to the rest of the nervous system.
   b. are highly sensitive to specific types of stimulation.
   c. sometimes have dendrites that merge directly into the axon, with the soma located on a stalk off the main trunk.
   d. all of the above.

9. Intrinsic neurons
   a. have multiple axons extending to numerous structures.
   b. have dendrites and axons confined within a structure.
   c. are afferent to a given structure.
   d. are efferent to a given structure.

10. Glia
   a. are larger as well as more numerous than neurons.
   b. are found in only a few areas of the brain.
   c. got their name because early investigators thought they glued neurons together.
   d. form synaptic connections with neurons and other glia.

11. Which of the following is not a function of glia?
   a. guiding the migration of neurons and the regeneration of peripheral axons
   b. exchanging chemicals with adjacent neurons
   c. forming myelin sheaths
   d. transmitting information over long distances to other cells

12. The blood-brain barrier
    a. allows some substances to pass freely, while others pass poorly or not at all.
    b. is formed by Schwann cells.
    c. is completely impermeable to all substances.
    d. keeps the blood from washing away neurons.

13. Which of the following is true of the blood-brain barrier?
    a. Electrically charged molecules are the only molecules that can cross.
    b. It results from tight junctions between endothelial cells.
    c. Fat soluble molecules cannot cross at all.
    d. An active transport system pumps blood across the barrier.

14. If a virus enters the brain,
    a. it survives in the infected neuron.
    b. a particle of it is exposed through the neuron's membrane so the infected cell can be killed.
    c. it is immediately removed by glia before it can enter a neuron.
    d. it is impossible for any virus ever to enter the brain.

15. Which of the following undergo active transport from blood into the brain?
    a. Amino acids
    b. Purines
    c. Iron
    d. All of the above.

16. Adult neurons
    a. are like all other cells of the body in depending heavily on glucose.
    b. depend heavily on glucose because they do not have enzymes to metabolize other nutrients.
    c. depend heavily on glucose because other nutrients cannot cross the blood-brain barrier in significant amounts.
    d. cannot use glucose because they do not receive enough oxygen or thiamine through the blood-brain barrier to metabolize it.

17. Potassium
    a. is found mostly outside the neuron.
    b. is pumped into the resting neuron by the sodium-potassium pump, but some flows out as a result of the concentration gradient.
    c. is actively pumped outside the neuron during the action potential.
    d. more than one of the above.

18. The sodium-potassium pump
    a. creates a negative potential inside the neuron by removing 3 sodium ions for every 2 potassium ions that it brings in.
    b. creates a negative potential inside the neuron by removing 2 sodium ions for every 3 potassium ions that it brings in.
    c. creates a positive potential inside the neuron by removing 3 sodium ions for every 2 potassium ions that it brings in.
    d. is basically a passive mechanism that requires no metabolic energy.

19. The resting potential
    a. prepares the neuron to respond rapidly to a stimulus.
    b. is negative inside the neuron relative to the outside.
    c. can be measured as the voltage difference between a microelectrode inside the neuron and a reference electrode outside the neuron.
    d. all of the above.

20. Sodium ions
    a. are found largely inside the neuron during the resting state because they are attracted in by the negative charge there.
    b. are found largely inside the neuron during the resting state because they are actively pumped in.
    c. are found largely outside the neuron during the resting state because they are actively pumped out, and the membrane is largely impermeable to their reentry.
    d. are actively repelled by the electrical charge of the neuron's resting potential.

21. Hyperpolarization
    a. refers to a shift in the cell's potential in a more negative direction.
    b. refers to a shift in the cell's potential in a positive direction.
    c. can trigger an action potential if it is large enough.
    d. occurs in an all-or-none fashion.

22. Depolarization of a neuron can be accomplished by having
    a. a negative ion, such as chloride (Cl-), flow into the cell.
    b. potassium (K+) ions flow out of the cell.
    c. sodium (Na+) ions flow into the cell.
    d. sodium ions flow out of the cell.

23. The all-or-none law
    a. applies only to potentials in dendrites.
    b. states that the amplitude and velocity of the action potential are independent of the intensity of the stimulus that initiated it.
    c. makes it impossible for the nervous system to signal intensity of a stimulus.
    d. all of the above.

24. When a neuron receives a threshold depolarization
    a. an action potential occurs, the size of which reflects the size of the stimulus that gave rise to it.
    b. so much sodium comes in that it almost completely depletes the extracellular fluid of sodium.
    c. sodium flows in only until the potential across the membrane is zero.
    d. the membrane becomes highly permeable to sodium ions for a brief time.

25. The down slope of the action potential graph
    a. is largely a result of sodium ions being pumped back out again.
    b. is the result of potassium ions flowing in briefly.
    c. is the result of sodium ions flowing in briefly.
    d. usually passes the level of the resting potential, resulting in a brief hyperpolarization, due to potassium freely leaving the cell.

26. Which of the following is true?
    a. Local anesthetics block nerve transmission by blocking sodium channels.
    b. Scorpion venom also blocks sodium channels.
    c. Local anesthetics keep sodium channels open and close potassium channels.
    d. None of the above is true.

27. The absolute refractory period is the time during which
    a. a stimulus must exceed the usual threshold in order to produce an action potential.
    b. a neuron is more excitable than usual.
    c. the sodium gates are firmly closed and no new action potentials can be generated.
    d. sodium and potassium ions are rapidly flowing.

28. Propagation of an action potential
    a. is analogous to the flow of electrons down a wire.
    b. is almost instantaneous.
    c. is inherently unidirectional because positive charges can flow only in one direction.
    d. depends on passive diffusion of sodium ions inside the axon, which depolarize the neighboring areas to their threshold.

29. Myelin sheaths
    a. would be much more efficient if they were not interrupted with a lot of leaky nodes.
    b. are interrupted about every 1 mm by a short unmyelinated segment.
    c. are much less effective in speeding transmission than a simple increase in axon size.
    d. are composed primarily of protein.

30. Saltatory conduction refers to
    a. the salt ions used in the action potential.
    b. sodium ions jumping into the neuron, once the sodium channels are opened.
    c. the impulse jumping from one node of Ranvier to the next.
    d. the impulse jumping from one myelin sheath to the next.

31. Myelin sheaths
    a. slow conduction of the impulse by blocking sodium's entry to the cell; their advantage lies in making the impulse all-or-none.
    b. are destroyed in multiple sclerosis.
    c. are found on dendrites.
    d. are found on cell bodies.

32. Which of the following is true regarding the diameter of an axon?
    a. The diameter of an axon does not influence the flow of ions.
    b. The smaller its diameter the faster the ions flow.
    c. The greater its diameter the faster the ions flow.
    d. The greater its diameter the slower the ions flow.

33. Nodes of Ranvier
    a. are interruptions of the myelin sheath at about 1 mm intervals.
    b. are sites of abundant sodium channels.
    c. are sites where an action potential is regenerated.
    d. all of the above.

34. Local neurons utilize
   a. graded potentials to convey information over short distances.
   b. graded potentials to convey information over long distances.
   c. action potentials to transmit information over long distances.
   d. action potentials to transmit information over short distances.

Helpful Hints

1. To remember the relative locations of sodium and potassium ions during the resting potential, remember that sodium (Na+) is "Not allowed" inside the neuron and potassium (K+) is labeled "Keep".

2. To appreciate the difference between fast electrical conduction inside the membrane and slow regenerative potentials across the membrane, think of ions simply elbowing their like-charged neighbors a short distance away inside the membrane, while sodium and potassium ions have to swim their equivalent of the length of a pool to cross the membrane.

Solutions

True/False Questions

1.	F	5.	T	9.	T	13.	F
2.	F	6.	F	10.	T	14.	F
3.	T	7.	T	11.	T	15.	T
4.	F	8.	F	12.	F	16.	F

Fill In The Blanks

1. nucleus; mitochondria; ribosomes; endoplasmic reticulum
2. Dendrites
3. Myelin sheaths
4. afferent
5. Oligodendrocytes; Schwann cells
6. Astrocytes
7. Radial glia
8. increased
9. blood-brain barrier
10. phospholipids
11. outside; inside
12. strong; fast
13. hyperpolarization;decreases
14. axon hillock.
15. all-or-none
16. node; Ranvier
17. Saltatory
18. action potentials

Matching Items

1.	d	5.	e	9.	m	13.	i
2.	f	6.	b	10.	g	14.	l
3.	a	7.	j	11.	n		
4.	h	8.	c	12.	k		

Multiple Choice Questions

1.	b	10.	c	19.	d	28.	d
2.	a	11.	d	20.	c	29.	b
3.	d	12.	a	21.	a	30.	c
4.	b	13.	b	22.	c	31.	b
5.	c	14.	a	23.	b	32.	c
6.	a	15.	d	24.	d	33.	d
7.	c	16.	c	25.	d	34.	a
8.	d	17.	b	26.	a		
9.	b	18.	a	27.	c		

CHAPTER 3

Synapses

Introduction

C. S. Sherrington inferred from careful behavioral observations that neurons do not merge with each other but communicate across tiny gaps called synapses. Reflex arcs that have one or more synapses are slower than simple transmission along the same distance of unbroken axon. Sherrington also inferred that complex integration of stimuli, including spatial and temporal summation of both excitation and inhibition, occurs at synapses. Most of his inferences were later confirmed by electrophysiological recordings by John Eccles, using microelectrodes inserted inside neurons. Inhibitory postsynaptic potentials (IPSPs) hyperpolarize the postsynaptic cell, making it more difficult to produce an action potential. Excitatory postsynaptic potentials (EPSPs) depolarize the postsynaptic neuron and may summate spatially and temporally with other EPSPs to reach triggering threshold for an action potential. Most neurons fire action potentials at a spontaneous rate, even without synaptic input. EPSPs increase firing above that rate, whereas IPSPs decrease the firing rate.

EPSPs and IPSPs result from the release of neurotransmitters from presynaptic terminals. The most widely studied neurotransmitter systems are those of the amino acids glutamate, gamma-aminobutyric acid (GABA), glycine, and aspartate; the monoamines dopamine, norepinephrine, epinephrine, and serotonin; neuropeptides, including endorphins, substance P, and neuropeptide Y; acetylcholine (a modified amino acid); purines, including adenosine and ATP; and gases, such as nitric oxide. Levels of some neurotransmitters can be affected by diet.

The neurotransmitter diffuses to and combines with receptor sites on the postsynaptic neuron, giving rise to either ionotropic or metabotropic changes that produce the postsynaptic potentials. Ionotropic mechanisms involve a brief flow of ions; metabotropic processes are mediated by a G-protein and second messenger system and have a slower onset and longer duration. Although each particular synapse is always excitatory or always inhibitory, each neuron receives many synapses, some of which are excitatory and some of which are inhibitory. Most neurons are thought to release the same neurotransmitter or combination of neurotransmitters at all of their terminals, although spinal cord motor neurons, and perhaps others, are an exception. Neuropeptides are sometimes described as neuromodulators. They are released from cell bodies and dendrites, as well as axon terminals, and diffuse widely. They act at metabotropic receptors and modulate the effects of other neurotransmitters. Hormones are different from neurotransmitters in that they are released from various organs into the blood, which carries them throughout the body where they may coordinate long-lasting changes. However, some hormones act like metabotropic neurotransmitters, binding to receptors on the cell membrane and activating an enzyme. The anterior pituitary and posterior pituitary are controlled by the hypothalamus in different ways and secrete different sets of hormones.

After interacting with its receptor, the neurotransmitter detaches and is either transported back into the presynaptic terminal and reused or broken by enzymes into inactive components. Neuropeptides simply diffuse away from the site of release. It is important to remove the neurotransmitter from the synapse in order to prevent it from having a prolonged effect on the postsynaptic neuron, which would make it incapable of responding to new stimuli. The effect on the postsynaptic cell depends on the type and amount of neurotransmitter, the nature and number of receptors, the amount of deactivating enzyme present at the synapse, the rate of reuptake, and probably other factors. Neurons can be prevented from releasing excessive amounts of neurotransmitter, either by using autoreceptors that detect the released transmitter and inhibit further release, or by having the postsynaptic cell release a chemical that diffuses back to the presynaptic cell and inhibits release.

Drugs typically either impede or facilitate chemical transmission at a given type of synapse. It may seem surprising that many drugs are derived from plants. Plants may have evolved these chemicals to entice or repel insects or other animals. Indeed, many of the same chemicals are used for communication throughout both the plant and animal kingdoms. Drugs may either block or activate a certain type of receptor, or they may affect release, reuptake, or enzyme inactivation of the neurotransmitter. Drugs that activate a receptor are agonists; those that block a receptor are antagonists. Affinity refers to the ability of a drug to bind to a particular receptor; efficacy refers to the ability to activate that receptor. Since different neurotransmitters have different behavioral and physiological effects, we can frequently predict the effect of a drug on behavior or physiology if we know its synaptic effect. However, there are individual differences in the effectiveness and side effects of drugs, due in part to differences in the numbers and distributions of the subtypes of receptors affected by the drug.

Almost all abused drugs increase dopamine release in the nucleus accumbens either directly or indirectly. However, dopamine release in the nucleus accumbens may increase *wanting* of something, but not necessarily *liking* it. Amphetamine increases release of dopamine from the presynaptic terminal, while cocaine blocks the reuptake of dopamine, norepinephrine, and serotonin, thereby prolonging their effects. Methylphenidate (Ritalin) also blocks dopamine reuptake; however, at the low doses prescribed for attention deficit disorder (ADD), orally-administered methylphenidate does not produce a rush of excitement or addiction. Methylphenidate used for ADD may even decrease later drug use, although it may also lead to increased fearfulness. Methylenedioxymethamphetamine (MDMA, or "ecstasy") increases release of dopamine and, at high doses, of serotonin, thereby altering perception and cognition. It may also destroy serotonin neurons. Nicotine stimulates nicotinic acetylcholine receptors, which increase dopamine release in the nucleus accumbens. Opiate drugs stimulate the same receptors as do endorphins (*endo*genous m*orphin*es); they increase (disinhibit) dopamine release and also have effects independent of dopamine. Marijuana leaves contain Δ^9-tetrahydrocannabinol (Δ^9-THC) and other cannabinoids, which intensify sensory experience, cause memory and cognitive impairments, and cause time perception to be slowed. Cannabinoid receptors are also stimulated by endogenous chemicals such as anandamide and sn-2-arachidonylglycerol (2-AG), which are released from the postsynaptic cell to the presynaptic cell and decrease neurotransmitter release. Hallucinogenic drugs, such as lysergic acid diethylamide (LSD) stimulate serotonin type 2A (5-HT_{2A}) receptors.

Alcohol is the most commonly abused drug. Alcohol inhibits brain activity by facilitating responses at $GABA_A$ receptors and blocking glutamate receptors; it also increases stimulation at dopamine and opiate receptors. There are two major types of alcoholism. Type I alcoholism is less dependent on genetics, develops gradually, and is equally common in women and men. Type II alcoholism has a stronger genetic basis, a rapid, early onset, and a great preponderance of men. Several genes have been associated with alcoholism, including one for a variant of the dopamine type 4 receptor and another for a more active version of COMT, which breaks down dopamine more rapidly. They may decrease the effectiveness of dopamine and increase impulsiveness. Sons of alcoholics feel less intoxication from small to moderate amounts of alcohol and greater than average relief from stress after drinking alcohol. In addition, sons of alcoholics tend to have a smaller than normal amygdala in the right hemisphere, even before starting to drink.

Initial experiences with abused drugs may be pleasant, but repeated use results in tolerance to both the drug's effects and other types of reinforcement. In addition, abstinence from opiates, alcohol, nicotine, and even videogames can lead to unpleasant withdrawal symptoms. Even after withdrawal symptoms have subsided, people and rats continue to crave the substance, especially when confronted with cues associated with the substance or when under stress. These prolonged effects may be due to rewiring of the nucleus accumbens, so that it responds more to the drug and less to other incentives. One hypothesis suggests that increased background inhibition in the prefrontal cortex decreases its ability to facilitate the nucleus accumbens's responses to reinforcing experiences.

Antabuse (disulfiram) is used to treat alcoholism; it inactivates acetaldehyde dehydrogenase, the enzyme that converts acetaldehyde (the toxic metabolic product of alcohol) to acetic acid (a source of energy). A person who drinks after taking Antabuse will become sick. However, many persons who use Antabuse never drink, and therefore never become ill; they use Antabuse as a daily reminder not to drink alcohol. Methadone is used to treat addiction to heroin and morphine. It has effects similar to those of heroin and morphine, but because it is taken as a pill, its effects rise and fall slowly and do not produce a "rush." The opiate antagonist naloxone (Revia) is also used to treat alcoholism. Acamprosate (Campral) blocks glutamate receptors and helps people get through the withdrawal period. Methadone, buprenorphine, and levomethadyl acetate (LAAM) are used to treat addictions to opiates; they are opiate receptor agonists, but when taken orally, they enter the blood slowly, thereby avoiding the "rush" experience. Chronic use of all abused drugs results in decreased responsiveness of nucleus accumbens cells that mediate reinforcement. However, we do not understand *why* dopamine in the nucleus accumbens is reinforcing.

Learning Objectives

Module 3.1 The Concept of the Synapse

1. Be able to describe Sherrington's inferences concerning the speed of a reflex and temporal and spatial summation.
2. Understand the mechanisms underlying the excitatory and inhibitory postsynaptic potentials.
3. Understand how synaptic potentials contribute to the firing rates of neurons and the integration of information.

Module 3.2 Chemical Events at the Synapse

1. Be able to describe the contributions of T.R. Elliott and O. Loewi to the question of whether most synaptic transmission is electrically or chemically mediated.
2. Be able to list the six major types of neurotransmitters.
3. Understand the role of diet in the synthesis of neurotransmitters.
4. Understand the processes of transport, release, and diffusion of neurotransmitters.
5. Understand the differences between ionotropic and metabotropic effects of neurotransmitters.
6. Be able to describe the similarities and differences between neurotransmitters and hormones.
7. Understand the difference in control mechanisms of the anterior and posterior pituitary and be able to list some of the hormones released from each.
8. Understand why inactivation of neurotransmitters is important and the two major ways in which this is achieved.
9. Understand the two mechanisms for producing negative feedback.

Module 3.3 Drugs and Synapses

1. Understand why our brains have receptors for plant chemicals.
2. Understand the difference between agonists, antagonists, and mixed agonist-antagonists and the difference between a drug's affinity for a receptor and its efficacy at that receptor.
3. Be able to explain the common mechanism of action of nearly all abused drugs.
4. Understand the relation of dopamine in the nucleus accumbens to motivation ("wanting") and why dopamine does not seem to be related directly to pleasure ("liking").
5. Be able to explain the differences between the effects of amphetamine, cocaine, and methylphenidate.
6. Understand the different ways of increasing dopamine release in the nucleus accumbens used by nicotine, opiates, and marijuana.
7. Understand the relationship of the prefrontal cortex to the nucleus accumbens in the facilitation of reinforcing experiences and how repeated drug use changes that.
8. Know the physiological effects of alcohol and the effects of Antabuse on alcohol metabolism.
9. Understand the two types of alcoholism and the differences between sons of alcoholics and sons of non-alcoholics.
10. Be able to describe the genetic variations that may contribute to alcoholism.
11. Know why methadone can be used to treat addiction to heroin or morphine and why it does not end the addiction.

Key Terms and Concepts

Module 3.1 The Concept of the Synapse
    1.   The properties of synapses
Ramón y Cajal: gap between neurons
Charles Sherrington's inferences
    Reflex arc
    Coordinated flexing and extending
Speed of a reflex and delayed transmission at the synapse
Temporal summation
    Presynaptic neuron
    Postsynaptic neuron
    John Eccles
    Microelectrode
Excitatory postsynaptic potential (EPSP)
    Graded potential
    Open gates for sodium (Na^+) to enter
Spatial summation
Inhibitory synapses
    Role of interneurons
Inhibitory postsynaptic potential (IPSP)
    Open gates for potassium (K^+) to leave or for chloride (Cl^-) to enter
    2.   Relationship among EPSP, IPSP, and action potentials
Combination of temporal and spatial summation
Spontaneous firing rate
    3.   In closing: The neuron as decision maker
Integration of information

Module 3.2 Chemical Events at the Synapse
1.   The discovery of chemical transmission at synapses
    T. R. Elliott
        Adrenalin
        Sympathetic nervous system
    O. Loewi
        Vagus nerve
        Accelerator nerve
2.   The sequence of chemical events at a synapse
    Types of neurotransmitters
        Amino acids
            Acids containing an amine group (NH_2)
            Glutamate, GABA, glycine, aspartate
        Neuropeptides
            Chains of amino acids
            Endorphins, substance P, neuropeptide Y
        Acetylcholine
            A modified amino acid

Monoamines
    Neurotransmitters containing one amine group
    Indoleamine: Serotonin
    Catecholamines: dopamine, norepinephrine, epinephrine
Purines
    Adenosine, ATP, maybe others
Gases
    Nitric oxide (NO), maybe others
    Control of blood flow
Synthesis of transmitters
    Acetylcholine
        Precursor: choline
            In milk, eggs, peanuts
    Catecholamines
        Dopamine, norepinephrine, epinephrine
        Precursors: phenylalanine, tyrosine
            In proteins
    Serotonin
        Precursor: tryptophan
            In soy
            Phenylalanine competes
        Role of insulin
Transport and storage of transmitters
    Neuropeptides
        Synthesized in cell body
        Slow transport to axon terminal or dendrites
    Small neurotransmitters
        Synthesized in terminals
    Vesicles
        Exception: nitric oxide released as soon as formed
        Some transmitter outside of vesicles
    Monoamine oxidase (MAO)
        Breaks down serotonin, dopamine, norepinephrine
Release and diffusion of transmitters
    Voltage-dependent calcium gates
    Exocytosis
    Diffusion across cleft
    Combination of transmitters
        Motor neurons: different transmitters from different branches
        Ability to respond to numerous neurotransmitters, though it releases only
        one or a few
Activation of receptors of the postsynaptic cell
    Scaffolding proteins: hold neurons together; guide neurotransmitter to receptor
    Multiple receptor subtypes
    Ionotropic effects (rapid, short-lived)
        Transmitter-gated (ligand-gated) ion channels

Glutamate
GABA
Glycine
Acetylcholine
Metabotropic effects and second messenger systems (slow, long-lasting)
G-protein (coupled to guanosine triphosphate, GTP)
Second messenger: cyclic AMP
Open or close ion channel
Activate portion of chromosome
Neuropeptides (neuromodulators)
Released by cell bodies and dendrites
Release usually requires repeated stimulation
Stimulation of other dendrites to release additional neuropeptide
Wide diffusion
Hormones
Released from endocrine glands, travel via blood
Coordinate multiple long-lasting effects
Protein hormones, peptide hormones
Some chemicals: both hormone and neurotransmitter
Anterior pituitary (glandular tissue)
Releasing hormones from hypothalamus
Adrenocorticotropic hormone (ACTH)
Thyroid stimulating hormone (TSH)
Prolactin
Somatotropin (growth hormone, GH)
Gonadotropins: follicle stimulating hormone (FSH), luteinizing hormone (LH)
Posterior pituitary (neural tissue, extension of hypothalamus)
Oxytocin
Vasopressin (antidiuretic hormone)
Inactivation and reuptake of neurotransmitters
Acetylcholinesterase: acetylcholine → acetate + choline
Choline: taken up by presynaptic cell, connects with another acetate
Reuptake for serotonin and catecholamines
Transporter
Conversion to inactive chemicals
COMT (catechol-o-methyltransferase)
Neuropeptides: diffuse away
Negative feedback from the postsynaptic cell
Presynaptic autoreceptors: negative feedback
Chemical from postsynaptic cell: travels back to presynaptic cell
Nitric oxide, anandamide, 2-AG
3. In closing: Neurotransmitters and behavior
Similarities across species

Module 3.3 Synapses, Drugs, and Addictions

1.   Types of mechanisms
       Why are our brains sensitive to plant chemicals?
            Plants evolved chemicals to affect animals' behavior
       Antagonist
       Agonist
       Mixed agonist-antagonist
       Ways to influence synaptic activity
            Increase or decrease synthesis of neurotransmitter
            Cause neurotransmitter to leak from vesicles
            Increase neurotransmitter release
            Decrease neurotransmitter reuptake
            Block neurotransmitter breakdown
            Directly stimulate or block receptors
       Affinity: ability to bind to a receptor
       Efficacy: tendency to activate a receptor
       Variability of responses to drugs
            Differences in abundance of receptor subtypes
2.   What abused drugs have in common
       Electrical self-stimulation of the brain
            James Olds and Peter Milner
                 Self-stimulation in several brain areas → dopamine release in nucleus
                 accumbens
       Other reinforcing experiences also → dopamine release in nucleus
            accumbens
       Addiction as increased "wanting," not necessarily "liking"
            Paychecks, videogames, gambling don't → happiness
            Drug addicts: Work hard for drug, even if drug does not → pleasure
3.   A survey of abused drugs
       Stimulant drugs
            Amphetamine
                 Reversal of dopamine transporter → release of dopamine
                 Also → release of serotonin, norepinephrine, etc.
            Cocaine
                 Blocks reuptake of dopamine, norepinephrine, serotonin
                 "Crash" after amphetamine or cocaine: depletion of dopamine
                 Impair attention and learning
                 Genetically "impulsive" rats self-administer more cocaine
                      Cocaine → more impulsive
                 Long-term problems in humans: memory impairment, increased risk of stroke,
                 epilepsy,
            Methylphenidate (Ritalin)
                 Blockade of dopamine reuptake
                 Treatment for attention-deficit disorder (ADD)
                 Low dose oral pills → slower increase in dopamine than cocaine, not addictive
                 Prolonged use in childhood → less likely to abuse drugs in adolescence

May lead to increased fearfulness

Methylenedioxymethamphetamine (MDMA, "ecstasy")

Low doses → dopamine release

High doses → also serotonin release and destruction of serotonin neurons

Increase temperature and hydrogen peroxide

Nicotine → stimulation of nicotinic acetylcholine receptors → dopamine release in nucleus accumbens

Repeated exposure → cells that produce reinforcement are less responsive to nicotine and other reinforcers

Opiates (morphine, heroin, methadone) → relaxation, less sensitivity to pain and problems

Taken for pain relief under medical supervision: rarely abused

Candace Pert and Solomon Snyder: neuropeptides: endorphins

Inhibit ventral tegmental neurons that release GABA → disinhibition of dopamine neurons

Other effects independent of dopamine

Marijuana (Δ^9-tetrahydrocannabinol, Δ^9-THC) and other cannabinoids

Decrease pain, nausea, glaucoma, increase appetite

Intensifies sensation, illusion of time passing slowly

Impairs memory, cognition

Cannabinoid receptors: abundant except in medulla: little effect on breathing, heartbeat

Endogenous cannabinoids: anandamide, sn-2 arachidonylglycerol (2-AG)

Presynaptic receptors → decrease both glutamate and GABA release

Disinhibit dopamine neurons in ventral tegmental area → increase dopamine in nucleus accumbens

Relieve nausea: inhibition of serotonin type 3 receptors (5-HT$_3$)

Marijuana → time seems to pass more slowly in rats and humans

Hallucinogenic drugs → stimulation of serotonin 5-HT$_{2A}$ receptors

Lysergic acid diethylamide (LSD)

4. Alcohol and alcoholism

Alcoholism (alcohol dependence): continued use of alcohol despite medical or social harm

Physiological effects

Facilitates GABA$_A$ receptor

Blocks glutamate receptors

Increases dopamine and opiate receptor activity

Genetics

Strong genetic basis for early-onset alcoholism, especially in men

Type I (or Type A) alcoholism

Later onset

Develops gradually

Less dependence on genetics

Fewer genetic relatives are alcoholic

Type II (or Type B) alcoholism

Rapid, early onset

Stronger genetic basis

Mostly men

Evidence for genetic basis

"Longer" version of dopamine D4 receptor (less sensitive): stronger cravings for alcohol

Gene for more active COMT: more impulsive

Other genes affect risk-taking, responses to stress

Maternal drinking during pregnancy also a factor

Risk factors

Impulsive, risk-taking, easily bored, sensation-seeking, outgoing

Son of alcoholic father

Less than average intoxication after moderate amount of alcohol

Greater decrease in stress by alcohol

Smaller amygdala in right hemisphere

5. Addiction

Seeking pleasure and avoiding displeasure

Tolerance with repeated use

Less responsive to reinforcers in general

Withdrawal symptoms → motivation to avoid displeasure

Craving even after end of withdrawal symptoms

Learning: drug can be strongly reinforcing during time of stress

Cravings in response to cues

Also in response to stress

Brain reorganization

Increased release of dopamine in nucleus accumbens by cocaine

Decreased response to other incentives

Increased background inhibition in prefrontal cortex → no longer facilitates reinforcement

6. Medications to combat substance abuse

Medications to combat alcohol abuse

Liver enzymes metabolize alcohol to acetaldehyde (a poisonous substance)

Acetaldehyde dehydrogenase metabolizes acetaldehyde to acetic acid (source of energy)

Slower acetaldehyde metabolism → unpleasant symptoms

Disulfiram (Antabuse) antagonizes acetaldehyde dehydrogenase

Naloxone (Revia) blocks opiate receptors

Acomprosate (Campral) antagonizes glutamate receptors

Medications to combat opiate abuse

Methadone: taken orally → slow onset and offset

Buprenorphine

Levomethadyl acetate (LAAM) (longer-lasting)

7. In closing: Drugs and behavior

Importance of reuptake transporters, retrograde signalling

Why is dopamine reinforcing?

Why does stimulation of serotonin 5-HT$_{2A}$ receptors → hallucinations?

Short-Answer Questions
Module 3.1 The Concept of the Synapse

1. *The properties of synapses*

    a. What is a reflex?

    b. What experimental evidence did Sherrington have for synaptic delay? For temporal summation?

    c. What evidence did he have for spatial summation? For coordinated excitation and inhibition?

    d. Describe John Eccles's experimental support for Sherrington's inferences.

    e. What is an EPSP, and what ionic flow is largely responsible for it?

    f. What is an IPSP, and what ionic flows can produce it?

2. *Relationship among EPSP, IPSP, and action potentials*

    a. What influence do EPSPs and IPSPs have on neurons with a spontaneous rate of firing?

3. *In closing: The neuron as decision maker*

    a. What factors influence a cell's "decision" whether or not to produce an action potential?

Module 3.2 Chemical Events at the Synapse

1. *The discovery of chemical transmission at synapses*

    a. What did T. R. Elliott propose?

    b. Describe Loewi's experiment with the two frogs' hearts.

2. *The sequence of chemical events at a synapse*

    a. What are the major events, in sequence, at a synapse?

    b. List the major neurotransmitters.

    c. How is nitric oxide unlike most other neurotransmitters?

    d. How is the synthesis of neuropeptides different from that of most other neurotransmitters?

    e. List the three catecholamines in the order of their synthesis. What is their amino acid precursor?

    f. How might one increase the amount of acetylcholine in the brain? Serotonin?

    g. How quickly can neuropeptides be transported to the terminal? Why is this not a problem for smaller neurotransmitters?

    h. Describe the process of exocytosis.

    i. What generalization can be drawn regarding the release of neurotransmitter(s) at the terminals of a given neuron? What type of neurons provides an exception to this generalization?

j. Contrast ionotropic and metabotropic synaptic mechanisms. List three ionotropic neurotransmitter receptors.

k. Discuss the role of second messengers in producing the metabotropic effects of neurotransmitters. What kinds of changes can they exert?

l. What is a G-protein? What is the "first messenger"? What is one common second messenger?

m. What is a neuromodulator? Through what type of receptor (ionotropic or metabotropic) are neuromodulator's effects produced?

n. What is a major difference between the function of neurotransmitters and hormones? Through what kind of receptor (ionotropic or metabotropic) do many hormones act?

o. Contrast the control of the anterior pituitary and posterior pituitary. What are some hormones released from each?

p. How does the control of the anterior pituitary differ from that of the posterior pituitary?

q. Which two hormones are released from the posterior pituitary? Name six hormones released from the anterior pituitary.

r. How are acetylcholine, serotonin, and the catecholamines inactivated? Why is inactivation important? Are peptide neurotransmitters inactivated after they are released?

s. What are autoreceptors? What is their function?

t. What is the function of chemicals released by the postsynaptic cell that travel back to the presynaptic terminal? Name two such chemicals.

Module 3.3 Synapses, Drugs, and Addictions

1. *Types of mechanisms*

    a. What is a possible explanation for why our brains are sensitive to plant chemicals? How common are neurotransmitter molecules throughout the animal kingdom?

    b. What is an agonist? An antagonist?

    c. List six ways in which drugs may affect synaptic function.

    d. Distinguish between a drug's affinity and efficacy at a receptor.

    e. How can one drug be an agonist at a given receptor, while another drug, with similar affinity for that receptor, can fail to stimulate it?

    f. What may explain individual differences in responsiveness to drugs?

2. *What abused drugs have in common*

    a. How were the brain mechanisms of pleasure and reinforcement discovered?

    b. Which brain area is especially important for reinforcement and addiction? What is the effect of electrical self-stimulation and drugs of abuse on dopamine release there?

    c. What other kinds of activities are associated with release of dopamine there?

d. Is dopamine release always associated with pleasure? Describe Berridge and Robinson's distinction between "wanting" and "liking." To which of these is nucleus accumbens dopamine more closely linked?

3. *A survey of abused drugs*

   a. What is the common neural mechanism of nearly all drugs of abuse?

   b. Describe a way in which inhibitory effects on neurons could result in excitation of a behavior.

   c. Contrast the actions of amphetamine and cocaine. What accounts for the "crash" that occurs after taking amphetamine or cocaine?

   d. Why is methylphenidate (Ritalin), taken orally as prescribed, less addictive than cocaine? Is there evidence that taking it for attention-deficit disorder in childhood promotes drug addiction in adolescence?

   e. What are the neuronal effects of low and high doses of MDMA ("ecstasy")? What psychological effects are observed after MDMA use in humans?

   f. How does nicotine affect dopamine release? How are nucleus accumbens cells altered after repeated exposure to nicotine?

   g. What are the psychological effects of opiate drugs? What are endorphins? Who discovered them?

   h. How do opiates affect cells in the ventral tegmental area that release GABA? What is the resultant effect on dopamine neurons?

   i. What is the major chemical in the marijuana plant that produces psychological changes? Name some of the medical and psychological changes produced by marijuana.

   j. What receptors mediate marijuana's effects? Why does marijuana have little effect on breathing and heartbeat?

   k. Name two endogenous chemicals that bind to cannabinoid receptors. Where are cannabinoid receptors located (pre- or postsynaptic)?

   l. How does stimulation of cannabinoid receptors result in an increase in dopamine release in the nucleus accumbens?

   m. How does marijuana affect appetite?

   n. What type of receptor is activated by hallucinogenic drugs?

4. *Alcohol and alcoholism*

   a. What type of receptor is facilitated by alcohol? Which other three neurotransmitters are affected?

   b. List the differences between Type I and Type II alcoholism.

   c. Which genes have been implicated as risk factors for alcoholism?

   d. What are three differences between sons of alcoholics and sons of non-alcoholics?

   e. What aspect of the prenatal environment also affects risk for alcoholism?

5. *Addiction*

   a. Describe the development of tolerance to a drug. Does the tolerance also extend to other reinforcers?

   b. Describe the symptoms of withdrawal from opiates, alcohol, and nicotine.

   c. After the symptoms of withdrawal have abated, what two environmental factors can reinstate craving?

   d. What is one hypothesis about the relation between the prefrontal cortex and nucleus accumbens in the filtering out of responses to reinforcers other than the drug?

6. *Medications to combat substance abuse*

   a. Describe the metabolism of alcohol.

   b. What is the biochemical effect of Antabuse? What is its physiological effect when combined with alcohol use?

   c. How may Antabuse work, in addition to its physiological effect?

   d. What are two other medications used to treat alcoholism? How does each work?

   e. What is methadone and how is it used? What other two drugs have similar effects? Do these drugs provide an end to addiction?

True/False Questions

1. Reflex arcs always consist of activation of motor neurons by sensory neurons within a single segment of the spinal cord.

   TRUE or FALSE

2. C. S. Sherrington discovered the concepts of spatial and temporal summation in simple experiments involving pinching a dog's foot.

   TRUE or FALSE

3. EPSPs and action potentials are similar in that both result from the influx of sodium ions.

   TRUE or FALSE

4. IPSPs and EPSPs are also similar in that both result from the influx of sodium ions.

   TRUE or FALSE

5. Otto Loewi discovered that synaptic conduction is almost always electrical in nature.

   TRUE or FALSE

6. The three catecholamine neurotransmitters are dopamine, epinephrine, and serotonin.

   TRUE or FALSE

7. Brain levels of acetylcholine may be increased by eating a lot of milk, eggs, and peanuts.

   TRUE or FALSE

8. Nitric oxide is a gaseous transmitter that is synthesized at the time it is needed, rather than being stored in vesicles; it is different from "laughing gas."

   TRUE or FALSE

9. Potassium, flowing in through voltage-dependent potassium channels in axon terminals, directly stimulates the release of vesicles containing neurotransmitter.

   TRUE or FALSE

10. Each neuron releases only one or a few neurotransmitters.

    TRUE or FALSE

11. Ionotropic effects result from ions crossing the membrane through cylindrical channels; these effects are faster, but more short-lived, than metabotropic effects.

    TRUE or FALSE

12. A second messenger is one that is sent out if the first messenger has no effect.

    TRUE or FALSE

13. Neuropeptides usually require repeated action potentials to release them.

    TRUE or FALSE

14. Neuropeptides are released only from axon terminals and only in the immediate vicinity of the ionotropic receptors that they activate.

    TRUE or FALSE

15. Receptors for protein and peptide hormones are in the cell membrane and activate second messenger systems similar to those of metabotropic neurotransmitters.

    TRUE or FALSE

16. The anterior pituitary is composed of neural tissue; neurons in the hypothalamus send axons into the anterior pituitary, from which hormones are released into the general blood circulation.

    TRUE or FALSE

17. Hormones released from the anterior pituitary include adrenocorticotropic hormone (ACTH), thyroid-stimulating hormone (TSH), prolactin, somatotropin (growth hormone, GH), and gonadotropins (follicle-stimulating hormone, FSH; luteinizing hormone, LH).

    TRUE or FALSE

18. Inactivation of neurotransmitters is accomplished almost exclusively by enzymes that convert them into inactive chemicals.

    TRUE or FALSE

19. Levels of some hormones and neurotransmitters are regulated by negative feedback systems.

    TRUE or FALSE

20. Species differences in neurotransmitters and receptors are so large that it is impossible to make useful generalizations about them across species.

TRUE or FALSE

21. Affinity and efficacy are really just two different words for the same factor—the ability of a drug to bind to a receptor.

TRUE or FALSE

22. Electrical stimulation of the brain is usually reinforcing only if it activates dopamine release, especially in the nucleus accumbens.

TRUE or FALSE

23. Dopamine release in the nucleus accumbens is now thought to be synonymous with pleasure: It always occurs with pleasant stimuli and promotes "liking."

TRUE or FALSE

24. Nearly all drugs of abuse either directly or indirectly increase the extracellular levels of dopamine in the nucleus accumbens.
    TRUE or FALSE

25. Both methylphenidate (Ritalin) and cocaine block reuptake of dopamine; however, methylphenidate, taken orally in low doses, produces a more gradual and smaller increase in dopamine levels and is therefore not usually addictive.

TRUE or FALSE

26. The drug methylenedioxymethamphetamine (MDMA, or "ecstasy") acts via nicotinic receptors and is relatively harmless.

TRUE or FALSE

27. Cannabinoid receptors are a type of opioid receptor.

TRUE or FALSE

28. Endorphins increase dopamine release by inhibiting inhibitory neurons in the ventral tegmental area that contain GABA.

TRUE or FALSE

29. Anandamide is an endogenous chemical that activates cannabinoid receptors and can thereby inhibit the release of both glutamate and GABA.

TRUE or FALSE

30. Hallucinogenic drugs exert their effects primarily by increasing dopamine release in the nucleus accumbens.

TRUE or FALSE

31. Alcohol facilitates the $GABA_A$ receptor, blocks activity at glutamate receptors, and increases stimulation at dopamine and opiate receptors.

TRUE or FALSE

32. Type II alcoholism has a more rapid onset than Type I, is more prevalent in men than in women, and has a relatively strong genetic basis.

TRUE or FALSE

33. Antabuse (disulfiram) stimulates acetaldehyde dehydrogenase, thereby decreasing the effects of alcohol.

TRUE or FALSE

Fill In The Blanks

1. _____, in the late 1800s, showed that neurons do not physically merge with one another.

2. _____ discovered the properties of spatial and temporal summation using behavioral experiments on dogs' reflexes.

3. Temporal summation in single cells was demonstrated by _____, using microelectrodes inserted into neurons.

4. EPSPs and action potentials are similar in that they both result from an inflow of _____ ions.

5. EPSPs and IPSPs are similar in that they are both _____.

6. IPSPs result from the outflow of _____ ions and/or the inflow of _____ ions.

7. The periodic production of action potentials without synaptic input is referred to as a(n) _____.

8. Otto Loewi found that when he stimulated the vagus nerve of one frog and then placed fluid collected from around that heart onto a second frog's heart, the second heart _____.

9. Amino acid neurotransmitters include _____, _____, _____, and _____.

10. Monoamine neurotransmitters include _____, _____, _____, and _____.

11. Some neuropeptides are _____, _____, and _____.

12. Insulin release, as a result of eating carbohydrates, can increase the production of _____ in the brain.

13. Enzyme-mediated effects that emerge about 30 ms or more after the release of a neurotransmitter are referred to as _____ effects.

14. _____ and _____ hormones activate metabotropic receptors that activate second messenger systems in a cell.

15. Two hormones released from the posterior pituitary are _____ and _____.

16. Six hormones released from the anterior pituitary are _____,

_____, _____, _____, _____, and

_____.

17. The enzyme that inactivates acetylcholine is _____.

18. Symptoms of _____ can be alleviated by drugs that block acetylcholinesterase.

19. Serotonin and the catecholamines are inactivated by _____, which occurs through membrane proteins called _____, in addition to being broken down by COMT.

20. _____ are receptors on presynaptic terminals that are sensitive to the same transmitter they release.

21. Chemicals released from the postsynaptic neuron that provide negative feedback to the presynaptic neuron include _____, _____, _____.

22. A(n) _____ is a drug that mimics or increases the effects of a neurotransmitter; a(n) _____ is a drug that blocks the effects of a neurotransmitter.

23. The degree to which a drug binds to a receptor is called its _____; the degree to which the drug is able to activate the receptor is called its _____.

24. _____ and _____ discovered that rats will work for electrical stimulation of certain brain areas.

25. Almost all drugs of abuse increase extracellular levels of _____ in the

_____.

26. _____ reverses the dopamine transporter and blocks receptors that inhibit dopamine release; it also increases release of norepinephrine and serotonin.

27. _____ blocks the reuptake of dopamine, serotonin, and norepinephrine.

28. _____ is used to treat attention-deficit disorder; its effects are similar to those of cocaine, but have a slower onset and offset and therefore less potential for addiction.

29. Long-term use of methylenedioxymethamphetamine (_____) destroys _____ neurons, increases anxiety, depression, sleep problems, memory deficits, attention problems, and impulsiveness.

30. Nicotine stimulates nicotinic receptors, which are a type of _____ receptor and are found, among other places, on neurons that release _____ in the nucleus accumbens.

31. Neuropeptides known as _____ are the brain's endogenous morphines. They inhibit ventral tegmental neurons that release _____, and thereby inhibit an inhibitor of dopamine neurons.

32. Marijuana stimulates _____ receptors, which are also stimulated by endogenous peptides such as _____ and sn-2 arachidonylglycerol (_____).

33. Hallucinogenic drugs stimulate _____ receptors.

34. Alcohol facilitates _____ receptors, blocks _____ receptors, and increases stimulation of _____ and _____ receptors.

35. Those with Type _____ alcoholism have a more rapid onset of alcoholism, are more likely to be men, and tend to have more relatives with alcohol problems.

36. Two genes that have been implicated in alcoholism control the _____ receptor and _____, the enzyme that breaks down dopamine.

37. Sons of alcoholic fathers show _____ intoxication after drinking a moderate amount of alcohol, report _____ decrease in stress after drinking, and have a smaller than normal _____ in the right hemisphere.

38. After repeated drug use, the pleasure derived from the drug and other activities decreases, a process referred to as _____.

39. A possible explanation for the decrease in motivation for other, non-drug experiences is increased background inhibition in the _____, which results in less facilitation of the _____ responses to reinforcing experiences.

40. The enzyme that metabolizes acetaldehyde to _____ is _____.

41. The drug _____ (_____) antagonizes the effects of acetaldehyde dehydrogenase, resulting in illness if the person drinks alcohol.

42. _____, _____, and _____ are used to treat opiate abuse; they have effects similar to those of morphine and heroin, but are taken orally and therefore have slower onset and offset.

Matching Items

1. _____ Sherrington
2. _____ Eccles
3. _____ Loewi
4. _____ EPSP
5. _____ IPSP
6. _____ amino acid
7. _____ Methadone
8. _____ catecholamine
9. _____ neuropeptide
10. _____ gaseous transmitter
11. _____ rapid, early onset; more men than women
12. _____ ionotropic effect
13. _____ metabotropic effect
14. _____ treatment for myasthenia gravis
15. _____ affinity
16. _____ efficacy
17. _____ agonist
18. _____ sulfiram (Antabuse)
19. _____ inhibited by cocaine

a. nitric oxide
b. acetylcholinesterase inhibitor
c. mimics or increases effects of transmitter
d. dopamine
e. ability to bind to a receptor
f. transmitter activation of G protein, enzyme
g. inhibits acetaldehyde dehydrogenase
h. inferred major properties of synapses
i. used to treat heroin addiction
j. showed temporal summation in single neurons
k. graded potential due to potassium out or chloride in
l. ability to activate a receptor
m. endorphin
n. glutamate
o. graded potential due to sodium influx
p. opening of ion channel by transmitter
q. showed synaptic conduction is chemical
r. Type II alcoholism
s. dopamine transporter

Multiple-Choice Questions

1. C. S. Sherrington
   a. did extensive electrophysiological recording of synaptic events.
   b. inferred the existence and properties of synapses from behavioral experiments on reflexes in dogs.
   c. was a student of John Eccles.
   d. found that conduction along a single axon is slower than through a reflex arc.

   Which of the following was NOT one of Sherrington's findings?
   a. The speed of conduction through a reflex arc was significantly slower than the known speed of conduction along an axon.
   b. Repeating a subthreshold pinch several times in rapid succession elicited leg flexion.
   c. Simultaneous subthreshold pinches in different parts of the foot elicited flexion.
   d. Reflex arcs are limited to one limb and are always excitatory.

3. Electrophysiological recording from a single neuron
   a. utilizes a microelectrode inserted into the neuron.
   b. supported Sherrington's inferences.
   c. is a field pioneered by John Eccles.
   d. all of the above.

4. IPSPs
   a. may summate to generate an action potential.
   b. are always hyperpolarizing under natural conditions.
   c. are characterized mainly by a large influx of potassium ions.
   d. are characterized mainly by a large influx of sodium ions.

5. Which of the following is true?
   a. The size of EPSPs is the same at all excitatory synapses.
   b. The primary means of inactivation for all neurotransmitters is degradation by an enzyme.
   c. The size, duration, and direction (hyperpolarizing or depolarizing) of a postsynaptic potential are functions of the type and amount of transmitter released, the type and number of receptors present, and perhaps other factors.
   d. A given neuron releases either an excitatory or an inhibitory transmitter (at different times), depending on whether it was excited or inhibited by a previous neuron.

6. EPSPs and action potentials are similar in that
   a. sodium is the major ion producing a depolarization in both.
   b. sodium is the major ion producing a hyperpolarization in both.
   c. potassium is the major ion producing a depolarization in both.
   d. both decay as a function of time and space, decreasing in magnitude as they travel along the membrane.

7. EPSPs
   a. result from a flow of potassium (K+) and chloride (Cl-) ions.
   b. are always depolarizing in natural conditions.
   c. are always large enough to cause the postsynaptic cell to reach triggering threshold for an action potential; otherwise there would be too much uncertainty in the nervous system.
   d. are the same as action potentials.

8. EPSPs and IPSPs
   a. may alter a neuron's spontaneous firing rate.
   b. are always the same size.
   c. usually occur one at a time, so that the neuron does not get confused.
   d. all of the above

9. T. R. Elliott discovered that
   a. adrenalin slowed a frog's heart.
   b. synaptic transmission is electrical rather than chemical.
   c. adrenalin could mimic the effects of the sympathetic nervous system.
   d. all of the above

10. Otto Loewi discovered that a substance collected from the vagus nerve innervating one frog's heart and transferred to a second frog's heart
    a. slowed the second frog's heart.
    b. speeded the second frog's heart.
    c. either speeded or slowed the second frog's heart, depending on the quantity applied.
    d. had no effect, thereby showing that synaptic transmission is not chemically mediated.

11. The level of acetylcholine in the brain can be increased by increasing dietary intake of
    a. acetylcholine.
    b. tyrosine.
    c. choline.
    d. tryptophan.

12. Serotonin levels in the brain can be increased by eating a meal that is high in
    a. choline.
    b. tyrosine.
    c. fat.
    d. carbohydrates.

13. The speed of transport of substances down an axon
    a. is fast enough that even the longest axons require only a few minutes for substances synthesized in the nucleus to reach the terminal.
    b. limits the availability of small neurotransmitters more than that of neuropeptides.
    c. limits the availability of neuropeptides more than that of small neurotransmitters.
    d. is a severe limitation on the availability of all neurotransmitters.

14. Vesicles
    a. are tiny nearly-spherical packets filled with neurotransmitters.
    b. are especially important for storing nitric oxide.
    c. are the only places where transmitters are found in axon terminals.
    d. store only excitatory neurotransmitters; inhibitory neurotransmitters are never stored in vesicles.

15. Calcium
    a. is responsible for exocytosis of neurotransmitters.
    b. enters the terminal when an action potential opens voltage-dependent calcium gates.
    c. causes the release of neurotransmitters within 1 to 2 milliseconds after entry into the terminal.
    d. all of the above

16. Each terminal of a given axon
    a. releases a different neurotransmitter, thus providing a rich repertoire of effects.
    b. usually releases the same neurotransmitter or combination of neurotransmitters at every terminal of that axon, although one exception to that rule is the motor neurons of the spinal cord.
    c. releases only one neurotransmitter, so as not to "confuse" the postsynaptic cell.
    d. releases all of the neurotransmitters known to exist in the brain.

17. Ionotropic synaptic mechanisms
    a. have slow-onset, long-lasting effects.
    b. use a cyclic AMP second messenger response.
    c. are exemplified by glutamate, GABA, and acetylcholine receptors.
    d. frequently use hormones as transmitters.

18. Metabotropic synapses
    a. may have effects that significantly outlast the release of the transmitter.
    b. are activated when a neurotransmitter binds to its receptor site and thereby induces a change in an intracellular part of the receptor that is coupled to a G-protein.
    c. are characterized by initiation of changes in proteins by cyclic AMP, which in turn open or close ion gates or alter the structure or metabolism of the cell.
    d. all of the above

19. Neuromodulators
    a. are usually neuropeptides that diffuse widely enough to affect many cells.
    b. are carried in the blood throughout the entire body.
    c. are usually monoamine neurotransmitters.
    d. usually have ionotropic effects.

20. Hormones
    a. are released in small quantities close to the target cells.
    b. may exert their effects through metabotropic receptors on the surface of cells.
    c. usually exert their effects through ionotropic receptors on the surface of cells.
    d. none of the above

21. The posterior pituitary
    a. is composed of glandular tissue.
    b. releases ACTH, TSH, prolactin, somatotropin, FSH, and LH into the blood stream.
    c. releases oxytocin and vasopressin into the blood stream.
    d. all of the above

22. Acetylcholinesterase
    a. promotes reuptake of acetylcholine into cholinergic terminals.
    b. is the enzyme that cleaves acetylcholine into two inactive parts.
    c. is the enzyme that produces acetylcholine.
    d. blocks reuptake of choline into cholinergic terminals.

23. Reuptake of neurotransmitters
    a. is the major method of inactivation of acetylcholine.
    b. is a major method of inactivation of serotonin and the catecholamines.
    c. is speeded up by COMT.
    d. is completely blocked by MAO.

24. An antagonist is a drug that
    a. has no affinity for a receptor.
    b. changes EPSPs into IPSPs.
    c. mimics or strengthens the effects of a neurotransmitter.
    d. blocks the effects of a neurotransmitter.

25. Which of the following is true?
    a. Some plant-derived drugs are chemicals used by the plants to attract or repel animals.
    b. Most transmitters used in humans have no counterpart in other species.
    c. A drug with high affinity for a given receptor will always elicit a response from that receptor.
    d. Release of neuropeptides requires only one action potential, unlike other neurotransmitters, which require multiple action potentials.

26. Negative feedback can be provided by
    a. autoreceptors that detect the amount of transmitter released and inhibit further synthesis and release.
    b. nitric oxide produced by the postsynaptic cell.
    c. anandamide and 2-AG produced by the postsynaptic cell.
    d. all of the above

27. James Olds and Peter Milner discovered that
    a. rats would press a lever in order to stimulate certain areas of their brains.
    b. only electrical stimulation could increase dopamine release in the nucleus accumbens; naturally motivated behaviors were reinforced only by release of GABA in the nucleus accumbens.
    c. dopamine is most important for producing a feeling of "liking" or pleasure, rather than "wanting."
    d. all of the above

28. Almost all drugs of abuse
    a. activate serotonin 2A receptors.
    b. increase dopamine release in the nucleus accumbens.
    c. activate cannabinoid receptors.
    d. activate opioid receptors.

29. Methylphenidate (Ritalin)
    a. blocks the reuptake of dopamine.
    b. is used to treat attention-deficit disorder (ADD).
    c. may decrease adolescent drug addiction after treatment of childhood ADD.
    d. all of the above

30. Which of the following is true of nicotine?
    a. It stimulates nicotinic acetylcholine receptors on neurons that release dopamine in the nucleus accumbens.
    b. After withdrawing from repeated exposures to nicotine, neurons are more sensitive to all kinds of events, showing that they are more reinforcing than ever.
    c. It is produced naturally in postsynaptic neurons and is used to provide negative feedback to the presynaptic cell.
    d. It stimulates nicotinic serotonin receptors.

31. Endorphins
    a. were discovered by James Olds and Peter Milner.
    b. inhibit GABA-containing neurons in the ventral tegmental area that otherwise would inhibit dopamine-containing neurons there; therefore, they disinhibit dopamine neurons.
    c. relieve pain by acting on receptors in the skin, or wherever pain is felt.
    d. work only by disinhibiting dopamine neurons.

32. Anandamide
    a. is an opioid peptide.
    b. is sometimes known as "ecstasy."
    c. is an endogenous chemical that activates cannabinoid receptors.
    d. stimulates serotonin 2A receptors and thereby induces hallucinations.

33. Alcohol
    a. makes $GABA_A$ receptors more responsive.
    b. inhibits glutamate receptors.
    c. increases stimulation of dopamine and opiate receptors.
    d. all of the above

34. Type II alcoholism
    a. has a stronger genetic basis than does Type I.
    b. develops gradually over the years.
    c. affects men and women about equally.
    d. all of the above

35. Acetaldehyde dehydrogenase
    a. is the generic name for Antabuse.
    b. controls the rate of conversion of acetic acid, a toxic product of alcohol metabolism, into acetaldehyde, a source of energy.
    c. controls the rate of conversion of acetaldehyde, a toxic product of alcohol metabolism, into acetic acid, a source of energy.
    d. if present in high levels, would make us feel very ill after drinking alcohol.

36. Which of the following is true?
    a. Sons of alcoholics experience less than average relief from stress after drinking alcohol.
    b. Antabuse acts as a supplement to the alcoholic's commitment to stop drinking.
    c. Sons of alcoholics show greater than average intoxication after drinking a small to moderate amount of alcohol.
    d. Sons of alcoholics tend to have an unusually large amygdala in the right hemisphere.

37. Methadone
    a. is frequently abused because it acts rapidly when taken in pill form, producing a sudden rush of excitement.
    b. is an antagonist at opiate receptors.
    c. has effects similar to heroin, but when given in pill form its effects occur gradually, without a "rush."
    d. cures addiction after the first few doses, with no need for further treatment.

Solutions

True/False Questions

1.	F	10.	T	19.	T	28.	T
2.	T	11.	T	20.	F	29.	T
3.	T	12.	F	21.	F	30.	F
4.	F	13.	T	22.	T	31.	T
5.	F	14.	F	23.	F	32.	T
6.	F	15.	T	24.	T	33.	F
7.	T	16.	F	25.	T		
8.	T	17.	T	26.	F		
9.	F	18.	F	27.	F		

Fill In The Blanks

1. Ramón y Cajal
2. Charles Sherrington
3. John Eccles
4. Na+ (sodium)
5. graded potentials
6. K+ (potassium); Cl- (chloride)
7. spontaneous firing rate
8. slowed
9. glutamate; GABA; glycine; aspartate
10. dopamine; norepinephrine; epinephrine; serotonin.
11. endorphins; substance P; neuropeptide Y
12. serotonin
13. metabotropic
14. Protein; peptide
15. oxytocin; vasopressin.
16. adrenocorticotropin; thyroid-stimulating hormone; prolactin; growth hormone; follicle-stimulating hormone; luteinizing hormone.
17. acetylcholinesterase
18. myasthenia gravis
19. reuptake; transporters
20. Autoreceptors
21. nitric oxide; anandamide; and 2-AG.
22. agonist; antagonist
23. affinity; efficacy
24. James Olds; Peter Milner
25. dopamine; nucleus accembens.
26. Amphetamine
27. Cocaine
28. Methylphenidate
29. MDMA or "ecstasy"; serotonin
30. acetylcholine; dopamine
31. endorphins; GABA
32. cannabinoid; anandamide; 2-AG
33. serotonin 2A
34. $GABA_A$; glutamate; dopamine; opiate
35. II
36. dopamine type 4; COMT
37. less; greater; amygdala
38. tolerance
39. prefrontal cortex; nucleus accumbens's
40. acetic acid; acetaldehyde dehydrogenase
41. disulfiram (Antabuse)
42. Methadone; buprenorphine; LAAM

Matching Items

1. h	6. n	11. r	16. l
2. j	7. i	12. p	17. c
3. q	8. d	13. f	18. g
4. o	9. m	14. b	19. s
5. k	10. a	15. e	

Multiple Choice Questions

1. b	11. c	21. c	31. b
2. d	12. d	22. b	32. c
3. d	13. c	23. b	33. d
4. b	14. a	24. d	34. a
5. c	15. d	25. a	35. c
6. a	16. b	26. d	36. b
7. b	17. c	27. a	37. c
8. a	18. d	28. b	
9. c	19. a	29. d	
10. a	20. b	30. a	

CHAPTER 4

Anatomy of the Nervous System

Introduction

The vertebrate nervous system consists of two major divisions, the central (CNS) and the peripheral (PNS) nervous systems. The CNS is composed of the brain and the spinal cord. The PNS is divided into the somatic and the autonomic nervous systems. The somatic system consists of sensory nerves that convey information from sense organs to the spinal cord, and motor nerves carrying messages from the spinal cord to muscles and glands. A pair of sensory nerves enters (one from each side) and a pair of motor nerves exits from the spinal cord through each pair of openings in the vertebral canal. The sensory nerves enter the spinal cord from the dorsal direction, and the motor axons leave from the ventral aspect. Cell bodies of sensory neurons lie in the dorsal root ganglia; those of the motor neurons are in the spinal cord. The autonomic nervous system also sends neurons through the vertebral openings; they synapse in ganglia outside the spinal cord. Ganglia of the sympathetic division of the autonomic nervous system are arranged in an interconnected chain along the thoracic and lumbar sections of the spinal cord. Ganglia of the parasympathetic division of the autonomic nervous system receive input from the cranial nerves and the sacral section of the cord and are located near the organs they innervate. The interconnections of the sympathetic system promote unified action by the body in a fight-or-flight situation, whereas the relative independence of the parasympathetic innervations allows for more discrete energy-saving responses. Most of the final synapses of the sympathetic nervous system use the neurotransmitter norepinephrine, while the final parasympathetic synapses use acetylcholine.

The brain is divided into the hindbrain, the midbrain, and the forebrain. The hindbrain is composed of the medulla, the pons, and the cerebellum. The medulla contains numerous nuclei that control life-preserving reflexes. The pons has many fibers that cross from one side to the other, going to the cerebellum, which is directly behind the pons. The cerebellum helps control movement and is important for shifting attention and for timing. The reticular formation and the raphe system, which modify the brain's readiness to respond to stimuli, have diffusely branching neurons throughout the medulla, pons, and midbrain and send diffusely branching axons throughout the brain. The midbrain is composed of the tectum (or roof), on which are the two superior colliculi and the two inferior colliculi, involved in sensory processing; and the tegmentum, containing cranial nerve nuclei, parts of the reticular formation, extensions of neural systems of the hindbrain, and the substantia nigra, degeneration of which causes Parkinson's disease. The forebrain includes the limbic system, a number of interlinked structures important for motivational and emotional behaviors; the thalamus, which is the main source of sensory input to the cerebral cortex; the hypothalamus, important for motivational and hormonal regulation; the pituitary or "master gland"; the basal ganglia, which influence motor movements, emotional expression, memory, and reasoning; the hippocampus, important in memory functions; and the cerebral cortex, which surrounds the rest of the brain and is responsible for complex sensory analysis and integration, language processing, motor control, and social awareness. The ventricles are fluid-filled cavities within the brain.

The cerebral cortex consists of up to six laminae, or layers, of cell bodies parallel to the surface of the brain. The cells are organized into columns, perpendicular to the laminae; each column contains cells with similar response properties. The occipital lobe of the cerebral cortex is the site of primary visual processing. The parietal lobe processes somatosensory and numerical information and contributes to our spatial sense. The temporal lobe processes auditory information and is important for perception of complex visual patterns, comprehension of language, and emotional and motivated behaviors. The frontal lobe contains the motor cortex, which controls fine movements, and prefrontal cortex, which contributes to social awareness, the expression of emotion, memory for recent details (working memory), and calculation of actions and their outcomes.

Each part of the brain accomplishes a set of more or less specific functions; yet, a sense of unified experience emerges from these separate operations. The question of how the brain integrates various kinds of sensory information into the perception of a unified object is known as the binding problem. How are the various aspects bound together? One possibility is that binding depends on precisely simultaneous activity (gamma waves) in the different brain areas. However, we still do not understand how synchronized gamma waves bind the different aspects into a unified perception. The inferior temporal cortex may contribute to binding by assigning aspects of a perception to a common location in space.

Describing the structure of the brain can be tedious, but understanding the functions of the various structures is daunting. Images of the whole brain can be obtained by computerized axial tomography (CAT or CT scans) or magnetic resonance imaging (MRI). Localized brain activity can be recorded with an electroencephalograph (EEG), which records either spontaneous activity or evoked potentials. Activity can also be recorded by a magnetoencephallograph (MEG), which measures faint magnetic fields. In addition brain activity can be recorded during a task, using electrodes or positron emission tomography (PET), which detects radioactivity from labeled chemicals taken up by the most active brain areas. A less expensive and less dangerous method is functional magnetic resonance imaging (fMRI), which detects changes in hemoglobin molecules as they release oxygen to the most active brain areas. The functions of brain areas can also be inferred from accidental (in humans) or deliberate (in animals) damage or temporary inactivation. Such inferences can be compared with those from electrical or magnetic stimulation of those areas in an intact brain. One problem with inferences about the function of a brain area from correlations between its size or activity and behavior is that correlation does not imply causation. An example of this arises when comparing size differences between the brain of men and women. On average, the size of the brain and certain brain structures is different between the two. Despite this fact, differences in several aspects of behavior are small or non-existent.

Learning Objectives

Module 4.1   Structure of the Vertebrate Nervous System
1.   Be able to identify the directional terms for anatomical structures.
2.   Be able to describe the structure of the spinal cord and the locations of its sensory inputs and motor outputs.

3. Know the functions, locations, and organization of the two main branches of the autonomic nervous system.
4. Know the three main divisions of the hindbrain and both their unique and their shared functions.
5. Know the two divisions of the midbrain and the major structures in each.
6. Be able to identify the main structures and functions of the diencephalon, the limbic system, the basal ganglia, and the basal forebrain.

Module 4.2 The Cerebral Cortex
1. Know the locations and functions of the four lobes of the cerebral cortex.
2. Understand the "binding problem" and a possible means of coordinating neural activity throughout a large portion of the brain to form a unified perception.

Module 4.3 Research Methods
1. Understand the uses of and principles underlying the techniques of computerized axial tomography (CAT), magnetic resonance imagine (MRI), electroencephalography (EEG), magnetoencephalography (MEG), positron emission tomography (PET), and functional magnetic resonance imaging (fMRI).
2. Be able to identify the major ways of inactivating parts of the brain, temporarily or permanently, and of stimulating parts of the brain.
3. Understand the problems of interpretation of the effects of lesions.
4. Understand gender-specific differences in size of brain and brain structures, including the limitations of interpreting these correlation data.

Key Terms and Concepts

Module 4.1 Structure of the Vertebrate Nervous System
1.   Terminology that describes the nervous system
    Central nervous system (CNS): Brain and spinal cord
    Peripheral nervous system (PNS): Somatic and autonomic nervous systems
    Dorsal (toward the back)
    Ventral (toward the stomach)
    Dorsal-ventral axis of human brain at right angles to dorsal-ventral axis of spinal cord

2.   The spinal cord
    Bell-Magendie Law
        Sensory nerves: Enter dorsally
        Motor nerves: Exit ventrally
    Dorsal root ganglia: Clusters of cell bodies of sensory neurons
    Gray matter: Cell bodies and dendrites
    White matter: Myelinated axons

3.   The autonomic nervous system
    Sympathetic nervous system ("fight or flight")
        Sympathetic chains of ganglia
        Thoracic and lumbar regions of spinal cord
        Norepinephrine

Parasympathetic nervous system (energy conserving)
    Cranial and sacral regions (craniosacral system)
    Ganglia near organs
    Acetylcholine

4.   The hindbrain (rhombencephalon): Medulla, pons, cerebellum
  Brain stem (medulla, pons, midbrain, some forebrain structures)
  Medulla
    Vital reflexes
    Cranial nerves
    Reticular formation
    Raphe system
  Pons ("bridge")
    Cranial nerves
    Fibers crossing
    Reticular formation
    Raphe system
  Cerebellum
    Control of movement
    Balance and coordination
    Shifting attention
    Timing

5.   The midbrain (mesencephalon)
  Tectum ("roof")
    Superior and inferior colliculi
  Tegmentum ("covering")
    Cranial nerves
    Reticular formation
  Substantia nigra

6.   The forebrain (prosencephalon)
  Cerebral hemispheres
  Cerebral cortex
  Limbic system (important for motivation and emotions): Borders around brain stem
    Olfactory bulb
    Hypothalamus
    Hippocampus
    Amygdala
    Cingulate gyrus of cerebral cortex
  Thalamus (part of diencephalon)
    Transmits sensory information (except olfaction) to cortex
  Hypothalamus (part of diencephalon, ventral to thalamus)
    Comprised by several nuclei
    Motivated behaviors
    Control of pituitary gland

Pituitary gland
    Controls other glands
Basal ganglia
    Caudate nucleus
    Putamen
    Globus pallidus
    Connections with frontal cortex
    Control of movement
    Aspects of memory and emotional expression
    Parkinson's disease
    Huntington's disease
Basal forebrain
    Nucleus basalis: acetylcholine to cortex
        Arousal, wakefulness, attention
    Parkinson's disease
    Alzheimer's disease
Hippocampus ("sea horse")
    Storing new memories

7.   The ventricles
    Central canal of spinal cord
    Two lateral ventricles, third and fourth ventricles
    Cerebrospinal fluid (CSF)
        Produced by choroid plexus
        Cushion, buoyancy, reservoir of hormones and nutrition
    Meninges: Membranes surrounding brain and spinal cord
    Subarachnoid space: Reabsorption of CSF into blood vessels
    Hydrocephalus

8.   In closing: Learning neuroanatomy

Module 4.2 The Cerebral Cortex
1. Connections between hemispheres
        Corpus callosum
        Anterior commissure
    Cortex: Higher percentage of brain in primates

2. Organization of the cerebral cortex
    Laminae: Layers parallel to surface
    Columns: Perpendicular to laminae

3.   The occipital lobe (posterior, or caudal, end of cortex)
    Primary visual cortex
    Striate cortex
    Cortical blindness

4. The parietal lobe (between occipital lobe and central sulcus)
   Central sulcus
   Postcentral gyrus: Primary somatosensory cortex
       Four bands parallel to central sulcus
           Two light-touch bands
           One deep-pressure band
           One light-touch and deep-pressure band
   Interpretation of visual and auditory input, numerical information

5. The temporal lobe (lateral, near temples)
   Primary auditory cortex
   Language comprehension
   Complex visual patterns
   Klüver-Bucy syndrome

6. The frontal lobe (from central sulcus to anterior end of brain)
   Precentral gyrus: Primary motor cortex
   Prefrontal cortex
       Prefrontal lobotomies
           Lack of initiative
           Memory disorder
           Loss of emotional expression
           Failure to inhibit unacceptable impulses
   Modern view of functions of the prefrontal cortex
       Working memory: Memory for recent events
       Delayed-response task
       Follow two or more rules at same time
       Fail to modify behavior according to context

7. How do the parts work together?
   Operation as a whole vs. collection of parts
   The binding problem (large-scale integration problem)
       How brain areas influence one another to produce perception of single object was thought
       to occur in "association areas."
           Advanced processing on a particular sensory system, not combining 2 systems
8. In closing: Functions of the cerebral cortex
   Elaborating sensory material

Module 4.3 Research Methods
1. Correlating brain anatomy with behavior
   Phrenology
   Computerized axial tomography (CT or CAT scan)
       Pass x-rays through the head
       Helps detect tumors or structural abnormalities
   Magnetic resonance imaging (MRI)
       Atoms with odd-numbered atomic weights: inherent rotation

Magnetic field aligns rotation of atoms

Brief radio frequency field → tilt axes

Field turned off → atoms relax, give off electromagnetic energy

Advantage: good spatial resolution without radioactivity

Disadvantage: lie motionless in confining, noisy apparatus

Problem: Correlation does not mean causation

2. Recording brain activity

Laboratory animals: Activity may be measured using electrodes or by staining for certain proteins.

Electroencephalograph (EEG)

Spontaneous brain activity

Evoked potentials (evoked responses)

Magnetoencephalograph (MEG)

Minute magnetic fields generated by brain activity

Good temporal resolution, but poor spatial resolution

Positron emission tomography (PET)

Radioactive chemical absorbed by most active neurons

Radioactive decay → positron collides with electron → two gamma rays

Gamma ray detectors

High spatial resolution

Dangerous because of radioactivity

Functional magnetic resonance imaging (fMRI)

Changes in hemoglobin molecules as they release oxygen in active areas

Less dangerous and less expensive than PET

Problem with interpretation of results

What is comparison task?

Experience alters results

Issues of consciousness are being investigated using fMRI

3. Effects of brain damage

Paul Broca

Part of left frontal lobe: Broca's area → ability to speak

Lesion: Damage to an area

Ablation: Removal of an area

Stereotaxic instrument, atlas

Sham lesion

Gene-knockout approach: directed mutation of a gene

Transcranial magnetic stimulation: Disruption of local activity by intense magnetic field

Difficulty of determining exact function

4. Effects of brain stimulation

Electrical stimulation in animals

Brief, moderate intensity magnetic fields in humans

5. Differences in brain size and structure
    Comparisons across species
        Brain-to-body ratio

        Accurately weighing brain is difficult
    Comparisons among humans
        Moderate positive correlation between brain size and IQ
        Significant correlation between IQ and specific brain areas
        General intelligence correlates with amount of gray matter throughout most cortical
        regions
        The genes controlling brain size also influence IQ
    Comparisons of men and women
        Men: Larger brains than women, but equal IQs
        Women: more and deeper gyri → more surface area
        Men and women: equal gray matter; men: more white matter
        Behavioral differences are small
            No differences in the number of words used per day
        Some cognitive differences exist

6. In closing: Methods and their limits

Short-Answer Questions

Module 4.1 Structure of the Vertebrate Nervous System

1. *The spinal cord*

    a. Draw a cross section of the spinal cord, including sensory and motor nerves, dorsal root
        ganglia, and dorsal and ventral directions.

    b. What is the Bell-Magendie Law?

    c. What makes up gray matter? White matter?

2. *The autonomic nervous system*

    a. Of what two parts does the autonomic nervous system consist? Give the location and basic
        function of each.

    b. Which transmitter is used by the postganglionic parasympathetic nerves? Which is used by
        most sympathetic postganglionic nerves?

3. *The hindbrain*

    a. What are the three components of the hindbrain? Give one "specialty" of each.

    b. What are cranial nerves? Where are their nuclei?

    c. What are the anatomical locations and functions of the reticular formation and the raphe
        system?

4. *The midbrain*

   a. What are the two major divisions of the midbrain? Name two structures in each division.

5. *The forebrain*

   a. What are the major structures comprising the limbic system? What are the general functions of this interconnected system?

   b. Describe the relationship of the thalamus to the cerebral cortex.

   c. Where is the hypothalamus, and what kinds of behavior does it help regulate?

   d. Where is the pituitary? What is its function? What structure largely controls it?

   e. Where are the basal ganglia? Which structures make up the basal ganglia? Briefly describe their function.

   f. Where is the hippocampus? To what psychological process has it been linked?

6. *The ventricles*

   a. What are the ventricles? Where is cerebrospinal fluid (CSF) formed? In which direction does it flow? Where is it reabsorbed into blood vessels?

   b. What are the functions of CSF?

Module 4.2 The Cerebral Cortex

1. *Organization of cerebral cortex*

   a. What is the relationship of gray matter to white in the cortex? Compare this relationship to that in the spinal cord.

   b. How many layers (laminae) does human neocortex have? Describe the input to lamina IV and the output from lamina V.

   c. What is the relationship of columns to laminae? What can be said about all the cells within one column?

2. *The occipital lobe*

   a. What are the location and functions of the occipital lobe?

3. *The parietal lobe*

   a. What are the location and functions of the parietal lobe?

4. *The temporal lobe*

   a. Where is the temporal lobe? What are some temporal lobe functions?

5. *The frontal lobe*

   a. What are the location and functions of the frontal lobe? Distinguish between the precentral gyrus and the prefrontal cortex.

   b. What were the results of prefrontal lobotomies?

   c. What is working memory? What is one task that shows impairment after prefrontal lesions?

6. *How do the parts work together?*

    a. What is the binding problem?

    b. What are gamma waves? What may be the role of the inferior temporal cortex in binding the different aspects of sensory objects?

Module 4.3 Research Methods

1. *Correlating brain activity with behavior*

    a. What was phrenology?

    b. Describe computerized axial tomography (CAT).

    c. What is the basis for magnetic resonance imaging? What is one drawback of this method?

    d. What is a limitation of inferences of function from correlations with measurable features of the brain?

2. *Recording brain activity*

    a. Describe the process of electroencephalography (EEG). What two types of activity can it measure?

    b. How does magnetoencephalography (MEG) differ from electroencephalography? Does it have better spatial or temporal resolution than EEG?

    c. What is the principle on which positron emission tomography (PET) is based?

    d. What are two advantages of functional magnetic resonance imaging (fMRI) over PET? What is the physical basis for fMRI?

    e. What is a problem with inferring function from records of brain activity?

3. *Effects of brain damage*

    a. What did Paul Broca discover?

    b. What is a stereotaxic instrument used for?

    c. What are four methods of deliberately inactivating some type or location of brain activity?

    d. What is the main problem with inferences about function based on these approaches?

4. *Effects of brain stimulation*

    a. Compare the magnetic stimulation used to stimulate certain brain areas with that used to inactivate brain areas.

    b. What is a problem with inferences about the functions of brain areas based on localized stimulation?

5. *Differences in brain size and structure*

    a. What are implications of brain-to-body ratio for animal intelligence?

    b. Understand the implications and limitations of data correlating brain size with intelligence.

    c. What brain areas differ in size between men and women? What are possible limitations presented when interpreting these differences?

True/False Questions

1. Sensory nerves enter the spinal cord from the dorsal side, and motor nerves exit from the ventral side.

   TRUE or FALSE

2. Ganglia of the sympathetic nervous system lie along the cervical and sacral parts of the spinal cord.

   TRUE or FALSE

3. The postganglionic transmitter of the parasympathetic nervous system is norepinephrine.

   TRUE or FALSE

4. The reticular formation and raphe system are found in the pons and medulla; they regulate arousal and the readiness to respond, respectively.

   TRUE or FALSE

5. The substantia nigra is found in the tectum of the midbrain and controls vital reflexes.

   TRUE or FALSE

6. The limbic system comprises the olfactory bulb, the hypothalamus, the hippocampus, the amygdala, and the cingulate gyrus of the cerebral cortex.

   TRUE or FALSE

7. The main function of the hypothalamus is to transmit information to the cortex.

   TRUE or FALSE

8. The basal ganglia are concerned with the control of movement and also some aspects of memory, reasoning, and emotional expression.

   TRUE or FALSE

9. A major function of the hippocampus is control of the pituitary gland.

   TRUE or FALSE

10. The ventricles contain cerebrospinal fluid (CSF) that is produced by the choroid plexus and provides cushioning and buoyancy to the brain.

    TRUE or FALSE

11. Laminae of the cerebral cortex are the same thing as columns.

    TRUE or FALSE

12. The occipital lobe is the site of primary auditory cortex.

    TRUE or FALSE

13. The temporal lobe is essential for the understanding of spoken language and also contributes to complex visual perceptions.

    TRUE or FALSE

14. The prefrontal cortex is the primary motor cortex.

TRUE or FALSE

15. Magnetoencephalography is a technique that detects the electromagnetic energy given off after atoms with odd numbers of electrons relax after a strong radiofrequency field is turned off.

TRUE or FALSE

16. Functional magnetic resonance imaging (fMRI) detects emission of radioactivity.

TRUE or FALSE

17. PET scans are safer and less expensive than fMRI scans.

TRUE or FALSE

18. Performing a task requiring constant attention increases activity in the posterior cingulated cortex.

TRUE or FALSE

19. Paul Broca discovered that people who had lost their ability to speak usually had damage to a part of the left frontal lobe.

TRUE or FALSE

20. A stereotaxic instrument is used to direct electrodes to a precise area of the brain.

TRUE or FALSE

21. Genetic factors do not influence intellectual performance.

TRUE or FALSE

22. The size of certain brain areas is different between males and females.

TRUE or FALSE

Fill In The Blanks

1. The Bell-Magendie Law states that sensory neurons enter the spinal cord from the _____ direction, and motor neurons exit the spinal cord from the _____ direction.

2. The autonomic nervous system consists of the _____ nervous system, with ganglia located _____, and the _____ nervous system, with ganglia located _____.

3. The hind brain consists of the _____, the _____, and the _____.

4. In addition to containing the reticular formation and the raphe system, the medulla contains cranial nerve nuclei that control _____.

5. The pons gets its name (Latin for "bridge") from _____.

6. The cerebellum was originally thought to be important only for controlling _____; however, we now know that it also contributes to _____ and _____.

7. The _____ of the midbrain contains the superior and inferior colliculi; the _____ of the midbrain contains nuclei of cranial nerves, part of the reticular formation, and the substantia nigra.

8. The main structures that comprise the limbic system are the _____, the _____, the _____, the _____, and the _____ of the cerebral cortex.

9. The main function of the _____ is to transmit sensory information (except olfaction) to the cerebral cortex.

10. The hypothalamus sends hypothalamic hormones to the _____ gland, and also helps to regulate various _____ behaviors.

11. The basal ganglia comprise the _____, the _____, and the _____.

12. The basal ganglia have important connections with the _____ and are important for the control of _____ and aspects of _____, _____, and _____.

13. The _____ in the basal forebrain sends acetylcholine to the cortex and promotes arousal, wakefulness, and attention.

14. The main function of the _____ is storing new memories.

15. The _____ forms cerebrospinal fluid.

16. A swelling of blood vessels in the _____ results in pain associated with migraine headaches.

17. The _____ of the cerebral cortex are layers of cell bodies that lie parallel to the surface of the cortex; the _____ of the cortex are perpendicular to the laminae and contain neurons that have similar properties.

18. Primary visual cortex is located in the _____ lobe.

19. The parietal lobe contains the postcentral gyrus, which is the primary _____ cortex.

20. A tumor in the temporal lobe may give rise to _____ or _____ hallucinations.

21. The main divisions of the frontal lobe are the _____, which serves as the primary motor cortex, and the _____, which contributes to working memory and modifies behavior according to the context.

22. The question of how the various areas of the brain work together to form a unitary perception is known as the _____. This function may be mediated by _____ waves of neural firing throughout much of the cortex.

23. The technique of _____ records magnetic fields generated by brain activity. It has good _____ resolution, but poor _____ resolution.

24. The technique of _____ (_____) uses the inherent rotation of atoms with odd-numbered atomic weights. A powerful magnetic field aligns the axes of rotation, which are tilted by a radiofrequency field. When the radiofrequency field is turned off, the atoms release electromagnetic energy as they relax. This technique has good _____ resolution.

25. By using the _____ approach, researchers demonstrated that mice lacking the gene for _____ receptors did not respond to cocaine as reinforcement.

26. The method of recording brain activity that measures changes in hemoglobin molecules as they release oxygen in active brain areas is _____ (_____).

27. Paul Broca discovered that loss of speech was frequently correlated with brain damage in the _____.

28. Different intensities and durations of magnetic fields can be used either to _____ or to _____ localized brain areas.

Matching Items

1. _____ CAT scans
2. _____ Intense, prolonged magnetic fields
3. _____ Brief, moderate intensity magnetic fields
4. _____ PET scans
5. _____ fMRI
6. _____ Dorsal root ganglia
7. _____ Motor axons
8. _____ Sympathetic nervous system
9. _____ Medulla
10. _____ Pons
11. _____ Midbrain
12. _____ Thalamus
13. _____ Hypothalamus
14. _____ Basal ganglia
15. _____ Occipital lobe
16. _____ Temporal lobe
17. _____ Parietal lobe
18. _____ Frontal lobe

a. Contains "vital nuclei"
b. Site of axons crossing to other side
c. Contains primary motor cortex
d. X-rays used to show brain structure
e. Exit through the ventral side of the spinal cord
f. Hemoglobin molecules releasing oxygen
g. Relays information to cerebral cortex
h. Method of temporarily inactivating an area
i. Movement, memory, emotional expression
j. Primary visual cortex
k. "Fight or flight" system
l. Cell bodies of sensory neurons
m. Primary somatosensory cortex
n. Site of tectum and tegmentum
o. Primary auditory cortex
p. Method of stimulating a brain area
q. Motivated behaviors, controls pituitary
r. Radioactive chemicals in most-active areas

16. Which of the following is true of cortical columns?
    a. Columns run parallel to the laminae, across the surface of the cortex.
    b. There are six columns in the human brain, and only one or two in other mammals.
    c. Cells within a column have similar response properties.
    d. The properties of cells within a column change systematically from top to bottom; cells at the top may respond to one stimulus, while those at the bottom respond to a different one.

17. Which is true of the occipital lobe?
    a. It is located at the posterior end of the cortex and contains the primary visual cortex.
    b. It is located at the sides of the brain and is concerned mostly with perception of complex visual patterns.
    c. It is located immediately behind the central sulcus and contains the postcentral gyrus.
    d. It is located at the top of the brain and contributes to somatosensory processing.

18. Which is true of the parietal lobe?
    a. It contains the primary receiving area for axons carrying touch sensations and other skin and muscle information.
    b. It has 4 bands on the postcentral gyrus that receive light-touch, deep-pressure, or both.
    c. It contributes to our sense of our body in space, relative to visual and auditory stimuli.
    d. All of the above are true.

19. The temporal lobe
    a. is located immediately in front of the central sulcus.
    b. is involved in some complex aspects of visual processing as well as auditory processing.
    c. has as its only function the processing of simple auditory information.
    d. none of the above.

20. Damage to the frontal lobe
    a. may cause losses of initiative and of social inhibitions and produce difficulties with delayed response tasks.
    b. is still a widely used surgical technique for mental patients because of its remarkable calming and normalizing tendencies without noticeable side effects.
    c. produces drastic impairments in intelligence.
    d. all of the above.

21. Gamma waves
    a. are synchronized waves of activity (30 to 80 per second) in various brain areas, which may reflect binding of sensory aspects into a unified perception.
    b. are synchronized by the prefrontal cortex, indicating that prefrontal cortex is the site of unified experience.
    c. are especially important for our numerical sense.
    d. are synchronized waves of activity localized within a specific brain area, and are important for shifting attention to the sensory aspect that is processed by that area.

22. CAT scans
    a. use intense magnetic fields to inactivate brain areas temporarily.
    b. use x-rays to describe brain structure.
    c. use changes in hemoglobin as it releases oxygen to areas with high metabolic activity.
    d. use brief, moderate magnetic fields to stimulate brain areas.

23. A problem in trying to infer behavioral function from measures of brain structure or activity is:
   a. Correlation does not imply causation.
   b. Cases of brain damage often are not specifically localized to one area.
   c. It is difficult to determine which aspect of a complex task is controlled by the brain area that was inactivated.
   d. All of the above are true.

Helpful Hints

- To remember the 12 cranial nerves, use this mnemonic device:
   1. On (Olfactory)
   2. Old (Optic)
   3. Olympia's (Oculomotor)
   4. Towering (Trochlear)
   5. Tops, (Trigeminal)
   6. A (Abducens)
   7. Firm, (Facial)
   8. Staid (Statoacoustic)
   9. German (Glossopharyngial)
   10. Viewed (Vagus)
   11. A lot of (Accessory)
   12. Hops (Hypoglossal)

- To remember the functions of the hypothalamus, think of the "4 Fs": Fighting, Fleeing, Feeding, and Reproductive Behavior.

Solutions

True/False Questions

1. T	7. F	13. T	19. T
2. F	8. T	14. F	20. T
3. F	9. F	15. F	21. F
4. T	10. T	16. F	22. T
5. F	11. F	17. F	
6. T	12. F	18. F	

Fill In The Blanks

1. dorsal; ventral
2. sympathetic; along the spinal cord; parasympathetic; near the organs they innervate
3. medulla; pons; cerebellum
4. vital reflexes
5. axons crossing from one side to the other
6. movement; timing; shifting attention.
7. tectum; tegmentum
8. olfactory bulb; hypothalamus; hippocampus; amygdale; cingulate gyrus
9. thalamus
10. pituitary; motivated
11. caudate nucleus; putamen; globus pallidus
12. frontal lobe; movement; memory; reasoning; emotional expression
13. nucleus basalis
14. hippocampus
15. choroid plexus
16. meninges
17. laminae; columns
18. occipital
19. somatosensory
20. auditory; visual
21. precentral gyrus; prefrontal cortex
22. binding problem; gamma
23. magnetoencephalography; temporal; spatial
24. magnetic resonance imaging; (MRI)
25. spatial
26. gene-knockout; dopamine
27. functional magnetic resonance imaging; (fMRI)
28. left frontal lobe
29. inactivate; stimulate

Matching Items

1. d	6. l	11. n	16. o
2. h	7. e	12. g	17. m
3. p	8. k	13. q	18. c
4. r	9. a	14. i	
5. f	10. b	15. j	

Multiple Choice Questions

1. b	7. d	13. b	19. b
2. d	8. b	14. d	20. a
3. a	9. c	15. c	21. a
4. b	10. a	16. c	22. b
5. c	11. d	17. a	23. d
6. a	12. d	18. d	

CHAPTER 5

Development and Plasticity of the Brain

Introduction

The central nervous system develops from two long thin lips on the surface of the embryo that merge to form a fluid-filled tube. The forward end of the tube enlarges to become the forebrain, midbrain, and hindbrain; the rest becomes the spinal cord. Cerebrospinal fluid continues to fill the central canal of the spinal cord and four hollow ventricles of the brain.

There are five major stages in the development of neurons: proliferation, migration, differentiation, myelination, and synaptogenesis. During proliferation, cells lining the ventricles divide. Some of the new cells remain in place as stem cells and continue dividing, whereas others, destined to become neurons and glia, migrate to their new destinations. Differentiation includes formation of the axon and dendrites and determination of shape and chemical components. Myelination is the formation, by glia, of insulating sheaths around axons, which increase the speed of transmission. Synaptogenesis, the formation of functional synapses, continues throughout life. The traditional view that vertebrates do not generate any new neurons in adulthood has been shown to be inaccurate in at least some cases. New olfactory receptors are formed from stem cells in the olfactory bulbs. Undifferentiated stem cells in the interior of the brain continue to divide, and some daughter cells migrate to the olfactory bulb and hippocampus and become neurons or glia. New neurons also have also been found in the song control areas of songbirds. More of these new neurons survive during a time of new learning. However, there appear to be no new neurons in the cerebral cortex.

As the brain grows, axons must travel long distances to reach their appropriate targets. They are guided by concentration gradients of chemicals, such as the protein TOP_{DV}, which guides retinal axons to the appropriate part of the tectum. Axons are attracted by some chemicals and repelled by others. After axons reach the general area of their target, they begin to form synapses with postsynaptic cells. The target cells receive an overabundance of synapses; they gradually strengthen some synapses and reject others. Initially, there are many tentative connections between axons and target cells; later, fewer but stronger attachments develop. The overproduction of neurons and subsequent pruning of unsuccessful connections provide a process of selection of the fittest or most informative connections, a process referred to as neural Darwinism.

There is an initial overproduction of neurons; those that fail to form synapses with appropriate target cells die. The process of programmed cell death, or apoptosis, can be prevented if the neuron receives a neurotrophin from the target cell. Rita Levi-Montalcini discovered the first neurotrophin, nerve growth factor (NGF), which promotes survival of neurons of the sympathetic nervous system. Several additional neurotrophins have been discovered, including brain-derived neurotrophic factor (BDNF). In addition to preventing apoptosis, neurotrophins also enhance branching of axons and dendrites in adulthood. During maturation of the prefrontal cortex in adolescence, the number of neurons decreases while neuronal activity actually increases. Thus, more successful neurons and connections survive at the expense of less successful ones.

Developing brains are not only more responsive to environmental stimuli, they are also more vulnerable to malnutrition, toxic chemicals, and infection. For example, fetal alcohol syndrome is characterized by hyperactivity, attention deficits, impulsiveness, mental retardation and other physical and mental abnormalities. Children with fetal alcohol syndrome have neurons with smaller, less branching dendrites. Alcohol decreases the release of glutamate and neurotrophins and increases activity at inhibitory GABA synapses; as a result more neurons undergo apoptosis. Prenatal exposure to cocaine and to the effects of cigarette smoking also result in physical and intellectual deficits. Even maternal stress can change the mother's behavior in a way that results in emotional and behavioral problems in the offspring.

Environmental enrichment results in a thicker cortex, more dendritic branching, and enhanced performance on learning tasks. Effects of enrichment, or of sensory deprivation, have been observed in several species, including rats and humans, although it is sometimes difficult to determine cause and effect relationships. Early sensory input has even "rewired" brain areas, so that routing visual input to the auditory thalamus resulted in visual experiences. At least some of the effects of enrichment may be due to increased physical activity; exercise enhances growth of axons and dendrites and lessens the thinning of the neocortex in old age. People who have been blind since infancy have increased activity in their occipital cortex while performing either a touch discrimination task or a verbal task, and this activity helps them to outperform sighted people in those tasks. Thus, a brain area normally devoted to visual processing becomes reorganized to analyze tactile and auditory information. Extensive training may increase the amount of cortical area devoted to a skill. In professional musicians, one area in the right temporal lobe was larger than in nonmusicians, and subcortical areas responded faster to auditory input. However, cause and effect relationships are not clear. There was also a larger representation of the fingers of left hand in the right postcentral gyrus of people who play stringed instruments, and another study showed thicker gray matter in areas related to hand control and vision in musicians. While such an increase in cortical representation is usually beneficial, it can produce problems if the representations of two fingers overlap.

Brain damage can be caused by a variety of factors, including closed head injury and stroke. Stroke can result either from ischemia due to a blood clot that obstructs an artery or from hemorrhage, caused by rupture of an artery. Strokes kill neurons either by depriving them of oxygen and glucose or by overexcitation, which allows excess sodium and other positive ions to enter the neuron, blocking metabolism in mitochondria and killing the neurons. Cell death in an ischemic stroke can be minimized by the use of drugs that break up clots, if given early after the stroke. Potential new treatments include cooling the brain and administration of cannabinoids or omega-3 fatty acids.

Recovery from brain damage depends on a number of physiological mechanisms. Diaschisis, or decreased activity of neurons after loss of input, contributes to impairment following brain damage. It can be reduced by administration of stimulant drugs during the recovery phase or, later, by electrical stimulation of the central thalamus. Regrowth of axons can be guided by myelin sheaths in the periphery. However, axons in the central nervous system do not regenerate, in part because of the mechanical barrier of scar tissue and in part because of growth-inhibiting chemicals from glia. In addition, the two sides of the axon pull apart. Recent data suggest that a protein bridge may provide a path for axons to regenerate across a scar-filled gap. Sprouting of axons occurs continually and is increased after brain damage. Cells that lose their innervation secrete neurotrophins that stimulate nearby axons to develop collateral sprouts that attach to the vacant synapses. Unilateral damage to axons from the entorhinal cortex to the hippocampus elicits sprouting from the other hemisphere into the hippocampus of the damaged side and promotes recovery. However, bilateral damage results in sprouting from unrelated areas, which may be helpful, harmful, or neutral regarding recovery. Denervation (or disuse) supersensitivity refers to the increased sensitivity to a neurotransmitter by a postsynaptic cell that is deprived of synaptic input. It results from an increased number and/or sensitivity of receptors and can promote recovery or result in prolonged pain. Reorganization of sensory representations can occur by collateral sprouting, sometimes over surprisingly long distances, or by increased receptor sensitivity. However, these reorganizations may not be beneficial, as in the case of phantom-limb sensations. Therapies for brain damage include behavioral interventions that help people to reaccess memories or skills or to make better use of their unimpaired abilities. Learned adjustments in behavior allow an individual to make better use of abilities unaffected by the damage and to improve abilities that were impaired by the damage, but not lost. Therapy is most effective if it begins soon after a person's injury. However, recovery requires effort and is impaired by alcohol, exhaustion, stress, and old age.

Learning Objectives

Module 5.1 Development of the Brain
1. Understand the processes of growth and differentiation of the brain.
2. Understand why there is initial overproduction of neurons and how axons follow chemical paths to their destinations and make functional connections, thereby allowing them to survive.
3. Understand the competition between axons in forming functional synapses.
4. Understand the reasons why the developing brain is vulnerable to chemical insults.
5. Be able to describe the effects of experience on the brain.

Module 5.2 Plasticity after Brain Damage
1. Be able to describe the processes by which strokes damage the brain and several means of lessening the damage.
2. Understand the mechanisms of recovery after brain damage and how various therapies promote recovery.

Key Terms and Concepts

Module 5.1 Development of the Brain
1.   Growth and differentiation of the vertebrate brain
        Maturation of the vertebrate brain
            Neural tube → spinal cord, hindbrain, midbrain, forebrain
            Cavity of neural tube → central canal of spinal cord, ventricles of brain
                Cerebrospinal fluid (CSF)
        Growth and development of neurons
            Proliferation of new cells
                Cells lining ventricles divide
                    Some → primitive neurons and glia
                    Others → stem cells that remain in place
                Number of days of neuron proliferation: Longer in humans than in chimpanzee
                    Small genetic change → large difference in outcome
            Migration toward eventual destinations
                Guides: Immunoglobulins, chemokines
            Differentiation, forming axon first and then dendrites
            Myelination of some axons, continuing for years
                Spinal cord first, then brain stem, midbrain, forebrain
            Synaptogenesis, continues throughout life
                Slows in old age
        New neurons later in life
            Olfactory receptors
            Stem cells
            Hippocampal cells in songbirds and mammals
                More new cells survive in times of new learning
                May label memories formed at a given time
            Probably no new neurons in adult cerebral cortex
2.   Pathfinding by axons
        Chemical pathfinding by axons
            Specificity of axon connections
                Axons to extra leg of salamander
                Optic tract axons to tectum of newts
        Chemical gradients
            TOP_{DV}
        Competition among axons as a general principle
            Neural Darwinism
3.   Determinants of neuron survival
        Nerve growth factor (NGF)
            Sympathetic nervous system
            Rita Levi-Montalcini
            Promotes survival and growth, not neuronal birth
            Apoptosis vs. necrosis
            Make more neurons than necessary, discard the rest
        Other neurotrophins

Brain-derived neurotrophic factor (BDNF) and others

Overproduction of neurons and massive cell death

Release of neurotransmitter plus neurotrophin

Neurotrophins needed from both incoming axons and target cells

Match incoming axons to number of recipient cells

Functions of neurotrophins

Prevent apoptosis

Increase branching of both axons and dendrites

4. The vulnerable developing brain

Greater vulnerabililty to malnutrition, toxic chemicals, infections

Impaired thyroid function in infancy: Permanent mental retardation and slow body growth

Fever, low blood glucose → impair neuron proliferation

Fetal alcohol syndrome

Short, less branched dendrites

Alcohol: Inhibits glutamate & neurotrophin release; increases GABA activity

Maternal cocaine or cigarette smoking → multiple deficits

Maternal stress → less care of offspring → emotional, social problems in offspring

5. Differentiation of the cortex

Ferrets: optic nerves to auditory thalamus → vision

6. Fine-tuning by experience

Experience and dendritic branching

Enriched environment

Thicker cortex

More dendritic branches

Improved learning

Effect of exercise

Effects of special experiences

Brain adaptations in people blind since infancy

Occipital cortex: Increased responsiveness to touch, sound, verbal stimuli

Effects of music training

Magnetoencephalography (MEG) in professional musicians

Stronger response of auditory cortex to tones

Also stronger response to speech sounds, faster learning of speech

Magnetic resonance imaging (MRI): One area in right temporal cortex of musicians larger

MRI: Increased thickness of gray matter in areas for hand control and vision in musicians

Playing stringed instruments (fingering with left hand): Larger area in right postcentral gyrus

Earlier training → bigger effects

When brain reorganization goes too far

Difficulty distinguishing one finger from another

Focal hand dystonia ("musician's cramp"): due to overlap of cortical representation of two fingers

"Writer's cramp" due to similar problem

7.   In closing: Brain Development
     Many ways to disrupt development; wonder that it ever works normally

Module 5.2 Plasticity after Brain Damage

1.   Brain damage and short-term recovery
     Tumors, infections, radiation, toxic substances, degenerative conditions
     Closed head injury
         Rotational force
         Blood clots
     How woodpeckers avoid concussions: no rotational forces
     Reducing the harm from a stroke (cerebrovascular accident)
         Ischemia (blood clot closes artery)
             Loss of oxygen and glucose
         Hemorrhage (rupture of artery)
             Excess oxygen, calcium, blood products
         Both ischemia and hemorrhage
             Edema → increased pressure → possible additional strokes
             Impaired sodium-potassium pump →
                 Increased extracellular potassium, intracellular sodium →
                 Glutamate release →
                 Overstimulation →
                 Accumulation of sodium, other ions →
                 Block metabolism in mitochondria →
                 Neurons die, glia proliferate
     Immediate treatments
         Tissue plasminogen activator (tPA): Breaks up blood clots
             Use within 3 hours
             Harmful for hemorrhagic strokes
     After the first few hours
         Penumbra (area surrounding immediate damage): Decreased stimulation
             Glutamate antagonists: Disappointing results
         Cooling brain—most effective
         Animal studies: Cannabinoids → reduced glutamate release
         Omega-3 fatty acids: Help block apoptosis and other neural damage
2.   Later mechanisms of recovery
     Increased brain stimulation
         Diaschisis: decreased activity in surviving neurons
         Electrical stimulation of central thalamus
         Amphetamine → Enhanced recovery
         Blocking dopamine receptors → impaired recovery
         Tranquilizers (decrease dopamine release) → impaired recovery
     The regrowth of axons
         Myelin sheaths as guides in peripheral nervous system
         Mature mammalian CNS: Little regrowth; fish: much more
         Scar tissue: mechanical barrier
         Two sides pull apart

Glia → growth-inhibiting chemicals
Protein bridge → path for regenerating axons
Sprouting
Neurotrophins → collateral sprouts
Hippocampus: Input from entorhinal cortex
Cut axons from one entorhinal cortex → other hemisphere sprouts → recovery
Cut axons from both sides → sprouting from unrelated areas → helpful, harmful, or neutral effects
Denervation supersensitivity
Disuse supersensitivity
Increased receptors or effectiveness of receptors
Can induce prolonged pain
Reorganized sensory representations and the phantom limb
Sprouting of axons from denervated area of visual cortex
Cortical cells: more responsive to other fingers after loss of input from one finger
Deafferented arm → "arm" area of cortex responds to stimuli from face
Stimuli perceived as from arm
Sexual activity → feel phantom foot
Artificial or transplanted arm or hand → phantom sensations subside
Connections plastic throughout life
Learned adjustments in behavior
Deafferented limbs
One deafferented limb: Lack of spontaneous use
Two deafferented limbs: Monkey learns to use both
Cortical damage → difficulty finding memory trace
Early practice or therapy most helpful after damage
Recovery is precarious: Decreases with alcohol, exhaustion, stress, old age
Methods 5.1: Histochemistry
Horseradish peroxidase: Transported from axon terminal to cell body
3. In closing: Brain damage and recovery
Numerous experimental treatments, none fully effective now

Short-Answer Questions

Module 5.1 Development of the Brain

1. *Growth and differentiation of the vertebrate brain*

   a. Describe the formation of the central nervous system in the embryo. What happens to the fluid-filled cavity?

   b. What are the three main divisions of the brain?

   c. What are the five stages in the development of neurons? Describe the processes in each.

   d. Which two kinds of chemicals guide neuron migration? Excesses of one of these kinds of chemicals has been linked to which psychiatric disorder?

e. Where in the brain are new neurons found in adulthood in black-capped chickadees? In mammals? What are stem cells?

f. Describe the evidence that few or no new neurons are found in the cerebral cortex of humans.

2. *Pathfinding by axons*

a. What did Weiss observe in his experiments on salamanders' extra limbs? What principle did he conclude directed the innervation of the extra limb? Is this principle still thought to be correct?

b. What did Sperry observe when he damaged the optic nerve of newts? What happened when he rotated the eye by 180 degrees? How did the newt with the rotated eye see the world?

c. What conclusion did these results suggest?

d. What is TOP_{DV}? What is its role in directing retinal axons to the tectum?

e. What happens to axons that form active synapses? What happens to axons that do not form active synapses?

f. Describe the principle of neural Darwinism. How does this relate to the initial overproduction and subsequent death of large numbers of neurons?

3. *Determinants of neuronal survival*

a. Who discovered nerve growth factor? What happens if a neuron in the sympathetic nervous system does not receive enough nerve growth factor?

b. What is apoptosis? What type of chemical can prevent apoptosis?

c. What is another neurotrophin besides nerve growth factor? What functions do neurotrophins serve in adulthood?

4. *The vulnerable developing brain*

a. What are the effects of thyroid deficiency in adulthood? Compare these with the effects of thyroid deficiency in infancy.

b. Describe fetal alcohol syndrome. How are dendrites affected? What effects of alcohol on synaptic activity may explain the neural deficits.

c. What are the effects of prenatal cocaine exposure? Cigarette smoking during pregnancy?

d. How does stress affect the mother, and how does her behavior influence her offspring?

5. *Differentiation of the cortex*

a. When a hamster's optic nerve connected to the auditory thalamus, because of lesions of its normal targets, did the animals respond to a light as if it were a visual or an auditory stimulus? What can we conclude from this experiment?

6. *Fine-tuning by experience*

a. Describe the effects of environmental enrichment.

b. How may exercise contribute to the effects of enrichment?

c. Describe the changes that occur in the occipital cortex in people who have been blind since infancy. Are these changes helpful?

d. What brain area is larger in professional musicians? What can we conclude about cause and effect in the relationship of brain size, musical ability, and experience?

e. What area is larger in people who had extensive experience playing stringed instruments? What is focal hand dystonia, and what is its physiological basis?

Module 5.2 Plasticity after Brain Damage

1. *Brain damage and short-term recovery*

   a. What is the most common cause of brain damage in young people? What are two factors that actually produce the brain damage in these cases?

   b. How do woodpeckers avoid concussions?

   c. What are the two types of stroke and the cause of each? How does each kill neurons?

   d. Describe the sequence of destructive processes in the penumbra.

   e. What are three treatments that may minimize damage from stroke?

2. *Later mechanisms of recovery*

   a. List six potential mechanisms for recovery from brain damage.

   b. What is diaschisis? How is recovery from diaschisis affected by amphetamine or a dopamine antagonist?

   c. How may crushed, but not cut, axons in the peripheral nervous system form appropriate connections when they regenerate? Why don't axons in the central nervous system regenerate?

   d. Under what conditions is sprouting most likely to be useful?

   e. What is denervation supersensitivity? What are two mechanisms of supersensitivity?

   f. What evidence suggests that sensory representations may be reorganized during recovery? What surprised investigators about the brain of a monkey whose limb had been deafferented 12 years earlier?

   g. What are some sources of sensory input that can give rise to phantom limbs?

   h. How may behavioral interventions facilitate recovery from brain damage?

3. *Methods box*

   a. What is histochemistry? How is horseradish peroxidase used?

True/False Questions

1. The cavity of the neural tube fills in with neural tissue as the brain develops.

   TRUE or FALSE

2. The five stages of neural development are proliferation, migration, differentiation, myelination, and synaptogenesis.

   TRUE or FALSE

3. Nerve growth factor (NGF) primarily promotes neuronal birth.

   TRUE or FALSE

4. Apoptosis is the process of increasing the branching of dendrites.

   TRUE or FALSE

5. In addition to preventing programmed cell death, neurotrophins increase the branching of axons and dendrites in adulthood.

   TRUE or FALSE

6. Massive cell death early in development is a sign of a profound disorder.

   TRUE or FALSE

7. Axons follow chemical gradients to get to the area where they can make functional synaptic connections.

   TRUE or FALSE

8. Rats that were reared in an enriched environment had thicker cortex, more dendritic branching, and improved learning.

   TRUE or FALSE

9. Mammals are born with all the neurons they will ever have.

   TRUE or FALSE

10. Professional musicians have a larger area in the right temporal lobe than do non-musicians.

    TRUE or FALSE

11. Fetuses are generally more affected by malnutrition, toxic chemicals, and infections than are adults.

    TRUE or FALSE

12. The two kinds of stroke are ischemic and hemorrhagic.

    TRUE or FALSE

13. The penumbra is the area of most direct damage from a stroke; neurons in the penumbra are killed almost immediately.

    TRUE or FALSE

14. Two compounds that may decrease damage soon after a stroke are cannabinoids and omega-3 fatty acids.

TRUE or FALSE

15. Tissue plasminogen activator (tPA) should be administered after a hemorrhagic stroke, but not after an ischemic stroke.

TRUE or FALSE

16. Heating the brain, mimicking a fever, is the most effective treatment for a stroke.

TRUE or FALSE

17. A dopamine antagonist is an effective treatment for diaschisis.

TRUE or FALSE

18. Three factors that limit axon regeneration in mammals are the formation of a barrier by scar tissue, pulling apart by the two sides, and the release of growth-inhibiting chemicals by glia.

TRUE or FALSE

19. After damage to the hippocampus, sprouting from unrelated areas into the damaged area almost always leads to a full recovery.

TRUE or FALSE

20. After one limb was deafferented, the monkey stopped using it; if both arms were deafferented, the monkey learned how to use both arms.

TRUE or FALSE

Fill In The Blanks

1. Early in development the _____ differentiates into the spinal cord, the hindbrain, the midbrain, and the forebrain.

2. The five stages of neural development are _____, _____, _____, _____, and _____.

3. The principle of competition among axons is referred to as _____.

4. _____ discovered the first neurotrophin, _____.

5. Programmed cell death, also called _____, occurs if neurons do not receive sufficient neurotrophins.

6. The cells that give rise to new neurons in the adult brain are called _____.

7. The developing brain is more vulnerable than is the adult brain to _____, _____, and _____.

8. An area in the _____ lobe of the _____ hemisphere was larger in professional musicians. An area of the _____ gyrus of the _____ hemisphere was larger in people who play stringed instruments.

9. The two types of stroke are _____ and _____.

10. The area surrounding the direct damage from a stroke is called the _____.

11. Some potential means of lessening the damage, if applied immediately after a stroke, are _____ and administration of _____ or _____.

12. _____ refers to the decreased activity of surviving neurons after other neurons are damaged. Two potential treatments for this condition are electrical stimulation of the _____ and administration of _____ drugs during recovery.

13. Regrowth of axons in the central nervous system of mammals is impeded by _____, the two sides pulling apart, and chemicals secreted by _____ that inhibit growth.

14. Vision has been partially restored in hamsters with severed optic nerves by building a _____, which formed a path across a scar-filled gap.

15. Denervation _____ depends on increased receptors or efficacy of receptors.

16. Phantom limb sensations arise primarily because of collateral _____ of axons.

Matching Items

1. _____ cavity of neural tube
2. _____ Rita Levi-Montalcini
3. _____ apoptosis
4. _____ necrosis
5. _____ neural Darwinism
6. _____ stem cells
7. _____ ischemic
8. _____ hemorrhagic
9. _____ overexcitation
10. _____ diaschisis

a. cell death due to injury or toxic chemical

b. decreased activity of surviving neurons after damage to other neurons

c. stroke caused by ruptured blood vessel

d. a cause of damage immediately after a stroke

e. programmed cell death

f. stroke caused by blood clot

g. cerebral ventricles and spinal central canal

h. discovered nerve growth factor

i. undifferentiated cells that can become neurons

j. axons competing for synapses and survival

Multiple-Choice Questions

1. The neural tube
   a. arises from a pair of long thin lips that merge around a fluid-filled cavity.
   b. develops into the spinal cord; the brain arises from a separate structure.
   c. eventually merges to form a solid structure, squeezing out the primitive cerebrospinal fluid.
   d. none of the above

2. The five major stages in the development of neurons, in order, are
   a. proliferation, differentiation, migration, myelination, synaptogenesis.
   b. proliferation, growth, synaptogenesis, myelination, migration.
   c. proliferation, migration, myelination, synaptogenesis, growth.
   d. proliferation, migration, differentiation, myelination, synaptogenesis.

3. Which of the following is true?
   a. Myelination is complete by the end of the first year in humans.
   b. Immunoglobulins and cytokines guide neuron migration.
   c. Dendrites usually form before axons, and are usually fully formed before migration begins.
   d. Neurons are incapable of conducting action potentials until they are fully myelinated.

4. Stem cells
   a. are hippocampal neurons that are especially resistant to damage.
   b. are undifferentiated cells in the interior of the brain that generate daughter cells that migrate to the olfactory bulb or hippocampus and become glia or neurons.
   c. are glia that guide neurons during migration.
   d. are neurons that develop especially long axons that resemble the stems of plants.

5. When Paul Weiss grafted an extra leg onto a salamander,
   a. the extra leg received no neurons and therefore could not move.
   b. the extra leg moved in the opposite direction from the normal adjacent leg.
   c. the extra leg moved in synchrony with the normal adjacent leg.
   d. the leg degenerated because the immune system rejected it.

6. Sperry's work with the eyes of newts led him to conclude that
   a. neurons attach to postsynaptic cells randomly, and the postsynaptic cell confers specificity.
   b. axons follow a chemical trail that places them in the general vicinity of their target.
   c. innervation in a sensory system is guided by specific genetic information, whereas that in the motor system is random.
   d. neurons follow specific genetic information that directs each of them to precisely the right postsynaptic cell.

7. TOP_{DV}
   a. is a trophic factor necessary for the survival of neurons of the sympathetic nervous system.
   b. is a protein that guides axons to the developing legs of newts.
   c. is a protein that causes a group of neurons that possess it to fire together, thereby increasing their chance of survival.

    d. is a protein that is more concentrated in neurons of the dorsal retina and the ventral tectum than in the ventral retina and dorsal tectum.

8. Neural Darwinism
    a. was formulated by Roger Sperry.
    b. has recently been shown to be false.
    c. proposes that synapses form somewhat randomly at first; those that work best are kept, while the others degenerate.
    d. all of the above

9. Nerve growth factor
    a. was discovered by Roger Sperry.
    b. is important for the survival and growth of sympathetic neurons.
    c. determines the number of neurons that will be formed.
    d. all of the above

10. Apoptosis
    a. is caused by an excess of neurotrophin.
    b. occurs in only a few areas of the brain.
    c. is the "suicide program" of the cell.
    d. was the first neurotrophin to be discovered.

11. Massive cell death early in development
    a. would be so maladaptive that it hardly ever occurs.
    b. occurs only with sensory deprivation or when the fetus has been exposed to toxins.
    c. occurs as a result of genetic mistakes, which fail to direct the cells to their genetically programmed target. As a result the neurons wander aimlessly until they die.
    d. is a normal result of unsuccessful competition for synapses and growth factors.

12. Mental retardation
    a. can be caused by thyroid deficiency during adulthood.
    b. can be caused by thyroid deficiency in infancy.
    c. is not due to lack or excess of chemicals during development, because the young brain is very plastic and can repair itself easily.
    d. all of the above

13. Fetal alcohol syndrome
    a. results in hyperactivity, impulsiveness, difficulty maintaining attention, varying degrees of mental retardation, motor problems, heart defects, and facial abnormalities.
    b. occurs because alcohol increases glutamate release and decreases GABA release.
    c. results from excessively long, heavily branched dendrites.
    d. all of the above

14. Children of mothers who smoked during pregnancy have greater risk for
    a. attention-deficit disorder.
    b. aggressive behavior.
    c. impaired memory and intelligence.
    d. all of the above

15. Environmental enrichment
    a. produces greater dendritic branching and a thicker cortex.
    b. produces changes in the structure of neurons, but no changes in neural function.
    c. produces changes in the function of neurons, but no changes in neural structure.
    d. has beneficial effects only in primates.

16. Which of the following is true?
    a. After practice of specific skills, connections relevant to those skills proliferate, while others retract.
    b. Physical activity can improve learning and memory.
    c. Exercise can decrease the rate of decline in brain volume and activity in older people.
    d. All of the above are true.

17. Which of the following is true?
    a. Professional musicians have a larger area in the right temporal lobe than do nonmusicians.
    b. Exercise generates waste products that are harmful to neural survival.
    c. The occipital cortex in people who have been blind since infancy continues to be selective only to visual stimuli.
    d. All of the above are true.

18. Which of the following is true?
    a. The increase in representation of the left hand in the right postcentral gyrus of stringed instrument players is always beneficial.
    b. There was decreased thickness of gray matter in brain areas for hand control and vision in musicians, because those areas became totally devoted to auditory function.
    c. Stressing a mother rat changes her behavior in ways that increase fearfulness in her offspring.
    d. none of the above

19. The most common cause of brain damage in young adults is
    a. stroke.
    b. disease.
    c. a sharp blow to the head.
    d. a brain tumor.

20. Which of the following occurs in the penumbra around the area of direct damage from stroke?
    a. Edema increases pressure on the brain and increases the probability of additional strokes.
    b. The combination of edema and impairment of the sodium-potassium pump results in glutamate release.
    c. Positive ions accumulate inside neurons, block metabolism in mitochondria and kill neurons.
    d. All of the above are true.

21. Damage from strokes may be minimized by
    a. activating glutamate synapses immediately after the stroke.
    b. giving tissue plasminogen activator (tPA), if the stroke is due to ischemia.
    c. creating a fever, which will increase the temperature of the brain and enhance repair processes.
    d. all of the above

22. Stimulants administered after the first few days following a stroke improves recovery by
    a. producing denervation supersensitivity.
    b. reducing diaschisis.
    c. relieving stress.
    d. stimulating regrowth of axons.

23. Adequate regrowth of an axon does not occur if
    a. the damaged axon is in the spinal cord of fish.
    b. an axon in the peripheral nervous system of mammals is crushed.
    c. the damaged axon is in the central nervous system of mammals.
    d. all of the above

24. Research on regrowth of axons in mammals has shown that
    a. scar tissue provides an effective guide for axon regrowth.
    b. myelin in the peripheral, but not central, nervous system can help axons regenerate.
    c. the mammalian central nervous system has evolved advanced chemical stimuli to promote better axon regrowth than that seen in fish.
    d. the reason that axons in the central nervous system fail to regrow is that there are no myelin sheaths there.

25. Sprouting
    a. occurs only in response to traumatic brain damage.
    b. is always maladaptive, since the wrong axons make connections.
    c. may be adaptive if sprouts come from closely related axons.
    d. is enhanced by dopamine antagonists.

26. Denervation supersensitivity is the result of
    a. increased output from other presynaptic cells adjacent to the one that has been damaged.
    b. postsynaptic neurons producing receptors for a different transmitter.
    c. changes in the chemical composition of the transmitter, making it more potent.
    d. an increased number of receptors on the postsynaptic cell and increased effectiveness of the receptors.

27. After denervation of a monkey's arm 12 years earlier,
    a. neurons that had previously responded to it died because of lack of input.
    b. neurons that had previously responded to it became responsive to stimuli in the face.
    c. no reorganization could occur because all connections are determined only genetically.
    d. no reorganization could occur because connections become permanently fixed during the early critical period.

28. Research on recovery from brain damage has shown that
    a. recovery can occur when an individual is forced to make full use of remaining capabilities.
    b. phantom limbs result from irritation in the remaining stump of the limb.
    c. monkeys with only one arm denervated showed better recovery in the use of that arm than when both arms were denervated.
    d. it is better to wait several weeks after a brain injury before beginning therapy.

Solutions

True/False Questions

1.	F	6.	F	11.	T	16.	F
2.	T	7.	T	12.	T	17.	F
3.	F	8.	T	13.	F	18.	T
4.	F	9.	F	14.	T	19.	F
5.	T	10.	T	15.	F	20.	T

Fill In The Blanks

1. neural tube
2. proliferation; migration; differentiation; myelination; synaptogenesis
3. neural Darwinism
4. Rita Levi-Montalcini; nerve growth factor
5. apoptosis
6. stem cells
7. malnutrition; toxic chemicals; infections
8. temporal; right; postcentral; right
9. ischemic; hemorrhagic
10. penumbra
11. cooling the brain; cannabinoids; omega-3 fatty acids.
12. Diaschisis; central thalamus; stimulant
13. scar tissue; glia
14. protein bridge
15. supersensitivity
16. sprouting

Matching Items

1.	g	4.	a	7.	f	10.	b
2.	h	5.	j	8.	c		
3.	e	6.	i	9.	d		

Multiple Choice Questions

1.	a	8.	c	15.	a	22.	b
2.	d	9.	b	16.	d	23.	c
3.	b	10.	c	17.	a	24.	b
4.	b	11.	d	18.	c	25.	c
5.	c	12.	b	19.	c	26.	d
6.	b	13.	a	20.	d	27.	b
7.	d	14.	d	21.	b	28.	a

CHAPTER 6

Vision

Introduction

Sensory systems, including vision, are concerned with reception (absorption) of physical energy and transduction of that energy into neural activity that encodes some aspect of the stimulus. The structure of each kind of sensory receptor allows it to be stimulated maximally by one kind of energy, and little or not at all by other forms of energy. The brain interprets any information sent by nerves that synapse with those receptors as being about that form of energy. This principle was described by Müller as the law of specific nerve energies. Much of sensory coding depends on the absolute or relative frequency of firing of sensory neurons. The brain's activity does not duplicate the shape of the object, but it is not clear how the brain makes sense of the coded information.

The retina contains two kinds of receptors. Cones are most densely packed in the fovea, an area in the center of the retina with the most acute (detailed) vision. This acuity arises largely because each cone connects to only one bipolar cell, which in turn connects to only one ganglion cell. Also, blood vessels and ganglion cell axons are routed around the fovea, leaving the fovea in a "pit" with its view unimpeded. Rods are located more peripherally in the retina and are more sensitive to low levels of light. Furthermore, each bipolar cell receives input from a large number of rods. This improves sensitivity to dim light but sacrifices acuity.

All mammalian photopigments contain 11-cis-retinal bound to one of several opsins. Light converts 11-cis-retinal to all-trans-retinal, which in turn activates second-messenger molecules. The trichromatic theory states that cones mediate color vision because three different photopigments are found in three types of cones. Each photopigment is maximally sensitive to one wavelength of light but responds less readily to other wavelengths. Thus, each wavelength produces a certain ratio of responses from the three receptor types; the ratio remains essentially constant regardless of brightness. Rods, in contrast to cones, contain only one photopigment and therefore do not contribute directly to our perception of colors. Processing of color vision beyond the receptor level depends on an opponent-process mechanism, in which a given cell responds to one color with increased firing and to another color with a decrease below its spontaneous rate of firing. In addition, color constancy, the ability to recognize the color of an object despite changes in lighting, depends on an area of the cortex that compares colors across all the objects in the visual field. Color vision deficiency occurs when an individual lacks, or has low numbers of, long-, medium-, and/or short-wavelength cones. Red-green color deficiency is the most common type; it is due to a gene on the X chromosome that causes the long- and medium-wavelength cones to make the same photopigment, instead of different ones.

Visual input is processed neurally in order to provide an organized, useful representation of the environment. The direct route of information in the retina is from receptor to bipolar to ganglion cell. Ganglion cell axons exit through the blind spot of the retina and project primarily to the lateral geniculate nucleus of the thalamus, although a few axons go to the superior colliculus or to an area of the hypothalamus that controls waking and sleeping. However, a visual receptor is able not only to stimulate its own bipolar(s) but also to inhibit activity in neighboring bipolars. It accomplishes this feat through the cooperation of horizontal cells, which receive input from a number of receptors and synapse with a number of bipolars. Electrical activity can flow in all directions in horizontal cells. The advantage of this arrangement is that borders are enhanced at the expense of redundant input. The process is called lateral inhibition.

A receptive field of a neuron in the visual system is that area of the visual field in which the presence or absence of light affects that neuron's activity. A receptive field beyond the receptor level represents a composite of the receptive fields of neurons that provide its input. Many contain both excitatory and inhibitory regions. The receptive fields of bipolar, ganglion, and geniculate cells are concentric circles. For some cells light in the center is excitatory, and for other cells it is inhibitory; light in the surround has the opposite effect. Cells in the visual cortex (occipital lobe) have bar shaped receptive fields as a result of summing the receptive fields of their lateral geniculate cell inputs.

Ganglion cells have been divided into three types. Parvocellular neurons are relatively small cells, located in or near the fovea, that respond differentially to colors. Because they have small receptive fields, they are highly sensitive to details. Magnocellular neurons are larger, are spread evenly across the retina, and respond best to moving stimuli and overall patterns. Because their receptive fields are large, they are not sensitive to small details; they also do not respond differentially to colors. A smaller group of cells, koniocellular neurons, have several functions and are poorly understood.

Most of the input from the lateral geniculate goes to the primary visual cortex (area V1), which is necessary for conscious vision, visual imagination, and visual dreams. V1 in turn projects to secondary visual cortex (area V2), which sends reciprocal input back to V1. From area V2, information branches out to numerous additional areas. At the cortex, the input is split into three pathways. A ventral pathway in the temporal lobe processes shape, movement, and brightness information primarily from the parvocellular system. It is referred to as the ventral stream, or the "what" pathway, because it is critical for identifying and recognizing objects. A primarily magnocellular pathway projects dorsally to the parietal cortex and integrates vision with action. It is referred to as the dorsal stream or "where" or "how" pathway. It primarily helps the motor system to find objects and manipulate them. The third pathway, with mixed input, analyzes primarily color and brightness.

David Hubel and Torsten Wiesel received the Nobel Prize for their pioneering work on feature detectors in the visual cortex. They distinguished three categories of neurons: simple, complex, and end-stopped or hypercomplex. Simple cells respond maximally to a bar oriented in a particular direction and in a particular location on the retina. Their receptive fields can be mapped into fixed excitatory and inhibitory areas. Complex cells, on the other hand, have larger receptive fields, respond to correctly oriented bars located anywhere within the field (i.e., they do not have fixed excitatory and inhibitory areas), and respond best to stimuli moving perpendicular to the receptive field axis. End-stopped, or hypercomplex, cells are like complex cells, except for an area of strong inhibition at one end of the field. Cortical cells with similar properties are grouped in columns perpendicular to the surface.

It has been suggested that neurons in area V1 are feature detectors. However, although each neuron has a preferred stimulus, it will respond to other similar stimuli. Therefore, the response of any cell must be compared with responses of many other cells. Furthermore, many cells in V1 respond best to sine wave gratings; however, it is obvious that we do not perceive the world as an assembly of sine waves. Therefore, the role of V1 in visual perception is probably to provide preliminary analyses for other areas that actually identify objects.

After V1, receptive fields become even larger and more specialized. Some cells in V2 respond best to lines, edges, and sine wave gratings; however, others prefer circles, right angles, or other complex patterns. Additional processing of shape information is accomplished by the inferior temporal cortex (in the ventral stream, or "what" pathway), which responds preferentially to highly complex shapes. Cells in this area ignore changes in location, size, and perspective; they may contribute to our capacity for shape constancy. Damage to the pattern pathway results in visual agnosia, the inability to recognize visual objects. An area in the inferior temporal lobe (the fusiform gyrus), especially in the right hemisphere, and part of the prefrontal cortex are activated during recognition of faces and, to a lesser degree, other complex figures. Damage there results in prosopagnosia, the inability to recognize faces.

Area V4, or a nearby area, is especially important for color constancy. Animals with damage to this area retain some color vision, but lose the ability to recognize the color of an object across lighting conditions. Area V4 also contributes to visual attention. Some cells in the magnocellular system detect motion. They project to middle temporal cortex, or MT (area V5), and an adjacent area (medial superior temporal cortex, MST). Neurons in these areas respond preferentially to different speeds and directions of movement, without analyzing the object that is moving. Many cells in MT respond best to moving borders of single objects, while cells in the dorsal part of MST prefer expanding, contracting, or rotating large scenes. These two types of cells send their output to the ventral part of MST, which allows us to perceive the motion of an object relative to its background. Nearby temporal lobe areas detect biological motion, such as swinging of arms and legs, or distinguish between moving objects and visual changes due to head or eye movements (saccades). Damage to MT can result in motion blindness, in which a person sees only a series of still scenes. Other people receive input from MT, but have extensive damage to V1; they can detect motion but cannot see the object that is moving.

Although a single neuron may not consistently detect a given stimulus, it contributes to the analysis by a population of neurons. Redundancy allows the system to work well, even when individual neurons fail. Simultaneous activity in many brain areas gives rise to visual perception.

Human infants are predisposed to pay more attention to faces than to other stimuli. Although cells in the mammalian visual cortex are endowed at the individual's birth with certain adultlike characteristics, normal sensory experience is necessary to develop these characteristics fully and to prevent them from degenerating. If only one eye is deprived of vision during an early sensitive period, the brain becomes unresponsive to that eye. Input from the active eye displaces the early connections made by the inactive eye. If both eyes are kept shut, however, cortical cells remain at least somewhat responsive to both eyes, though their responses are sluggish. Apparently, the changes that occur during the sensitive, or critical, period require GABA, the main inhibitory transmitter. Therefore, both excitatory and inhibitory influences are required to sculpt the neural mechanisms of vision.

Stereoscopic depth perception requires the detection of retinal disparity, the slight discrepancy between the images on the two eyes. Strabismus ("lazy eye") is a condition in which the eyes point in slightly different directions, so that cortical cells do not receive synchronized images from both eyes. Usually, children with this condition attend to only one eye. Using a patch on the good eye can increase attention to the other eye, but still does not produce depth perception. However, having the child play a videogame that requires three-dimensional binocular processing has helped. Other aspects of vision that require early experience for proper development are stereoscopic depth perception, ability to see lines of a given direction, and motion perception. A cataract on the left eye during the early sensitive period can impair recognition of faces, because the left eye projects primarily to the right side of the brain during early development, and the right fusiform gyrus is specialized for facial recognition. Furthermore, a lack of detailed vision for many years, due to cataracts or damaged corneas, can result in impaired ability to see details after surgical correction. We are born with pre-wired connections for visual processing; however, we need experience to maintain and develop visual perception.

Learning Objectives

Module 6.1 Visual Coding
1. Be able to describe the parts of the eye and its connections to the brain.
2. Understand the process by which three types of cones, and the neurons they connect with, can produce a rich spectrum of perceived color.
3. Understand the trade-off between acuity for detail and sensitivity to dim light.

Module 6.2 The Neural Basis of Visual Perception
1. Understand the concept of receptive fields and how they change from the retina to the various areas of the visual cortex.
2. Understand the inputs to the dorsal and ventral streams of cortical processing and what each pathway analyzes.
3. Know the contributions of areas V1, V2, and inferior temporal cortex to shape perception.
4. Be able to describe the brain areas that process color and motion.

Module 6.3 Visual Development
1. Be able to describe the effects of early experiences and of visual deprivation on the development of the visual system.

Key Terms and Concepts

Module 6.1 Visual Coding
1.   General principles of perception
     Law of specific nerve energies: Activity by a given nerve always sends same kind of information to brain
          Mechanical pressure on eye → perception of light
          Strength of stimulus → amount of receptor's depolarization or hyperpolarization → rate and timing of firing of next neuron
     From neuronal activity to perception
          Coding does not duplicate shape of object in brain
2.   The eye and its connections to the brain
     Route within the retina
          Cornea → pupil → lens → retina
          Image inverted and reversed
          Receptors → bipolar cells → ganglion cells
          Amacrine cells
          Optic nerve
          Blind spot
     Fovea and periphery of the retina
          Fovea (Latin for "pit")
               Blood vessels and ganglion cell axons nearly absent
               Midget ganglion cells: Input from single cone
               Good acuity: Sensitivity to detail
               Poor sensitivity to dim light
          Periphery
               More receptors converge on bipolar and ganglion cells
                    Better sensitivity to dim light
                    Poorer acuity
          Birds: Two foveas per eye
               Predatory birds: Greater receptor density on top half of retina (looking down)
               Prey animals: Greater receptor density on bottom half of retina
3.   Visual receptors: Rods and cones
     Rods
          Most abundant in periphery
          Responsive to faint light, bleached out by bright light
     Cones
          Most abundant in and around fovea
          Essential for color vision, less active in dim light
     Ratio of rods to cones: 20 to 1 in humans; 15,000 to 1 in South American oilbirds
     Photopigments
          11-cis-retinal
          Opsins
          Conversion of 11-cis-retinal to all-trans-retinal releases energy

4. Color vision
    "Visible" wavelengths vary with species
    No single neuron can encode both brightness and color
    Dependent on patterns of responses by different neurons
    The trichromatic (Young-Helmholtz) theory
        Three types of cone, each maximally sensitive to a different set of wavelengths
        Color matching
        Ratio of activity across three cone types
        More long- and medium-wavelength than short-wavelength cones
        Random distribution of cone types
    The opponent-process theory (Hering)
        Negative color afterimage
        Red vs. green, yellow vs. blue, white vs. black
    The retinex theory
        Color constancy
        Edwin Land
        Dale Purves: Perception requires inference
    Color vision deficiency
        Most common form: Difficulty distinguishing red from green
            Red and green cones make same photopigment
            Sex linked (gene on X chromosome)
        Women with four cone types
5. In closing: Visual receptors
    Vision requires complicated processing

Module 6.2 Neural Basis of Visual Perception
1. An overview of the mammalian visual system
    Retina
        Receptors (rods and cones)
        Horizontal cells
        Bipolar cells
        Amacrine cells
        Ganglion cells
            Axons form optic nerve
            Optic chiasm
    Lateral geniculate nucleus of the thalamus
    Superior colliculus
    Hypothalamus
    Cerebral cortex: Many visual areas with distinct functions
        Axons from cortex back to thalamus
2. Processing in the retina
    Lateral inhibition
    Heightens contrast
        Horizontal cells (local cells)
        Bipolar cells

3. Pathways to the lateral geniculate and beyond
    Receptive fields
        That part of visual field to which a given neuron responds
        Receptive field of ganglion cell
            Composed of receptive fields of its inputs
            Circular center with antagonistic doughnut-shaped surround
    In the retina and lateral geniculate
        Parvocellular cells
            Small cell bodies
            Small receptive fields
            Located in or near fovea
            Good acuity and color discrimination
        Magnocellular cells
            Larger cell bodies
            Larger receptive fields
            Even distribution
            Best response to moving stimuli
            No color discrimination
        Koniocellular cells
            Small cell bodies
            Found throughout retina
            Axons terminate in several locations
            Least understood
        Ganglion cell axons: Optic nerve → optic chiasm (half cross there in humans)
        Lateral geniculate nucleus of the thalamus
            Receptive fields resemble those of ganglion cells
4. Pattern recognition in the cerebral cortex
    Primary visual cortex, striate cortex (V1)
        Necessary for conscious vision, visual imagination, visual dreams
        Blindsight: After V1 damage, people respond to light they report not seeing
            Due to input to other brain areas, such as superior colliculus?
            Due to undamaged islands of V1?
    Pathways in the visual cortex
        Secondary visual cortex (V2)
            Reciprocal connections
        Ventral stream, mostly parvocellular: "What" pathway
            Temporal cortex → details of shape
        Dorsal stream, mostly magnocellular: "Where" or "how" pathway
            Parietal cortex → aids motor system
        Mixed parvocellular and magnocellular: Color and brightness
    The shape pathway
        Hubel and Wiesel's cell types in the primary visual cortex
            Simple cells (V1)
                Fixed excitatory and inhibitory zones in receptive fields
                Bar- or edge-shaped receptive fields
                Mostly horizontal or vertical receptive fields

Complex cells (V1 and V2)
    Do not respond to exact location of a stimulus
    Responds to moving bar of light in a particular orientation anywhere in receptive field
    End-stopped or hypercomplex cells
    Strong inhibitory area at one end of bar-shaped receptive field
The columnar organization of the visual cortex
    Columns perpendicular to surface
    Similar response properties within a column
Are visual cortex cells feature detectors?
    Prolonged exposure: Decreased sensitivity to feature
    Ambiguity of response of a single cell
    Spatial frequencies, sine-wave gratings
    Fourier analysis: combination of sine waves → unlimited variety of other patterns
    We perceive objects, not sine waves: preliminary step in analysis
Shape analysis beyond area V1
    Area V2
        Lines, bars, sine wave gratings
        Circles, right angles, other complex patterns
    Inferior temporal cortex
        Shape constancy
        Respond to reversal of contrast or mirror image
        Do not respond to figure-ground reversal

Methods 6.1: Microelectrode recordings

Anesthetize animal → drill small hole in skull → insert thin electrode next to or into a single cell → record activity in response to stimuli

1. Disorders of object recognition
    Visual agnosia
    Prosopagnosia
        Fusiform gyrus in inferior temporal cortex (especially right side)
        Part of prefrontal cortex
        Some specialization for faces and some general expertise
2. The color, motion, and depth pathways
    Structures important for color perception
        Input from parvocellular (color) and koniocellular pathways
        Area V4
            Color constancy
            Visual attention
    Motion perception
        Middle temporal cortex (MT, area V5)
            Cells respond best to movement at a particular speed in a particular direction
            Detect acceleration or deceleration
            Adjust for eye position
            Respond to implied movement
        Medial superior temporal cortex (MST)

Cells in dorsal MST: Best response to expansion, contraction, or rotation of large scene

Cells in ventral MST: Best response to movement of object relative to background

Distinguish between result of eye movements and result of object movements

Area near MT: Biological motion

Suppressed vision during eye movements

Suppression of visual cortex activity during saccades

Motion blindness

Also opposite: Movement detection without seeing object

3. In closing: From single cells to vision

Redundancy: Simultaneous processing of different aspects by different brain areas

Module 6.3 Visual Development

1. Vision by human infants

Attention to faces and face recognition

More time looking at faces

No preference for realistic vs. distorted faces, as long as eyes on top

Gradual development of face recognition

Ability matures into adolescence

Improved recognition with practice, especially at 6-9 months of age

2. Early experience and visual development

Deprived experience in one eye

Binocular input to cortex, normally

Experience necessary for fine-tuning

Blindness in deprived eye

Deprived experience in both eyes

Cortical cells

Sluggish response to both eyes after more than three weeks

Lose well-defined receptive fields

Not much orientation selectivity

Sensitive period

Lasts longer with complete visual deprivation

Depends on availability of GABA

Need for excitation of some synapses and inhibition of others

Ends with onset of chemicals that stabilize synapses and inhibit axon sprouting

Duration of sensitive period different for different functions

Local rearrangements vs. axon growth over longer distances

Uncorrelated stimulation in the two eyes

Stereoscopic depth perception

Retinal disparity: discrepancy between what left and right eyes see

Synchronous messages from two or more axons → stronger connections

Strabismus (strabismic amblyopia, "lazy eye")

Unrelated inputs from two eyes → cortical cell strengthens synapses with only one

Put patch over active eye: still no stereoscopic depth perception

Early treatment better than later treatment

Videogame that requires attention to binocular three-dimensional display →
encouraging results
Block GABA receptors in cortex → good results in animals
Ten days of complete darkness → good results in animals
Early exposure to a limited array of patterns
Astigmatism (asymmetric curvature of the eye) → blurred vision for lines in one
direction
Lack of seeing objects in motion
Stroboscopic illumination
Motion blindness
Impaired infant vision and long-term consequences
Cataracts removed at 2 – 6 months → subtle problems
Cataract on left eye of infants → worse problem than on right eye
Right fusiform gyrus
Crossed pathway develops faster
Cataract removal in adulthood → limited improvement
Infant plasticity greater than in adulthood
3.   In closing: The nature and nurture of vision
Some visual abilities at birth
Require experience to maintain and refine them

Short-Answer Questions

Module 6.1 Visual Coding

1. *General principles of perception*

   a. State the law of specific nerve energies. Who formulated it?

   b. How is the strength of a stimulus encoded?

   c. Is it necessary for the representation of an image in the brain to resemble the stimulus itself?

2. *The eye and its connections to the brain*

   a. Trace the path of visual information from a receptor to the optic nerve. What is the blind spot?

   b. What is the fovea? How did it get its name?

   c. How have many bird species solved the problem of getting detailed information from two different directions?

3. *Visual receptors: Rods and cones*

   a. Compare foveal and peripheral vision with regard to acuity, sensitivity to dim light, and color vision.

   b. What is the specific role of light in the initiation of a response in a receptor? What is a photopigment?

   c. What is the relationship of 11-cis-retinal to all-trans-retinal? What is an opsin?

4. *Color vision*

    a. How did Young and Helmholtz propose to account for color vision? On what kind of data was their theory based?

    b. Why does color vision necessarily depend on the pattern of responses of a number of different neurons?

    c. What kind of theory did Hering propose? What observations supported his theory?

    d. What visual ability does the retinex theory explain?

    e. What is the genetic basis for the most common form of color vision deficiency? Why do more males than females have this form of color deficiency?

Module 6.2 Neural Basis of Visual Perception

1. *An overview of the mammalian visual system*

    a. Draw a diagram showing the relationships among the rods and cones, the bipolar and horizontal cells, and the ganglion and amacrine cells.

    b. Axons of which kind of cell form the optic nerve? What is the name of the site where the right and left optic nerves meet? What percentage of axons cross to the opposite side of the brain in humans? What percentage of axons cross to the opposite side of the brain in species with eyes far to the sides of their heads?

    c. Where do most axons in the optic nerve synapse? Where do some other optic nerve axons synapse?

    d. What is the destination of axons from the lateral geniculate nucleus?

2. *Processing in the retina*

    a. What is lateral inhibition? How does it enhance contrast?

    b. How is lateral inhibition accomplished in the retina?

3. *Pathways to the lateral geniculate and beyond*

    a. What is the definition of the receptive field of a neuron in the visual system?

    b. If several bipolar cells provide input to a certain ganglion cell, what can be said about the location of their receptive fields relative to that of the ganglion cell?

    c. Describe the characteristics of parvocellular neurons.

    d. How do they differ from magnocellular neurons? What are koniocellular neurons?

    e. What happens at the optic chiasm?

    f. Describe the receptive fields of lateral geniculate cells.

4. *Pattern recognition in the cerebral cortex*

    a. Describe the evidence that Area V1 is necessary for conscious vision.

    b. What is blindsight? What are two hypotheses that may explain it?

c. In what cortical area does the ventral stream of visual input end? Describe the three types of information that are analyzed by the "what" pathway. Does this pathway have mostly parvocellular or magnocellular input?

d. In what cortical area does the dorsal stream of visual input end? What is its functional contribution? Does it have mostly parvocellular or magnocellular input?

e. For what accomplishment did David Hubel and Torsten Wiesel share the Nobel Prize?

f. Describe the receptive fields of simple cells.

g. What is the major difference between responses of simple and complex cells?

h. Describe the receptive field of an end-stopped, or hypercomplex, cell?

i. What can be said about the receptive fields of neurons in a column in the visual cortex?

j. What is a feature detector?

k. What evidence suggests that neurons in area V1 are feature detectors?

l. What is a problem with that interpretation?

m. What is the evidence for spatial frequency detectors? What is the problem with the view that neurons in V1 are primarily spatial frequency detectors?

n. Which areas, beyond V1, are important for shape analysis? What are their major contributions?

o. Describe shape constancy.

5. *Disorders of object recognition*

a. Describe the symptoms of visual agnosia. What is prosopagnosia?

b. Which area in the inferior temporal lobe increases its activity when people with intact brains recognize faces?

c. What other kinds of things can activate that area?

6. *The color, motion, and depth pathways*

a. What appears to be the special function of area V4? To what other function does area V4 contribute?

b. Which two areas of the cortex are specialized for motion perception? How "picky" are cells in these areas regarding the specific characteristics of the stimulus that is moving?

c. Describe the response characteristics of some cells in area MT.

d. Describe the preferred stimuli for many cells in the dorsal part of area MST.

e. What is the role of cells in the ventral part of MST?

f. Why don't we see a blur when we move our eyes? What is a saccade?

g. Describe the symptoms of motion blindness. Damage to what area might cause motion blindness?

h. How can we explain blindness *except* for the ability to detect motion?

Module 6.3 Visual Development

1. *Vision by human infants*
   a. To what type of stimuli do infants pay most attention? What aspect of such a stimulus is important for this preference?
   b. Which brain area develops tuning to the "average" face?

2. *Early experience and visual development*
   a. What is the effect of depriving only one eye of pattern vision during the critical period?
   b. What happens if both eyes are kept shut early in life?
   c. What is a sensitive or critical period? What neurotransmitter is important for establishing organization during the critical period?
   d. Define retinal disparity. How does the brain use this information to produce stereoscopic depth perception?
   e. What is strabismus? What ability do people with strabismus lack? What is the usual treatment for this condition? What is a promising alternative treatment?
   f. What happens to the response characteristics of visual cortical cells in a kitten exposed to only horizontal lines early in life? What is astigmatism?
   g. What was the effect of rearing kittens in an environment illuminated only by a strobe light?
   h. What visual deficit was observed after cataracts were removed at ages 2-6 months? Why does a cataract on the left eye result in greater deficits in face perception than a cataract on the right eye?

True/False Questions

1. In order to perceive the shape of an object, the pattern of neural activity in the cortex must duplicate the shape of the object.

   TRUE or FALSE

2. The law of specific nerve energies states that the activity of a given nerve always sends the same kind of information to the brain.

   TRUE or FALSE

3. The order of information transmission in the retina is receptor → ganglion cell → bipolar cell → amacrine cell.

   TRUE or FALSE

4. The fovea is the site at which ganglion cell axons exit the retina.

   TRUE or FALSE

5. The reason that peripheral vision has relatively low acuity, but good sensitivity to dim light, is that many rods send input to each bipolar, and many bipolars synapse with each ganglion cell.

TRUE or FALSE

6. Conversion of all-trans-retinal to 11-cis-retinal releases energy that controls the receptor's activity.

TRUE or FALSE

7. The trichromatic theory was proposed by Young and Helmholst on the basis of color matching experiments.

TRUE or FALSE

8. A likely physiological basis for the opponent-process theory is the depolarization of bipolar cells by some wavelengths and their hyperpolarization by other wavelengths.

TRUE or FALSE

9. The retinex theory was proposed by Edwin Land to explain color and brightness constancy.

TRUE or FALSE

10. People who have four types of cones are almost always men; they have much better color discrimination than others.

TRUE or FALSE

11. The receptive field of a ganglion cell is composed of the receptive fields of the cells that send input to it.

TRUE or FALSE

12. Lateral inhibition is produced by horizontal cells, which inhibit nearby bipolar cells.

TRUE or FALSE

13. Parvocellular neurons are large cells that are especially important for motion detection.

TRUE or FALSE

14. The ventral stream ("what") pathway terminates in the temporal cortex.

TRUE or FALSE

15. The dorsal stream ("where" or "how") pathway also terminates in the temporal lobe.

TRUE or FALSE

16. Hubel and Wiesel received the Nobel Prize for discovering that cells in the primary visual cortex respond preferentially to bars or edges, rather than spots of light.

TRUE or FALSE

17. Complex cells have receptive fields that can be mapped into excitatory and inhibitory areas, and those areas recognize complex shapes, such as triangles, squares, or faces.

TRUE or FALSE

18. Columns in the visual cortex are spread horizontally across the surface of the cortex and have response characteristics that vary systematically across the column.

    TRUE or FALSE

19. Sine wave gratings of specific spatial frequencies elicit even greater responses from cells in primary visual cortex than do bars and edges; however, we don't perceive the world as a series of gratings, suggesting that these neurons provide an early stage of analysis.

    TRUE or FALSE

20. Prosopagnosia is a degenerative condition leading to total blindness.

    TRUE or FALSE

21. Cells in the inferior temporal cortex contribute to our capacity for shape constancy.

    TRUE or FALSE

22. Area V4 is especially important for color constancy and visual attention.

    TRUE or FALSE

23. Cells in the MT and MST respond primarily to faces.

    TRUE or FALSE

24. A cataract on the left eye during early development can lead to problems with face recognition, even after the cataract is removed, because the right fusiform gyrus did not get proper stimulation during the early sensitive period.

    TRUE or FALSE

Fill In The Blanks

1. The strength of a stimulus is encoded as the amount of a receptor's _____ or _____, which then affects the rate and timing of firing of the next neuron.

2. The _____ cells receive input from the retinal receptors and provide input to the _____ cells.

3. The _____ is an area in the center of the retina that provides the most acute vision, as a result of tight packing of receptors and near absence of _____ and _____ in front of it.

4. Compared to the fovea, the periphery has _____ sensitivity to dim light and _____ acuity because more receptors converge on bipolar and ganglion cells.

5. _____-retinal is converted to _____-retinal by light; this releases energy that leads to a receptor potential.

6. Helmholtz proposed the _____ theory, based on color matching experiments.

7. Hering proposed the _____ theory, based on negative color afterimages.

8. Land proposed the _____ theory to account for color and brightness constancy.

9. Axons of _____ cells form the optic nerve, which exits the retina at the _____.

10. The _____ receives input from ganglion cell axons and sends its output to the primary visual cortex.

11. Lateral inhibition is produced by _____ cells; it is useful for enhancing _____.

12. _____ ganglion cells in the retina have small cell bodies and small receptive fields and are located in or near the fovea.

13. _____ ganglion cells have larger cell bodies and larger receptive fields and are located more evenly across the retina.

14. In the cortex a mostly parvocellular pathway, referred to as the ventral stream provides _____ information and ends in the _____ lobe.

15. A mostly magnocellular pathway, referred to as the dorsal stream, is sensitive to _____ and integrates vision with _____.

16. A mixed parvocellular and magnocellular pathway is sensitive to _____ and _____.

17. The brain area that confers shape constancy is the _____ cortex.

18. The brain area that confers color constancy is area _____.

19. The area of the cortex that responds best to moving borders and may record the movement of single objects is the _____ cortex (_____) or _____.

20. The cortical area that responds best to expansion, contraction, or rotation of large scenes is the _____ cortex (_____).

21. Blindsight may be mediated by the _____ or by islands of healthy tissue in otherwise damaged cortex.

22. The neurotransmitter that is important for establishing neural connections during the early critical period is _____.

23. A human condition similar to that of animals that were deprived of vision in one eye for several days is _____.

24. Animals raised with uncorrelated stimulation of the two eyes lacked _____ perception.

25. Animals that were raised with only stroboscopic lighting had _____ blindness.

26. People with a cataract on the left eye early in life had problems with _____ even after the cataract was removed.

Matching Items

1. _____ horizontal cells
2. _____ blind spot
3. _____ ganglion cells
4. _____ fovea
5. _____ rods
6. _____ cones
7. _____ parvocellular neurons
8. _____ magnocellular neurons
9. _____ columns of cortex
10. _____ simple cells
11. _____ hypercomplex cells
12. _____ area MST
13. _____ area MT
14. _____ area V4
15. _____ inferior temporal lobe
16. _____ superior colliculus

a. small cells, small receptive fields → detailed vision
b. detects movement of simple objects
c. detects expansion, contraction, or rotation of field
d. possible mediator of blindsight
e. color constancy, visual attention
f. cells with similar responses, perpendicular to surface
g. site where ganglion cells exit the retina
h. cells in V1 with fixed excitatory & inhibitory areas
i. lateral inhibition
j. cells with large receptive field and inhibitory area at 1 end
k. receptors more sensitive to dim light
l. shape constancy
m. cells that send axons to lateral geniculate nucleus
n. receptors with 3 different pigments → color vision
o. "pit" in retina, all cones, most acute vision
p. large cells, large receptive fields, detect movement

Multiple-Choice Questions

1. The law of specific nerve energies
   a. was proposed by Hering.
   b. states that any activity of a given nerve always conveys the same kind of information to the brain.
   c. states that the information carried by a given nerve changes, depending on the kind of stimulus that gave rise to the nerve's activity.
   d. is no longer thought to be true, and is now only of historical interest.

2. The fovea
   a. is completely blind because axons from ganglion cells exit from the retina there.
   b. covers approximately half the retina.
   c. contains no rods and is bypassed by most blood vessels and axons of distant ganglion cells.
   d. is color blind because it contains no cones but has good sensitivity to dim light.

3. Which of the following is true?
   a. The fovea is more sensitive to dim light than is the periphery.
   b. The fovea has more detailed vision because each receptor synapses with just one bipolar, which in turn synapses with just one ganglion cell.
   c. Cones mediate more detailed vision because of their shape.
   d. Cones are situated peripherally in the retina, rods more centrally, though there is overlap.

4. A photopigment molecule absorbs a photon of light whose energy converts
   a. all-trans-retinal to 11-cis-retinal.
   b. opsin to all-trans-retinal.
   c. 11-cis-retinal to all-trans-retinal.
   d. 11-cis-retinal to opsin.

5. The opponent-process theory
   a. was proposed by Hering to account for negative afterimages; for example, excitation of a bipolar cell could lead to the experience of blue, whereas inhibition could lead to the experience of yellow.
   b. was proposed by Young and Helmholtz based on color matching experiments; any color could be matched by a combination of three lights.
   c. states that each receptor is sensitive only to a narrow band of wavelengths of light and that wavelength bands of different receptor groups do not overlap.
   d. is true only for rods, not cones.

6. The most common form of color vision deficiency
   a. is more common in women than in men.
   b. has been well known since the earliest civilizations.
   c. is characterized by difficulty distinguishing blue from yellow.
   d. is characterized by difficulty distinguishing red from green.

7. Which of the following best describes the main route of visual information in the retina?
   a. receptor→ganglion cell→bipolar cell
   b. receptor→bipolar cell→ganglion cell
   c. receptor→ganglion cell→amacrine cell
   d. receptor→horizontal cell→amacrine cell

8. Which of the following is true concerning receptive fields?
   a. They are always defined as an area surrounding "their" neuron; the receptive field for a simple cortical cell is itself in the cortex.
   b. The presence of both excitatory and inhibitory areas in the same receptive field is maladaptive and is a holdover from an earlier, inefficient way of processing information.
   c. Receptive fields of simple cortical cells are circular.
   d. For mammalian ganglion cells, they are generally doughnut-shaped, with the center being either excitatory or inhibitory and the surround being the opposite.

9. Lateral inhibition
   a. increases sensitivity to dim light.
   b. decreases contrast at borders.
   c. heightens contrast at borders.
   d. interferes with processing of color information.

10. Horizontal cells
    a. send axons out of the retina through the blind spot.
    b. send graded inhibitory responses to neighboring bipolar cells.
    c. are located behind the receptors so that they are out of the way of incoming light.
    d. all of the above

11. Parvocellular ganglion cells
    a. are highly sensitive to both detail and color.
    b. are located primarily in the periphery of the retina.
    c. are among the largest ganglion cells in the retina.
    d. respond only weakly to visual stimuli.

12. Koniocellular ganglion cells
    a. have large cell bodies and are the most important cells for detection of movement.
    b. have small cell bodies, occur throughout the retina, and are the least understood type.
    c. are the most important ganglion cells for shape perception.
    d. are located only in the fovea.

13. Simple cells in the visual cortex
    a. respond maximally to bars of light oriented in one direction but not to bars of light oriented in another direction.
    b. respond to "correctly" oriented bars of light only when the bars are in the "correct" part of the retina.
    c. were first described by Hubel and Wiesel.
    d. all of the above

14. Simple and complex cells differ in that
    a. the receptive field of a simple cell is larger than that of a complex cell.
    b. the receptive field of a complex cell cannot be mapped into fixed excitatory and inhibitory zones, but that of a simple cell can.
    c. simple cells respond only to bars of light, whereas complex cells respond best to small spots of light.
    d. all of the above

15. Simple and complex cells are similar in that
    a. both may be found in the striate cortex.
    b. most respond maximally to bars of light oriented in a particular direction.
    c. both a and b
    d. none of the above

16. End-stopped, or hypercomplex, cells
    a. have extremely small receptive fields.
    b. are similar to complex cells, except for an inhibitory area at one end of the receptive field.
    c. respond only to very complex stimuli, such as faces.
    d. respond best to small spots of light.

17. Neurons along the track of an electrode inserted perpendicular to the surface of visual cortex
    a. have response characteristics that vary widely, but systematically, from the top to the bottom.
    b. have a random distribution of response characteristics.
    c. have certain response characteristics in common.
    d. cannot have their responses recorded, since the electrode damages them severely.

18. The hypothesis that neurons in the visual cortex are feature detectors
    a. is supported by the observation that prolonged exposure to a given feature seems to fatigue the relevant detectors.
    b. is supported by the finding that each cell in the primary visual cortex responds only to one very precise stimulus, so its response is not at all ambiguous.
    c. is disproved by the observation that visual cortical cells respond only to sine-wave gratings, and not at all to bars and edges.
    d. is now known to be true for hypercomplex cells, but not for any other cells.

19. The inferior temporal cortex
    a. has cells that detect objects, not the amount of light or darkness on the retina.
    b. is concerned with more complex shapes than the bars or edges that are detected in V1 and V2.
    c. may provide our sense of shape constancy.
    d. all of the above

20. A person with visual agnosia
    a. may have lost recognition for only a few kinds of stimuli, such as faces, as in prosopagnosia.
    b. has lost the ability to read.
    c. is blind.
    d. has had damage limited to the primary visual cortex (area V1).

21. Area V4
    a. seems to be especially important for face recognition.
    b. seems to be especially important for color and brightness constancy.
    c. seems to be especially important for shape constancy.
    d. receives input only from the magnocellular system.

22. Occipital area V5 (MT, middle-temporal cortex) analyzes
    a. complex shapes.
    b. colors.
    c. speed and direction of movement.
    d. stereoscopic depth cues.

23. Cells in the dorsal part of MST that respond to expansion, contraction, or rotation of a large visual scene
    a. probably help to record the movement of the head with respect to the world.
    b. probably help to keep track of a single object.
    c. are very particular about the specific objects in their receptive field.
    d. receive input primarily from the parvocellular system.

24. Cells in the ventral part of MST
   a. receive input from cells that record movement of single objects.
   b. also receive input from cells that record movement of the entire background.
   c. respond whenever an object moves in a certain direction relative to its background.
   d. all of the above

25. Which of the following is true?
   a. Cells in V4 contribute to visual attention, in addition to color constancy.
   b. Recognition of complex objects, especially faces, is associated with activity in the fusiform gyrus of the inferior temporal cortex, especially on the right side.
   c. Several visual areas of the brain decrease their activity during saccades.
   d. all of the above

26. Human infants
   a. are unable to see any patterns for at least several weeks.
   b. spend more time looking at patternless displays than at faces.
   c. during the first few days infants look more at a face with the eyes on top, whether or not it is realistic.
   d. all of the above

27. If a kitten's eyelid is sutured shut for the first 6 weeks of life, and the sutures are then removed, the kitten
   a. is blind in the inactive eye only if the other eye had normal visual input.
   b. is blind in the inactive eye regardless of the other eye's visual experience.
   c. is able to see horizontal and vertical lines, but not diagonal lines or curves.
   d. sees normally out of the eye, since all of its connections were formed before birth.

28. Children with "lazy eye" (strabismus, or strabismic amblyopia)
   a. should have the active eye covered continuously until adulthood.
   b. may be helped by covering the good eye as early as possible or by having the child play a videogame that requires attention to a three-dimensional display.
   c. should have the active eye covered only after they have reached normal adult size, in order to avoid reorganization of connections.
   d. should not be treated at all, since they will eventually outgrow the condition.

29. Retinal disparity
   a. is an abnormal condition that should be treated as early as possible.
   b. is a cue for depth perception only in people with strabismus.
   c. can be used as a cue for depth perception regardless of the organism's early experience.
   d. can normally be used for stereoscopic depth perception because cortical cells respond differentially to the degree of retinal disparity.

30. Experiments on abnormal sensory environments have shown that
   a. if kittens are reared in an environment in which they see only horizontal lines, at maturity all cells are completely normal because receptive field characteristics are fully determined at birth.
   b. if kittens are reared with only horizontal lines, they will become so habituated to that stimulus that they soon lose their ability to see horizontal lines.
   c. if kittens are reared with only horizontal lines, they will lose the ability to see vertical lines.

   d. if the environment is illuminated only with a strobe light during development, kittens lose their ability to see either horizontal or vertical lines.

31. Astigmatism
   a. is caused by asymmetric curvature of the eyes and results in blurring of vision for lines in one direction.
   b. is caused by strabismus and results in color blindness.
   c. is caused by strabismus and results in loss of binocular cells in the cortex.
   d. is caused by too much retinal disparity and results in loss of depth perception.

32. A cataract on the left eye that was present for several months during infancy
   a. did not result in any noticeable problem, as long as it was removed by age 9 or 10.
   b. resulted in mild impairments in face recognition.
   c. caused less impairment than a cataract on the right eye.
   d. resulted in a great facility for skiing.

Helpful Hint

Here is an analogy of the selective absorption of different wavelengths by the three types of cones: Think of three tennis nets with different-sized holes. The one with the largest holes will easily "catch" a red foam-rubber ball about the same size as its holes. Larger or smaller balls will tend to either bounce back off the net or to go through it, though if they are hit just right, they may be caught in the net. A net with medium-sized holes will easily catch a yellow tennis ball, and a net with even smaller holes will catch a blue golf ball.

Solutions

True/False Questions

1.	F	7.	T	13.	F	19.	T
2.	T	8.	T	14.	T	20.	F
3.	F	9.	T	15.	F	21.	T
4.	F	10.	F	16.	T	22.	T
5.	T	11.	T	17.	F	23.	F
6.	F	12.	T	18.	F	24.	T

Fill In The Blanks

1. depolarization; hyperpolarization
2. bipolar; ganglion
3. fovea; blood vessels; ganglion cell axons
4. greater; worse
5. 11-cis; all-trans
6. trichromatic
7. opponent-process
8. retinex
9. ganglion; blind spot
10. lateral geniculate nucleus
11. horizontal; contrast
12. Parvocellular
13. Magnocellular
14. shape; temporal
15. movement; action
16. color; brightness
17. inferior temporal
18. V4
19. middle temporal; MT; V5
20. medial superior temporal; MST
21. superior colliculus
22. GABA
23. strabismus (strabismic amblyopia or "lazy eye")
24. stereoscopic depth
25. motion
26. face recognition

Matching Items

1.	i	5.	k	9.	f	13.	b
2.	g	6.	n	10.	h	14.	e
3.	m	7.	a	11.	j	15.	l
4.	o	8.	p	12.	c	16.	d

Multiple Choice Questions

1.	b	9.	c	17.	c	25.	d
2.	c	10.	b	18.	a	26.	c
3.	b	11.	a	19.	d	27.	a
4.	c	12.	b	20.	a	28.	b
5.	a	13.	d	21.	b	29.	d
6.	d	14.	b	22.	c	30.	c
7.	b	15.	c	23.	a	31.	a
8.	d	16.	b	24.	d	32.	b

CHAPTER 7

The Other Sensory Systems

Introduction

Sensory systems have evolved to provide information most useful for each species. Although humans can perceive a relatively wide range of stimuli, our sensory systems also show certain specializations.

The sense of hearing uses air vibrations to move the tympanic membrane and three middle ear bones (the hammer, anvil, and stirrup), which focus the force of the vibrations so that they can move the heavier fluid inside the cochlea. The basilar membrane forms the floor of a tunnel, the scala media. Receptor cells are embedded in the basilar membrane; hairs in the top of the receptors are in contact with the overlying tectorial membrane. Inward pressure of the stirrup on the oval window increases pressure in scala vestibuli, which presses down on scala media, which in turn bulges downward into scala tympani and pushes the round window outward. The opposite happens when the stirrup moves outward. The movement of the basilar membrane (the floor of scala media) relative to the tectorial membrane produces a shearing action that bends the hair cells, thereby generating a potential.

Pitch perception depends on a combination of three mechanisms. At low frequencies, neurons can fire with each vibration. At medium frequencies, neurons split into volleys, one volley firing with one vibration, another with the next, and so on. At higher frequencies the area of the basilar membrane with greatest displacement is used as a place code. The characteristics of the basilar membrane vary along the length of the cochlea. At the basal end a bony shelf occupies most of the floor of scala media, and the basilar membrane, which attaches to the shelf, is thin and stiff. At the apex, there is almost no bony shelf, and the basilar membrane is larger and floppier, even though the cochlea as a whole is smaller. The size and stiffness of the basilar membrane determine which part of the basilar membrane will respond to various frequencies of sound with the greatest-amplitude traveling wave. High-pitched tones cause maximal displacement near the base, and low-pitched tones cause maximal displacement closer to the apex. There is considerable overlap of pitches coded by frequency of firing and by place.

After passing through several subcortical structures, auditory information reaches the primary auditory cortex in the temporal lobes. Neurons in one area respond selectively to the location of sound, and those in another area respond selectively to tones. Neurons with similar preferred tones cluster together there. Damage to the primary auditory cortex does not impair responses to simple sounds but does impair responses to combinations or sequences of sounds.

There are two categories of hearing impairment. Conductive, or middle ear, deafness results from failure of the middle ear bones to transmit sound waves to the cochlea. It can be caused by diseases, infections, or tumorous growths in the middle ear. Nerve, or inner ear, deafness is caused by damage to the cochlea, the hair cells, or the auditory nerve. Prenatal infections or toxins, inadequate oxygen during birth, diseases, reactions to drugs, and exposure to loud noises are frequent causes of nerve deafness.

Sound localization is accomplished by three methods. The difference in loudness between the two ears is used for high-frequency sounds, while the phase difference for sound waves arriving at the two ears is used for low-frequency sounds. In addition, time of arrival at the two ears is useful for sounds with a sudden onset. However, for animals with small heads, there is little phase difference in the sound waves reaching the two ears. Therefore, it is difficult for them to localize low-frequency tones. These animals have evolved the ability to perceive sounds that they can localize easily.

Our auditory system may have evolved from the touch receptors of primitive animals. Vestibular sensation, contributes to our sense of balance and guidance of our eye movements.

The sense of touch is composed of several modalities, some of which are fairly well correlated with activity in specific receptor types. For example, free nerve endings are involved in sensations of pain, warmth, and cold. Hair-follicle receptors respond to movement of hairs; Meissner's corpuscles and Pacinian corpuscles signal sudden displacement of skin. Merkel's disks produce a prolonged response to steady indentation of the skin, while Ruffini endings respond to skin stretching.

Sensory nerves enter and motor nerves exit the spinal cord through each of 31 openings in the vertebral canal. These nerves innervate overlapping segments of the body (dermatomes). Several well defined pathways ascend from the spinal cord to separate areas of the thalamus, and thence to appropriate areas of somatosensory cortex in the parietal lobe. Thus, the various aspects of somatosensation are at least partially separate, from the receptor level to the cerebral cortex. Bodily sensations are mapped onto four parallel strips, two of which respond mostly to touch and the other two, to deep pressure and movement of joints and muscles. In some patients damage to the somatosensory cortex may result in impairment of body perception.

Pain information is transmitted to the spinal cord by axons that use glutamate and substance P as their transmitters. Mild pain releases only glutamate; stronger pain releases both. Pain sensations can be inhibited by release of the brain's endogenous opiates (endorphins). However, one endorphin, dynorphin A, increases pain. Changes in levels of circulating estradiol also influence opiate activity and mediate sensitivity to pain. According to the gate theory, various kinds of nonpain stimuli can modify pain sensations. Endorphins released in the periaqueductal gray area of the midbrain result in excitation of neurons that block the release of substance P in the spinal cord and brainstem.

Capsaicin, derived from hot peppers, elicits the release of substance P and thereby produces a sensation of pain or heat. However, following application of capsaicin, there is a prolonged decrease in pain sensations. Placebo procedures may decrease the emotional response to painful stimuli by inhibiting a pathway through the hypothalamus, amygdala, and cingulate cortex. Nocebos procedures worsen pain. Pain may be increased as a result of sensitization in damaged or inflamed tissue. Histamine, nerve growth factor, and other chemicals that promote healing also increase sodium gates in pain receptors and may thereby enhance pain sensitivity. Anti-inflammatory drugs, such as ibuprofen, and the neurotrophin GDNF decrease pain by reducing the release of chemicals from damaged tissue. Morphine administered for serious pain is almost never addictive. It is more effective at blocking thin axons that carry dull post-surgical pain than the larger axons that carry sharp pain. Cannabinoids act primarily in the periphery to block only certain kinds of pain. As a last resort, electrical stimulation in or near brain pathways carrying messages of pain may disrupt synapses and relieve pain. However, benefits of this procedure are generally brief. The sensation of itch is poorly understood. It is generated by the release of histamines in the skin that activate a very slow-conducting path in the spinal cord. It can be relieved by mild pain from scratching.

Taste and olfactory stimuli activate some receptors better than others; however, vertebrate sensory systems do not have any pure "labeled lines." Instead, the brain analyzes patterns of firing across populations of neurons. Studies of cross-adaptation suggest that we have at least four types of taste receptor: sweet, sour, salty, and bitter. There may also be a receptor for glutamate, termed umami by the Japanese, and additional receptors for bitter and sweet. The mechanisms of activation of some taste receptors have been discovered. Sodium ions activate salty receptors; acids close potassium channels in sour receptors; and sweetness, bitterness, and umami receptors respond to molecules that activate G proteins, which then release a second messenger within the cell. The anterior two-thirds of the tongue sends information via the chorda tympani, a branch of the seventh cranial nerve (facial nerve) to the nucleus of the tractus solitarius in the medulla. The posterior third of the tongue and the throat send input via branches of the ninth and tenth cranial nerves to different parts of the nucleus of the tractus solitarius. From there the information is sent to numerous areas, including the pons, lateral hypothalamus, amygdala, ventral-posterior thalamus, and two areas of the cerebral cortex. There are individual differences in sensitivity to tastes. "Supertasters" have more fungiform papillae near the tip of the tongue. Estradiol increases women's taste sensitivity at mid-cycle and during the early stages of pregnancy.

Olfactory cells have cilia that extend into the mucous lining of the nasal passages. Odorant molecules must diffuse through a mucous fluid in order to reach the receptor sites on the cilia. Humans have several hundred types of olfactory receptor proteins, whereas rats and mice have about 1000 olfactory receptor proteins, which operate on the same principles as metabotropic neurotransmitter receptors. When activated by an odorant molecule, the receptor triggers a change in a G protein, which in turn elicits chemical activities within the cell. Because there are so many types of receptor, olfaction has more of a labeled-line system of coding than does, for example, color vision, which has only three types of cones. However, even in olfaction, each receptor responds to other odorants that are similar to its preferred stimulus. Therefore, a single receptor can provide an approximate classification of an odorant, but related receptors provide more exact information. A population of varied receptors can provide information about complex mixtures of odors. Pheromones are chemicals released by members of a species that affect the behavior of other members of that species. They are detected by the vomeronasal organ (VNO), located near, but separate from the olfactory receptors. Each VNO receptor responds to only one pheromone and is linked to a G-protein. The VNO in humans is vestigial; however, humans do respond to pheromones, perhaps via receptors in the main olfactory mucosa.

Learning Objectives

Module 7.1 Audition
1. Be able to describe the physical structures of the ear and their contributions to hearing.
2. Understand the mechanisms of pitch perception and sound localization.
3. Know the types of hearing loss and the conditions that can cause them.

Module 7.2 The Mechanical Senses
1. Understand the roles of the otoliths and semicircular canals in vestibular sensation.
2. Be able to describe the somatosensory receptors and the stimuli they respond to.
3. Be able to describe the cortical processing of somatosensory information.
4. Understand the roles of the various neurotransmitters in the production and the alleviation of pain and itch sensations.

Module 7.3 The Chemical Senses
1. Understand the concepts of the labeled-line and across-fiber pattern principles and how they apply to each of the senses.
2. Understand the mechanisms of the taste receptors and be able to describe the pathways of taste coding in the brain.
3. Be able to describe the operation and numbers of olfactory receptors, and the implications of the numbers of receptors for coding olfactory information.
4. Understand the types of stimuli that the vomeronasal organ responds to and differences between the vomeronasal and olfactory systems.
5. Be able to describe synesthesia and its possible anatomical basis.

Key Terms and Concepts

Module 7.1 Audition
1.　Sound and the ear
　　Physical and psychological dimensions of sound
　　　Sound waves: Periodic compressions of air, water, or other media
　　　Amplitude (physical intensity)
　　　　　Loudness (perception of intensity)
　　　Frequency (compressions per second, hertz: Hz)
　　　　　Pitch (perception related to frequency)
　　Structures of the ear
　　　Outer ear
　　　　Pinna → helps localize source of a sound
　　　Middle ear
　　　　Tympanic membrane (eardrum)
　　　　　　Middle ear bones
　　　　　　Hammer (malleus)
　　　　　　Anvil (incus)
　　　　　　Stirrup (stapes)
　　　　　Tympanic membrane: 20 X larger than footplate of stirrup → greater pressure on oval window
　　　Inner ear

Oval window
Cochlea
Scala vestibuli
Scala tympani
Scala media
Basilar membrane
Hair cells (auditory receptors)
Tectorial membrane
Auditory nerve (part of eighth cranial nerve)

2. Pitch perception
Frequency theory and place theory
Place theory
Each frequency activates hair cells at only one place on basilar membrane
Problem: Basilar membrane parts bound too tightly
Frequency theory
Action potentials in synchrony with sound
Problem: Neurons cannot fire fast enough
Volley principle: Effective to ~4000 Hz
Compromise: Frequency theory below 4000 Hz, place theory above that
Amusia ("tone deafness"): Difficulty recognizing tones
Genetic predisposition
Abnormal migration of auditory neurons during development
Thicker auditory cortex and less white matter in right hemisphere
Absolute pitch ("perfect pitch"): Ability to hear and identify notes
Genetic predisposition
Early musical training
Common in those using tonal languages

3. The auditory cortex
Primary auditory cortex (area A1: Superior temporal cortex)
Includes area MT
Important for visual motion
Damage to parts of superior temporal cortex → motion deafness
Auditory imagery: Fills in gaps in familiar songs
Requires experience for development
Damage to A1 → deficits in advanced processing, not total deafness
Unlike damage to V1, which → blindness
Cells → prolonged response to preferred sound
Tonotopic map
Complex sounds better than pure tones for many cells
Other areas that detect motion of sounds
Part of parietal cortex ("where" stream) → location of sounds and visual stimuli
Areas surrounding A1
Respond more to changes in sounds than to single prolonged sound
"Auditory objects": Animal cries, machinery noises, music
Interpret a sound's meaning

4. Hearing loss
    Conductive deafness (middle-ear deafness)
      Certain diseases or infections
      Tumorous bone growth in middle ear
      Sometimes temporary
      Can be corrected
      Can hear sounds that bypass middle ear, including own voice
    Nerve deafness (inner-ear deafness)
      Damage to cochlea, hair cells, or auditory nerve
      May be inherited
      Prenatal exposure to rubella, syphilis, or other contagious diseases or to toxins
      Inadequate oxygen to brain during birth
      Inadequate thyroid activity
      Diseases, including multiple sclerosis and meningitis
      Childhood reactions to drugs, including aspirin
      Repeated exposure to loud noises
    Tinnitus: Frequent or constant ringing in ears
      Similarity to phantom limb

5. Sound localization
    Difference in intensity
      Sound shadow
      High frequencies
    Difference in time of arrival
      Sudden onset sounds
      Useful for any frequency
    Phase difference
      Depends on frequency, head size, and sound direction
      Low frequencies

6. In closing: Functions of hearing

Module 7.2 The Mechanical Senses

1. Mechanical senses
      Includes touch, pain, other body sensations, and vestibular sensations
2. Vestibular sensation
    Vestibular organ (adjacent to cochlea)
          Saccule
          Utricle
          Semicircular canals
          Otoliths: calcium carbonate particles next to hair cells
      Semicircular canals (three planes): Filled with jellylike substance, lined with hair cells
    Eighth cranial nerve, vestibular component
      Brain stem and cerebellum

3. Somatosensation
    Somatosensory receptors
      Bare (or free) nerve ending

Pain, warmth, cold
Hair-follicle receptors
    Movement of hairs
Meissner's corpuscles
    Sudden displacement of skin, low frequency vibration
Pacinian corpuscles
    Sudden displacement of skin, high frequency vibration
Merkel's disks
    Indentation of skin
Ruffini endings
    Stretch of skin
Krause end bulbs
    Uncertain function
Touch receptors (bare nerve endings, Ruffini endings, Meissner's corpuscles, Pacinian corpuscles): Opening of sodium channels → Action potential
Heat receptors: Also respond to capsaicin
Coolness receptors: Also respond to menthol and mint
Tickle: Poorly understood
    Can't tickle oneself
    Motor areas signal somatosensory areas
Input to central nervous system
  31 sets of spinal nerves
  Dermatome
Somatosensory thalamus
Somatosensory cortex
  Parietal lobe
  Four parallel strips
    Two for touch
    Two for deep pressure and joint and muscle movement
Damage to somatosensory cortex → impaired perception of body

4.   Pain
Pain stimuli and pain pathways
  Bare nerve endings
  Capsaicin
  Axons carrying pain messages have little or no myelin (conduct information relatively slowly)
    Thicker and faster axons convey sharp pain
    Thinner and slower axons convey duller pain
  The brain responds more rapidly to pain stimuli than touch
  Pain axons release neurotransmitters in spinal cord
  Glutamate (mild pain)
  Substance P and glutamate (strong pain)
  Spinal pathways
    Painful stimuli, memories of pain, and impending pain: Spinal cord → ventral posterior nucleus of the thalamus → somatosensory cortex

Pain and touch: Parallel, pain path crosses contralateral, touch path travels ipsilateral but crosses in medulla

Pain → activation of hypothalamus, amygdala, hippocampus, and cingulate cortex, in addition to somatosensory cortex → Emotional responses

Cingulate cortex: Response increases when watching someone else experiencing pain, and decreases with hypnotic suggestion to feel no pain

Somatosensory cortex: Response decreases slightly or not at all

Ways of relieving pain

Opioids and endorphins

Opioid mechanisms: Inhibit pain

Candace Pert and Solomon Snyder

Receptors in spinal cord and periaqueductal gray area

Inhibit effects of substance P

β-endorphin (endogenous morphine)

Dynorphin A increases pain

Estradiol mediates opiate activity → influences pain sensitivity in women

Gate theory: Nonpainful stimuli decrease pain

Morphine blocks activity of thin, unmyelinated axons → blocks postsurgical pain

Doesn't block acute pain carried by large-diameter axons

Placebo: drug or procedure with no pharmacological effects

Decrease pain, primarily effects on emotion not sensation

Decreases response in cingulated cortex, but not somatosensory cortex

Decrease pain in part by influencing opiates

Nocebos (anti-placebos) worsen pain

Anti-anxiety drugs decrease effects of nocebos

Cannabinoids

Blocks certain kinds of pain

Act in periphery

Delete receptors in periphery (but not in CNS) → Cannabinoids lost ability to decrease pain

Endorphins in periaqueductal gray area → medulla

Both areas → spinal cord → block release of substance P

Capsaicin (induces release of substance P, stimulates heat receptors)

Depletes substance P → analgesia

High doses → damage to pain receptors

Electrical stimulation of the nervous system

Pioneered in the 1970s

Last resort to relieve pain

Stimulation in or near pain pathways in spinal cord or thalamus

Disrupts pain synapses

Benefits are brief, most do not experience long-lasting benefits

Sensitization of pain

Damage to tissue → release of histamine, nerve growth factor → repair damage

Also increase sodium gates → magnify pain response

Facilitate activity at capsaicin receptors

Nonsteroidal anti-inflammatory drugs → reduce release of chemicals in damage tissue

Potentiation of receptors after barrage of stimulation

Similar to learning and memory

5. Itch

Histamines in skin → slow-conducting pathway

Mild pain (scratching) → blocks itch

Certain plants (e.g. cowhage) produce itch

Capsaicin, but not antihistamines, relieves cowhage itch

Some axons conveying sensation of itch respond to histamine, while others respond to cowhage

Axons also respond to heat

Itch axons → gastrin-releasing peptide

Block gastrin-releasing peptide → decrease scratching

Opiates decrease pain, increase itch

Novocain effects wear off faster for itch than touch and pain

Therefore, itch not form of pain

6. In closing: The mechanical senses

Module 7.3 The Chemical Senses

1. General issues about chemical coding

Labeled-line principle

Across-fiber pattern principle

2. Taste

Taste receptors (modified skin cells)

Taste buds (about 50 receptors per taste bud)

Papillae (0-10 taste buds per papilla)

How many kinds of taste receptors?

Four main types: Sweet, sour, salty, bitter

Chemicals that alter taste buds

Miracle berries and modification of taste receptors

Miraculin: Acids → sweet

Sodium laurel sulfate: Intensifies bitter, decreases sweet

Gymnena sylvestre: Blocks sweet

Aspartame (NutraSweet®): Sweetness only partially blocked

Therefore, must stimulate additional receptor

Adaptation within a taste; little cross-adaptation

Monosodium glutamate

Umami

Fat receptors in taste buds of rats and mice

Different rhythms of action potentials

Mechanisms of taste receptors

Salty: Sodium influx

Amiloride: blocks sodium entry → decreases salty taste

Sour: Acid closes potassium channels → depolarize membrane
Sweet, bitter, umami: G protein and second messenger
    Multiple bitter receptors
  Taste coding in the brain
    Pattern across fibers
    Information from anterior two-thirds of tongue
        Chorda tympani: Branch of seventh cranial nerve (facial nerve)
    Information from posterior third of tongue and throat
        Ninth and tenth cranial nerves
        Anesthetize chorda tympani
            Lose taste in anterior tongue
            Increase bitter and salt sensitivity in posterior tongue
            "Phantoms" due to release from inhibition
    Nucleus of the tractus solitarius (NTS, in medulla)
    Pons
    Lateral hypothalamus
    Amygdala
    Ventral-posterior thalamus
    Two areas of cerebral cortex
        Insula → taste
        Somatosensory → touch
    Mostly ipsilateral input
    Cells in cerebral cortex intermingle with cells responsive to other tastes
  Individual differences in taste
    Phenylthiocarbamate (PTC)
        Bitter, very bitter, or little taste
        Supertasters: Most fungiform papillae
    Women's taste sensitivity correlated with estrogen

3. Olfaction
  Olfactory receptors
    Olfactory cells
    Olfactory epithelium
    Cilia: From cell body into mucous surface
    Similar to metabotropic neurotransmitter receptors
        Seven transmembrane sections
        G proteins
    About 1000 receptor proteins in rodents
    Several hundred in humans
    One receptor type per cell
    Inhibition of less strongly activated receptors

  Implications for coding
    Each receptor: Identify approximate nature of molecule
    Receptor population: More precise; identify complex mixture
    Variety of airborne chemicals, not one single dimension
  Messages to the brain

Olfactory bulb
>Coding by area of olfactory bulb excited

Several parts of cortex
>Clusters of neurons responsive to similar smells
>Similar across individuals
>Naturally occurring objects (e.g. food) activate a larger population of cells
>Brain's ability to distinguish similar smells improves with experience

Olfactory receptors susceptible to damage
>Average survival: ~ one month
>Stem cell → new neuron in same place
>Axon contains receptor protein → find target in olfactory bulb
>Damage to entire olfactory surface → incomplete recovery

Individual differences
>Women more sensitive and attentive to odors
>Young adult women become more sensitive with experience
>>Effect of hormones
>Perception of androstenone is influenced by genetic variations in olfactory receptors (OR7D4)
>Deletion of gene for potassium channel → increased sensitivity

4.   Pheromones
>Vomeronasal organ (VNO): Receptors located near, but separate from, olfactory receptors
>Pheromones: Chemicals released by animals, affect conspecifics
>>Fewer receptor types
>>>Each receptor responds to one pheromone
>>Nonadapting
>>Lack of vomeronasal receptors → impaired mating in mice
>>Vestigial in humans
>>>Pheromone receptors in olfactory mucosa
>>Human pheromones
>>>Skin secretions → increased activity in hypothalamus → autonomic responses
>>>Male sweat → increases release of cortisol in women
>>>Unconscious effects
>>>Synchronized menstrual cycles
>>>Man's pheromones → more regular cycles in partner

5.   Synesthesia
>1:500 people
>Experience one sense in response to stimulation of a different sense
>fMRI: Speech activated both auditory and visual cortex

6.   In closing: Different senses offer different ways of knowing the world
>Taste and smell more important than we realize

Short-Answer Questions

Module 7.1 Audition

1. *Sound and the ear*

    a. What is the relationship between amplitude and loudness? Between frequency and pitch?

    b. What is the role of the tympanic membrane and the hammer, anvil, and stirrup?

    c. Where are the auditory receptors located? How are they stimulated?

2. *Pitch perception*

    a. What led to the downfall of the frequency theory of pitch discrimination in its simple form?

    b. What is the volley theory?

    c. What observation led to the downfall of the place theory as originally stated?

    d. What is the current compromise between the place and frequency theories of pitch discrimination?

    e. At which end of the cochlea is the basilar membrane stiffest?

    f. Describe the location of the primary auditory cortex. To what two aspects of auditory stimuli do parts of primary auditory cortex respond?

    g. What are the effects of damage to the primary auditory cortex?

3. *Hearing loss*

    a. For which type of deafness can one hear one's own voice, though external sounds are heard poorly?

    b. For what type of deafness is hearing impaired for a limited range of frequencies?

    c. What are some causes of nerve deafness? Of conductive deafness?

4. *Localization of sounds*

    a. For which frequencies is the "sound shadow" method of localization best? Why?

    b. What characteristic of sound is necessary to be able to localize sounds on the basis of difference in time of arrival? Are some frequencies easier to localize on this basis than others?

    c. Describe localization on the basis of phase difference. For which frequencies is it most effective?

    d. Which method of sound localization is best for a species with a small head? Why?

Module 7.2 The Mechanical Senses

1. *Vestibular sensation*

    a. What are the main parts of the vestibular organ? What are otoliths? What is their function?

    b. What are the semicircular canals?

2. *Somatosensation*

    a. List the somatosensory receptors and their probable functions.

    b. How many sets of spinal nerves do we have?

    c. What is a dermatome?

    d. Describe briefly the cortical projections of the somatosensory system.

    e. Describe the loss of body sense that may accompany Alzheimer's disease.

3. *Pain*

    a. What is the role of glutamate in pain sensation? What is substance P?

    b. What is capsaicin? How does it work? What food contains capsaicin?

    c. What theory did Melzack and Wall propose to account for variations in pain responsiveness? What is its main principle?

    d. What are endorphins? How was the term derived? Do all endorphins exert similar effects?

    e. How does estradiol influence pain sensitivity in women?

    f. Where are endorphin synapses concentrated? What is their function there?

    g. What is a placebo? What aspect of pain does it sometimes relieve? Which areas of the brain are important for this effect? What are nocebos?

    h. How do cannabinoids influence pain? Where do they act to influence pain?

    i. Briefly describe how electrical stimulation may help relieve pain.

    j. Describe the process by which tissue damage results in pain sensitization. Which drugs or natural chemicals can decrease pain sensitization?

    k. In which type of axons does morphine decrease activity? How addictive is morphine when used for pain relief in hospital settings?

4. *Itch*

    a. What is the physiological mechanism of itch sensation?

Module 7.3 The Chemical Senses

1. *General issues about chemical coding*

    a. Describe the labeled-line type of coding. Do vertebrate sensory systems have any pure labeled-line systems?

    b. Describe the across-fiber pattern type of coding. Give an example.

2. *Taste*

    a. Where are the taste receptors located? What is the relationship between taste buds and papillae?

    b. How can cross-adaptation be used to help determine the number of taste receptors?

    c. What are the four major kinds of taste receptor? What additional kinds may we have?

d. What are the mechanisms of activation of salty, sour, sweet, bitter, and umami receptors? How does amiloride affect salty tastes?

e. Describe the changes in taste sensitivity that occur if the chorda tympani is anesthetized.

f. Which structures in the brain process taste information? Is taste analysis primarily ipsilateral or contralateral?

g. Describe the individual differences in taste of phenylthiocarbamate (PTC). What is the physiological basis of increased sensitivity in supertasters?

3. *Olfaction*

a. Describe the olfactory receptors. Where do their axons project.

b. How are olfactory receptors similar to neurotransmitter receptors? How many olfactory receptor proteins are estimated to exist in rodents, based on isolation of these proteins? in humans?

c. What can we say about the labeled-line theory vs. the across-fiber pattern theory for smell?

d. What is the vomeronasal organ? What type of molecules does it detect?

e. What are some functions of pheromones in mice?

f. What are two functions of pheromones that have been demonstrated in humans?

4. *Synesthesia*

a. What is synesthesia? What is one possible explanation for it?

True/False Questions

1. The function of the middle ear bones is to focus the force of vibrations of the eardrum onto the smaller oval window, in order to move the viscous fluid behind the oval window.

   TRUE or FALSE

2. The basilar membrane at the base of the cochlea is larger and floppier than at the smaller apex of the cochlea.

   TRUE or FALSE

3. Two areas of the primary auditory cortex are sensitive to location and frequency of sounds.

   TRUE or FALSE

4. Extensive damage to the primary auditory cortex results in profound deafness for all sounds.

   TRUE or FALSE

5. People with inner-ear deafness can hear their own voices.

   TRUE or FALSE

6. Localization of high-frequency sounds depends mainly on a sound shadow created by the head.

   TRUE or FALSE

7. Pacinian corpuscles are the primary receptors for heat and pain.

   TRUE or FALSE

8. A dermatome is an area on the cortex that receives input from a peripheral structure, such as an arm.

   TRUE or FALSE

9. The somatosensory cortex receives input primarily from the contralateral side of the body, although many neurons also receive input via the corpus callosum from the ipsilateral side.

   TRUE or FALSE

10. Mild pain releases only glutamate in the spinal cord; intense pain releases both glutamate and substance P.

    TRUE or FALSE

11. Endorphins in the periaqueductal gray lead to the activation of neurons that decrease the release of substance P in the spinal cord.

    TRUE or FALSE

12. Capsaicin is an endorphin that that is released in the spinal cord and immediately decreases the release of substance P.

    TRUE or FALSE

13. Dynorphin A, an endorphin, inhibits the effects of substance P and decreases pain.

    TRUE or FALSE

14. A placebo decreases the emotional response to pain by decreasing activity in a pathway through the hypothalamus, amygdala, and cingulate cortex.

    TRUE or FALSE

15. Anti-anxiety drugs decrease the effects of nocebos.

    TRUE or FALSE

16. Electrical stimulation in or near pain pathways in the spinal cord or thalamus will increase pain.

    TRUE or FALSE

17. Histamine, nerve growth factor, and other chemicals released from inflamed tissue inhibit pain in the area.

    TRUE or FALSE

18. Opiates are even more effective at inhibiting itch than at inhibiting pain.

    TRUE or FALSE

19. Capsaicin relieves itch caused by cowhage.

    TRUE or FALSE

20. Blocking gastrin-releasing peptide increases itch.

    TRUE or FALSE

21. Saltiness receptors permit sodium ions on the tongue to cross their membrane and depolarize the neuron.

    TRUE or FALSE

22. Sweet, bitter, and umami receptors close potassium channels, keeping more of the positive ions inside the cell and thereby depolarizing it.

TRUE or FALSE

23. Taste nerves project to the nucleus of the tractus solitarius in the medulla, which in turn projects to the pons, lateral hypothalamus, amygdala, ventral-posterior thalamus, and two areas of cerebral cortex.

TRUE or FALSE

24. Each olfactory axon branches widely to provide input to a large percentage of the olfactory bulb.

TRUE or FALSE

25. Vomeronasal receptors respond to species-specific pheromones that regulate sexual interest, and, in humans, timing of the menstrual cycle.

TRUE or FALSE

Fill In The Blanks

1. The three middle ear bones are the _____ (_____), the _____ (_____), and the _____ (_____).

2. The basilar membrane in located in the scala _____.

3. Pitch perception depends on aspects of both the _____ theory and the _____ theory.

4. The two kinds of deafness are _____ (_____) and _____ (_____) deafness.

5. Phase differences are most useful for localizing _____-frequency sounds.

6. The vestibular organs consist of the _____, the _____, and the _____.

7. Bare (or free) nerve endings convey information about _____, _____, and _____. Stimulation of these neurons opens _____ channels.

8. The transmitters that convey pain information are _____ and _____.

9. According to the _____ theory, nonpainful stimuli can decrease the intensity of pain by releasing endorphins in the _____ of the midbrain.

10. _____ is a chemical found in red peppers that activates pain and heat receptors.

11. A drug or procedure that has no pharmacological effect, but that can ease the psychological distress of pain is called a _____.

12. Sensitization of pain occurs when _____, _____, and other chemicals that promote healing also increase the number of _____ gates in pain neurons.

13. Itch is occasioned by release of _____ in the skin.

14. Taste buds are located in _____ on the surface of the tongue.

15. _____ receptors are activated by sodium on the tongue; _____ receptors respond by closing potassium gates; _____, _____, and _____ receptors activate G-proteins that release second messengers within the cell.

16. Olfactory receptors are located on _____ that extend into the mucous surface of the nasal passage.

17. Olfactory coding relies more on a _____ principle than does taste coding, because there are so many types of receptor proteins, and each receptor projects to a specific area of the olfactory bulb.

18. Exposing women to male sweat increases circulating levels of _____.

19. Receptors sensitive to pheromones are located in the _____ organ.

Matching Items

1. _____ Amplitude
2. _____ Frequency
3. _____ Sound shadow
4. _____ Time of arrival
5. _____ Phase difference
6. _____ Capsaicin
7. _____ Endorphins
8. _____ Histamine
9. _____ Substance P
10. _____ Pheromone
11. _____ Experience of one sense after stimulation of a different sense

a. Localize low-frequency sounds
b. Localize high-frequency sounds
c. Localize sudden onset sounds
d. Stimulates heat and pain receptors
e. Synesthesia
f. Pitch
g. Loudness
h. Decrease pain
i. Major transmitter for intense pain
j. Increases both healing and pain in sensitization
k. Vomeronasal organ

Multiple-Choice Questions

1. Which of the following is true of auditory perception?
   a. Loudness is the same thing as amplitude.
   b. Pitch is the perception of intensity.
   c. Perception of low frequencies decreases with age and exposure to loud noises.
   d. Perception of high frequencies decreases with age and exposure to loud noises.

2. The function of the tympanic membrane and middle-ear bones is to
   a. directly stimulate the auditory receptors.
   b. move the tectorial membrane to which the stirrup is connected.
   c. focus the vibrations on a small area, so that there is sufficient force to produce pressure waves in the fluid-filled cochlea.
   d. none of the above.

3. The auditory receptors
    a. are called hair cells.
    b. are embedded in the basilar membrane below and the tectorial membrane above.
    c. are stimulated when the basilar membrane moves relative to the tectorial membrane; displacement of the hair cells by about the diameter of one atom opens ion channels in the membrane of the neuron.
    d. all of the above.

4. The frequency theory
    a. in its simplest form cannot describe coding of very high-frequency tones because the refractory periods of neurons limit their firing rates.
    b. can be modified by the volley principle to account for pitch discrimination of all frequencies, up to 20,000 Hz.
    c. is now thought to be valid for high-frequency tones, whereas the place theory describes pitch coding of lower tones.
    d. is a form of labeled-line theory.

5. The place theory
    a. received experimental support from demonstrations that the basilar membrane was composed of a series of separate strings.
    b. has been modified so that a given frequency produces a greater displacement at one area of the basilar membrane than at others.
    c. cannot be true at all, because the basilar membrane is the same throughout its length and therefore cannot localize vibrations.
    d. cannot be true at all, because the basilar membrane is too loose and floppy to show any localization.

6. The basilar membrane
    a. is smallest and stiffest at the apex (farthest, small end) of the cochlea.
    b. is smallest and stiffest at the base (large end) of the cochlea.
    c. has the same dimensions and consistency throughout its length.
    d. shows maximum displacement for low tones near its base.

7. Pitch discrimination
    a. depends on a combination of mechanisms: frequency coding for low pitches, place coding for high pitches, and both mechanisms for intermediate pitches.
    b. depends on a combination of mechanisms: frequency coding for high pitches, place coding for low pitches, and both mechanisms for intermediate pitches.
    c. cannot be satisfactorily explained by any theory.
    d. is accomplished only by place coding.

8. Damage to primary auditory cortex results in
    a. inability to hear anything.
    b. inability to hear high tones, but not low tones.
    c. inability to hear low tones, but not high tones.
    d. inability to recognize combinations or sequences of sounds, as in music or speech.

9. Inner-ear deafness
   a. is frequently temporary; if it persists, it can usually be corrected by surgery.
   b. is characterized by total deafness to all sounds.
   c. may result from exposure of one's mother to rubella or other contagious diseases during pregnancy.
   d. is characterized by being able to hear one's own voice but not external sounds.

10. A "sound shadow"
   a. is useful for sound localization only for low-pitched sounds.
   b. is useful for sound localization only for wavelengths shorter than the width of the head.
   c. is a means of sound localization that uses differences in time of arrival between the two ears.
   d. cannot be used at all by small-headed species such as rodents.

11. Which of the following pairs of receptors and sensations is most correct?
   a. free nerve endings: pain, warmth, cold
   b. Merkel's disks: sudden movement across skin
   c. Pacinian corpuscles: steady indentation of skin
   d. Ruffini endings: movement of hairs

12. Which of the following is true regarding effects of placebos on pain?
   a. They decrease pain primarily by influencing emotion.
   b. They decrease pain primarily by influencing sensation.
   c. They decrease response in the somatosensory cortex
   d. They have little or no influence on opiates.

13. Dermatomes
   a. are sharply defined, nonoverlapping areas innervated by single sensory spinal nerves.
   b. are overlapping areas innervated by single sensory spinal nerves.
   c. are symptoms of a skin disorder, much like acne.
   d. are found only on the trunk of the body, not the arms, legs, or head.

14. Somatosensory information
   a. travels up a single pathway to one thalamic nucleus, which projects to one strip in the parietal lobe.
   b. travels up different pathways to separate thalamic areas, which project to four parallel strips in the parietal lobe.
   c. travels directly from the spinal cord to the parietal lobe, without any synapses on the way.
   d. travels to separate thalamic areas, which project to four parallel strips in the temporal lobe.

15. Substance P
   a. is an endogenous opiate.
   b. activates receptors that are normally blocked by capsaicin.
   c. is a neurotransmitter that signals intense pain.
   d. none of the above.

16. The gate theory of pain
   a. was proposed by Melzack and Wall.
   b. states that nonpain input can close the "gates" for pain messages.
   c. can be demonstrated by gently rubbing the skin around an injury or concentrating on something else.
   d. all of the above.

17. The labeled-line principle
    a. states that each receptor responds to a wide range of stimuli and contributes to the perception of each of them.
    b. states that each receptor responds to a narrow range of stimuli and sends a direct line to the brain.
    c. describes color coding better than does the across-fiber pattern principle.
    d. describes most sensory systems in vertebrates.

18. Which of the following is true concerning taste receptors?
    a. There are about 50 receptor cells in each taste bud, and 0 to 10 or more taste buds in each papilla.
    b. Each receptor has its own taste bud.
    c. Taste receptor cells are true neurons that send axons directly to the thalamus.
    d. In adult humans taste buds are located mainly in the center of the tongue.

19. Cross-adaptation studies have suggested that
    a. there are at least four kinds of taste receptors.
    b. there may be a separate receptor for monosodium glutamate.
    c. there may be more than one kind of receptor for both bitter and sweet tastes.
    d. all of the above.

20. Which of the following is an appropriate pairing of receptor type with its method of activation?
    a. salty: sodium inflow
    b. sweet: closing potassium channels
    c. sour: activation of G protein
    d. bitter: sodium outflow

21. The across-fiber pattern principle of taste
    a. assumes that there are seven basic taste qualities.
    b. holds that taste is coded in terms of a pattern of neural activity across many neurons.
    c. has been disproven by the finding that every receptor responds only to one taste.
    d. none of the above.

22. The nucleus of the tractus solitarius (NTS)
    a. is located in the medulla and sends taste information to the pons, lateral hypothalamus, amygdala, thalamus, and cerebral cortex.
    b. is responsible for analyzing pheromones.
    c. is located in the medulla and sends its output primarily to cranial nerves.
    d. is located in the cerebral cortex and projects to the medulla.

23. Olfactory receptors
    a. are not replaceable, once they die.
    b. each responds to only one specific odor.
    c. respond equally well to a great many odors.
    d. are located on cilia that extend into the mucous surface of the nasal passage.

24. Which of the following is true of olfactory receptors?
    a. They are similar to metabotropic neurotransmitter receptors in that they have seven transmembrane sections and trigger changes in a G protein, which then provokes chemical activities inside the cell.
    b. There are as many as 1000 olfactory receptor proteins in mice and several hundred in humans.
    c. They send their axons to specific areas of the olfactory bulb.
    d. All of the above are true.

25. Pheromones
    a. are detected by standard olfactory receptors, which have an especially rapid adaptation.
    b. can synchronize or regularize women's menstrual cycles.
    c. are used in lower mammals, but not in humans.
    d. are especially important for locating sources of food.

Solutions

True/False Questions

1. T	8. F	15. T	22. F
2. F	9. T	16. F	23. T
3. T	10. T	17. F	24. F
4. F	11. T	18. F	25. T
5. F	12. F	19. T	
6. T	13. F	20. F	
7. F	14. T	21. T	

Fill In The Blanks

1. hammer; malleus; anvil; incus; stirrup; stapes
2. media
3. frequency; place
4. conductive; middle-ear; nerve; inner-ear)
5. low
6. saccule; utricle; semicircular canals
7. pain; heat; cold; sodium
8. glutamate; substance P
9. gate; periaqueductal gray
10. Capsaicin
11. placebo
12. histamine; nerve growth factor; sodium
13. histamine
14. papillae
15. Saltines; sourness; sweetness; bitterness; umami
16. cilia
17. labeled-line
18. cortisol
19. vomeronasal

Matching Items

1. g	4. c	7. h	10. k
2. f	5. a	8. j	11. e
3. b	6. d	9. i	

Multiple Choice Questions

1. d	8. d	15. c	22. a
2. c	9. c	16. d	23. d
3. d	10. b	17. b	24. d
4. a	11. a	18. a	25. b
5. b	12. a	19. d	
6. b	13. b	20. a	
7. a	14. b	21. b	

CHAPTER 8

Movement

Introduction

All movements of the body result from muscle contractions. Acetylcholine is the neurotransmitter released at the neuromuscular junction; it always results in contraction of the recipient muscle. Myasthenia gravis is a disease characterized by weakness and fatigue. It results from autoimmune destruction of acetylcholine receptors on muscle fibers. We manage to move our limbs in two opposite directions by alternately contracting antagonistic muscles, such as flexors and extensors. There are three categories of muscle: smooth, skeletal (or striated), and cardiac. Skeletal muscles may be either fast or slow. Fish have three types of muscle: red, slow, fatigue-resistant; pink, intermediate-speed, moderately fatigue-resistant; and white, fast, easily fatigued. Mammals have muscles composed of mixed fast-twitch and slow-twitch fibers. Muscles consist of many fibers, each of which is innervated by one axon; however, each axon can innervate more than one fiber. Greater precision of movement can be achieved if each axon innervates few muscle fibers.

Two kinds of receptors signal change in the state of muscle contraction. The muscle spindle is a stretch receptor located in fibers parallel to the main muscle. Whenever the main muscle and spindle are stretched, the spindle sends impulses to the spinal cord that excite the motor neurons innervating the main muscle. This results in contraction of the main muscle, opposing the original stretch. The Golgi tendon organ is located at both ends of the main muscle and responds to increased tension in the muscle, as when the muscle is contracting or being actively stretched by an external stimulus. Its impulses to the spinal cord inhibit the motor neuron, leading to relaxation of the muscle. Combinations of activity in these two receptors allow one to maintain steady positions, to resist external forces, and to monitor voluntary movement.

Most behaviors are complex mixtures of voluntary and involuntary, or reflexive, components. Some movements are ballistic, which means that they proceed automatically once triggered. Other movements require constant sensory feedback. Central pattern generators control rhythmic movements, such as wing flapping and scratching. Motor programs are fixed sequences of movements; they may be learned or innate, rhythmic or not.

The cerebral cortex coordinates complex plans of movement. The primary motor cortex sends axons to the brainstem and spinal cord, which in turn innervate the muscles. It has overlapping areas that control different parts of the body. These areas are activated even when we imagine movements. "Mirror neurons" in the inferior parietal cortex of monkeys respond during a movement and when the animal watches another monkey perform the same movement. They enable the observer to identify with the other individual's movements. Neurons in the posterior parietal cortex respond to visual and somatosensory input, to future or current movements, or to a mixture of sensory input and the upcoming response. This area is important for converting perception into action. The primary somatosensory cortex provides the primary motor cortex with sensory information and also sends axons directly to the spinal cord. It is especially active when the hand grasps an object, responding to the object's shape and the type of movement. Several other cortical areas guide the preparation for movement. Prefrontal cortex responds mostly to sensory stimuli that lead to movement; it also calculates the likely outcome of the movement. Premotor cortex is active before a movement and, to some extent, during the movement. Supplementary motor cortex helps plan and organize a rapid series of movements. There is evidence that the motor cortex begins planning a movement even before we are aware of making a decision to act.

Output from the cortex to the spinal cord can be divided into two tracts. The lateral corticospinal tract controls movements in the periphery of the opposite side of the body. It includes axons from the primary motor cortex and adjacent areas and from the red nucleus, all of which cross from one side to the other in bulges in the medulla called the pyramids. These axons extend without synapsing to targets in the medulla and spinal cord. The medial corticospinal tract controls movements near the midline of the body that require bilateral control. It consists of some axons from primary and supplementary motor cortex, others from widespread areas of cortex, and those from the midbrain tectum, reticular formation, and vestibular nucleus. Axons branch to both sides of the cord; they control muscles of the neck, shoulders, and trunk, whose movements are necessarily bilateral.

The cerebellum is important for learning, planning and coordinating complex movements, especially rapid sequences that require accurate timing and aiming. It also contributes to sensory and cognitive processes. Damage to the cerebellum impairs rapid alternating movements, saccades, the ability to touch one's nose with one's finger, and the ability to shift attention. Parallel fibers in the cerebellar cortex activate Purkinje cells, which in turn inhibit the cerebellar and vestibular nuclei. Inhibiting these nuclei for shorter or longer times determines the duration and distance of a movement. Information from these nuclei is then sent to the midbrain and thalamus.

The basal ganglia are a group of subcortical structures that contribute to the selection and organization of movements and to habit learning. The caudate nucleus and putamen receive input from the cerebral cortex and send information to the globus pallidus, which in turn sends output to the thalamus, which finally sends its output to motor and prefrontal cortex. The globus pallidus constantly inhibits the thalamus; the caudate nucleus and putamen select certain movements by telling the globus pallidus to stop inhibiting them. The basal ganglia are especially important for self-initiated movements not controlled by an external stimulus. They are also important for learning motor skills.

The symptoms of Parkinson's disease include muscle rigidity and tremor, slow movement, difficulty initiating physical or mental activity, depression, and cognitive deficits. Parkinson's disease results from degeneration of dopamine neurons ascending from the substantia nigra in the midbrain to the caudate nucleus and putamen, which are part of the basal ganglia. Loss of dopamine in the basal ganglia results ultimately in less excitation of the cortex. Therefore, the cortex is less able to initiate movements. Several genes have been implicated in early-onset Parkinson's disease, but they have little influence on the much more common late-onset disease. A possible cause of this disease is MPTP in the environment, possibly in the form of herbicides and pesticides. MPTP is converted in the body to MPP+, which accumulates in dopamine neurons and destroys them. On the other hand, nicotine and caffeine may decrease risk of the disease. Damage to mitochondria, caused by clusters of α-synuclein, is the ultimate cause of Parkinson's disease. The symptoms of Parkinson's disease can be lessened with L-dopa, the precursor of dopamine, although such treatment frequently results in undesirable side effects. Furthermore, L-dopa does not prevent further loss of neurons. Other possible treatments include antioxidants, drugs that stimulate dopamine receptors, drugs that inhibit glutamate or adenosine receptors, drugs that block specific calcium channels, drugs that decrease apoptosis, and high-frequency stimulation of the globus pallidus. Brain grafts of fetal substantia nigra tissue have produced promising results in laboratory animals, but have produced only modest benefits in humans. Research is continuing on the possible use of genetically altered stem cells and neurotrophins.

Whereas Parkinson's disease results from degeneration of the dopaminergic input to the basal ganglia, Huntington's disease results from degeneration of the postsynaptic neurons there and in the cortex. Symptoms begin with a facial twitch and progressively lead to tremors in other parts of the body and to writhing movements and psychological disorders. An autosomal dominant gene on chromosome 4 has been identified as the ultimate cause of the disease. In people with Huntington's disease this gene contains extra repetitions of a sequence of bases (CAG) in the genetic code for a protein called huntingtin. These repetitions lead to production of long chains of glutamine, which aggregate into clusters that impair mitochondria. Cells with abnormal huntingtin also fail to release BDNF, which results in impaired function of other cells. Several drugs for treatment of this disorder show promise in animal models.

Learning Objectives

Module 8.1 The Control of Movement
1. Be able to list the three categories of muscle and understand the need for antagonistic muscles.
2. Understand the difference between fast and slow muscles and conditions under which each is most useful.
3. Be able to name and know the functions of proprioceptors.

Module 8.2 Brain Mechanisms of Movement
1. Understand the roles of the primary motor cortex, inferior parietal cortex, posterior parietal cortex, and the prefrontal, premotor, and supplementary motor cortex in the control of movement.
2. Understand the implications of the timing of the readiness potential before the person is aware of making a decision.
3. Understand the functions and cellular organization of the cerebellum.
4. Be able to list the structures that comprise the basal ganglia and know the function of each and the general contribution of the whole system.

Module 8.3 Disorders of Movement
1. Know the symptoms and immediate physiological cause of Parkinson's disease.
2. Understand the genetic and environmental causes of Parkinson's disease.
3. Know the most common treatment for Parkinson's disease and a problem with that treatment.
4. Be able to describe the symptoms and immediate physiological cause of Huntington's disease.
5. Understand the genetic cause of Huntington's disease.

Key Terms and Concepts

Module 8.1 The Control of Movement
1.   Muscles and their movements
    Categories of muscle
      Smooth
      Skeletal or striated
      Cardiac
    Precise movements: Few muscle fibers innervated by each axon
    Neuromuscular junction
      Acetylcholine → excitation and muscle contraction
    Antagonistic muscles
      Flexor
      Extensor
    Myasthenia gravis
      Autoimmune attack on acetylcholine receptors at neuromuscular junctions
      Progressive weakness and rapid fatigue
      Depletion of acetylcholine after several action potentials in rapid succession
    Fast and slow muscles
      Fish
        Red, slow, resistant to fatigue
        Pink, intermediate speed, moderately resistant to fatigue
        White, fast, forceful, fatigue quickly
      Humans and other mammals: Mixed fibers in each muscle
        Fast-twitch fibers
          Anaerobic → oxygen debt → muscle fatigue
          Use fatty acids
        Slow-twitch fibers
          Aerobic → slow to fatigue
          Use glucose, activate gene to inhibit further glucose use when supplies dwindle
        People: Varying percentages of fast- and slow-twitch fibers

    Muscle control by proprioceptors
      Proprioceptor: Receptor that detects position or movement
        Stretch reflex
        Muscle spindle: Stretch receptor parallel to muscle that responds to stretch
          When stretched, causes muscle to contract → decreases stretch
          Contributes to walking: Raise upper leg → lower leg moves forward
        Golgi tendon organ
          Responds to increased muscle tension
          In tendons at opposite ends of muscle
          Inhibits muscle: Brake against too vigorous contraction

2.   Units of movement
    Voluntary and involuntary movements
      Reflexes: Consistent automatic responses to stimuli
        Involuntary
        Infant reflexes

Grasp reflex

Babinski reflex

Rooting reflex

Cerebral cortex damage in adults → infant reflexes released from inhibition

Allied reflexes: Several reflexes elicited together

Many behaviors: mixture of voluntary and involuntary influences

Movements varying in sensitivity to feedback

Ballistic movement: Executed as a whole; cannot be altered after initiated

Reflexes

Contraction of pupil

High sensitivity to feedback

Threading needle

Singing

Delayed auditory feedback

Sequences of behaviors

Central pattern generators

Rhythmic movements

Frequency of repetition governed by spinal cord

Cat scratch: 3 to 4 strokes per second

Motor program: Fixed sequence of movements

Learned or built in

Birds: Wing extension when dropped

Humans: Yawning

3.   In closing: Categories of movement

Spinal motor neuron: Final common path

Many brain areas control different patterns

Module 8.2 Brain Mechanisms of Movement

1.   The cerebral cortex

Primary motor cortex: Precentral gyrus

No direct connections to muscles

Axons synapse in brainstem and spinal cord

General movement plans

Each movement associated with activity in scattered population of cells

Brief electrical stimulation of cortex → twitches

Longer (.5 sec) stimulation → complex movements

Active when people "intend" a movement

Inferior parietal cortex

Mirror neurons: Active during movement and while watching another monkey do same movement

Areas near the primary motor cortex

Posterior parietal cortex

Position of body relative to the world

Converting perception into action

Planning movement

Primary somatosensory cortex

Sensory information to motor cortex

Direct output to spinal cord

Prefrontal cortex

Response to sensory signals that lead to a movement

Calculates probable outcome, plans movement

Inactive during dreams

Premotor cortex

Preparation for movement

Gets information about target relative to body

Output to primary motor cortex and spinal cord

Supplementary motor cortex

Planning and organizing sequence of movement in order

Essential for inhibiting habitual actions when doing something else

Preparation for rapid series of movements

Light stimulation → urge to move body part, expectation of movement

Stronger stimulation → movements

Mirror neurons

Mirror neurons: active in preparation for movement and while watching same or similar movement performed by someone else

Observed in premotor cortex of monkeys and in other areas in humans

Develop mirror quality by learning

Important for imitation

Conscious decisions and movements

Decision to move: ~200 ms before actual movement

Readiness potential: ~500 ms before movement

~300 ms before conscious decision

Damage to parietal cortex → intention at same time as movement

Parietal cortex → feeling of intention to move before actual move

Don't realize that they can't move left arm or leg

Motor cortex normally monitors feedback from muscles

Connections from the brain to the spinal cord

Corticospinal tracts

Lateral corticospinal tract

Primary motor cortex

Red nucleus (midbrain area controlling arm muscles)

Targets spinal cord

Crosses to contralateral side of spinal cord in pyramids of the medulla

Hands and feet

Medial corticospinal tract

Cerebral cortex

Midbrain tectum

Reticular formation

Vestibular nucleus

Targets contralateral and ipsilateral spinal cord

Neck, shoulders, and trunk

Stroke in left primary motor cortex → loss of control of right side of body

Some recovery: A few undamaged neurons in lateral corticospinal tract, learned use of medial corticospinal tract and connections between left and right spinal cord

2. The cerebellum ("little brain")
More neurons than rest of brain combined
Rapid movements that require accurate aim and timing
Effects of damage to the cerebellum
Difficulty with aiming and timing
Difficulty imagining sequences of movement
Normal at continuous motor activity
Tests of cerebellar functioning
Saccades
Finger-to-nose test
Move function: Cerebellar cortex
Hold function: Nuclei of the cerebellum
Slow movement: Not dependent on cerebellum
Damage → effects similar to alcohol intoxication
Role in functions other than movement
Response to sensory stimuli that direct movement
Precise timing of brief intervals
Aspects of attention
Programming sequence of actions as a whole
Cellular organization
Input from spinal cord, sensory cranial nerve nuclei, and cerebral cortex
Cerebellar cortex: Precise geometrical pattern with multiple repetitions of same units
Purkinje cells (flat cells in sequential planes) inhibit nuclei of the cerebellum and vestibular nuclei of brain stem
These then send information to midbrain and thalamus
Controls duration of response
Parallel fibers (axons parallel to each other) activate Purkinje cells one after another

3. The basal ganglia
Component structures
Caudate nucleus
Putamen
Globus pallidus
Input from cerebral cortex → caudate nucleus and putamen → globus pallidus → thalamus → motor and prefrontal cortex
Transmitter from globus pallidus to thalamus: GABA
Much spontaneous activity → constant inhibition of thalamus
Input from caudate nucleus and putamen → which movements to *stop inhibiting*
Damage to globus pallidus → lack of inhibition → involuntary, jerky movements
Functions
Select correct movement and inhibit other movements
Self-initiated behaviors
Not activated if action is guided by a stimulus

4.   Brain areas and motor learning
   All motor areas important for learning new skills
   Motor cortex
>   Increased firing rate and consistency
>   Increased signal-to-noise ratio
   Basal ganglia
>   Critical for learning new habits
>   Organizing sequences of movement into a whole
>   Alter response patterns as skills become automatic

5.   In closing: Movement control and cognition
   Behavior: Integrated contributions of numerous areas
   Posterior parietal cortex → position of body in visual space → guides movement
>   Sensory, cognitive, and motor functions
>   Cerebellum → both motor functions and timing sensory processes
>   Basal ganglia → select or start movement, enhance cognitive function
   Selecting and organizing a movement: Intertwined with sensory and cognitive processes

Module 8.3 Disorders of Movement
1.   Parkinson's disease
   Symptoms
>   Rigidity
>   Muscle tremors
>   Slow movements
>   Difficulty initiating physical and mental activity
>   Depression and cognitive deficits
>   Less problem if external stimuli guide action
   Movements require more effort
   Possible causes
   Degeneration of dopamine projections from substantia nigra to caudate nucleus and putamen
>   Increased inhibition of thalamus → decreased excitation of cerebral cortex → slow movement onset
>   Steady loss of substantia nigra neurons after age 45
>   Less than 20-30% of normal → Parkinson's disease

>   Early-onset Parkinson's disease: Several genes implicated
>   Low heritability of late-onset Parkinson's disease
>   Exposure to toxins
>   Heroin-like drug: MPTP → MPP+
>   Postsynaptic neurons increase dopamine receptors
>   Herbicides, pesticides (including rotenone): One factor
>   Cigarette smoking, caffeine: Decrease risk
>   Marijuana: Increases risk
>   Common factor: α-synuclein → damage to mitochondria
>   Dopamine neurons more vulnerable
   L-dopa treatment
>   Precursor to dopamine
>   Effectiveness varies
>   Main treatment for Parkinson's disease
>   Does not prevent loss of dopamine neurons

g. From what structures does the medial corticospinal tract originate? What is the relationship between this tract and the two sides of the spinal cord?

h. Which movements are controlled by the lateral corticospinal tract, and which by the medial corticospinal tract?

i. What happens to the partially bilateral innervation by the primary motor cortex during the first year and a half of life? How may that be affected by cerebral palsy? What is the behavioral result?

2. *The cerebellum*

   a. What kinds of movements are especially affected by cerebellar damage?

   b. What are saccades? Describe the effect of cerebellar damage on the control of saccades.

   c. Describe the motor control required to touch one's finger to one's nose as quickly as possible.

   d. Why may a police officer use the finger-to-nose test to check for alcohol intoxication?

   e. Describe the evidence for a broad role for the cerebellum, beyond motor performance.

   f. From what sources does the cerebellum receive input?

   g. Describe the relationship between the Purkinje cells and the parallel fibers. How does this affect movement?

3. *The basal ganglia*

   a. What structures comprise the basal ganglia?

   b. Which are the main receptive areas? The main output area? Where does the major input come from, and where does the output go?

   c. Describe the way in which the basal ganglia select movements. Which transmitter does the globus pallidus release?

   d. Are the basal ganglia more important for self-initiated or stimulus guided movements?

   e. What is the role of the basal ganglia in the learning of motor patterns?

Module 8.3 Disorders of Movement

4. *Parkinson's disease*

   a. Describe the symptoms of Parkinson's disease.

   b. What is its immediate cause? How does loss of dopamine in the caudate nucleus and putamen affect activity in the cortex?

   c. How strong is the evidence for a genetic predisposition for Parkinson's disease?

   d. How did the experience with a heroin substitute lead to suspicion of an environmental toxin as a cause of this disease?

   e. How may herbicides and pesticides be implicated?

   f. What is a problem with the toxin-exposure hypothesis?

   g. What was the unexpected finding concerning cigarette smoking, coffee drinking, and Parkinson's disease?

h. What is the role of α-synuclein in causing damage to dopamine neurons?

i. What is the rationale for treatment of Parkinson's disease with L-dopa? What are the side effects of this treatment?

j. List some other possible treatments for Parkinson's disease.

k. How successful have brain grafts been in treating Parkinson's disease in humans? What are some of the problems with the use of fetal tissue? From where in the brain is fetal tissue taken?

l. What other kinds of tissue have been used for brain grafts to treat Parkinson's disease? What are some potential additional sources for tissue for such grafts?

5. *Huntington's disease*

a. What are the physical and psychological symptoms of Huntington's disease?

b. Which neurons degenerate in Huntington's disease?

c. Discuss the role of genetics in Huntington's disease. On which chromosome is the gene for Huntington's disease located?

d. What is huntingtin? What do we know about the base sequence of the gene that codes for it? What may it do inside the cell?

e. What are two potential treatments for Huntington's disease that have shown promise in animal models?

True/False Questions

1. Acetylcholine is the transmitter at all neuromuscular junctions; however, it has excitatory effects at some muscles, and inhibitory effects at others, depending on the type of receptor on the muscle.

TRUE or FALSE

2. Myasthenia gravis is caused by an autoimmune attack on acetylcholine receptors.

TRUE or FALSE

3. Muscle spindles are receptors at opposite ends of a muscle; activation of them inhibits muscle contraction.

TRUE or FALSE

4. Ballistic movements are those that have especially high sensitivity to feedback while they are being executed.

TRUE or FALSE

5. The primary motor cortex is located in the precentral gyrus, at the posterior end of the frontal lobe.

TRUE or FALSE

6. The posterior parietal cortex is especially important for preparation for a rapid series of movements.

TRUE or FALSE

7. The prefrontal cortex responds to signals that lead to a movement.

   TRUE or FALSE

8. Mirror neurons may play an important role in imitation.

   TRUE or FALSE

9. The lateral corticospinal tract descends from primary motor cortex and surrounding cortical areas and from the red nucleus; its axons cross in the pyramids of the medulla.

   TRUE or FALSE

10. The medial corticospinal tract controls peripheral movements on the opposite side of the body.

    TRUE or FALSE

11. The cerebellum is especially important for linking motions rapidly and smoothly, especially those that require accurate aim and timing. However, it is also important for aspects of attention.

    TRUE or FALSE

12. Purkinje cells in the cerebellar cortex inhibit parallel fibers, which are the main output cells of the cerebellum.

    TRUE or FALSE

13. The globus pallidus is the main receiver of input to the basal ganglia; the caudate nucleus and the putamen provide the main output.

    TRUE or FALSE

14. Parkinson's disease results from degeneration of dopamine projections from substantia nigra to the caudate nucleus and putamen.

    TRUE or FALSE

15. L-dopa provides some relief from symptoms of Parkinson's disease.

    TRUE or FALSE

16. Inhibiting glutamate or adenosine receptors may have therapeutic effects on Parkinson's disease.

    TRUE or FALSE

17. Only the earliest-onset form of Huntington's disease shows any heritability.

    TRUE or FALSE

18. Genes that regulate glutamate receptors influence the age of onset of Huntington's disease.

    TRUE or FALSE

19. Huntington's disease is characterized by excessively long repeats of CAG in the gene that codes for huntingtin.

    TRUE or FALSE

20. Sleeping pills improved deficiencies of learning and memory in mice with Huntington's disease mutation.

    TRUE or FALSE

Fill In The Blanks

1. The three categories of muscle are _____, _____ (_____), and _____.

2. Antagonistic skeletal muscles are _____ and _____.

3. Myasthenia gravis results from the loss of _____ receptors, as a result of autoimmune attack.

4. In humans a high ratio of _____ to _____ fibers is more characteristic of sprinters than marathon runners.

5. A stretch receptor located in parallel to a muscle, and that causes the muscle to contract, is called a _____.

6. A receptor located in tendons at opposite ends of a muscle, and that inhibits muscle contraction, is called a _____.

7. A movement executed as a whole, without intervening feedback, is a _____ movement.

8. A fixed sequence of movements is called a _____.

9. The primary motor cortex is located in the _____ gyrus.

10. The brain area that helps to convert perception into action is the _____ cortex.

11. The brain area that responds to sensory signals that lead to a movement and calculates the outcome of that movement is the _____ cortex.

12. Neurons in the inferior parietal cortex that fire when a monkey performs an act, and also when it watches another monkey perform the same act, are called _____.

13. Neurons in the _____ cortex respond to visual or somatosensory stimuli or to current or future movements and keep track of the body in relation to the world.

14. The brain area in front of primary motor cortex that receives information about the position of the target in space as well as the position of the body is the _____ cortex.

15. The supplementary motor cortex is especially important for planning and organizing _____.

16. The _____ tract controls peripheral movements on the opposite side of the body; the _____ tract controls midline movements that require bilateral influence.

17. The brain area that links movements rapidly and smoothly and contributes to aspects of attention is the _____.

18. The three structures that comprise the basal ganglia are the _____, the _____, and the _____.

19. Parkinson's disease results from degeneration of the tract from the _____ to the _____ and _____.

20. The usual treatment for Parkinson's disease is _____.

21. _____ disease is characterized by twitches and tremors, writhing movements, and impaired ability to learn new movements.

22. Genes influencing _____ receptors influence the age of onset for Huntington's disease.

23. This disorder results from mutation in the gene on chromosome _____ that codes for the protein called _____; as a result a mutant form of the protein is produced, which impairs the neuron's mitochondria and its release of _____.

Matching Items

1. _____ Long-distance running
2. _____ Golgi tendon organ
3. _____ Muscle spindle
4. _____ Primary motor cortex
5. _____ Posterior parietal cortex
6. _____ Primary somatosensory cortex
7. _____ Lateral corticospinal tract
8. _____ Medial corticospinal tract
9. _____ Cerebellum
10. _____ Caudate nucleus, putamen
11. _____ Globus pallidus
12. _____ Parkinson's disease
13. _____ L-dopa
14. _____ Hunington's disease

a. Causes associated muscle to contract
b. Precentral gyrus
c. Receive dopamine from substantia nigra
d. Disease with excessive CAG repeats in a gene
e. Treatment for Parkinson's disease
f. Contains Purkinje cells and parallel fibers
g. Inhibits contraction of associated muscle
h. Keeps track of the body relative to the world
i. Provides sensory information to motor cortex
j. Degeneration of dopamine neurons
k. A human specialization for locomotion
l. Crosses in the pyramids of medulla
m. Main output from basal ganglia
n. Controls midline movements

Multiple-Choice Questions

1. Which of the following is true of nerves and muscles?
    a. There is always a one-to-one relationship between axons and muscle fibers.
    b. Each axon innervates several or many muscle fibers.
    c. Each muscle fiber receives many axons.
    d. Some muscle fibers are not innervated by any axons.

2. Acetylcholine
    a. has only inhibitory effects on skeletal muscles.
    b. has excitatory effects on some skeletal muscles and inhibitory effects on others.
    c. has only excitatory effects on skeletal muscles.
    d. is released only onto smooth muscles, never onto skeletal muscles.

3. Myasthenia gravis
    a. results from destruction of acetylcholine receptors at neuromuscular junctions by an autoimmune process.
    b. is characterized by excessive, jerky movements.
    c. is helped by drugs that greatly increase the production of antibodies to acetylcholine receptors.
    d. all of the above.

4. Which of the following is a type of skeletal muscle in fish?
    a. slow, white, fatigue-resistant
    b. fast, white, fatigue-resistant
    c. slow, pink, fatigue-prone
    d. slow, red, fatigue-resistant

5. Mammalian muscles
    a. can be classified as red, pink, and white, as in fish.
    b. contain either fast-twitch or slow-twitch fibers, but not both.
    c. contain both fast-twitch and slow-twitch fibers in the same muscles.
    d. show only genetic, and not any environmental, determination of the ratio of fast-twitch to slow-twitch fibers.

6. The muscle spindle
    a. is a stretch receptor located in parallel to the muscle.
    b. inhibits the motor neuron innervating the muscle when it is stretched; this leads to relaxation of the muscle.
    c. responds only when the muscle contracts.
    d. synapses onto the muscle to excite it directly.

7. The Golgi tendon organ
    a. is also located in the muscle spindle.
    b. affects the motor neuron in the same way as the muscle spindle, thereby enhancing its effect.
    c. responds when the muscle contracts.
    d. excites the motor neuron that innervates the muscle.

8. Ballistic movements
    a. are required when a singer holds a note for a long time.
    b. require feedback as they are being executed.
    c. are always highly complex and never simple reflexes.
    d. proceed automatically once triggered.

9. The frequency of repetition of a cat's scratch reflex
   a. varies, and is controlled by pattern generators in the brain.
   b. is constant at three to four scratches per second, and is determined by cells in the lumbar spinal cord.
   c. is constant and is determined by pattern generators in the brain.
   d. is an example of feedback control.

10. Which of the following is true?
   a. Feedback control must be at the root of all movements; otherwise we would be unable to modify our behavior.
   b. Singing a single note does not require feedback, although singing several notes in a sequence does require feedback.
   c. Even ballistic movements are in reality feedback controlled.
   d. There are involuntary components of many voluntary behaviors.

11. Which of the following is true of motor programs?
   a. Grooming behavior of mice is an example of a built-in motor program.
   b. Grooming behavior of mice is an example of a learned motor program.
   c. Species of birds that have not used their wings for flight for millions of years still extend their wings when dropped.
   d. Humans have only learned, and not built-in, motor programs.

12. The primary motor cortex
   a. sends axons to the brainstem and the spinal cord to execute movements.
   b. includes the somatomotor, prefrontal, premotor, and supplementary motor cortex, as well as the basal ganglia.
   c. controls isolated movements of individual muscles.
   d. all of the above.

13. The order of activity in preparing for and executing a movement is
   a. primary motor, premotor, prefrontal cortex.
   b. prefrontal, premotor, primary motor cortex.
   c. premotor, primary motor, prefrontal cortex.
   d. primary motor, prefrontal, premotor cortex.

14. The posterior parietal cortex
   a. is the main receiving area for somatosensory information.
   b. helps us to program a series of rapid movements.
   c. helps us to keep track of the position of the body relative to the world and convert perception into action.
   d. is part of the primary motor cortex.

15. A readiness potential
   a. has been recorded in people's motor cortex several hundred milliseconds before their conscious decision to move.
   b. has been recorded in supplementary motor cortex several hundred milliseconds after the conscious decision to move.
   c. has been recorded in the cerebellum several hundred milliseconds after the movement began.
   d. all of the above.

16. The lateral corticospinal tract of the spinal cord
    a. originates mostly in the primary motor cortex and adjacent areas and in the red nucleus of the midbrain.
    b. controls movements in the periphery of the body.
    c. controls movements on the side of the body opposite the brain area where the fibers originate.
    d. all of the above.

17. The medial corticospinal tract of the spinal cord
    a. contains crossed fibers from the primary motor cortex and adjacent areas and from the red nucleus of the midbrain.
    b. controls movements near the midline of the body that are necessarily bilateral.
    c. controls movements on the side of the body opposite the brain area where the fibers originate.
    d. works independently from the lateral corticospinal tract.

18. The pyramids of the medulla
    a. contain the cell bodies of the lateral corticospinal tract.
    b. contain the cell bodies of the medial corticospinal tract.
    c. are the site where axons of the lateral corticospinal tract cross from one side to the other.
    d. are the site where axons of the medial corticospinal tract cross from one side to the other.

19. The cerebellum
    a. is especially important for performance of movement sequences that require accurate aiming and timing.
    b. is more important for continuous motor activities than for movements that require rhythmically starting and stopping.
    c. is important only for innate, not learned, motor responses.
    d. contains relatively few neurons and synapses, compared to the cerebral hemispheres.

20. Damage to the cerebellum produces
    a. Parkinson's disease.
    b. Huntington's disease.
    c. deficits in saccadic movements of the eyes.
    d. deficits in slow feedback-controlled movements.

21. In executing the "finger-to-nose" movement quickly
    a. the cerebellar cortex is important in the initial rapid movement.
    b. the nuclei of the cerebellum are important in maintaining the brief hold pattern.
    c. other structures are important in the final slow movement.
    d. all of the above.

22. Purkinje cells in the cerebellum
    a. receive input from parallel fibers.
    b. send output to parallel fibers.
    c. excite cells in the nuclei of the cerebellum.
    d. send output to the basal ganglia and cerebral cortex.

23. The cerebellum
    a. shows most activity during purely motor tasks.
    b. contributes to any motor, perceptual, or cognitive task that requires careful timing of brief intervals.
    c. is now thought to contribute only to cognitive tasks, and not to motor tasks.
    d. is especially important for controlling muscle force and determining which tone is louder.

24. The basal ganglia consist of
    a. the caudate nucleus, the cerebellum, and the thalamus.
    b. the cerebellum, the putamen, and the thalamus.
    c. the caudate nucleus, the putamen, and the globus pallidus.
    d. the putamen, the globus pallidus, and the pyramids of the medulla.

25. Which of the following is true?
    a. Neurons in the globus pallidus send GABA-containing axons to the thalamus.
    b. Neurons in the globus pallidus show much spontaneous activity.
    c. The caudate nucleus and putamen tell the globus pallidus which movements to stop inhibiting.
    d. All of the above are true.

26. The basal ganglia are important for
    a. actions guided by a stimulus.
    b. learning motor skills, selecting movements, and organizing them into a whole.
    c. wing flapping in birds.
    d. fine control of movement.

27. Parkinson's disease
    a. results from too much dopamine in the basal ganglia.
    b. results from too little acetylcholine at the neuromuscular junction.
    c. results from too little dopamine in the basal ganglia.
    d. is almost completely determined genetically.

28. MPTP
    a. has been used with some success in treating Parkinson's disease.
    b. may be an environmental cause of Parkinson's disease.
    c. may be an environmental cause of myasthenia gravis.
    d. has been used with some success in treating Huntington's disease.

29. α-synuclein
    a. is a promising new treatment for Parkinson's disease.
    b. is a promising new treatment for Huntington's disease.
    c. clots into clusters that damage neurons containing dopamine.
    d. results in destruction of acetylcholine receptors.

30. Which of the following is **not** a current or potential treatment for Parkinson's disease?
    a. dopamine pills.
    b. L-dopa.
    c. neurotrophins.
    d. antioxidants.

31. Which of the following may be forms of therapy for Parkinson's disease?
    a. L-dopa.
    b. Stimulation of cannabinoid receptors.
    c. Inhibiting glutamate receptors.
    d. All of the above are true.

32. Brain grafts
    a. are currently the best treatment for Parkinson's disease.
    b. are most effective if they use tissue from the patient's own adrenal gland in order to prevent rejection.
    c. are able to produce beneficial effects only if the implanted tissue survives and makes functional synapses.
    d. currently use fetal substantia nigra tissue, but may someday use stem cells genetically altered to produce large quantities of L-dopa.

33. Huntington's disease
    a. results from destruction of dopaminergic input to the basal ganglia.
    b. is characterized by great weakness.
    c. is caused by a dominant gene on human chromosome number 4.
    d. is caused by a recessive gene on human chromosome number 10.

34. Which of the following are not symptoms of Huntington's disease?
    a. weakness and difficulty initiating movements
    b. depression, anxiety, memory impairment, hallucinations, and delusions
    c. poor judgment, alcoholism, and drug abuse
    d. facial twitch and tremors

35. The gene associated with Huntington's disease
    a. in its normal form, contains a sequence of bases repeated at least 40 times; many of those repeats are lost in patients with Huntington's disease.
    b. in its normal form, does not contain any repeated sequences of bases.
    c. is now known to code for acetylcholine receptors.
    d. is now known to code for huntingtin, a protein, the mutant form of which has long chains of glutamine, which form clusters that impair the neuron's mitochondria.

36. Cells with abnormal huntingtin
    a. release an excessive amount of BDNF, thereby causing uncontrolled growth.
    b. fail to release BDNF along with their neurotransmitter, thereby impairing the function of other cells.
    c. produce as much damage throughout the body as it does in the brain.
    d. produce too little glutamine for normal function.

Solutions

True/False Questions

1. F	6. F	11. T	16. T
2. T	7. T	12. F	17. F
3. F	8. T	13. F	18. T
4. F	9. T	14. T	19. T
5. T	10. T	15. T	20. T

Fill In The Blanks

1. Smooth; skeletal; striated; cardiac
2. Flexors; extensors
3. acetylcholine
4. fast-twitch; slow-twitch
5. muscle spindle
6. Golgi tendon organ
7. ballistic
8. motor pattern
9. precentral
10. posterior parietal
11. prefrontal
12. mirror neurons
13. posterior parietal
14. premotor
15. a rapid series of movements.
16. lateral corticospinal
17. medial corticospinal
18. cerebellum.
19. caudate nucleus; putamen; globus pallidus
20. substantia nigra; caudate nucleus; putamen
21. L-dopa
22. Huntington's
23. glutamate
24. 4; huntingtin; BDNF

Matching Items

1. k	5. h	9. f	13. e
2. g	6. i	10. c	14. d
3. a	7. l	11. m	
4. b	8. n	12. j	

Multiple Choice Questions

1. b	10. d	19. a	28. b
2. c	11. a	20. c	29. c
3. a	12. a	21. d	30. a
4. d	13. b	22. a	31. d
5. c	14. c	23. b	32. d
6. a	15. a	24. c	33. c
7. c	16. d	25. d	34. a
8. d	17. b	26. b	35. d
9. b	18. c	27. c	36. b

CHAPTER **9**

Wakefulness and Sleep

Introduction

Animals ranging from insects to humans exhibit endogenous rhythms of behavior. Circannual (approximately year-long) cycles govern hibernation, migration, and seasonal mating in some species. Circadian (approximately 24-hour) cycles regulate activity and sleep as well as other bodily functions. The "clock" governing these cycles generates the rhythm internally, although the external light cycles affect the specific settings. Light influences the suprachiasmatic nucleus (SCN) of the hypothalamus, which provides the main control of rhythms of sleep and temperature. If the SCN is isolated from the rest of the brain, it continues to generate a circadian rhythm of approximately 24 hours. The biochemical mechanism of the clock is based on two genes, initially discovered in fruit flies. These genes, *period* (*per*) and *timeless* (*tim*) produce protein products (Per and Tim) that build up during the day and produce sleepiness. High levels then feed back to decrease production of the proteins. Similar genes have been found in mammals. Melatonin, a hormone produced by the pineal gland, is one means by which the SCN regulates sleeping and waking. Increased melatonin secretion begins 2 to 3 hours before the onset of sleepiness. The SCN can be reset by various stimuli, including light, tides, exercise, noises, meals, etc. Light is the most important stimulus (zeitgeber: time giver) for most mammals. People traveling across several time zones suffer from jet lag, which is worse traveling east than traveling west. People who work night shifts are also stressed and are plagued by more errors and injuries than people who work during their normal waking period. Very bright lights during the new day time and complete darkness during the new night help travelers and shift workers adapt to their schedules. Some axons in the optic nerve form the retinohypothalamic path, which innervates the SCN. Even animals with little or no vision can use retinal ganglion cells that contain their own photopigment (melanopsin) to regulate the biological clock.

The electroencephalogram (EEG) is used to record the average of the electrical potentials of neurons near each electrode on the scalp. Relaxed wakefulness (with the eyes closed) is characterized by alpha waves at a frequency of 8 - 12 per second. Stage 1 of sleep is signaled by irregular, low-voltage waves, after which progression through stages 2, 3, and 4 is correlated with increasingly slow, large-amplitude waves. Throughout the night, there is a cyclic progression back and forth through the four stages approximately every 90 minutes. However, after the first period of stage 1, each return to stage 1 is correlated with rapid eye movements, relaxed muscles, and rapid and variable heart rate and breathing. Rapid eye movement (REM) sleep has also been called paradoxical sleep, because the EEG shows fast, low amplitude waves, as during wakefulness, and heart rate and breathing are variable, but the postural muscles are completely relaxed. Dreams during REM sleep tend to be more intense than those during non-

REM (NREM) sleep. Stages 3 and 4 of slow wave sleep predominate early in the night, whereas REM periods are longer and comprise a larger portion of sleep time late in the night.

Wakefulness and behavioral arousal depend, in part, on the reticular formation, a group of large, branching neurons running from the medulla into the forebrain. The pontomesencephalon is the part of the reticular formation that contributes to cortical arousal. It receives input diffusely from many sensory systems and generates spontaneous activity of its own. It sends cholinergic and glutamatergic output to the basal forebrain, which then activates the hypothalamus, thalamus, and forebrain. The locus coeruleus, in the pons, is active in response to meaningful events and may help to form memories. It sends widely branching axons containing norepinephrine to the cortex. A path from the hypothalamus increases arousal by releasing the neurotransmitter histamine; antihistamine drugs for allergies lead to drowsiness. Another path from the hypothalamus releases orexin (hypocretin) widely throughout the forebrain and brainstem. Orexin allows an individual to remain awake for a longer time, as opposed to alternating between sleep and wakefulness. The basal forebrain is the site of neurons that activate GABA-containing axons in the thalamus and cortex; GABA inhibits neurons there and promotes sleepiness. The basal forebrain also sends acetylcholine-containing axons to the thalamus and cortex; these neurons promote wakefulness.

During REM sleep, high-amplitude potentials can be recorded in the pons, geniculate, and occipital cortex (PGO waves). Animals maintain nearly constant amounts of PGO waves. If deprived of REM, PGO waves intrude into other sleep stages and even wakefulness. Animals compensate for lost PGO waves when allowed to sleep freely. In addition to initiating REM episodes, cells in the pons inhibit the motor neurons that control postural muscles. Other sites that are active during REM are the limbic system and parts of parietal and temporal cortex. However, the primary visual, motor, and dorsolateral prefrontal cortex, become less active during REM. Acetylcholine induces the onset of REM, as well as of wakefulness, and serotonin and norepinephrine interrupt or shorten it.

Insomnia may be caused by uncomfortable environmental conditions, abnormalities of biological rhythms, and withdrawal from tranquilizers. A phase-delayed temperature rhythm may cause difficulty getting to sleep, whereas a phase-advanced rhythm may cause early awakening. Sleep apnea, the inability to breathe during sleep, may be caused by obesity, genetics, hormones, old age, or alcohol, or tranquilizers. People with sleep apnea often have brain areas that have lost neurons. It is not clear whether the apnea is the cause or the result of the brain damage, but animal studies suggest that apnea causes the damage. Narcolepsy refers to periods of extreme sleepiness during the day. Additional symptoms of narcolepsy are cataplexy (extreme muscle weakness while awake), sleep paralysis (inability to move during transition into or out of sleep), and hypnagogic hallucinations (dreamlike experiences that are difficult to distinguish from reality). All of these symptoms can be interpreted as intrusions of REM sleep into wakefulness. Narcolepsy results from a deficit in orexin (hypocretin), which maintains wakefulness. Orexin is not necessary for waking up, but it is needed for staying awake for prolonged periods. Periodic limb movement disorder, in which the legs kick every 20 to 30 seconds for minutes or hours, can lead to insomnia. In REM behavior disorder people appear to act out their dreams, possibly as a result of damage to the neurons in the pons that inhibit movement during REM. Nightmares are unpleasant dreams that occur during REM sleep; night terrors are experiences of extreme anxiety, occurring during NREM sleep, from which a person wakens in terror. Sleep talking occurs with similar probability in REM and NREM sleep, whereas sleepwalking and sleep sex (sexomnia) occur mostly during stages 3 and 4 slow-wave sleep.

Sleep serves several functions. The primary function of sleep during early evolution was to conserve energy during times when activity would be either inefficient or dangerous. Both body temperature and energy expenditure are decreased during sleep, and animals that hibernate decrease energy needs even more. Animals that eat nutrition-rich foods and face little threat from attack sleep longer than those that eat plants and must avoid predators. Some species have developed specializations in their sleep, such as decreasing the need for sleep during migration or sleeping with one side of the brain at a time. Another function of sleep is rebuilding proteins the brain. People who sleep irregularly or poorly often feel depressed and have decreased alertness and performance. Immune responses may also be altered. Another function of sleep is to promote memory storage. People who slept after learning a task performed better than those who stayed awake. The brain apparently activates the same areas during sleep that were used in the initial learning. One way of strengthening memories is to weed out less successful connections, so that they do not compete with the new memories

The function of REM sleep is not well understood. In general, the percentage of sleep spent in REM correlates positively with the total amount of sleep. REM deprivation has resulted in increased REM time on subsequent uninterrupted nights. REM may facilitate the consolidation of motor skills; whereas NREM sleep may strengthen verbal memories. The eye movements that characterize REM may also increase oxygen supply to the corneas. Dreams may result from the brain's attempt to make sense of its increased activity during REM episodes (activation-synthesis hypothesis). A clinico-anatomical hypothesis rests in part on the observations that during REM, neural activity in primary visual, motor, and prefrontal cortex is suppressed. Therefore, normal visual input cannot compete with self-generated stimulation, and motor activity is suppressed. Also, the prefrontal cortex is inhibited, resulting in sudden scene changes in dreams and poor memory of the dreams. On the other hand, increased activity in inferior parietal cortex and higher visual areas may increase spatial perception and visual imagery. Finally, increased activity in the hypothalamus, amygdala, and other areas may increase the emotional intensity of dreams.

Learning Objectives

Module 9.1 Rhythms of Waking and Sleeping
1. Understand the functions of endogenous rhythms and our difficulty with altered rhythms.
2. Be able to describe the anatomical location of the biological clock and its biochemical and hormonal signals.
3. Be able to explain how light can reset the biological clock.

Module 9.2 Stages of Sleep and Brain Mechanisms
1. Know the characteristics of the stages of slow-wave and REM sleep.
2. Know the brain areas and neurotransmitters that promote wakefulness, slow-wave sleep and REM sleep.
3. Know the various sleep disorders, their possible causes, and their treatments.

Module 9.3 Why Sleep? Why REM? Why Dreams?
1. Understand the proposed functions of sleep in general and of REM sleep.

Key Terms and Concepts

Module 9.1 Rhythms of Waking and Sleeping
1. Endogenous cycles
    Endogenous circannual and circadian rhythms
      Bird migration
      Squirrel food storage and fat deposition
      Student sleepiness and wakefulness
      Flying squirrel in total darkness
      Naval personnel on submarines: Difficulty with 18-hour schedule
      Mammalian rhythms in wake/sleep, eat/drink, urination, hormones, drug sensitivity, temperature
    Individual differences
      "Morning people" and "evening people"
      Age differences in circadian rhythms
2. Setting and resetting the biological clock
    Free-running rhythm
    Zeitgeber ("time giver") resets clock
      Light (most effective for land animals), tides, exercise, noises, meals, temperature
      Eastern Germany: Sleep midpoint ~30 minutes earlier than western Germany
      Blind people: Some are sensitive to other zeitgebers, others less so
    Jet lag
      Worse going east
      Phase-delay going west
      Phase-advance going east
      Stress of jet lag → cortisol → degeneration of hippocampus neurons
    Shift work
      Work at night: Exposure to bright lights helps, sleep in dark room in day
3. Mechanisms of the biological clock
    Interfering with the biological clock
      Curt Richter
        Lack of effect of most procedures
    The suprachiasmatic nucleus (SCN)
      Main control of rhythms of sleep and temperature
      Endogenous rhythm
        Disconnected SCN still generates rhythms
        Single SCN cells generate rhythm
          Less steady than group of cells
        Genetic mutation that produces 20-hour rhythm
        Transplant mutant or normal SCN: Animals followed rhythm of SCN
    How light resets the SCN
      Retinohypothalamic path
        Axons from optic nerve
        Animals with little or no vision: Light still resets rhythms
          Mice with genetic defects
          Blind mole rats

Retinal ganglion cells with own photopigment (melanopsin)
Also receive some input from rods and cones
Respond slowly to average amount of light
The biochemistry of the circadian rhythm
Drosophila genes
Period (per)
Timeless (tim)
Proteins Per and Tim build up during day
Interact with Clock protein → sleepiness
Light at night → inactivate Tim → decrease sleepiness → reset clock
Similar genes in mammals (slight differences)
Per and Tim → increase activity of certain neurons in SCN
Mutations → altered rhythms
Mice with mutation in *overtime* gene → 26 hour rhythm
Humans: mutation of *per* → earlier cycles, depression
Melatonin
Pineal gland
Peaks 2 to 3 hours before sleepiness
Melatonin pill in afternoon → phase advance
Repeated melatonin pills in morning → phase delay
Antioxidant
Impaired learning and reproduction in rats
4. In closing: Sleep-wake cycles
Sleepiness not voluntary

Module 9.2 Stages of Sleep and Brain Mechanisms

1. Sleep and other interruptions of consciousness
Coma: Extended period of unconsciousness due to head trauma, stroke, or disease
Steady, low level of brain activity
Vegetative state: Alternation between sleep and moderate arousal
No awareness of surroundings
May have some cognitive activity
Minimally conscious state: Brief periods of purposeful actions, limited speech comprehension
Can last months or years
Brain death: no sign of brain activity, no response to any stimulus
After 24 hours, considered to be ethical to remove life support
2. The stages of sleep
Electroencephalogram (EEG)
Average of electrical potentials of neurons near scalp electrode
Polysomnograph: EEG + eye-movement records
Alpha waves (8 – 12 per second): Relaxed wakefulness
Stage 1 sleep
Irregular, low-voltage EEG waves
Stage 2 sleep
Sleep spindle: 12 – 14-Hz waves in bursts of 0.5 second

K-complex: Sharp, high-amplitude negative wave
Stages 3 and 4 slow-wave sleep (SWS)
Synchronized EEG: Slow, large amplitude waves
Less input to cortex
3. Paradoxical or REM sleep
Discovered by Michel Jouvet
Paradoxical sleep
In some ways deepest and in some ways lightest sleep
Nathaniel Kleitman & Eugene Aserinsky
Rapid eye movement (REM) sleep
Characteristics
Rapid eye movements (REM)
Irregular, low-voltage fast EEG
Postural relaxation
Erections in males, vaginal moistening in females
Variable heart rate, blood pressure, and breathing
Facial twitches
Sleep cycles
90-minute cycles
Stages 3 and 4 predominate early in night
REM predominant late in night
Governed by time, not length of sleep
Depressed people: REM soon after going to sleep
REM sleep and dreaming
Dement & Kleitman: Dreams reported on 80 - 90% of awakenings from REM
Some kind of thought process during non-REM sleep (NREM)
REM: intensifies dreams but not synonymous with dreaming
4. Brain mechanisms of wakefulness and arousal
Brain structures of arousal and attention
Cut through midbrain → prolonged sleep
Not due to loss of sensory input
Reticular formation: Network from medulla into forebrain
Pontomesencephalon
Widespread sensory input
Spontaneous activity
Axons to basal forebrain
Acetylcholine and glutamate → excitatory effects in hypothalamus, thalamus, and forebrain
Arousal then relayed to cortex
Locus coeruleus ("dark blue place") in pons
Bursts of impulses in response to meaningful events
Norepinephrine
May aid in memory formation, increase wakefulness
Hypothalamus
Histamine pathway → excitatory effects throughout the brain
Antihistamine drugs → drowsiness

Orexin (hypocretin) axons to basal forebrain and other areas

    Necessary for staying awake, not for waking up

    Nasal spray of orexin → increased alertness

Basal forebrain nuclei (anterior and dorsal to hypothalamus)

    Provides input to thalamus and cortex

    Some neurons: Acetylcholine → mostly excitatory effects → arousal

    Damage (including Alzheimer's disease) → impairments of alertness and attention

    Some neurons: Stimulate local GABA neurons → inhibitory effects → sleep

        Input from anterior and preoptic hypothalamus

        Decrease temperature and metabolic rate

5. Brain function in REM sleep

    Increased activity in pons and limbic system and in parietal and temporal cortex

        Pons → onset of REM

    Decreased activity in primary visual, motor, and dorsolateral prefrontal cortex

    PGO (pons-geniculate-occipital) waves

        Compensation for lost PGO waves

    Pons → spinal cord → inhibition of motor neurons

    Neurotransmitters

        Acetylcholine → REM onset

            Carbachol

            Important for both waking and REM → activate brain

        Serotonin and norepinephrine interrupt REM

6. Sleep disorders

    Insomnia

        Causes: Noise, uncomfortable temperatures, stress, pain, diet, medications

            Also epilepsy, Parkinson's disease, brain tumors, depression, anxiety

        Trouble falling asleep

            Possible cause: Phase-delayed temperature rhythm

        Awakening too early

            Possible cause: Phase-advanced temperature rhythm

        Withdrawal from tranquilizers

    Sleep apnea (stop breathing for about a minute)

        Low oxygen → loss of neurons

        Causes: Genetics, hormones, old age, obesity; worsened by alcohol, tranquilizers

        Treatments: Lose weight, avoid alcohol & tranquilizers, surgery, mask that delivers air under pressure

    Narcolepsy

        Attacks of daytime sleepiness

        Cataplexy: Muscle weakness while awake

        Sleep paralysis

        Hypnagogic hallucinations

        May be due to intrusion of REM into wakefulness

        Orexin

            Peptide neurotransmitter → maintain wakefulness

            Cells in hypothalamus

Huntington's disease: Loss of cells in basal ganglia and hypothalamus, including orexin-containing cells

Treated with stimulants like methylphenidate (Ritalin)

Periodic limb movement disorder (mostly during NREM sleep)

May be treated with tranquilizers

REM behavior disorder

Acting out dreams

Damage in pons

Motor neurons no longer inhibited

Night terrors, sleep talking, and sleepwalking

Night terrors different from nightmares (bad dreams)

Occur in NREM sleep

Night terrors, sleep talking, and sleepwalking

Sleep talking

Occurs in REM or NREM sleep

Sleepwalking

Most common in children

Mostly in Stages 3 and 4 (not during REM)

May occur after sleep deprivation, alcohol, or drugs

Sleep sex or sexomnia

7. In closing: Stages of sleep

Usefulness of EEG recordings in identifying internal experiences

Module 9.3 Why sleep? Why REM? Why dreams?

1. Functions of sleep

Sleep and energy conservation

Decreased temperature and muscle activity → save energy

Similar to hibernation

Hibernation: Brain activity almost lost; neurons smaller

Hibernation retards aging

Decreases vulnerability to infection and trauma

Time required for food search

Safety from predators

Dolphins: Sleep on one side of the brain at a time

Migratory birds: Decreased need for sleep during migration

Swifts

First flight ~ two years

Both days and nights in the air

Need for sleep and effects of deprivation

Accumulation of GABA during deprivation → impairs concentration

Major cause of accidents, comparable to alcohol

Effects of sleep deprivation

One night deprivation→ increased immune function (similar to illness)

Astronauts on long trips or winter living in Antarctica → poor sleep, depression, impaired performance

"Evening people" adapt more easily, also show more brain arousal

Caffeine: Blocks adenosine receptors → increased arousal

Sleep and memory

Sleep → enhanced memory

After a nap: Memory better than before nap

Increased ability to reanalyze memories

During sleep: Increased activity in same brain areas activated while learning a skill

Correlation between amount of activity during sleep and amount of improvement

Rose odor during learning & during sleep → better memory than with the odor during learning & waking

Weeding out less successful connections

Increased sleep spindles during Stage 2 sleep after learning

Sleep spindles correlated with nonverbal IQ

2. Functions of REM sleep

Individual and species differences

Percent of time in REM correlated with length of sleep

Hypotheses

Memory storage

Deprivation of sleep early in night (mostly SWS) → impaired verbal learning

Deprivation of sleep late in night (much REM) → impaired consolidation of motor skills

MAO inhibitors (antidepressants) → decrease REM, but don't impair memory

Increase oxygen to eyeballs

No clear answer

3. Biological perspectives on dreaming

The activation-synthesis hypothesis

Cortex synthesizes story from stimuli processed in activated areas of cortex

Primary visual and primary somatosensory cortex inactivated

No sensory input to interfere

Pons → amygdala → emotional content

Vague and hard to test

A clinico-anatomical hypothesis

Arousing stimuli processed in unusual ways

Suppression of activity in primary visual, motor, and prefrontal cortex and spinal cord

No normal visual stimuli or motor responses

Prefrontal cortex inactivated → can't remember dreams, sudden scene changes in dreams

Increased activity in inferior parietal cortex

Damage there → poor visual-spatial perception and no dreams

Increased activity in "higher" visual areas → visual imagery

Increased activity in hypothalamus, amygdala, and other areas that process emotions

Also vague and hard to test

4. In closing: Our limited self-understanding

No need for conscious understanding of evolutionary reasons for behavior

Short-Answer Questions

Module 9.1 Rhythms of waking and sleeping

1. *Endogenous cycles*

   a. What do we know about the factors that do, or do not, initiate migration in birds?

   b. What are endogenous circannual rhythms? endogenous circadian rhythms? How consistent are circadian rhythms within individuals in a given environment? between individuals?

   c. How can circadian rhythms be demonstrated experimentally? What are some bodily and behavioral changes that occur in circadian rhythms?

   d. How easily can humans adapt to a new cycle length? What are the limits of adaptation?

2. *Mechanisms of the biological clock*

   a. What sorts of attempted interference with the biological clock were not effective?

   b. What brain structure is the source of the circadian rhythms? What is its relationship to the visual system?

   c. What is the evidence that the suprachiasmatic nucleus (SCN) generates rhythms itself?

   d. What happened when SCN tissue from hamsters with a mutant gene for a 20-hour rhythm were transplanted into normal hamsters?

   e. What two genes, discovered in Drosophila (fruitflies), govern circadian rhythms? How do they work? How common is this mechanism in other animals?

   f. What is melatonin? From which gland is it secreted? When does increased secretion of melatonin occur?

3. *Setting and resetting the biological clock*

   a. What is a zeitgeber? What is the most effective zeitgeber for land animals? for many marine animals?

   b. Is it easier to cross time zones going east or west? Why?

   c. What is the best way to reset the biological clock when working a night shift?

   d. By what path does the retina influence the SCN? What is unusual about the ganglion cells whose axons make up this path? How rapidly do they respond to light? How are blind mice and mole rats able to use light to reset their SCN?

Module 9.2 Stages of Sleep and Brain Mechanisms

1. *The stages of sleep*

   a. Briefly state the defining characteristics for coma, vegetative state, minimally conscious state, and brain death.

   b. What is an electroencephalogram?

   c. What accounts for rapid, low-voltage EEG activity? Slow, high-voltage activity?

d. Describe the usual behavioral correlate of alpha waves. What is their frequency?

e. Describe the EEG in stage 1 sleep.

f. What are the EEG characteristics of stage 2 sleep?

g. Which stages of sleep are classed as slow-wave sleep (SWS)?

2. *Paradoxical or REM sleep*

a. Why is REM sleep sometimes called paradoxical sleep? What are its characteristics?

b. What is a polysomnograph?

c. What is the typical duration of the sleep cycle? During which part of the night is REM predominant? During which part are stages 3 and 4 SWS predominant?

d. How good is the correlation between REM and dreaming?

3. *Brain mechanisms of wakefulness and arousal*

a. What is the effect of a cut through the midbrain on sleep and waking cycles? Was this result due simply to loss of sensory input or to damage to a particular brain structure?

b. Describe the input and output of the pontomesencephalon. What is its relation to the reticular formation?

c. Give the location, neurotransmitter, and a major function of the locus coeruleus.

d. What is the neurotransmitter of one path from the hypothalamus that stimulates arousal? What is the implication of this for allergy treatments?

e. What is the location of neurons that produce orexin? What is the main function of orexin?

f. What is the major neurotransmitter released by neurons in the basal forebrain that contributes to sleep? To arousal?

4. *Brain function in REM sleep*

a. What are PGO waves? Where are they recorded? What happens to PGO waves after a period of REM deprivation?

b. What brain area inhibits motor activity during REM sleep?

c. Which neurotransmitter is important for REM onset? Which two neurotransmitters interrupt or shorten REM? What is one effect of the drug carbachol?

5. *Sleep disorders*

a. How may shifts in circadian rhythm cause insomnia? Describe the different effects of phase advanced vs. phase delayed rhythms.

b. How may sleeping pills contribute to insomnia?

c. Describe the symptoms of sleep apnea. What are four factors that may contribute to sleep apnea?

d. What four symptoms are commonly associated with narcolepsy?

e. Define cataplexy. What tends to trigger it?

f. Define hypnagogic hallucinations.

g. The lack of what transmitter has been associated with narcolepsy?

h. Describe the symptoms of periodic limb movement disorder. What is one treatment?

i. What are the symptoms and a possible cause of REM behavior disorder?

j. How do night terrors differ from nightmares? During which type of sleep are night terrors most common?

k. During which stages does sleep talking occur? Sleepwalking? What is sexomnia?

Module 9.3 Why sleep? Why REM? Why Dreams?

1. *Functions of sleep*

    a. What was probably the original function of sleep?

    b. In what ways does sleep conserve energy?

    c. What are some advantages of hibernation?

    d. How do dolphins manage their need for sleep and their prolonged time under water?

    e. How is the need for sleep altered in migrating birds?

    f. What is the effect of sleep deprivation on GABA? How can that affect one's ability to concentrate?

    g. What are some effects of sleep deprivation in humans? in rats?

    h. What did researchers discover when they recorded brain activity while people learned a motor skill and then again while the people slept?

    i. What process may account for at least some of the beneficial effects of sleep on memory?

    j. What is the relationship between sleep spindles and learning? Between sleep spindles and nonverbal IQ?

2. *Functions of REM sleep*

    a. What is the relationship between percentage of time in REM and total sleep time?

    b. To what kind of learning may REM sleep contribute? To what kind of learning may NREM contribute?

    c. Do the effects of MAO inhibitors (antidepressant drugs) on REM sleep and memory support or bring into question a role of REM sleep in memory formation?

    d. How may REM contribute to oxygen supply for the cornea?

3. *Biological perspectives on dreaming*

    a. State the activation-synthesis hypothesis. What evidence supports this hypothesis?

    b. Summarize the basic ideas of the clinico-anatomical hypothesis.

    c. What three cortical areas are suppressed during dreams? What would be the effects of these suppressions?

d. Which two cortical areas are active during dreams? What would they contribute to dreams?

e. Which subcortical areas are active during dreams? What do these areas contribute?

True/False Questions

1. Day length is the most powerful stimulus for bird migration; if birds are kept in a constant environment, they might eventually migrate, but only after a delay of months.

    TRUE or FALSE

2. Humans can adapt to 25-hour days, but not to rhythms far from the 24-hour norm.

    TRUE or FALSE

3. The suprachiasmatic nucleus can generate circadian rhythms, even if it is disconnected from the rest of the brain.

    TRUE or FALSE

4. The genes *per* and *tim* produce proteins, high levels of which interact with the Clock protein to induce wakefulness.

    TRUE or FALSE

5. Melatonin is a hormone produced by the pituitary gland that induces sleepiness within minutes after being introduced into the body.

    TRUE or FALSE

6. A zeitgeber resets the circadian rhythm, but is not the actual generator of the rhythm.

    TRUE or FALSE

7. Jet lag is worst traveling east.

    TRUE or FALSE

8. The main input to the SCN is from branches of the same axons that project to the lateral geniculate nucleus of the thalamus and carry normal visual information.

    TRUE or FALSE

9. Sleep spindles and K-complexes are characteristic of REM sleep.

    TRUE or FALSE

10. Sleep stages 3 and 4 predominate early in the night, and REM periods take up more time late in the night.

    TRUE or FALSE

11. Narcolepsy may result from a lack of orexin neurons in the hypothalamus.

    TRUE or FALSE

12. GABA-containing neurons of the basal forebrain produce arousal.

    TRUE or FALSE

13. Acetylcholine triggers the onset of REM sleep, and serotonin and norepinephrine inhibit REM sleep.

    TRUE or FALSE

14. REM deprivation may impair primarily verbal learning.

    TRUE or FALSE

15. Falling asleep easily but awakening early may be caused by a phase-delayed temperature rhythm.

    TRUE or FALSE

16. People with sleep apnea may be helped by losing weight, avoiding alcohol and tranquilizers, having surgery to remove tissue obstructing the trachea, and/or using a mask that delivers air under pressure.

    TRUE or FALSE

17. Activity in primary visual cortex (V1) is increased in REM sleep, thereby giving rise to the visual content of dreams.

    TRUE or FALSE

Fill In The Blanks

1. The site of the biological clock is the _____.

2. The drosophila genes _____ (_____) and _____ (_____) produce proteins that interact with the _____ protein to induce sleepiness.

3. Melatonin is produced by the _____ gland and peaks _____ before the onset of sleepiness.

4. A stimulus that resets the circadian rhythm is called a(n) _____.

5. The tract that carries input concerning light to the biological clock is the _____ path, which arises from _____ cells with their own photopigment, _____.

6. The EEG waves characteristic of relaxed wakefulness are _____ waves.

7. Sleep cycles last approximately _____ minutes.

8. _____ and _____ are characteristic of stage _____ sleep.

9. The _____ is a part of the reticular formation that sends axons to the thalamus and basal forebrain that release _____ and _____ to produce arousal.

10. REM sleep is associated with high-amplitude electrical potentials called _____.

11. The transmitter that stimulates REM onset is _____; two that inhibit REM are _____ and _____.

12. _____ is a peptide neurotransmitter that stimulates neurons responsible for maintaining wakefulness.

13. _____ or _____ is a condition in which a person engages in sexual behavior, either with a partner or by masturbation, during a sleeplike state and does not remember it afterward.

14. A chemical that builds up during waking and induces sleepiness is _____; caffeine increases arousal by blocking its receptors.

15. The theory that dreams are caused by the brain's attempt to make sense out of neural activity is the _____ theory.

16. The clinico-anatomical hypothesis observes that suppressed activity in primary _____, _____ and _____ cortex leaves the brain without normal sensory input and motor output and without normal working memory.

Matching Items

1. _____ Suprachiasmatic nucleus
2. _____ Pineal gland
3. _____ Zeitgeber
4. _____ Retinohypothalamic path source
5. _____ Alpha waves
6. _____ Sleep spindle
7. _____ Pontomesencephalon
8. _____ Locus coeruleus
9. _____ Basal forebrain GABA neurons
10. _____ PGO waves
11. _____ Acetylcholine
12. _____ Serotonin
13. _____ Adenosine
14. _____ Trouble falling asleep
15. _____ Awakening too early
16. _____ Orexin

a. EEG sign of REM sleep
b. A transmitter that inhibits REM
c. EEG sign of stage 2 sleep
d. A transmitter that → waking & REM
e. Site of norepinephrine neurons→memory, wakefulness
f. EEG sign of relaxed wakefulness
g. Ganglion cells with own photopigment
h. Site of biological clock
i. Phase-delayed temperature rhythm
j. Transmitter that maintains wakefulness
k. Phase-advanced temperature rhythm
l. Part of reticular formation that → arousal
m. Structure that releases melatonin
n. Stimulus that resets circadian rhythm
o. Neurons that induce sleep
p. Chemical that builds up to → sleepiness

Multiple-Choice Questions

1. Curt Richter suggested the revolutionary idea that
    a. nearly all behavior is a reaction to a stimulus.
    b. the body generates its own cycles of activity and inactivity.
    c. temperature fluctuations are the best zeitgeber.
    d. animals wait till the first frost before preparing for winter so that they can enjoy summer longer.

2. Migratory birds
    a. respond only to temperature signals to begin migration.
    b. respond only to the ratio of light to dark, especially in spring.
    c. respond only to the availability of food.
    d. become more active in the spring, even in the absence of external cues, and fly north if released from captivity.

3. Circadian rhythms
    a. cannot be demonstrated if lights are always on or always off.
    b. always average within a minute or two of 24 hours in length, regardless of the light cycle.
    c. include cycles of waking and sleeping, eating and drinking, temperature, hormone secretion, and urine production.
    d. are very flexible and can be changed as soon as a different light cycle is established.

4. Which of the following can totally disrupt the biological clock?
    a. food or water deprivation
    b. anesthesia
    c. lack of oxygen
    d. none of the above

5. The suprachiasmatic nucleus (SCN)
    a. if transplanted from fetal hamsters that have a mutant gene producing a 20-hour cycle into normal hamsters, will produce 20-hour cycles in the recipients.
    b. no longer generates a rhythm if it is disconnected from input from the optic nerve.
    c. is located in the brain stem.
    d. is concerned only with the resetting of the clock, not with generating the rhythm.

6. Two genes in Drosophila known as *period (per)* and *timeless (tim)*
    a. produce proteins that are present in only small amounts early in the day, but increase
    b. throughout the day.
    c. produce proteins that make the fly sleepy, when present in high levels.
    d. are similar to genes found in mice.
    e. all of the above

7. Melatonin
    a. is secreted by the pituitary gland just before awakening.
    b. is secreted by the pituitary gland 2 - 3 hours before the time of sleep onset.
    c. is secreted by the pineal gland 2 - 3 hours before the time of sleep onset.
    d. is secreted by the pineal gland at the time of sleep onset.

8. The human circadian rhythm
   a. can easily adjust to 22- or 28-hour days, but not to 20- or 30-hour days.
   b. has a mean of 24.2 hours, but can adjust to 25-hour days.
   c. can be most easily reset by using only dim lights in the evening.
   d. cannot be reset at all.

9. Which of the following is true?
   a. It is easier to adjust our biological rhythms to longer cycles and to travel across time zones going west.
   b. It is easier to adjust our biological rhythms to shorter cycles and to travel across time zones going east.
   c. People on irregular shifts tend to sleep the longest when they go to sleep in the morning or early afternoon.
   d. People on night shifts that were exposed to normal levels of room lighting found it easy to adjust their cycles.

10. Alpha waves are characteristic of
    a. REM sleep.
    b. alert mental activity.
    c. relaxed wakefulness.
    d. slow-wave sleep.

11. Stages 3 and 4 sleep
    a. are characterized by sleep spindles and K-complexes.
    b. together are known as slow-wave sleep.
    c. are characterized by irregular, jagged, low-voltage waves.
    d. are the stages during which REM occurs.

12. Which of the following is **not** a sign of REM sleep?
    a. tenseness in postural muscles
    b. extreme relaxation of postural muscles
    c. variable heart and breathing rates
    d. irregular, low-voltage, fast EEG activity

13. Paradoxical sleep is paradoxical because brain waves suggest
    a. slow-wave sleep, when one is really dreaming.
    b. dreaming, when one is really in slow-wave sleep.
    c. sleep, when one is really awake.
    d. activation, when one's postural muscles are most relaxed.

14. REM sleep occurs
    a. only early in a night's sleep.
    b. cyclically, about every 90 minutes.
    c. randomly throughout the night.
    d. only after a period of physical exercise.

15. Dreams
    a. are highly correlated with sleep talking.
    b. are of greater duration and frequency during the early part of the night.
    c. may occur in NREM, but are more likely to include vivid visual imagery during REM.
    d. all of the above

16. A cut through the midbrain
    a. produced prolonged sleep because an area that promotes wakefulness was cut off from the rest of the brain.
    b. left the animal sleeping constantly because most sensory input was cut off from the brain.
    c. left the animal sleeping and waking normally, since structures that control these functions are anterior to the midbrain.
    d. left the animal more wakeful than usual because much of the reticular formation was still connected to the brain, but a sleep-promoting system had been damaged.

17. The pontomesencephalon, a part of the reticular formation,
    a. is the site of neurons that contain orexin.
    b. is important in generating slow-wave sleep.
    c. is primarily concerned with sensory analysis.
    d. none of the above

18. The locus coeruleus
    a. is very active during REM sleep.
    b. is very active during slow wave sleep.
    c. is very active during meaningful events and may be important for strengthening recent memories.
    d. got its name from its bright red color.

19. Sleep-inducing nuclei in the basal forebrain
    a. stimulate other neurons that use GABA as their neurotransmitter.
    b. use acetylcholine as their neurotransmitter.
    c. use histamine as their neurotransmitter.
    d. have very restricted projections to specific cortical areas.

20. Neurons in the basal forebrain that promote arousal
    a. use GABA as their transmitter.
    b. use acetylcholine as their transmitter.
    c. use serotonin as their transmitter.
    d. are increased in people with Alzheimer's disease..

21. PGO waves
    a. occur during REM sleep.
    b. are recorded in the pons, lateral geniculate, and occipital cortex.
    c. are compensated, if lost due to REM deprivation.
    d. all of the above

22. Which of the following is true?
    a. Histamine increases alertness and is released from neurons in the hypothalamus.
    b. Orexin is also released from neurons in the hypothalamus.
    c. Orexin is necessary, not for waking up, but for staying awake.
    d. all of the above

23. Inhibition of motor neurons during REM is induced by neurons in
    a. the dorsolateral prefrontal cortex.
    b. the reticular formation.
    c. the pons.
    d. the amygdala.

24. Which of the following is true?
    a. Acetylcholine promotes the onset of REM sleep.
    b. Acetylcholine promotes slow-wave sleep.
    c. Carbachol inhibits REM sleep.
    d. Serotonin promotes the onset of REM sleep.

25. People with phase-delayed temperature rhythms who try to fall asleep at the normal time may experience
    a. excess sleep.
    b. repeated awakenings throughout the night.
    c. awakening too early.
    d. difficulty falling asleep.

26. Which of the following is a cause of insomnia?
    a. narcolepsy
    b. cataplexy
    c. repeated use of tranquilizers
    d. hypnagogic hallucinations

27. Which of the following is more closely associated with REM sleep than NREM sleep?
    a. nightmares and other dreams
    b. night terrors
    c. sleep walking
    d. all of the above

28. When people are deprived of sleep for a week or more,
    a. they usually suffer severe consequences, including death.
    b. they report dizziness, irritability, and difficulty concentrating, but no drastic consequences.
    c. they actually fall asleep early in the deprivation period and only appear to be awake, because their sleepwalking and sleep talking appear to be very realistic.
    d. they report no symptoms whatever.

29. In our evolutionary history the original need for sleep was probably
    a. promotion of memory storage.
    b. rebuilding proteins in the brain.
    c. replenishing energy supplies.
    d. energy conservation at times when animals are relatively inefficient.

30. Adenosine
    a. is a major neurotransmitter producing arousal.
    b. builds up during wakefulness and increases drowsiness.
    c. is the component of coffee that keeps us awake.
    d. is produced by neurons in the cortex during REM sleep.

31. Which of the following is true?
    a. A major function of sleep may be weeding out less successful connections.
    b. Presentation of rose odor during both learning and sleep resulted in better memory than presentation of the odor during both learning and wakefulness.
    c. Sleep spindles increase during Stage 2 after learning.
    d. all of the above.

32. Comparisons of sleep patterns across individuals and across species indicate that
    a. percentage of time spent in REM remains the same, no matter how long the individual sleeps.
    b. percentage of time in REM decreases as total amount of sleep increases.
    c. percentage of time in REM increases as total amount of sleep increases.
    d. percentage of time spent in REM is extremely variable, and shows no relationship to the total amount of sleep.

33. The activation-synthesis hypothesis proposes that dreams result from
    a. unconscious wishes struggling for expression.
    b. the ego's attempt to gain control of the id.
    c. the brain's attempt to make sense of its activity.
    d. the brain's attempt to wake up.

34. The clinico-anatomical hypothesis is based on observations that during dreaming
    a. there is increased activity in the inferior parietal cortex, which contributes to visuo-spatial perception; in "higher" visual areas, which provide visual imagery; and in the hypothalamus and amygdala, which contribute to emotional intensity.
    b. there is increased activity in prefrontal cortex, which contributes to the fantasy-like experience of dreams.
    c. there is increased activity in primary visual cortex, which contributes to visual dreams.
    d. there is also increased activity in primary auditory cortex, which provides rich auditory content.

Solutions

True/False Questions

1. F	6. T	11. T	16. T
2. T	7. T	12. F	17. F
3. T	8. F	13. T	
4. F	9. F	14. F	
5. F	10. T	15. F	

Fill In The Blanks

1. suprachiasmatic nucleus
2. period; per; timeless; tim; Clock
3. pineal; 2-3 hours
4. zeitgeber
5. retino-hypothalamic; ganglion; melanopsin
6. alpha
7. 90
8. Sleep spindles; K-complexes; 2
9. Pontomesencephalon; acetylcholine; glutamate
10. PGO waves
11. acetylcholine; serotonin; norephinephrine.
12. Orexin
13. Sexomnia; sleep sex
14. adenosine
15. activation-synthesis
16. visual; motor; prefrontal

Matching Items

1. h	5. f	9. o	13. p
2. m	6. c	10. a	14. i
3. n	7. l	11. d	15. k
4. g	8. e	12. b	16. j

Multiple Choice Questions

1. b	10. c	19. a	28. b
2. d	11. b	20. b	29. d
3. c	12. a	21. d	30. b
4. d	13. d	22. d	31. d
5. a	14. b	23. c	32. c
6. d	15. c	24. a	33. c
7. c	16. a	25. d	34. a
8. b	17. d	26. c	
9. a	18. c	27. a	

Internal Regulation

CHAPTER 10

Introduction

Homeostatic drives are drives that tend to maintain certain biological conditions within a fixed range. Temperature regulation in mammals and birds is such a drive. Constant relatively high temperatures provide conditions in which chemical reactions can be regulated precisely and, by increasing the metabolic rate, increase capacity for prolonged activity. Several physiological mechanisms, including shivering, sweating, panting, and redirection of blood flow, raise and lower temperature appropriately. These are coordinated primarily by the preoptic area/anterior hypothalamus (POA/AH), which monitors both its own temperature and that of the skin and spinal cord. Behavioral regulation of temperature is used both by animals that are poikilothermic (body temperature matches that of environment) and by those that are homeothermic (body temperature is regulated within a few degrees of a constant setting). Fever is produced when leukocytes (white blood cells) release cytokines, which activate the vagus nerve, which in turn causes the preoptic area to raise body temperature. Moderate fevers are helpful in combating bacterial infections.

Water balance is critical, both for regulating the concentration of chemicals in our bodily fluids (and therefore the rate of chemical reactions) and for maintaining normal blood pressure. If we have ample supplies of palatable fluids to drink, we may drink a great deal of them and let the kidneys discard the excess. If there is a shortage of fluids to drink, or a large loss of water, the posterior pituitary releases vasopressin (also known as antidiuretic hormone, or ADH), which increases both blood pressure and water retention by the kidneys. There are two major types of stimuli for thirst: decreased water content inside cells and decreased blood volume. When there are increased solutes in the blood, the blood and extracellular fluid become more concentrated. Water tends to flow out of cells into the area of higher osmotic pressure (extracellular fluid). The resulting loss of water from cells surrounding the third ventricle, especially in the organum vasculosum laminae terminalis (OVLT) and subfornical organ (SFO), elicits neural responses that are relayed to several hypothalamic nuclei, including the supraoptic and paraventricular nuclei. Input from the stomach also informs the OVLT and SFO about high levels of sodium. The supraoptic and paraventricular nuclei, in turn, produce vasopressin (antidiuretic hormone, ADH), the hormone that is released from the posterior pituitary and that increases blood pressure and urine concentration. Receptors in the OVLT, SFO, and stomach also relay information to the lateral preoptic area and surrounding areas, which give rise to osmotic thirst. Thus, an increase in osmotic signals results in greater water retention, increased water intake, and higher blood pressure. If large amounts of whole blood are lost, the resulting hypovolemia (low volume of blood) is detected by receptors in the large veins. The kidney also detects the hypovolemia and releases renin, which acts in the blood to produce angiotensin II. This hormone causes constriction of blood vessels to maintain blood pressure. It also stimulates neurons in areas around the third ventricle that use angiotensin II as their transmitter to induce thirst. Thus, the cells around the third ventricle both respond to angiotensin II and release it.

Hypovolemic thirst is satisfied best by salt water. A hunger for sodium depends largely on two hormones, aldosterone and angiotensin II. Aldosterone, secreted by the adrenal glands, causes the kidneys, salivary glands, and sweat glands to conserve sodium; it also stimulates an increase in salt intake. Angiotensin II, as noted above, stimulates sodium hunger. The effects of aldosterone and angiotensin II are mediated by the nucleus of the tractus solitarius, which begins to respond to salt in nearly the same way as to sugar.

The factors regulating hunger, satiety, and the selection of specific foods are very complex. Food selection is influenced by the digestive system (including intestinal enzymes), cultural factors, taste, familiarity, and memories of the consequences of consuming a particular food. Hunger and satiety depend on stimuli from the mouth, stomach, and duodenum. Oral factors, stomach or duodenum distension, and nutrient contents of the stomach contribute to satiety. Cholecystokinin (CCK), released by the duodenum, inhibits stomach emptying. CCK also stimulates the vagus nerve, which activates neurons that release a short version of CCK in the brain. Thus, as with angiotensin II's roles in thirst, the brain and periphery use the same (or similar) chemicals to accomplish related tasks. Blood glucose levels are maintained in a relatively narrow range by varying amounts of insulin, which enables glucose to enter cells, and glucagon, which converts stored glycogen into glucose. Leptin is a peptide that is produced by fat cells; it serves as an indicator of the body's fat stores and is also increased after a meal. Therefore, it provides information about both long-term and short-term nutrient availability. It decreases eating, increases general activity and immune function, and can trigger the onset of puberty. However, leptin is not an effective treatment of obese people; apparently they produce leptin, but are insensitive to its effects.

Brain mechanisms use a complex array of signals to regulate food intake. Hunger-sensitive neurons in the arcuate nucleus of the hypothalamus receive input from the taste system and from axons that release ghrelin, a neurotransmitter that binds to the same receptors as growth-hormone releasing hormone (GHRH, from which it gets its name). Ghrelin is also released in the stomach, where it causes contractions. The arcuate nucleus also has satiety-sensitive neurons that receive inputs concerning intestine distention (using CCK as transmitter), blood glucose, and body fat (using leptin). Axons from satiety-sensitive neurons in the arcuate nucleus stimulate the paraventricular nucleus of the hypothalamus (PVN), using α-melanocyte stimulating hormone (αMSH). The PVN is important for ending a meal. In contrast, hunger-sensitive neurons in the arcuate nucleus send inhibitory input to the PVN, as well as to satiety-sensitive neurons in the arcuate itself, using GABA, neuropeptide Y (NPY), and agouti-related peptide (AgRP) as transmitters. Therefore, different groups of arcuate neurons can end a meal by stimulating the PVN with αMSH or elicit hunger by inhibiting the PVN with GABA, NPY, and AgRP. An additional pathway from the arcuate nucleus activates orexin-containing cells in the lateral hypothalamus that increase feeding and rewarding properties of food.

Output from the PVN goes to the lateral hypothalamus, which controls insulin secretion, alters taste responsiveness, and facilitates feeding in other ways. Damage to the lateral hypothalamus results in self-starvation, unless the animal is force-fed, in which case it will partially recover. The effects of lesions on feeding are due to cell bodies in the lateral hypothalamus, rather than to axons passing through, which are themselves important for arousal and activity. The intact lateral hypothalamus contributes to feeding by modifying activity in the nucleus of the tractus solitarius (NTS), which influences taste sensations and salivation, and also by increasing insulin release, facilitating ingestion, and increasing autonomic responses, such as the release of digestive juices. On the other hand, damage to the ventromedial hypothalamus (VMH) and surrounding areas results in obesity. This results from increased stomach motility and secretions, faster emptying of the stomach, and increased release of insulin, which promotes fat storage and inhibits its release for use as fuel. As a result, the animal consumes more frequent normal-sized meals. The problem is not so much that the rat gets fat because it overeats, but that it overeats because it is storing so much fat. The multiple messengers and pathways that control food intake and digestion provide an effective system of checks and balances.

Genes control body weight in many ways, including activity levels. Other genetic influences include the sensitivity to, or production of, peptides, such as melanocortin and ghrelin, that regulate eating. However, social and other environmental influences, as well as exercise and eating habits, are important determinants of body weight. Some appetite-suppressant drugs increase levels of norepinephrine, serotonin, and dopamine or block absorption of fats in the intestines.

Anorexia nervosa is a disorder in which people eat much less than they need, sometimes starving themselves to death. They are usually perfectionistic, most frequently women. They are interested in food, but are afraid of losing control and gaining weight. People with bulimia nervosa alternate between overeating and dieting, frequently eating a huge meal and then purging. People with bulimia have decreased release of CCK, increased release of ghrelin, and other changes in hormones and transmitters that affect eating. However, it is not clear whether transmitter abnormalities precede or result from the bulimia. Bulimia may have some similarities to drug addiction. Rats that consumed excessive glucose after a period of deprivation had increased release of dopamine and opiate-like chemicals and increased the levels of dopamine type 3 receptors in their brain. Furthermore, withdrawal from the glucose resulted in some of the symptoms of drug withdrawal.

Learning Objectives

Module 10.1 Temperature Regulation
1. Understand the advantages of constant high body temperatures and the brain mechanisms that maintain temperatures.
2. Know the advantage of moderate fevers and the physiological mechanisms that produce fever.

Module 10.2 Thirst
1. Understand the concepts of osmotic and hypovolemic thirst and stimuli that give rise to each.
2. Know the brain mechanisms that promote osmotic and hypovolemic thirst and salt appetite.

Module 10.3 Hunger
1. Know the functions of the various components of the digestive system and their roles in hunger and satiety.
2. Understand the functions, neurotransmitters, and outputs of the hunger- and satiety-sensitive neurons in the arcuate nucleus of the hypothalamus.
3. Know the functions of the paraventricular nucleus of the hypothalamus, the lateral hypothalamus, and the ventromedial nucleus of the hypothalamus and their major sources of input.
4. Know the various peripheral and central chemicals that contribute to satiety.
5. Know the evidence for genetic, environmental, and neurochemical contributions to obesity.
6. Know commonly use weight loss techniques.
7. Be able to describe the characteristics of anorexia nervosa and bulimia nervosa and the physiological correlates of bulimia nervosa.

Key Terms and Concepts

Module 10.1 Temperature Regulation
1. Homeostasis and allostasis
     Walter R. Cannon
     Set point
     Set range
     Negative feedback
         Role of behavior
     Differences from simple homeostasis
         Allostasis: Set points vary with situation
2. Controlling body temperature
     Basal Metabolism
     Poikilothermic: Body temperature same as environment
     Homeothermic: Body temperature almost constant
     Mechanisms for cooling
         Sweating
         Panting
         Licking
     Mechanisms for heating
         Shivering
         Increased metabolic rate in brown fat
         Decreased blood flow to skin
         Fluffed out fur
     Behavioral mechanisms
     Surviving in extreme cold
         Problem: Formation of ice crystals → tear blood vessels and cell membranes
         Some insects and fish: Glycerol and other antifreeze chemicals in blood
         Wood frogs: Do freeze
             Withdraw most fluid from organs and blood vessels, store it in extracellular space
             Chemicals that regulate ice crystal formation

Increased blood-clotting
The advantages of constant high body temperature
Warmer muscles work better
Hotter than $37^{\circ}C \rightarrow$ greater energy need
Hotter than $41^{\circ}C \rightarrow$ protein bonds break
Reproductive cells: Cooler environment
Brain mechanisms
Hypothalamus
Preoptic area/anterior hypothalamus (POA/AH)
Monitors own temperature
Monitors temperature of skin and spinal cord
Fever
Body's defense against infection
Leukocytes $\rightarrow$ cytokines $\rightarrow$ vagus nerve $\rightarrow$ hypothalamus $\rightarrow$ prostaglandins
Cytokines also attack intruders, some cross blood-brain barrier
Stimulation of prostaglandin receptors in hypothalamus is required for fever.
Moderate fevers helpful
Enhances activity of immune system
Physiological and behavioral means
High fevers harmful
3. In closing: Combining physiological and behavioral mechanisms
Redundancy of mechanisms

Module 10.2 Thirst
1. Mechanisms of water regulation
Increasing intake
Decreasing output
Vasopressin or antidiuretic hormone (ADH)
2. Osmotic thirst
Osmotic pressure
Semipermeable membrane
Increase in solute concentration outside cell
Water leaves cells $\rightarrow$ osmotic thirst + more concentrated urine
Brain areas around third ventricle
Leaky blood-brain barrier: Detect osmotic pressure
Organum vasculosum laminae terminalis (OVLT)
Subfornical organ (SFO)
Input from stomach: High levels of sodium
Output $\rightarrow$ supraoptic and paraventricular nuclei $\rightarrow$ vasopressin release from posterior pituitary
Output $\rightarrow$ lateral preoptic area $\rightarrow$ drinking
Input from mouth, stomach, intestines $\rightarrow$ inhibit thirst temporarily, limits drinking to not much more than needed
3. Hypovolemic thirst and sodium-specific hunger
Loss of blood volume
Vasopressin $\rightarrow$ constrict blood vessels

Hormones from kidneys

    Renin: Angiotensinogen in blood → Angiotensin II → constricts blood vessels

    Angiotensin II → areas around third ventricle → Angiotensin II as their transmitter → hypovolemic thirst

    Angiotensin II also → sodium-specific hunger

        Automatic, unlearned (unlike other specific hungers)

    Adrenal glands → aldosterone → salt retention and sodium hunger

    Angiotensin II + aldosterone → taste receptors + nucleus of the tractus solitarius (taste system) → prefer salt and increase salt intake

4.   In closing: The psychology and biology of thirst

    Both behavioral and autonomic controls

Module 10.3 Hunger

1.   How the digestive system influences food selection

    Mouth: Enzymes in saliva → carbohydrate digestion

    Stomach: Hydrochloric acid, enzymes → protein digestion

    Small intestine: Enzymes → protein, fat, and carbohydrate digestion

        Absorption of nutrients

    Large intestine

        Water and mineral absorption

        Lubrication

    Enzymes and consumption of dairy products

        Lactose, milk sugar

        Lactase enzyme

            Lack of lactase → inability to digest milk → stomach cramps, gas

        Genes for lactose digestion evolved independently in different regions

    Other influences on food selection

        Carnivore, herbivore, omnivore

        Culture, taste, familiarity, learning

            Select sweet, avoid bitter, eat salty and sour in moderation

            Familiar = safe

            Conditioned taste aversion

2.   Short- and long-term regulation of feeding

    Oral factors

        Desire to taste or chew

            Pump liquid diet into stomach → unsatisfying

        Sham feeding: Eat, swallow, eat more

        Mouth sensations contribute to satiety, but not sufficient

    The stomach and intestines

        Vagus nerve (cranial nerve X)

            Information about stretching of stomach: Sufficient but not necessary for satiety

        Splanchnic nerves

            Information about nutrient contents

        The duodenum

            Also sufficient but not necessary for satiety

            The hormone CCK (cholecystokinin)

CCK directly inhibits stomach emptying

CCK also → vagus nerve → short version of CCK released as neurotransmitter in brain

Short term effects only

Glucose, insulin, and glucagon

Glucose: Main fuel for brain, one of several for rest of body

Excess glucose

Liver: Glucose → glycogen

Fat cells: Glycogen → fat

Low glucose

Liver: Glycogen → glucose

Insulin: Facilitates glucose entry into cells (except in brain cells)

Rises when getting ready to eat

Decreases appetite

Glucagon → liver converts stored glycogen to glucose

Insulin drops → glucose enters cells slowly → hunger increases

Hibernating species: High insulin → store fat and glycogen

Diabetes: High blood glucose; little enters cells, most is excreted

Leptin

Limited to vertebrates

Produced by fat cells → signal to eat less, be more active, increase immune function

Triggers puberty onset

Obese people: High leptin levels, insensitive to it

3. Brain mechanisms

The arcuate nucleus and paraventricular hypothalamus

Arcuate nucleus ("Master area" for control of appetite)

Hunger-sensitive neurons

Input from taste system

Input from axons releasing ghrelin

Stomach releases ghrelin → stomach contractions

Ghrelin → hypothalamus to decreases appetite

Ghrelin → hippocampus enhance learning

Satiety-sensitive neurons

Intestine distention → CCK (short term signal)

Blood glucose (short term signal) → stimulates satiety cells in arcuate nucleus & increases insulin secretion

Body fat (long term signal) → leptin

Output to paraventricular nucleus (PVN) of the hypothalamus

Paraventricular nucleus of the hypothalamus

Inhibits lateral hypothalamus

Damage to PVN → larger meals

Interconnections

Arcuate satiety-sensitive cells excite PVN

α-melanocyte stimulating hormone (αMSH, a melanocortin) → end of meal

Arcuate hunger-sensitive cells inhibit paraventricular hypothalamus

Also inhibit satiety sensitive cells in arcuate itself

Transmitters: GABA, neuropeptide Y (NPY), agouti-related peptide (AgRP)
Additional pathway to cells in lateral hypothalamus that release orexin
Orexin increases food seeking behavior & responds to rewarding properties of food.

The lateral hypothalamus
Controls insulin secretion, alters taste responsiveness, facilitates feeding in other ways
Lesions: Starvation or weight loss
Neurons vs. dopamine axons passing through
Damage to cell bodies or lesions in very young rats → loss of feeding
Mechanisms
Axons to NTS (nucleus of the tractus solitarius in medulla) → taste, salivation
Increase insulin secretion
Axons to cerebral cortex → facilitate ingestion
Increase insulin secretion
Stimulation of autonomic responses, including digestive secretions

Medial areas of the hypothalamus
Ventromedial hypothalamus
Lesions → weight gain to a new high set point
Ventromedial hypothalamic syndrome: Includes damage to nearby cells and axons
Ventral noradrenergic bundle
Increased appetite
Finickiness, after weight gain
More normal-sized meals per day
Increased stomach motility and secretions
Faster stomach emptying
Increased insulin and fat storage
Problem not that rat gets fat from overeating; rat overeats because it's storing so much fat

4. Obesity and other eating disorders
Social and cultural factors
Genetics and body weight
High heritability of obesity
Melanocortin receptor
Mutation → obesity
Variant form of FTO gene → 2/3 greater probability of becoming obese
Prader-Willi syndrome
Mental retardation, short stature, obesity
Blood ghrelin levels 4 to 5 times higher than average
Multiple gene influences
Environment
Native American Pimas: Typical American diet → obesity
Inactive life style, fast-food restaurants, large helpings
High-fructose sweeteners
Less insulin or leptin release than with glucose or sucrose → less satiety
Stored as fat, not used for immediate needs

Weight loss
    Increase exercise & decrease eating
    Soft drinks increase likelihood of being overweight due to fructose
    Restraint of eating
        Fat-carbohydrate combinations: High calorie, taste good
        Appetite suppressant drugs
            "Fen-phen"
                        Fenfluramine →increase serotonin release and decrease
                        reuptake
                        Phentermine → block norepinephrine and dopamine
                        reuptake
                        Medical complications
            Sibutramine (Meridia):
                        Blocks reuptake of serotonin and
                        norepinephrine
            Orlistat (Xenical): Blocks fat absorption
    Gastric bypass
    Anorexia nervosa
            Interested in food, fear becoming fat
            Hardworking perfectionists (obsessive-compulsive)
            Similar to migrating elk
    Bulimia nervosa
        Eat enormous meal, then purge
        Many have another psychiatric disorder
        High levels of ghrelin
        Low levels of CCK
        Similar to drug addiction
            Food-deprive rats for first 4 hours of day, then offer glucose → great increase in
            eating
            Increased dopamine and opiate-like compounds in brain (similar to abused drugs)
            Increased dopamine type 3 receptors
            Deprived of glucose → withdrawal symptoms
5. In closing: The multiple controls of hunger
        Checks and balances

Short-Answer Questions

Module 10.1 Temperature Regulation

1. *Homeostasis and allostasis*

   a. What is a homeostatic process?

   b. What are some of the physiological processes that are controlled near a set point? What are some homeostatic processes that anticipate future needs or that change under various conditions?

   c. Why does the scrotum of most male mammals hang outside the body? Why should pregnant women avoid hot baths?

2. *Controlling body temperature*

   a. Define the terms poikilothermic and homeothermic.

   b. What prevents the temperature of most fish, amphibians, and reptiles from fluctuating wildly?

   c. How do some frogs, fish, and insects adapt to extreme cold?

   d. What is an advantage of a constant relatively high body temperature? What is the cost to the animal for maintaining homeothermy?

   e. What two kinds of stimuli does the preoptic area monitor for temperature control?

   f. What are leukocytes and cytokines? What are their roles in producing a fever?

   g. Of what benefit is a moderate fever?

Module 10.2 Thirst

1. *Mechanisms of water regulation*

   a. Describe the different mechanisms of maintaining water balance that have been developed by desert animals and by animals with an abundant water supply.

   b. What are the two functions of vasopressin when body fluids are low? What is its other name?

2. *Osmotic thirst*

   a. What is osmotic pressure?

   b. How does the body "know" when its osmotic pressure is low?

   c. What are the roles of the OVLT, the subfornical organ (SFO), the supraoptic and paraventricular nuclei, and the lateral preoptic area in osmotic thirst?

3. *Hypovolemic thirst*

   a. Why is hypovolemia dangerous?

   b. Under what circumstances does hypovolemic thirst occur?

   c. Describe the steps leading to the production of antiotensin II. What are its two main effects?

   d. Will an animal with hypovolemic thirst drink more pure water or more salt water with the same concentration as blood? Why?

   e. What two effects of aldosterone are beneficial in cases of sodium deficiency? What other hormone contributes to salt hunger? On what brain area do these two hormones act to increase salt hunger?

Module 10.3 Hunger

1. *How the digestive system influences food selection*

   a. Enzymes for the digestion of what type of nutrient(s) are present in saliva? In the stomach? In the small intestine?

   b. From which structure is digested food absorbed?

   c. Why do newborn mammals stop nursing as they grow older?

   d. Discuss the evidence that humans are a partial exception to the principle of lactose intolerance in adults.

   e. List the factors that may influence food selection.

2. *Short- and long-term regulation of feeding*

   a. Summarize the evidence for the importance of oral factors in hunger and satiety. What is the evidence that these factors are not sufficient to end a meal normally?

   b. How did Deutsch et al. demonstrate the importance of stomach distension in regulating meal size?

   c. Which two nerves convey the stomach's satiety signals?

   d. What is CCK? In what two places is it produced? What are two mechanisms by which it induces satiety?

   e. What is the effect of insulin on blood glucose? In what ways does insulin affect hunger? Compare the effects of glucagon with those of insulin.

   f. Why do people with untreated diabetes eat a lot but gain little weight? How is this similar to, and how is it different from, the effects of high levels of insulin?

   g. Where is leptin produced? What are three effects of leptin? Why may it be important for puberty onset? Why can't we treat most obese people with leptin?

3. *Brain mechanisms*

   a. What are the effects on hunger of two kinds of neurons in the arcuate nucleus? What kinds of input does each type receive?

   b. Which neurotransmitters relay the output of the two kinds of arcuate neurons to the paraventricular nucleus (PVN)?

   c. What is the main role of the PVN in the control of feeding? What is the effect of damage to the PVN?

   d. Describe the evidence that the lateral hypothalamus is important for hunger.

   e. What are four mechanisms by which the lateral hypothalamus contributes to feeding?

   f. What is the result of damage to lateral hypothalamic cell bodies? How did researchers separate the roles of cell bodies from those of dopamine-containing axons passing through.

   g. Describe the various behavioral changes produced by lesions of the ventromedial nucleus of the hypothalamus (VMH), ventral noradrenergic bundle, and surrounding areas.

   h. To what factors can we attribute the obesity induced by VMH lesions?

   i. How are the effects of damage to the paraventricular nucleus (PVN) different from those of VMH damage?

4. *Eating disorders*

   a. Give one example of a group of people who demonstrate the relationship of genetic and environmental factors in the control of weight. How important are exercise and restraint of eating?

   b. What are advantages and disadvantages of common weight loss techniques?

   c. Compare the symptoms of anorexia nervosa with those of bulimia nervosa.

   d. Describe the personality characteristics of many people with anorexia.

   e. What chemical differences are seen in bulimics, compared to other people? Can we determine whether these differences imply cause and effect relationships between the chemical and the disorder?

   f. What evidence suggests that excessive eating in bulimia has some parallels with drug addiction?

True/False Questions

1. Behavior can act as a negative feedback mechanism to correct homeostatic imbalances.

    TRUE or FALSE

2. Poikilothermic animals are those that maintain almost constant temperature.

    TRUE or FALSE

3. The POA/AH monitors its own temperature and that of the skin and spinal cord.

    TRUE or FALSE

4. During illness, leukocytes produce cytokines, which in turn stimulate the preoptic area to induce a fever.

    TRUE or FALSE

5. Cells in the supraoptic and paraventricular nuclei send input to the OVLT and subfornical organ concerning hypovolemic signals; the OVLT then releases vasopressin from the anterior pituitary.

    TRUE or FALSE

6. Hypovolemic thirst and osmotic thirst are both relieved best by drinking pure water.

    TRUE or FALSE

7. Aldosterone from the adrenal glands increases salt retention and salt hunger.

    TRUE or FALSE

8. Renin from the kidneys splits off a portion of angiotensinogen, forming angiotensin I, which enzymes then convert to angiotensin II, which in turn constricts blood vessels and stimulates drinking.

    TRUE or FALSE

9. Oral factors are sufficient to induce satiety.

    TRUE or FALSE

10. The splanchnic nerve carries information about the nutrient content of the stomach.

    TRUE or FALSE

11. CCK is a powerful stimulus to initiate eating.

    TRUE or FALSE

12. Diabetics have high levels of glucose, but little is able to enter cells.

    TRUE or FALSE

13. Leptin is produced by fat cells; it is a signal to decrease eating, become more active, and increase immune function.

    TRUE or FALSE

14. Ghrelin is a satiety signal in the stomach and the brain.

    TRUE or FALSE

15. Hunger-sensitive cells in the arcuate nucleus send axons containing GABA, neuropeptide Y (NPY), and agouti-related peptide (AgRP) to stimulate the paraventricular nucleus (PVN) in order to begin a meal.

    TRUE or FALSE

16. Satiety-sensitive cells in the arcuate nucleus send axons containing α-melanocyte stimulating hormone (αMSH, a melanocortin) to stimulate the paraventricular nucleus (PVN) in order to end a meal.

    TRUE or FALSE

17. Orexin induces both satiety and sleepiness.

    TRUE or FALSE

18. Lesions of cell bodies in the lateral hypothalamus result in a specific loss of feeding.

    TRUE or FALSE

19. Lesions of the ventromedial hypothalamus result in a voracious appetite that included even foods that were bitter or untasty and produce continued weight gain until the animals died.

    TRUE or FALSE

20. Lesions of the ventromedial nucleus result in more, normal-sized meals; lesions of the paraventricular nucleus result in an unchanged number of larger meals.

    TRUE or FALSE

21. Some cases of obesity may be linked to a mutation in the melanocortin receptor.

    TRUE or FALSE

22. The most successful weight loss treatments combine increase exercise and decreased eating.

    TRUE or FALSE

23. People with gastric bypass surgery eat smaller meals because stomach distention occurs quicker.

    TRUE or FALSE

24. People with Prader-Willi syndrome are severely underweight because they have insufficient ghrelin release.

    TRUE or FALSE

25. People with anorexia nervosa have no interest in food, as a result of a single-gene defect.

    TRUE or FALSE

26. Bulimia nervosa is in some ways like drug addiction.

    TRUE or FALSE

Fill In The Blanks

1. Walter R. Cannon introduced the term _____ to refer to the biological processes that keep certain body variables within a certain range.

2. Animals whose body temperature matches that of the environment are referred to as _____.

3. The _____ / _____ is the primary brain area that controls body temperature.

4. During illness leukocytes produce _____, which in turn result in an increase in body temperature.

5. The two kinds of thirst are _____ and _____.

6. The _____ and _____ (_____) are the main brain areas that detect osmotic pressure.

7. Activity in the _____ and _____ nuclei result in the release of vasopressin from the _____ pituitary.

8. Salt hunger is stimulated by _____ from the adrenal glands and by _____.

9. Low blood pressure stimulates the kidneys to release _____, which results in the production of _____ from angiotensinogen in the blood.

10. The _____ nerve carries information about stomach distension; the _____ nerve carries information about the stomach's nutrient content.

11. The duodenum releases _____ (_____), which inhibits stomach emptying and also acts via the vagus nerve to promote satiety.

12. _____ facilitates glucose entry into cells; _____ promotes the release of glucose from the liver.

13. Hunger-sensitive neurons in the _____ receive input from _____ –containing axons and inhibit the paraventricular nucleus via axons containing _____, _____, and _____.

14. Satiety-sensitive neurons in the arcuate nucleus stimulate the _____ by releasing _____, a(n) _____, thereby ending a meal.

15. Neurons in the _____ promote feeding by increasing insulin secretion, altering taste responsiveness, promoting ingestion, and increasing autonomic responses, such as secretion of digestive juices.

16. Lesions of the _____ hypothalamus increase stomach motility and secretions, increase insulin and fat storage, and speed stomach emptying.

17. _____ is a satiety signal produced by fat cells; it inhibits _____, increases _____, and increases _____ system activity. It can also trigger the onset of _____.

18. A mutation in the _____ receptor gene may underlie some cases of obesity.

19. Studies indicate that rats eating diet yoghurt will _____ weight.

20. The _____ syndrome is characterized by mental retardation, short stature, and obesity that is caused at least in part by high levels of ghrelin.

21. _____ has some characteristics similar to drug addiction.

Matching Items

1. _____ Poikilothermic
2. _____ Homeothermic
3. _____ POA/AH
4. _____ Vasopressin
5. _____ OVLT
6. _____ Osmotic thirst
7. _____ Hypovolemic thirst
8. _____ Renin
9. _____ Vagus nerve
10. _____ Splanchnic nerve
11. _____ Duodenum
12. _____ Lateral hypothalamus
13. _____ Ventromedial hypothalamus
14. _____ Paraventricular nucleus
15. _____ Leptin
16. _____ Bulimia nervosa

a. Brain area that controls temperature
b. Brain area that normally promotes eating
c. Brain area that detects osmotic pressure
d. Lesions → larger meals
e. Lesions → more normal-sized meals per day
f. Carries information about stomach distention
g. Hormone from kidney → angiotensin II
h. Releases CCK to inhibit stomach emptying
i. Peptide hormone produced by fat cells
j. Body temperature relatively constant
k. Result of increased extracellular solutes
l. Hormone → increases blood pressure, thirst
m. Result of loss of blood, vomiting, heavy sweating
n. Characterized by binge eating followed by purging
o. Body temperature similar to environment
p. Carries information about nutrient content

Multiple-Choice Questions

1. Temperature regulation
    a. is an example of a homeostatic mechanism.
    b. is important in mammals and birds for increasing capacity for muscle activity.
    c. maintains body temperature at levels that maximize the enzymatic properties of proteins.
    d. all of the above

2. The preoptic area monitors
    a. only its own temperature.
    b. only skin and spinal cord temperature.
    c. both its own and skin and spinal cord temperature.
    d. the temperature of internal organs via nerve input from those organs.

3. Behavioral means of temperature regulation
    a. are the only means of temperature regulation in poikilotherms.
    b. are the only means of temperature regulation in homeotherms.
    c. do not become functional until adulthood.
    d. are effective only for controlling temperature within the normal range, not to induce
        a fever.

4. Fever
    a. is harmful and should always be reduced with aspirin.
    b. is produced primarily by prostaglandins E1 and E2 acting on cells in the preoptic area.
    c. is produced directly by bacteria acting on the preoptic area.
    d. is especially high in baby rabbits, in response to infections.

5. Vasopressin
    a. raises blood pressure by constricting blood vessels.
    b. is also known as antidiuretic hormone, because it promotes water retention by the kidney.
    c. is secreted from the posterior pituitary, as a result of control by the supraoptic and
        paraventricular nuclei of the hypothalamus.
    d. all of the above.

6. The main reason that a salty meal makes us thirsty is that
    a. excess salt in extracellular fluid produces cellular dehydration; such dehydration of cells
        in the OVLT results in osmotic thirst.
    b. increased salt in extracellular fluid causes the fluid to enter OVLT cells, thus distending
        them and producing osmotic thirst.
    c. increased salt in the blood causes the liquid portion of the blood to enter cells throughout
        the body, thus producing hypovolemia.
    d. the salt enters cells in the OVLT and stimulates them directly.

7. The lateral preoptic area
    a. controls hypovolemic, but not osmotic, thirst.
    b. is the site of receptors for osmotic thirst.
    c. receives input from the OVLT and controls drinking.
    d. primarily responds to signals concerning dryness of the throat.

8. After its blood volume has been reduced, an animal
   a. will drink more pure water than salt water of the same concentration as blood.
   b. will drink more slightly salty water than pure water.
   c. will not drink any more than usual, since both liquid and solute have been removed.
   d. will drink only highly concentrated salt water.

9. Salt hunger
   a. depends in part on aldosterone secreted by the adrenal glands.
   b. is enhanced by angiotensin II.
   c. is mediated by neurons in the nucleus of the tractus solitarius that are activated by aldosterone and angiotensin II.
   d. all of the above

10. Angiotensin II
   a. is secreted by the kidney.
   b. causes water to leave cells in the preoptic area and thereby stimulates osmotic thirst.
   c. stimulates the subfornical organ, which relays the information to the preoptic area, which in turn induces drinking.
   d. all of the above

11. Which of the following is **not** likely to induce drinking?
   a. application of aldosterone to the lateral preoptic area
   b. application of angiotensin II to the subfornical organ
   c. low blood pressure signals from baroreceptors in the large veins
   d. a salty meal

12. In the stomach,
   a. food is mixed with hydrochloric acid and enzymes for the digestion of protein.
   b. food is mixed with hydrochloric acid and enzymes for the digestion of carbohydrates.
   c. food is mixed with enzymes that aid the digestion of fats.
   d. absorption of food through the walls of the stomach occurs.

13. Lactase
   a. is the sugar in milk.
   b. is an intestinal enzyme for the digestion of milk.
   c. is abundant in almost all adult humans, but is lacking in adults of other mammalian species.
   d. is abundant in birds and reptiles, but is lacking in mammals.

14. Oral factors
   a. contribute to satiety but are not sufficient to determine the amount of food consumed.
   b. are irrelevant to satiety.
   c. are the single most important factor in inducing satiety.
   d. include only the taste of food.

15. If a cuff closes the outlet from the stomach to the small intestine
    a. the animal will not eat because of the trauma of the cuff.
    b. the animal will continue eating, since food must pass beyond the stomach to trigger satiety.
    c. the animal will eat a normal-sized meal and stop.
    d. the animal will eat a normal meal, wait for it to be absorbed through the walls of the stomach, and then eat again.

16. Splanchnic nerves
    a. carry information about the nutrient contents of the stomach.
    b. carry information about the stretching of the stomach walls.
    c. are stimulated directly by cholecystokinin (CCK).
    d. secrete CCK into the circulatory system.

17. CCK
    a. is produced by the duodenum in response to the presence of food there.
    b. works, in part, by closing the sphincter muscle between the stomach and duodenum, thus allowing the stomach to fill faster.
    c. is also produced in the brain, where it tends to decrease eating.
    d. all of the above

18. Which of the following is true?
    a. Diabetes results from a deficit in glucagon.
    b. Obese people produce more insulin than do people of normal weight.
    c. Diabetic people produce more insulin than do non-diabetics.
    d. Glucose levels in the blood are elevated by insulin.

19. Insulin
    a. is secreted in response to low blood sugar.
    b. is released by the liver.
    c. is no longer secreted after VMH lesions.
    d. promotes entry of glucose into cells.

20. People with untreated diabetes eat more food because
    a. the vagus and splanchnic nerves are damaged.
    b. they store too much of their glucose, so it is unavailable for use.
    c. they excrete most of their glucose unused.
    d. their basal metabolic rate is too high.

21. Glucagon
    a. is high in the late autumn in migratory and hibernating species.
    b. is produced by the small intestine.
    c. stimulates the liver to convert stored glycogen to glucose for release into the blood.
    d. stimulates the liver to convert glucose to glycogen for storage.

22. Which of the following is true of lateral hypothalamic damage?
    a. It results in inactivity and decreased responsiveness to stimuli.
    b. At least some of the results are due to damage to axons passing through the area, rather than to cell bodies located there.
    c. At least some of the effects on eating are due to low levels of insulin and digestive juices.
    d. All of the above are true.

23. Obesity resulting from damage to the ventromedial hypothalamus and ventral noradrenergic bundle
    a. can be prevented by letting the animals eat only as much as they ate before the lesion.
    b. occurs because the stomach empties faster than usual and insulin secretion is increased.
    c. results from a dramatic increase in the palatability of all foods, resulting in overeating even of bitter or untasty food.
    d. results from eating much larger meals than usual, because of lack of satiety.

24. Which of the following is true of the paraventricular nucleus (PVN)?
    a. It is important for ending a meal.
    b. It is important for beginning a meal.
    c. NPY excites neurons in the PVN.
    d. Leptin increases eating by increasing NPY release in the PVN.

25. Leptin
    a. increases eating.
    b. is a neurotransmitter produced by the brain.
    c. is produced by fat cells.
    d. is reduced in quantity in overweight people.

26. Neuropeptide Y (NPY)
    a. is produced by fat cells and decreases feeding.
    b. directly increases metabolic rate.
    c. decreases fat storage by decreasing the production of leptin.
    d. inhibits activity in the PVN, thereby increasing meal size.

27. Microdialysis
    a. is a means of detecting the release of neurotransmitters.
    b. is a technique used primarily for damaging cell bodies while leaving axons intact.
    c. is a technique used primarily for damaging axons while leaving cell bodies intact.
    d. has been used to demonstrate that CCK is an important hunger signal.

28. Which of the following is true?
    a. Anorexics are frequently hardworking perfectionists.
    b. Bulimics have higher than normal levels of peptide YY (PYY).
    c. Bulimics have lower than normal levels of CCK and altered serotonin receptors.
    d. All of the above are true.

Solutions

True/False Questions

1. T	8. T	15. F	22. T
2. F	9. F	16. T	23. T
3. T	10. T	17. F	24. F
4. T	11. F	18. T	25. F
5. F	12. T	19. F	26. T
6. F	13. T	20. T	
7. T	14. F	21. T	

Fill In The Blanks

1. homeostasis
2. poikilothermic.
3. preoptic area; anterior hypothalamus
4. cytokines
5. osmotic; hypovolemic
6. OVLT; subfornical organ; SFO
7. Supraoptic; paraventricular; posterior
8. Aldosterone; angiotensin II
9. Rennin; angiotensin II
10. Vagus; splanchnic
11. Cholecystokinin; CCK
12. Insulin; glucagon
13. arcuate nucleus; ghrelin; GABA; neuropeptide Y; agouti-related peptide.
14. paraventricular nucleus; α-MSH; melanocortin
15. lateral hypothalamus
16. ventromedial
17. Leptin; eating; activity; immune; puberty
18. melanocortin
19. gain
20. Prader-Willi
21. Bulimia nervosa

Matching Items

1. o	7. m	13. e
2. a	8. g	14. d
3. j	9. f	15. i
4. l	10. p	16. n
5. c	11. h	
6. k	12. b	

Multiple Choice Questions

1. d	8. b	15. c	22. d
2. c	9. d	16. a	23. b
3. a	10. c	17. d	24. a
4. b	11. a	18. b	25. c
5. d	12. a	19. d	26. d
6. a	13. b	20. c	27. a
7. c	14. a	21. c	28. d

CHAPTER 11

Reproductive Behaviors

Introduction

Although sexual reproduction is less efficient than nonsexual reproduction, its major advantages may be shuffling genes to adapt to a changing environment and correcting genetic errors. Sexual reproduction and sex differences are regulated largely by steroid hormones, which are derived from cholesterol. Three types of sex steroid hormones are androgens, which are found in higher concentrations in males; estrogens, which are found in higher concentrations in females; and progesterone, which is found mostly in females and is critical for preparing for and maintaining pregnancy. A number of sex differences are produced by sex-limited genes, which are activated by estrogen or androgen. Hormones, released from endocrine glands, travel in the blood throughout the body. Because of their widespread effects, they are useful for coordinating long-lasting effects.

Sex hormones have two distinct kinds of effects, depending on the stage of development at which they are present. Organizing effects are produced during a sensitive period early in development and are permanent, whereas activating effects can be produced at any time and are temporary. The SRY (sex-determining region on the Y chromosome) gene causes the primitive gonads to develop as testes and to secrete testosterone, which increases growth of the testes and Wolffian ducts (seminal vesicles and vas deferens). The testes also secrete Müllerian inhibiting hormone (MIH), which causes the female reproductive tract to regress. In the absence of the SRY gene, mammals develop as females. Their gonads differentiate into ovaries, their Müllerian ducts differentiate into oviducts, uterus, and upper vagina, and their Wolffian ducts regress. Androgens administered to a genetic female during an early sensitive period masculinize her genitals and behavior, and the absence of androgens results in female-typical appearance and behavior. Numerous drugs, including alcohol, marijuana, an antipsychotic drug, cocaine, and even aspirin, can interfere with behavioral masculinization. Hormones also have organizing effects on the hypothalamus. A sexually dimorphic nucleus in the hypothalamus is larger in males, and a cyclic pattern of hormone release in females is also organized in the hypothalamus. In humans, testosterone itself produces organizing effects on the hypothalamus. However, in rodents androgen exerts its masculinizing effects on behavior mostly by being converted intracellularly to estrogen by the aromatase enzyme. A female is not masculinized by her own and her mother's estrogen because it is bound to alpha-fetoprotein, which prevents it from entering cells. However, small amounts of estrogen are necessary for development of female brains.

When sex hormones are administered during adulthood, they tend to activate whatever behavior patterns were organized during development. These effects can occur within 15 minutes. Also, behaviors can influence hormone secretions. Estrogens enhance sensory responsiveness of the pubic area of female rats. The ventromedial nucleus, medial preoptic area (MPOA), and sexually dimorphic nucleus (SDN) of the anterior hypothalamus are important brain areas for the activational effects of hormones. In female rats, activation of D_1 or D_5 receptors increases receptivity. However, female rats find sex reinforcing only if they control the timing. Similarly, in male rats sex hormones promote dopamine release in the MPOA, which enhances sexual behavior. Moderate levels of dopamine stimulate D_1 or D_5 receptors, which promote erection; higher levels stimulate D_2 receptors and promote ejaculation. Castrated males produce dopamine in the MPOA but fail to release it in response to a female. In humans a sudden increase in dopamine release in several brain areas at the time of orgasm resembles the "rush" produced by addictive drugs. The impairment of sexual arousal and orgasm by some antidepressant drugs results, at least in part, from their inhibition of dopamine release. Testosterone increases men's sexual interest, and their desire to seek sexual partners. Decreases in sex hormones may impair memory and affect the numbers of neurotransmitter receptors in numerous brain areas, as well as decrease sexual activity. However, low testosterone is not usually the source of impotence. Testosterone increases the production of the gaseous molecule nitric oxide (NO), which increases blood flow to the penis and also increases activity in the hypothalamus. The drug sildenafil (Viagra) prolongs the effects of nitric oxide. Although sex offenders are a diverse group, most of whom have average testosterone levels, treatments that reduce testosterone production or block its receptors have been used with some success. However, dropping out of treatment is a frequent problem.

In women and certain other female primates, menstrual cycles result from interaction between the hypothalamus, pituitary, and ovaries. Follicle-stimulating hormone (FSH) from the anterior pituitary stimulates the growth of ovarian follicles and the secretion of estrogen from the follicles. Increasing estrogen at first decreases the release of FSH, but near the middle of the cycle, it somehow causes a sudden surge of luteinizing hormone (LH) and FSH. These hormones cause an ovum to be released. They also cause the remnant of the follicle (the corpus luteum) to release progesterone, which causes the uterine lining to proliferate in preparation for implantation of a fertilized ovum. Progesterone inhibits release of LH; therefore, near the end of the cycle, all hormones are low, resulting in menstruation if fertilization does not occur. If the ovum is fertilized, estradiol and progesterone increase throughout the pregnancy. Combination birth-control pills contain estrogen and progesterone, which prevent the surge of LH and FSH necessary for the release of an ovum. They also thicken the cervical mucus and prevent implantation of an ovum in the uterus. Women's sexual interest is higher during the periovulatory period. Sex hormones also affect women's preference for somewhat masculinized, as opposed to feminized, men's faces, with a peak of preference for masculinized faces and more athletic, competitive men in the periovulatory period. Oxytocin stimulates uterine contractions during labor and stimulates milk release from the mammary glands. It is also released at orgasm and promotes complete relaxation shortly after orgasm.

Parental behavior in rodents can be rapidly induced by hormonal patterns characteristic of the time of delivery, including increased levels of estradiol, prolactin, and oxytocin. This suggests that the immediate maternal behavior that occurs with delivery may be under hormonal control.

Hormones increase activity in the medial preoptic area and anterior hypothalamus, which are important for parental behavior, as well as for temperature regulation, thirst, and sexual behavior. Vasopressin can induce male prairie voles to form long-term bonds with females and help rear their young. Repeated exposure to pups can induce parental behavior after about six days, even in females without ovaries. However, pheromones from the young animals initially suppress parental behavior; it is only after the adoptive mother becomes accustomed to their odors that parental behavior occurs. Thus, there are two phases of maternal behavior, an early phase that is elicited by hormones and a later phase that depends on familiarity with the young. However, hormonal changes are not necessary for parental behavior in humans, except to permit a woman to nurse a baby.

There are a number of differences between men and women in some aspects of their sexual activities and in the qualities that they prefer in their mates. An evolutionary explanation for men's greater interest in short-term sexual relationships with many partners suggests that males typically seek to spread their genes, whereas females have a greater investment in a small number of offspring. However, females may also benefit from having multiple sexual partners, including greater fertility and a chance for a better mate. Both men and women prefer a healthy, intelligent, honest, physically attractive mate. In addition, women seek good providers, especially in societies where women have little economic power. On the other hand, men tend to seek younger partners because they are more likely to be fertile. However, male chimpanzees prefer older, but still fertile, females that are more likely to have a higher social rank. Women are less concerned with age because men are fertile into old age. Women tend to prefer men with dissimilar body odor, which results from immune system genes that also regulate body odor. This preference may prevent inbreeding. Studies of responses in hypothetical situations have suggested that men are more likely to be upset by sexual infidelity, whereas women are more upset by emotional infidelity. However, a study of people's responses to actual situations found that both men and women were more upset by emotional infidelity. The fact that similar sex differences are found in many cultures does not necessarily imply that they have genetic bases.

Humans are variable in their sexual development and gender identity. Early fetal gonadal structures differentiate in either a male or a female direction, depending on the presence or absence of the SRY gene. Some XY males have a mutation of the SRY gene, resulting in poorly developed genitals. Some XX females have an SRY gene translocated from their father's Y chromosome to another chromosome, which may result in some ovary and some testis tissue. If a female is exposed to excess androgen during the critical period for sex differentiation, due to congenital adrenal hyperplasia (CAH), she may develop structures intermediate between those of a normal female and a normal male. Adolescent girls with CAH show more interest in sports magazines than glamour magazines and are more likely to show homosexual or bisexual interests or low interest in any sexual activity. These differences occurred in spite of parental encouragement of girl-typical play. A sexually ambiguous condition may occur if a genetic male has low levels of testosterone or is unresponsive to it. Such individuals are called intersexes or pseudohermaphrodites. Most intersexes have been reared as females, since it is easier to feminize the genitals surgically than to masculinize them. However, the surgery often impairs genital sensation and results in other physical problems. Many of those who had the surgery neonatally resent the deception by their parents and physicians. A genetic male may develop a relatively normal female appearance and gender identity because of testicular feminization (androgen insensitivity), due to a lack of androgen receptors. Genetic males with cloacal exstrophy, a defect in pelvic development that results in a very small penis, were often raised as girls. However, they developed male interests, and most asked to be reassigned as males. In the Dominican Republic some genetic males lack an enzyme (5-α reductase) that converts testosterone to dihydrotestosterone. Because dihydrotestosterone is more effective than testosterone for masculinizing the genitals, these boys appeared to be girls early in life; however, they became masculinized by high levels of testosterone at puberty. They then developed male gender identity, which was consistent with their prenatal testosterone. One genetic male, whose penis was accidentally removed at birth, did not develop a female identity, despite attempts by his parents to raise him as a girl. He later declared a male gender identity, married a woman, and adopted her children. Tragically, he later committed suicide. These cases suggest that prenatal hormones play an important role in determining gender identity, although environmental factors may have some influence.

Homosexual or bisexual behavior occurs in both humans and nonhumans. Several genetic and prenatal factors may predispose males to homosexuality. There is weaker genetic influence on female homosexuality, and more women are attracted to both women and men. There are studies in humans that show subtle sex differences in the length of bones, size or projections of brain structures, the tendency to give directions in terms of landmarks rather than compass directions, and the ability of a weak noise to suppress a startle response to a loud noise. In some of these comparisons homosexual men or women have measurements that resemble those of the opposite sex or fall between those of heterosexual men and women. Homosexuals may be shifted toward the opposite sex in some ways, but not others. These differences suggest that sexual orientation is not an arbitrary decision, but may be influenced by biological factors.

Genetic factors may promote homosexual orientation in both men and women. Monozygotic (identical) twins of homosexuals are more likely to be homosexual than are dizygotic (fraternal) twins or other biological or adopted siblings. One study suggested that a gene that contributes to male homosexuality is on the X chromosome, and therefore is inherited from the mother; however, later studies did not replicate these results. A gene that increases homosexuality, and therefore decreases reproductive success, would be expected to be selected against in the course of evolution. The theory that it may be perpetuated through kin selection has been discredited. There is evidence that the reproductive ability of women who carry the gene is increased, but not enough to offset the decreased reproduction of their gay brothers. Some genes may confer an advantage if present as a single copy (heterozygous), but may predispose to homosexuality if present in two copies (homozygous) or in the presence of other genes. Finally, homosexuality may be influenced by the methylation (attachment of a CH_3 molecule) of a gene, thereby inactivating it. Such inactivation of genes can be passed on to the next generation.

Homosexuality is not correlated with hormone levels in adulthood. However, animal studies suggest that pre- or early postnatal hormones can produce organizational effects on anatomy and sexual behavior. Men who have older brothers are more likely to be homosexual than are oldest sons. Perhaps the mother's immune system reacts to a protein in a son and then attacks that protein in later sons. In rats, prenatal stress or alcohol feminized the adult behavior of the male offspring; the combination of stress and alcohol demasculinized, as well as feminized, the offspring. These effects appeared to be mediated by endorphins, which antagonize the effects of testosterone, and by corticosterone, which decreases testosterone levels. There is some evidence for a similar effect of stress in humans, though the data are based on mothers' memories of events 20 years before. Some brain structures show sex differences in size. For some of these structures, including the anterior commissure, the suprachiasmatic nucleus, and the interstitial nucleus 3 of the hypothalamus, homosexual men have structures more similar in size to those of women than to those of heterosexual men. The smaller size of INAH3 in homosexual men is due to decreased size, but not number, of neurons and is not due to AIDS. We do not know whether these differences are a cause or an effect of homosexuality, or indeed, if they are relevant at all. However, a similar nucleus in female-oriented rams is larger than in male-oriented rams, and that difference is due to higher prenatal testosterone. This suggests that the hormonal difference led to the behavioral difference.

Learning Objectives

Module 11.1 Sex and Hormones
1. Know the three types of sex hormones and the three ways they can exert their effects.
2. Understand the roles of genes and hormones in the organization of physical and behavioral sex differences in mammals.
3. Understand the activating roles of hormones on reproductive behaviors and neurotransmitters in certain brain areas.
4. Understand the hormonal processes that control women's menstrual cycles and pregnancy, including the effects of birth-control pills.
5. Know the endocrine influences on parental behaviors.

Module 11.2 Variations in Sexual Behavior
1. Be familiar with evolutionary interpretations of mate choice and jealousy.
2. Know the genetic and hormonal factors that can produce intersexes and other discrepancies in sexual appearance.
3. Understand the genetic and hormonal influences on gender identity and sexual orientation.

Key Terms and Concepts

Module 11.1 Sex and Hormones
1. Organizing effects of sex hormones
    What good is sex?
        Reshuffles genes to adapt to changing environment
        Corrects genetic errors
    Steroid hormones
        Four carbon rings
        Derived from cholesterol
        Three ways to exert effects
            Bind to membrane receptors
            Enter cell, activate proteins in cytoplasm
            Activate or inactivate specific genes
        Types of sex hormones

Androgens
    Testosterone
Estrogens
    Estradiol
Progesterone
Sex differences
    Sex-limited genes: Activated by estrogen or androgen
        Estrogen → breast development
        Androgen → facial hair growth
        Hormones → different rates of apoptosis (cell death) in brain
    Three genes on Y chromosome: Active in specific brain areas
    One gene on X chromosome: Active only in female brains
    Y chromosome: Many sites that do not code for proteins but alter expression of genes on other chromosomes
Organizing effects of hormones
    Permanent change
    Sensitive stage of development
Activating effects
    Temporary activation of a response
    May last longer than hormone remains in organ, but not indefinitely
    Difference is not absolute
        Some temporary early differences
        Some long-lasting effects during puberty
Sex differences in the gonads
    Chromosomes
        Female: XX
        Male: XY
    Gonads: identical in very early stage
    Male (XY)
        SRY gene (sex-determining region on the Y) → testes → testosterone →
        Testes grow → more testosterone → Wolffian ducts → seminal vesicles and vas deferens
        MIH (Müllerian inhibiting hormone) → degeneration of Müllerian ducts
        Testosterone also → formation of penis, scrotum
    Female (XX)
        Ovaries (egg-producing organs)
        Müllerian ducts mature → oviducts, uterus, upper vagina
        Wolffian ducts degenerate
    Sensitive period for testosterone's effects
        Humans: Third and fourth months of pregnancy
        Rats: Last few days of pregnancy and first few postnatal days
        Masculinization of female rats by testosterone injections
        Low levels of sex hormones → female development
        Drugs that block androgen effects or remove hormones → demasculinization
            Alcohol, marijuana, haloperidol (antipsychotic drug), cocaine, aspirin
        Small amounts of estradiol necessary for female brain development

          Estradiol or estradiol-like compounds → malformation of prostate in males

       Sex differences in the hypothalamus

          Anterior hypothalamus

             Sexually dimorphic nucleus: Larger in males

          Cyclic pattern of hormone release in females

          Aromatization of testosterone to estradiol

             Alpha-fetoprotein: Protects some female mammals from prenatal estradiol

             Primates: Protected by metabolism of estradiol

             Estradiol injection → masculinizes female rodents

                Exceeds normal binding by alpha-fetoprotein or metabolism

2.   Activating effects of sex hormones

       Relationship to behavior

          Doves: Behavior → hormone change → behavior → hormone change, etc.

          Hormones → alter responsiveness of brain, peripheral structures to certain stimuli

       Rodents

          Sexual experience sensitizes response to future stimuli

          Dependent on hormones

          Testosterone and its metabolites, dihydrotestosterone and estradiol → masculine behavior

          Estrogen followed by progesterone → feminine behavior

          Pudendal nerve: Tactile stimulation from pubic area to brain

             Estrogens increase its sensitivity

          Ventromedial nucleus

          Medial preoptic area (MPOA)

             Sexually dimorphic nucleus: Exact importance unclear

                Stimulation → sexual behavior in rats

                Lesions → only mild deficits

             Dopamine

                Released in male MPOA in presence of female

                Facilitates copulation

                Males: Testosterone → release of dopamine in MPOA

                Castration → normal production of dopamine, but no release with female

                Moderate dopamine levels → D_1 and D_5 receptors → erection in male and receptivity in female

                Higher dopamine levels → D_2 receptors → ejaculation and orgasm

          Orgasm → dopamine in several brain areas similar to "rush" of addictive drugs

             Serotonin inhibits dopamine release and sexual behavior

             Antidepressant drugs increase serotonin, decrease sexual arousal, orgasm

          Female rats: Sex is reinforcing only if she controls the pace

       Humans

          Effects of hormones on brain

             Testosterone (and maybe estrogen) decreases pain and anxiety

             Decrease in sex hormones → memory impairment

             Estrogen → increased dendritic spines in hippocampus

             Estrogen → increased certain dopamine and serotonin receptors in several brain areas

Men
  Correlation of testosterone levels and sexual excitement
  Testosterone levels greater in unpaired men than in men with committed relationship
    Men with lower testosterone more likely to marry
    Men with high testosterone that marry still seek additional partners
  Impotence
    Not usually due to low testosterone
    Impaired blood circulation, neurological problems, reactions to drugs, psychological tension
  Mechanism of erection
    Testosterone → nitric oxide (NO) in hypothalamus and penis → blood flow to penis
  Sex offenders: Reduce testosterone → reduced sexual activities
    High testosterone levels don't explain offenders' behavior
    Child molesters do have higher testosterone
    If men take drugs that lower testosterone, they show decreased deviant behavior.
      Many drop out of the program
Women
  Menstrual cycle (~28 days)
  FSH (follicle stimulating hormone)
    Promotes growth of follicle, which nurtures ovum
    Increases secretion of estradiol by follicle
  Estradiol
    Decreases FSH, but follicle increases FSH receptors → increased estradiol → surge of LH (luteinizing hormone) and FSH
  LH and FSH
    Release ovum
    Increase secretion of progesterone by corpus luteum (remnant of follicle)
  Progesterone from corpus luteum
    Prepares lining of uterus
    Inhibits LH release
  Menstruation: Due to decreased hormone levels
  If pregnancy: Estrogen and progesterone increase
    Fluctuating activity at serotonin 5-HT$_3$ receptors → nausea
  Birth-control pills
    Combination pill: Both estrogen and progesterone
    Prevents FSH and LH surge
    Thickens cervical mucus → sperm can't reach egg
    Prevents ovum from implanting
  Periovulatory period
    Increased estrogen levels
    Maximum fertility and sexual interest
      Lap dancers: more tips

Prefer more masculine-looking faces & more athletic, competitive men during periovulatory period

Oxytocin

Stimulaltes uterine contractions during labor

Stimulates mammary gland to release milk

Released at orgasm → relaxation and decreased anxiety

Promotes pair bond formation between mating partners and between mom and baby

3. Parental behavior

Hormone-dependent early phase

Estradiol

Prolactin → milk production, maternal and paternal behavior

Oxytocin → maternal behavior, sexual arousal, social attachment, enhancement of learning

Hormones → paternal behavior in some species

Increased estrogen receptors in medial preoptic area, anterior hypothalamus → maternal behavior

Vasopressin: Synthesized in hypothalamus, secreted by posterior pituitary

Male prairie voles: Vasopressin → pair bonding, paternal behavior

Male meadow voles with increased activity of gene for vasopressin → preference for mate, paternal behavior

Experience-dependent later phase

Not hormone-dependent

Decreased response to aversive pheromones from pups

Vomeronasal organ

Hormones not necessary in humans

4. In closing: Reproductive behaviors and motivations

No need to understand purpose of behavior

Sexual activity feels good

Mother rat licks pups to get salt

Module 11.2 Variations in Sexual Behavior

1. Evolutionary interpretations of mating behavior

Birds: The sex with dull-colored feathers sits on nest

Interest in multiple mates

Men: More interest in short-term sexual relations with multiple partners → spread genes

Women: May sometimes gain from multiple partners

Infertile mate; gifts; "trade up"

What men and women seek in a mate

Both prefer healthy, intelligent, honest, attractive mate

Women

Prefer good provider

Women more cautious during courtship

Prefer man with dissimilar body odor

Major histocompatibility complex genes control immune system, body odor

Dissimilar odor may prevent inbreeding
Men
    Prefer younger partner: Greater fertility
    Women less concerned with age: men fertile into old age
Male chimpanzees prefer older but still fertile females
    Higher social rank
Differences in jealousy
    Men: Hypothetically more upset by sexual infidelity
    Women: Hypothetically more upset by emotional infidelity
    Actual infidelity: Both men and women more upset at emotional infidelity
Evolved or learned?
    Difficult to separate genetic influences from learned tendencies
Conclusions
    Morality different from scientific questions

2.   Gender identity and gender-differentiated behaviors
Coral goby: Changes sex if partner dies and no new partner of opposite sex appears
Sex differences: Biological
Gender differences: What we think of ourselves
Gender identity: Sexual identification
    Human characteristic
    Previously assumed to be mainly or entirely based on rearing
    Biological factors also important
Intersexes
    Atypical chromosomes
        XY, with mutation of SRY
        XX, with translocated SRY from father's Y onto another chromosome
    Atypical hormone pattern
        Males: Low testosterone, mutation of androgen receptors
        Excess androgens in females: Congenital adrenal hyperplasia (CAH)
            Adrenal glands: Insufficient cortisol → lack of feedback → excess ACTH → testosterone and other androgens from adrenal gland
    True hermaphrodites: Some testicular and some ovarian tissue
    Intersexes or pseudohermaphrodites: Intermediate appearance
Interests and preferences of CAH girls
    Genetic females with CAH: Usually reared as girls
        Intermediate preferences for girl-typical and boy-typical toys
            Parents had encouraged girl-typical play
        Slight increase in boy-typical toys even in normal girls whose mothers had high normal testosterone during pregnancy
    Adolescent CAH girls: more sports magazines, fewer glamour magazines
    Increased incidence of homosexual or bisexual activity
    Increased number with low interest in any sexual activity
Testicular feminization or androgen insensitivity
    XY genotype
    Lack of androgen receptors
    Varying degrees of feminization

Some appear to be normal females
    Puberty: Breast development, broadening hips, but no menstruation
    Internal testes: Testosterone → estradiol
    Sparse or absent pubic hair
Issues of gender assignment and rearing
    Cloacal exstrophy: Genetic male with defective pelvis development, elevated prenatal testosterone, small penis
    1950s: All intersexes reared as girls
        Surgery → genitals look normal
    Males with cloacal exstrophy and reared as girls: All developed male interests
        Most wanted reassignment as males
        Attracted to women, not men
    Girls with CAH
        Surgery to reduce clitoris and lengthen vagina → no sensation, much effort to prevent scarring over, significant sexual difficulty
        Many resent deception
        Recommendations
            Be honest, do nothing without informed consent
            Choose sex of rearing by predominant external appearance
            Rear the child consistently, but accept later choice to be different
            Do not perform surgery to "correct" genitals until adulthood
Discrepancies of sexual appearance
    Penis development delayed until puberty
        Decreased 5α-reductase 2 (enzyme that converts testosterone to dihydrotestosterone)
        Dihydrotestosterone more effective in masculinizing genitals
        Puberty → different enzyme to convert testosterone to dihydrotestosterone → masculinize genitals
        Male gender identity after puberty, perhaps due to early testosterone effects on brain
    Accidental removal of the penis, reared as a girl
        Preferred boys' toys
        Age 14: Wanted to live as a boy, was finally told truth
        Age 25: Married a woman, adopted her children
        Later: Committed suicide
3.   Sexual orientation
    Male homosexuality
        Several predisposing factors
        Several anatomical and behavioral correlates
    Female homosexuality
        Weaker genetic predisposition than in men
        Masculine-type behaviors less predictive
        More women: Attracted to both women and men
        More women: Switch orientations one or more times
    Behavioral and anatomical differences
        Arm, leg, and hand bones

Longer in heterosexual than homosexual men
Longer in homosexual than heterosexual women
Size of cortical hemispheres
Heterosexual women: Nearly equal
Heterosexual men: Slightly larger on right
Homosexual men: Similar to women
Homosexual women: Intermediate between heterosexual men and women
Connections of amygdala
Heterosexual women: More widespread on left side
Heterosexual men: More widespread on right side
Homosexual men: Similar to women
Homosexual women: Intermediate
Giving directions
Heterosexual women: Landmarks
Heterosexual men: North, south, east, west
Homosexual men: Similar to women
Prepulse inhibition
Weak noise decreases startle response to louder noise just after it
Usually stronger in men than in women
Homosexual men: No different from heterosexual men
Homosexual women: Shifted in male direction
Sexual orientation not an arbitrary decision
Complex situation
Homosexuals shifted toward opposite sex in some ways, not others
Differences apply only on average
Genetics
Greater similarity of orientation in monozygotic (identical) twins > dizygotic
(fraternal) twins > adopted siblings > population at large
Both genetic and environmental factors
Greater genetic influence in men than women
A few genes implicated
Gene on X chromosome may increase male homosexuality; inconclusive data
An evolutionary question
May be perpetuated by kin selection: Not supported by survey data
May increase reproductive success of women relatives: Supported by one study
Not enough to offset decrease in reproduction by gay brother
Some genes may → advantages if present alone (heterozygous), but may →
homosexuality if homozygous or coupled with other gene(s)
Activation vs. inactivation (via methylation) of genes
Methylation of genes passed on to offspring without changing the gene
Prenatal influences
No consistent differences in adult hormone levels between heterosexual and gay men
or heterosexual and lesbian women
Increased probability of homosexuality in men with older biological brothers
Mother's immune system attacks a certain protein in later sons?
Holds only for right-handed younger brothers

Prenatal stress <u>or</u> alcohol in rats → males' sexual behavior feminized
    Both stress <u>and</u> alcohol → sexual behavior also demasculinized
    Endorphins → antitestosterone effects
    Stress → corticosterone → decrease testosterone release
    Prenatal stress or alcohol → feminized brain structures
Prenatal stress in humans may predispose sons to homosexuality
    Data based on memories from 20 years before: May not be reliable
  Brain anatomy
  Anterior commissure
    Larger in women and homosexual men
  Suprachiasmatic nucleus (SCN)
    Larger in homosexual than heterosexual men
    Deprivation of testosterone during development of male rats
      Abnormalities in SCN
      Sexual advances to both males and females early in day, mostly to
      females later
  Interstitial nucleus 3 of anterior hypothalamus
    Larger in heterosexual men than in women and homosexual men
    Differences not due to AIDS, though AIDS may also decrease volume
    Heterosexual men: Larger neurons, but ~ same number
    Cause vs. effect of behavior?
    Functions unclear
    Anterior hypothalamic area in female-oriented rams larger > male-oriented rams,
    which is in turn larger > females
      Testosterone increases this area prenatally: Not due to behavior
4. In closing: We are not all the same
    Biological understanding may increase acceptance of diversity

Short-Answer Questions

Module 11.1 Sex and Hormones

1. *Organizing effects of sex hormones*

   a. What are two advantages of sexual, as opposed to asexual, reproduction?

   b. What is an advantage of hormonal communication, compared to communication by neurotransmitters at synapses?

   c. Name the three types of sex hormones. What are three ways in which they exert their effects?

   d. What is a sex-limited gene? How do sex-limited genes produce sex differences in physical characteristics and behavior?

   e. Distinguish between organizing effects and activating effects of hormones.

   f. What is the SRY gene? Describe the chain of events that result from its presence during development.

g. What are Müllerian ducts? What are Wolffian ducts? What directs the survival or regression of these ducts in males and females?

h. When is the sensitive period for testosterone's effects on humans? On rats?

i. Describe the effects of testosterone injections on female rats during the last few days before birth and the first few days after birth.

j. What is the external appearance of a mammal that was exposed to neither androgens nor estrogens during early development? Which hormone is required in low amounts for brain differentiation in females?

k. By what mechanism does testosterone exert its effects on the hypothalamus in rodents?

l. What are two sex differences in the structure or function of the hypothalamus?

m. What is the role of alpha-fetoprotein?

2. *Activating effects of sex hormones*

a. Which hormones can restore male-typical sexual behavior in rodents following castration? What is the most effective hormone treatment for restoring female-typical behavior?

b. What is the pudendal nerve? What are estrogen's effects on its function?

c. What brain area may facilitate male-typical behavior in males?

d. What neurotransmitter in the MPOA stimulates male sexual activity? How does castration affect the release of that neurotransmitter in the MPOA?

e. What may be the role of this neurotransmitter in the progression from the early stages of copulation, which require erection in males and the receptive posture in females, to the stage of orgasm?

f. How may antidepressant drugs that increase serotonin activity decrease sexual arousal and orgasm?

g. What factor is important in determining whether sexual activity is reinforcing in female rats?

h. Describe the relationship between testosterone levels and sexual activity in men. Which other hormone contributes to sexual pleasure?

i. How does nitric oxide contribute to erection? What is the role of sildenafil (Viagra)?

j. What type of drugs has been used to treat sex offenders? Have they been successful?

k. List the chain of hormonal processes in the menstrual cycle.

l. What are the two functions of the follicle?

m. Rising levels of which hormone cause a sudden surge of luteinizing hormone (LH) and follicle-stimulating hormone (FSH) near the middle of the cycle? What is the effect of that surge on the ovum?

n. What is the corpus luteum, and what hormone does it release?

o. What are the effects of progesterone? Describe the levels of the major hormones shortly before menstruation.

p. How do combination birth-control pills work?

q. Describe the effect of women's menstrual cycles on their sexual interest and their preference for masculinized vs. feminized faces and for athletic, competitive men.

r. What are four effects of oxytocin?

3. *Parental behavior*

a. Which three hormones have been shown to promote maternal behavior in birds and mammals? Can hormones also promote paternal behavior in some species? Which other behaviors are increased by oxytocin.

b. What brain area is important for these hormonal effects?

c. Describe the differences between male prairie voles and male meadow voles in their relationships to females with which they have mated and to their offspring. What hormone is responsible for this difference?

d. Compare the roles of hormones and experience in parental behavior of rodents. Are the effects of experience mediated by hormonal changes?

e. What are the effects of pheromones released by infant rats on females that have not had hormonal priming or previous maternal experience?

Module 11.2 Variations in Sexual Behavior

1. *Evolutionary interpretations of mating behavior*

a. What are some differences between men and women in mate preference?

b. Give an evolutionary explanation for each of these.

c. How did the results of studies of sex differences in jealousy differ when hypothetical vs. actual cases of infidelity were examined?

d. How certain can we be that sex differences that are fairly consistent across cultures have a genetic basis?

2. *Gender identity and gender-differentiated behaviors*

a. What is gender identity?

b. What is an intersex?

c. What are some developmental influences that may produce an intersex individual?

d. What is the most common cause of the intersex condition? Describe the normal relationship between the adrenal gland and the anterior pituitary. How is this relationship altered in congenital adrenal hyperplasia (CAH)?

e. What is the difference between a true hermaphrodite and an intersex?

f. Describe the choice of toys by girls with CAH. Is this a result of parental encouragement?

g. Describe the chromosomal pattern and the genital appearance of individuals with androgen insensitivity (testicular feminization). What causes the unresponsiveness to androgen? What two abnormalities appear at puberty?

h. What is cloacal exstrophy?

i. Why have most intersexes been reared as females?

j. How successful is the surgical treatment of intersexes?

k. Describe two situations in which children were exposed to the prenatal hormonal pattern of one sex and then reared as the opposite sex. What can we infer from these situations about the relative importance of early rearing experiences and hormones as determinants of gender identity?

3. *Sexual orientation*

a. In which sex is there a greater genetic predisposition towards homosexuality? In which sex is there a higher percentage of at least some attraction to both males and females?

b. Describe the findings regarding the length of arm, leg, and hand bones in heterosexual and homosexual men and women. Do these differences begin before or after puberty?

c. Describe the sex difference in the relative size of the cerebral hemispheres. How do homosexual men and women compare on this measure?

d. Describe the sex difference in the projections from the amygdala. How do homosexual men and women compare on this measure?

e. How do women tend to give directions to a given place? How do heterosexual men tend to give directions? How do homosexual men tend to give directions?

f. What is prepulse inhibition? Is it usually stronger in men or women? Are such measures in homosexual men or women shifted from those of heterosexual men or women?

g. What conclusions can we draw from twin studies about genetic and environmental influences on homosexuality?

h. Describe the evidence for increased incidence of homosexuality among maternal relatives of homosexual men. How would this implicate a gene on the X chromosome? Have the early findings been replicated?

i. Discuss the problems concerning evolutionary selection of any genes predisposing toward homosexuality.

j. What are four possible explanations for the continued existence of genes that predispose toward homosexuality? Which of these has received some support?

k. Can hormone levels in adulthood account for sexual orientation? What is a more plausible hypothesis concerning hormonal influence on sexual orientation?

l. What explanation may account for the greater probability of homosexuality in men with older brothers than in men who were the oldest son?

m. Describe the experiments on the effects of stress and alcohol on sex differentiation of rats. What were their results?

n. How may endorphins be implicated in the effects of stress? How may corticosterone mediate the effects of stress?

o. How good is the evidence regarding possible prenatal stress effects in homosexual men?

p. What are three brain structures that show a sex difference in size? In which direction is the size difference for each? How do homosexual men compare with heterosexual men and with women regarding the size of these structures?

q. Describe LeVay's evidence implicating the interstitial nucleus 3 of the hypothalamus in homosexuality. Was AIDS a likely cause of those differences?

r. If there is a consistent difference between homosexual and heterosexual men in the size of various brain nuclei, what can we conclude about the role of these nuclei in determining sexual orientation?

s. What brain area is larger in female-oriented than in male-oriented rams? What is the cause of this difference?

True/False Questions

1. Some receptors for steroid hormones are in the cell membrane and activate second messenger systems similar to those of metabotropic neurotransmitters; others activate proteins in the cytoplasm; and still others move to the nucleus when bound to hormone and alter gene expression.

   TRUE or FALSE

2. The Wolffian ducts are precursors to the internal female reproductive structures.

   TRUE or FALSE

3. The SRY gene on the Y chromosome causes the primitive gonads to differentiate into testes, which secrete testosterone, which in turn leads to masculine development of the genitals and, either directly or through its metabolites, of the brain.

   TRUE or FALSE

4. The sexually dimorphic nucleus (SDN) of the hypothalamus is larger in females, because it generates a cyclic pattern of hormone release.

   TRUE or FALSE

5. Female rodents are not masculinized by their own and their mother's estrogen because the aromatase enzyme rapidly converts it to progesterone.

   TRUE or FALSE

6. Hormones activate behavior, in part, by altering the responsiveness of certain brain areas and of the genitals to sexually relevant stimuli.

   TRUE or FALSE

7. Moderate concentrations of dopamine in rats stimulate D_1 and D_5 receptors, which facilitate erections in males and sexually receptive postures in females.

   TRUE or FALSE

8. Sildenafil (Viagra) promotes erections by increasing testosterone release.

    TRUE or FALSE

9. Birth-control pills containing estrogen and progesterone prevent the mid-cycle surge of LH and FSH and also thicken the mucus of the cervix and prevent implantation of an ovum.

    TRUE or FALSE

10. Hormones promote maternal behavior by increasing activity in the MPOA and anterior hypothalamus.

    TRUE or FALSE

11. Hormones that promote parental behavior in some species include estrogen, prolactin, oxytocin, and vasopressin.

    TRUE or FALSE

12. A major stimulus for maternal behavior is the detection of attractant pheromones produced by infant rats.

    TRUE or FALSE

13. Although both men and women seek mates that are healthy, intelligent, honest, and physically attractive, women also seek mates that will be good providers, and men seek mates that are young.

    TRUE or FALSE

14. Although men say that they would be more upset by sexual infidelity than emotional infidelity, a recent study found that both men and women are more upset by emotional infidelity.

    TRUE or FALSE

15. Intersexes have been usually reared as boys, because it has long been known that even moderate amounts of prenatal testosterone will lead to a male gender identity.

    TRUE or FALSE

16. Congenital adrenal hyperplasia (CAH) is the most common cause of the intersex condition.

    TRUE or FALSE

17. Testicular feminization occurs when the testes secrete large amounts of estrogen, rather than testosterone.

    TRUE or FALSE

18. The lack of the enzyme that converts testosterone to dihydrotestosterone results in children that appear to be boys at birth, but who start secreting estrogen at puberty, causing them to switch to a female identity.

    TRUE or FALSE

19. There is some evidence that female relatives of gay men have more offspring than do other women; however, that probably is not sufficient to offset the decreased reproduction of gay men.

    TRUE or FALSE

CHAPTER 11

20. It is now generally accepted that some gay men have inherited a gene on the Y chromosome, passed on to them from their father, which predisposed them to homosexuality.

TRUE or FALSE

21. A major factor in predisposing men to homosexuality is that they have low levels of testosterone in adulthood.

TRUE or FALSE

22. Prenatal stress may alter brain development, in part, by increasing the release of endorphins, which can affect the fetus's hypothalamus, and in part by increasing release of corticosterone, which decreases the release of testosterone.

TRUE or FALSE

23. The INAH-3 nucleus is larger in heterosexual men than in women and homosexual men.

TRUE or FALSE

Fill In The Blanks

1. The three types of sex hormones are _____, _____, and _____.

2. The gene that directs the primitive gonad to become a testis is the _____ gene.

3. The _____ ducts develop into the oviducts, uterus, and upper vagina.

4. The _____ ducts develop into the seminal vesicles and vas deferens.

5. The protein that binds estradiol in the blood of some immature animals, thereby protecting females from their own and their mother's estradiol, is _____.

6. The enzyme that converts testosterone to estradiol is _____.

7. The neurotransmitter _____ is released in the _____ of male rats and promotes sexual behavior.

8. Sildenafil (Viagra) prolongs the effects of _____ and thereby increases blood engorgement of the penis.

9. Antidepressant drugs that increase activity of the neurotransmitter _____ can interfere with sexual arousal and orgasm by decreasing release of the neurotransmitter _____.

10. Combination birth control pills work by preventing the surge of _____ and _____ that would normally release an ovum, by _____ the _____ of the cervix, and by preventing implantation of the ovum in the uterus.

11. Increased levels of _____, _____, and _____ around the time of birth increases maternal behavior by activating neurons in the _____ and _____.

12. _____ promotes pair bonding and paternal behavior in male prairie voles.

13. Men tend to prefer a _____ partner; women tend to prefer a mate who is a good _____.

14. A person who develops genitals intermediate between those of typical males and females is known as a(n) _____.

15. The condition in which insufficient cortisol production in fetuses results in excessive production of androgens by the adrenal gland is _____.

16. People with an XY chromosome pattern but who lack androgen receptors and appear to be female have a condition known as _____ or _____.

17. A defect in pelvis development that can result an unusually small penis is

    _____.

18. Delay of development of a penis until puberty can result from a genetic defect in the enzyme _____, which converts testosterone into _____.

19. Evidence favoring a genetic predisposition to homosexuality includes the observation that the concordance rate for homosexuality among _____ (or _____) twins is higher than that for _____ (or _____) twins; however, environmental factors are also important, because the concordance rate is less than 100%, and is higher in adopted siblings than in the population at large.

20. One means of producing a heritable influence on homosexuality without mutating a gene is to attach a(n) _____ group to it and thereby _____ it.

21. Prenatal stress increases the release of _____ and of _____, which can impair masculine development of the brain.

22. The _____ is a brain nucleus that is larger in heterosexual men than in women and homosexual men. However, the interpretation of this finding is not clear.

Matching Items

1. _____ Major histocompatibility complex genes
2. _____ Estrogen, prolactin, oxytocin
3. _____ Pudendal nerve
4. _____ Müllerian ducts
5. _____ Wolffian ducts
6. _____ Alpha-fetoprotein
7. _____ Aromatase
8. _____ Dopamine increases in brain
9. _____ LH and FSH surge
10. _____ Progesterone
11. _____ 5α-reductase
12. _____ INAH-3

a. Binds estradiol in blood during development
b. Seminal vesicles, vas deferens
c. Testosterone → estradiol
d. Hormones that promote maternal behavior
e. Carries tactile stimulation from pubic area to brain
f. Control immune system and body odor
g. Oviducts, uterus, upper vagina
h. Testosterone → dihydrotestosterone
i. Releases ovum
j. Facilitates male and female sex behavior
k. Larger in men than in women and gay men
l. Prepares uterus for embryo, inhibits LH

Multiple-Choice Questions

1. Which of the following is <u>not</u> true of sex hormones?
   a. They are peptide hormones.
   b. They are derived from cholesterol.
   c. They consist of androgens, estrogens, and progesterone.
   d. They mediate the effects of sex-limited genes.

2. The SRY gene
   a. is present on the X chromosome and is responsible for the tendency of mammals to become female, unless the gene's effects are overridden by high levels of testosterone.
   b. is present on the Y chromosome and causes the gonads to differentiate into testes, which then secrete testosterone, which in turn masculinizes the organism.
   c. has been linked to homosexuality.
   d. is the major gene that directly specifies the size of sexually dimorphic brain structures.

3. Wolffian ducts
   a. are the precursors of the oviducts, uterus, and upper vagina.
   b. are the precursors of the seminal vesicles and vas deferens.
   c. are the precursors of the external genitals.
   d. none of the above

4. Sex differences in the hypothalamus include
   a. the sexually dimorphic nucleus of the medial preoptic area, which is larger in males.
   b. parts of the hypothalamus that generate a cyclic pattern of hormone release in females.
   c. both a and b.
   d. none of the above.

5. If a female rat receives testosterone injections during the last few days before birth or the first few postnatal days, then in adulthood
   a. she will exhibit neither masculine nor feminine sexual behavior.
   b. she will exhibit normal feminine sexual behavior in spite of the full masculinization of her genitals.
   c. she will exhibit normal feminine sexual behavior, and her genitals will appear fully feminine.
   d. her pituitary and ovary will produce steady levels of hormones rather than cycling in the normal manner, and she will exhibit masculinized sexual behavior.

6. A female pattern of development can be produced
   a. by giving a mammal large amounts of estrogen during the sensitive period.
   b. in normal males by giving them estrogen in adolescence.
   c. in mammals of either sex by depriving the animal of testosterone during the sensitive period, although some estrogen is necessary for feminine differentiation of the brain.
   d. all of the above

7. Which of the following is true?
   a. Testosterone's organizing effects occur throughout the entire period of gestation.
   b. Alpha-fetoprotein is the enzyme that converts testosterone to estradiol.
   c. Estradiol masculinizes the hypothalamus largely by being aromatized to testosterone.
   d. Testosterone masculinizes the hypothalamus of rodents largely by being aromatized to estradiol.

8. High levels of androgens during prenatal development of females
   a. result in steady levels of sex hormones in adulthood, instead of the typical female cycles.
   b. will cause female rats to mount other females in adulthood.
   c. may contribute to choice of male-typical toys by girls.
   d. all of the above

9. The sexually dimorphic nucleus (SDN) of the MPOA
   a. is larger in males than in females.
   b. is necessary for males to be able to perform any male-typical behavior.
   c. is the area that controls the production of testosterone.
   d. all of the above

10. Activation of female sex behavior by hormones
    a. is most easily elicited by injections first of progesterone and then dihydrotestosterone in females whose ovaries were removed.
    b. may be mediated in part by increasing the sensitivity of the pudendal nerve, which transmits tactile stimulation from the pubic area to the brain.
    c. is mediated by a decrease in stimulation of D_1 and D_5 dopamine receptors in the brain.
    d. is mediated by an increase in serotonin activity.

11. Dopamine in the MPOA of male rats
    a. is released when a gonadally intact male is exposed to a receptive female.
    b. is not released in normal amounts by castrated males.
    c. may act through different receptors to promote erection first and then ejaculation.
    d. all of the above.

12. Drugs that decrease testosterone levels
    a. are common treatments for impotence.
    b. totally block the ability to have sex.
    c. can be used to decrease sexual activities of sex offenders, but offenders often drop out of the drug program.
    d. can be used to increase sexual interest in women.

13. The corpus luteum
    a. is the remnant of the ovarian follicle, which releases progesterone.
    b. releases estrogen during the early part of the cycle, which causes the pituitary to release a surge of progesterone at midcycle.
    c. is the primary source of FSH.
    d. is the primary source of LH.

14. FSH
    a. is secreted from the uterus.
    b. is secreted from the follicle.
    c. stimulates the follicle to grow, nurture the ovum, and produce estrogen.
    d. stimulates the follicle to grow and produce LH.

15. Combination birth control pills
    a. contain both estrogen and progesterone.
    b. suppress the release of FSH and LH.
    c. thicken cervical mucus.
    d. all of the above

16. Which of the following is true?
    a. During the periovulatory period women tend to prefer men who are more gentle and helpful.
    b. Women tend to prefer men with body odors different from their own; body odor is controlled by major histocompatibility genes that also affect the immune system. This preference may prevent inbreeding.
    c. The periovulatory period is characterized by high levels of progesterone, but low levels of estrogen.
    d. Estrogen is the hormone that stimulates uterine contractions during labor, milk release during nursing, relaxation after orgasm, and pair bond formation.

17. Which is true concerning rodent parental behavior?
    a. Maternal behavior depends on hormones for the first few days after giving birth.
    b. Hormones continue to be the most important factor in eliciting parental behavior throughout the entire period of care of the young.
    c. The odor of newborn rat pups is naturally very attractive to female rats.
    d. Parental behavior is enhanced by lesions of the MPOA, since that area is concerned only with male sexual behavior, which would interfere with parental behavior.

18. Which of the following is true of prairie voles and meadow voles?
    a. Male prairie voles form long-term pair bonds and help take care of their young.
    b. Male meadow voles tend to be loners and do not care for their young.
    c. Male meadow voles that have experimentally increased gene activity for vasopressin in one part of their brain form pair-bonds and help care for their young.
    d. all of the above

19. Which of the following is true of mate selection?
    a. It is now clear that women are more jealous about their husbands' sexual infidelity, whereas men are more jealous of their wives' emotional infidelity.
    b. Men tend to have a stronger preference for a young partner, whereas women prefer a mate who can be a good provider.
    c. Women never have anything to gain from having more than one sex partner, since they can have only a limited number of pregnancies.
    d. Among birds, it is the partner with the brightest colored feathers that sits on the nest.

20. Intersexes
    a. are extremely rare, no more than one in several million.
    b. usually have complete sets of both male and female structures.
    c. include genetic females who were exposed to elevated levels of androgens during fetal development, due to congenital adrenal hyperplasia (CAH).
    d. are usually genetic males who have been exposed to estrogens during fetal development.

21. Intersexes
    a. should always have surgical "correction" of their genitals immediately after birth.
    b. are sometimes resentful that surgical "correction" of their genitals destroyed sexual sensation and caused problems with scar formation.
    c. should be reared as males if they have an XY chromosome configuration, and as females if they have an XX configuration, regardless of the appearance of their external genitals.
    d. provide clear evidence that prenatal hormones are unimportant in gender identity.

22. Androgen insensitivity (testicular feminization)
    a. is characterized by normal testosterone levels, but a lack of androgen receptors.
    b. can result in an individual who appears to be completely female but fails to menstruate at puberty and has no pubic hair.
    c. cannot be alleviated by giving injections of testosterone.
    d. all of the above

23. Cloacal exstrophy
    a. is malformation of the pelvis, which often results in a very small penis.
    b. results in XX genetic females having male-typical genitals.
    c. is characterized mainly by abnormal hormone production by the adrenal glands.
    d. results from a lack of androgen receptors.

24. Certain genetic males in the Dominican Republic
    a. lack the enzyme that converts testosterone to dihydrotestosterone.
    b. lack the enzyme that converts testosterone to estradiol.
    c. are usually reared as boys, but adapt easily to a feminine sexual identity when they begin to produce high levels of estrogen at puberty.
    d. are usually reared as girls, but are completely unable to adapt to their new male gender identity when high levels of testosterone at puberty cause growth of a penis.

25. A genetic predisposition to homosexuality
    a. may be carried by a gene on the X chromosome that promotes homosexuality in males, although the evidence is not consistent.
    b. may be carried by a gene on the Y chromosome that promotes homosexuality in males, although the evidence is not consistent.
    c. is now known to be controlled by the same gene in male and female homosexuals.
    d. has been disproven, since evolution strongly selects against any genes that would interfere with reproduction.

26. Male homosexuality
    a. is highly correlated with low levels of testosterone in adulthood.
    b. is highly correlated with high levels of estrogen in adulthood.
    c. may be associated with increased stress during prenatal development.
    d. may be redirected to heterosexuality by injections of testosterone in adulthood.

27. Which of the following is true?
    a. It is now clear that low levels of testosterone during gestation are the major cause of homosexuality in males.
    b. There is considerable support for the hypothesis that kin selection has ensured the survival of genes for homosexuality, despite their apparent decrease in reproductive ability.
    c. Alcohol, administered prenatally during the same time as a stressor, may overcome the effects of stress, because it helps to calm the mother.
    d. The probability of a homosexual orientation is higher among men with older brothers, perhaps because the mother's immune system attacks a protein in the later sons.

28. The interstitial nucleus 3 (INAH-3) of the anterior hypothalamus
    a. is larger in women and homosexual men than in heterosexual men.
    b. is smaller in women and homosexual men than in heterosexual men.
    c. is smaller in homosexual men than in either women or heterosexual men, because the AIDS virus is known to kill neurons in that site more than in the rest of the brain.
    d. is now known to be the primary brain center that determines sexual orientation.

Solutions

True/False Questions

1.	T	7.	T	13.	T	19.	T
2.	F	8.	F	14.	T	20.	F
3.	T	9.	T	15.	F	21.	F
4.	F	10.	T	16.	T	22.	T
5.	F	11.	T	17.	F	23.	T
6.	T	12.	F	18.	F		

Fill In The Blanks

1. estrogens; androgens; progesterone.
2. SRY
3. Müllerian
4. Wolffian
5. alpha-fetoprotein.
6. aromatase
7. dopamine; medial preoptic area
8. nitric oxide
9. serotonin; dopamine
10. LH; FSH; thickening; mucus
11. estrogen; oxytocin; prolactin; medial preoptic area; anterior hypothalamus
12. Vasopressin
13. younger; provider
14. intersex
15. congenital adrenal hyperplasia
16. testicular feminization; androgen insensitivity.
17. cloacal exstrophy
18. 5α-reductase; dihydrotestosterone
19. monozygotic; identical; dizygotic; fraternal
20. methyl (CH_3); inactivate
21. endorphins; corticosterone
22. INAH-3

Matching Item

1.	f	4.	g	7.	c	10.	l
2.	d	5.	b	8.	j	11.	h
3.	e	6.	a	9.	i	12.	k

Multiple Choice Questions

1.	a	8.	d	15.	d	22.	d
2.	b	9.	a	16.	b	23.	a
3.	b	10.	b	17.	a	24.	a
4.	c	11.	d	18.	d	25.	a
5.	d	12.	c	19.	b	26.	c
6.	c	13.	a	20.	c	27.	d
7.	d	14.	c	21.	b	28.	b

Emotional Behaviors

Introduction

Emotional states include three aspects: cognition, readiness for action, and feeling. Readiness for action depends on the autonomic nervous system, composed of the sympathetic and parasympathetic divisions. Sympathetic activity prepares for vigorous or emergency activity, whereas the parasympathetic system promotes digestion and conserves energy. Each situation requires a different combination of sympathetic and parasympathetic activity. There has been debate about the role of autonomic arousal in emotions. The James-Lange theory proposes that autonomic and skeletal activity occurs first, and emotions result from our perception of those responses. There is evidence for the importance of physiological responses in determining the intensity of emotions, and extreme sympathetic nervous system arousal during panic attacks is interpreted as fear. However, it is possible to feel some blunted emotions, even after injuries that prevent autonomic responses. Also, there are no clear distinctions among autonomic responses that would allow us to identify specific emotions, based only on the autonomic responses.

The frontal and temporal lobes of the cerebral cortex are strongly activated during various emotions, and the insular cortex is activated during feelings of disgust and fear. The frontal and temporal lobes of the left hemisphere mediate what Jeffrey Gray termed the Behavioral Activation System. It includes low to moderate autonomic arousal, a tendency to approach new objects, which could portray happiness or anger. In contrast, the frontal and temporal lobes of the right hemisphere are associated with the Behavioral Inhibition System, which increases attention and arousal, decreases action, and elicits disgust and fear. People with greater activity in the left hemisphere tend to be happy and outgoing, while those with greater right hemisphere activity are more withdrawn and have more unpleasant emotions. The right hemisphere also helps to recognize emotions in others. Emotions provide a useful guide for quick decisions. Damage to the prefrontal cortex results in a lack of emotions. People with such damage make stupid decisions, despite being able to predict the outcomes; they are also impulsive and fail to behave morally. However, emotions can also prompt unwise decisions.

Many kinds of situations can trigger aggressive attacks, including pains, threats, and even dispassionate attacks for financial or other gains. Increased aggressiveness is influenced by heredity and by prenatal influences, including maternal smoking during pregnancy. Testosterone level is correlated with aggressiveness, although its effect is relatively weak. It may affect the way people react to various stimuli, by increasing emotional arousal and decreasing emotional regulation. Stimulation of some brain areas can promote aggressive responses. Low serotonin turnover is associated with aggressiveness in both animals and people. Turnover is inferred from levels of 5-HIAA, a serotonin metabolite. Low serotonin turnover was observed in mice that showed isolation-induced aggression and in monkeys that were naturally aggressive. Low serotonin turnover in humans may be associated with violent crimes and suicide. However, low serotonin turnover is also associated with impulsiveness and depression. Serotonin synthesis can be affected by diet. Tryptophan, the precursor of serotonin, competes with other amino acids for transport into the brain. Therefore, foods like maize (American corn) and aspartame (NutraSweet), which are high in the amino acid phenylalanine and low in tryptophan, can increase aggressive or suicidal tendencies. Similarly, several genes that control serotonin synthesis, its transport back into cells, or its breakdown can affect the amount of serotonin in synapses. Increases of serotonin typically decrease depression, aggressiveness, impulsiveness, and even drug cravings. Strangely, serotonin is also released during aggression, although it is also released during all social encounters in rats.

The basolateral and central nuclei of the amygdala are important for learned fear responses, including enhancement of the startle reflex. The amygdala receives input concerning pain, vision, and hearing. Its output to the hypothalamus controls autonomic responses; its output to the prefrontal cortex influences approach and avoidance responses, and its connections to the central gray in the midbrain elicit the startle response. Damage to the amygdala reduces or eliminates fears and also impairs the interpretation of social signals. The amygdala is activated by emotional expressions and scenes, even if the person does not consciously recognize the picture. The names of famous people who were liked or disliked are sufficient to elicit a response in the amygdala. People with Urbach-Wiethe disease suffer atrophy of the amygdala and have a resultant loss of the experience or perception of fear. One reason that people with damage to the amygdala fail to recognize fearful expressions may be that they focus on the nose and mouth, rather than the eyes. On the other hand, genes that enhance amygdala responsiveness are associated with fearful and anxious personalities.

Drugs that are used to control anxiety affect synapses in the amygdala. CCK (cholecystokinin) excites the amygdala and is also released in the prefrontal cortex in stressful situations. Injections of drugs that stimulate CCK receptors into the amygdala enhance the startle reflex, and drugs that block CCK type B receptors block anxiety. The main inhibitory transmitter in the amygdala is GABA; drugs that block GABA type B receptors produce panic. Anxiety is commonly treated with benzodiazepine tranquilizers. These drugs exert their effect at benzodiazepine binding sites on the $GABA_A$ receptor complex, thereby facilitating the binding of GABA to its own sites at the complex. The binding of GABA increases the flow of chloride ions across the membrane and thereby inhibits neural activity. Alcohol also binds to the $GABA_A$ complex and facilitates GABA binding. An experimental drug can block the effects of alcohol on the $GABA_A$ complex and on behavior. However, this drug is not marketed because of its potential for misuse. Diazepam-binding inhibitor (DBI) is an endozepine (endogenous antibenzodiazepine). It is released by glia cells and blocks the effects of diazepam and other benzodiazepines, thereby increasing anxiety. Changes in genes controlling endozepines may influence the development of anxiety disorders.

Stress was defined by Hans Selye as the nonspecific response of the body to any demand made upon it. In addition to specific responses to stressors, the body mounts a general adaptation syndrome, characterized by three stages: alarm, resistance and exhaustion. Stress activates the autonomic nervous system, especially the sympathetic "fight or flight" response, and also the HPA axis (the hypothalamus, pituitary gland, and adrenal cortex). During stress, the hypothalamus directs the anterior pituitary to secrete ACTH (adrenocorticotropic hormone), which in turn stimulates the adrenal gland to secrete cortisol. Cortisol shifts energy metabolism to increase blood sugar and metabolic activity. Moderate levels of cortisol improve attention and memory, but very high or low levels of cortisol impair these functions.

Three important elements of the immune system are B cells, which produce antibodies that attach to and inactivate specific antigens; T cells, which attack specific "foreign" cells or stimulate proliferation of other immune cells; and natural killer cells, which kill tumor cells and cells infected with viruses in a nonspecific way. These immune cells are leukocytes (white blood cells); they produce cytokines. Cytokines induce fever, which helps fight infections, and promote fatigue, which leads to conservation of energy. Although brief stressors activate the immune system, chronic stressors may depress its functioning and leave an individual more vulnerable to disease. Prolonged stress, with its high cortisol levels, can also increase the vulnerability of hippocampal neurons, with resultant impairment of memory. Post-traumatic stress disorder (PTSD) occurs in some people who have had traumatic experiences. They have flashbacks, nightmares, and exaggerated arousal to noises and other stimuli. We do not know why some people do, and others do not, succumb to PTSD. Those who do have been found to have a smaller than usual hippocampus and low cortisol levels. Although cause and effect have not been clearly established, there is evidence that in some cases the small hippocampus preceded, and may have increased vulnerability to, the PTSD. Additionally, Vietnam War veterans who experienced damage in their amygdala do not suffer from PTSD, suggesting a role for the amygdala in regulating the emotional impact associated with this disorder.

Learning Objectives

Module 12.1 What Is Emotion?
1. Be able to describe the influences of the autonomic nervous system on emotions.
2. Know the effects of damage or inactivation of cortical structures and of the right vs. left hemisphere on emotional responsiveness.
3. Understand the role of emotions in decision making and the brain areas that promote wise decision making.

Module 12.2 Attack and Escape Behaviors
1. Know the genetic, environmental, and hormonal contributions to aggressiveness.
2. Understand the roles of brain abnormalities and serotonin turnover in aggressive behavior.
3. Understand the ways in which the amygdala promotes fear and anxiety.
4. Be able to explain the effects of anxiety-reducing drugs.

Module 12.3 Stress and Health
1. Understand the concept of the General Adaptation Syndrome, including its three stages and its implications for today's crises.
2. Understand the components and functions of the hypothalamus-pituitary-adrenal (HPA) axis.
3. Know the components and functions of the immune system and the effects of brief or prolonged stressors on immune function.
4. Be able to list the symptoms of post-traumatic stress disorder (PTSD) and describe the relation between size of hippocampus, cortisol levels, and vulnerability to PTSD.

Key Terms and Concepts

Module 12.1 What Is Emotion?

1.   Emotions, autonomic arousal, and the James-Lange Theory
     Emotion: Three components
          Cognition
          Feelings
          Actions
     Autonomic nervous system arousal
          Sympathetic nervous system→ vigorous, emergency activity
          Parasympathetic nervous system → digestion, conservation of energy
          Each situation → mixture of sympathetic and parasympathetic activity
     James-Lange theory: Appraisal → action → emotional feeling
          Prefrontal cortex: Responds differently to "pleasant" or "unpleasant" photos within 1/8
          second
     Is physiological arousal necessary for emotions?
          Feedback from muscle movements unnecessary for emotion
          Autonomic response not affected by paralysis
          Pure autonomic failure
               Report cognitive aspects of emotions; decreased emotional intensity
     Is physiological arousal sufficient for emotions?
          Panic attack
               Extreme sympathetic nervous system arousal → interpreted as fear
          The sensation of smiling increases happiness.
               Möbius syndrome → unable to smile → yet experience happiness
          Smiling → increases happiness
          Brain stimulation during surgery → laughter interpreted as emotion
          Frowning → photographs rated more unpleasant
          Certain breathing patterns or postures → mild emotional feelings
          James-Lange correct: Perception of bodily reactions contribute to emotional feelings
               The autonomic nervous system, not muscle, is strongest contributor to
               this response.
2.   Brain areas associated with emotion
     Limbic system: forebrain areas critical for emotions
     Attempts to localize specific emotions
          The brain responds within milliseconds to faces showing emotional expressions
          PET or fMRI: Frontal or temporal cortex activated during varied emotions
               Variability
          EEG: Different emotions → different brain areas in first half-second
          Insular cortex (insula): Disgust
               Seeing disgusting picture or facial expression of disgust → activates   insular
               cortex
               Dis-gust = bad taste
               Damage to insular cortex → failed to experience or recognize disgust
               Also responds to frightening pictures
               Disgusting experiences activate other brain areas not only insula

Contributions of the left and right hemispheres
    Left hemisphere (especially frontal and temporal lobes)
        Behavioral Activation System (BAS)
            Low to moderate autonomic arousal
            Tendency to approach new objects: Happiness or anger
    Right hemisphere
        Behavioral Inhibition System (BIS)
            Right frontal and temporal lobes
            Increased attention and arousal
            Decreased action
            Increased fear and disgust
    Personality differences
        Greater activity in left frontal cortex → happier, outgoing, fun-loving
        Greater activity in right → shy, less satisfied, more unpleasant emotions
    Right hemisphere more responsive to emotional stimuli
        Listening to laughter or crying → activates right amygdala more than left
        Looking at emotional expressions → activates right temporal cortex
        Damage to right temporal cortex → difficulty identifying emotional expressions
    Left hemisphere damage → improved detection of others' emotions
        Inactivating right hemisphere (Wada procedure) → recall facts, not emotions

3.   The functions of emotions
    Emotions are evolutionarily adaptive
        Fear → escape danger
        Anger → attack intruder
        Disgust → avoid illness
    "Gut feelings" based on autonomic responses: Useful guide for quick decision

4.   Emotions and moral decisions
    Predicted emotional outcomes influence moral decisions

5.   Decision making after brain damage that impairs emotions
    Prefrontal cortex damage → lack of emotions
        Stupid decisions, despite predicting outcomes
        No moral behavior
        Phineas Gage
        Damage in infancy → failed to learn moral behavior
    Gambling task
        Damage to prefrontal cortex or amygdala → little or no emotion; choose riskier decks of cards
    Emotions can also interfere with good decisions

6.   In closing: Emotions and the nervous system

Module 12.2 Attack and Escape Behaviors
1.   Attack behaviors
    "Play" behavior: Compromise between attack and escape
    Corticomedial amygdala
        Priming for further attacks
    Heredity and environment in violence

Decreased lead in environment → correlates with decreased violent crimes

Maternal smoking during pregnancy

Effect compounded with complications during pregnancy

Correlational, not causational effect

Heritability

Monozygotic > dizygotic in adult crimes

Adopted children resemble biological parents

Genes: specific gene weakly linked

Genetic predisposition coupled with troubled early environment → greater predictor of increased violence

Genetic differences for monoamine oxidase A + severe childhood mistreatment → increased antisocial behavior

Hormones

Male-female differences

Aggressive behavior depends heavily on testosterone

More crime in young adult men: Highest testosterone levels

Higher testosterone correlated with more violent acts

Interpretation difficult

Testosterone may → attend longer, respond more vigorously to conflict

Injecting women with testosterone → decreased recognition of angry expressions

Testosterone → increased response of amygdala to angry expressions

Testosterone may increase emotional arousal and decrease emotional regulation

Serotonin synapses and aggressive behavior

Nonhuman animals

Social isolation of male mice → lower serotonin turnover, correlated with aggression

5-HIAA (5-hydroxyindoleacetic acid): Measure of serotonin turnover

Social isolation of female mice → no change in serotonin turnover or aggression

Serotonin activity is lower in juvenile rodents: aggression is higher

Male monkeys: Low serotonin turnover correlated with high aggression, short lives

Possible evolutionary explanations

Evolution → intermediate aggressiveness: Both fearless and highly fearful die young

High-risk → high-payoff → a few sire many young

Monkey who wins and survives several fights → dominant status

Humans

Low serotonin turnover: Correlation with violent crimes or suicide

Released prisoners with lower serotonin: greater probability of later conviction

Low tryptophan diet → increase in aggressiveness

Other amino acids compete with tryptophan for transport channel

Aspartame, maize (corn): High in phenylalanine → competes with tryptophan

Relevant genes

Gene for tryptophan hydroxylase: Tryptophan → serotonin

People with less active form of this gene → more aggressive

Complication: Brain releases serotonin with aggression

Possible explanation: Low basal levels may magnify serotonin's effects during aggressive encounter

Low serotonin → depression, aggression, impulsivity

    Addicts → drug craving

    Effects are complicated

2.   Escape, fear, and anxiety

    Nucleus accumbens

        Some cells more important for approach behavior or avoidance: determined by their anatomical location in the nucleus accumbens

    Fear, anxiety, and the amygdala

        Startle reflex

            Auditory input → cochlear nucleus of medulla → pons → tense muscles

            Stronger if already tense: posttraumatic stress disorder show enhanced response

        Studies in rodents

            Conditioning a stimulus with shock → stimulus becomes fear signal → fear stimulus then enhances startle response

            Stimulus conditioned to pleasant stimuli → decreases startle response

            Pain, vision, hearing → basolateral, central amygdala

            Cells in amygdala vary response: reward, punishment, or surprise

            Output to hypothalamus → autonomic responses

            Output to prefrontal cortex → approach and avoidance responses

            Output to midbrain → pons → skeletal responses

            Damage to amygdala → no enhancement of startle reflex by conditioned fear signal

            Damage to amygdala → interferes learning fear, less so with retention of fear response

            Protozoan parasite → reproduce in cat → excrete eggs in feces → rat picks up eggs from ground → new parasites → damage rat's amygdala → lose fear → eaten by cat → reproduce in cat

        Studies in monkeys

            Amygdala damage

                Klüver-Bucy syndrome: Little fear or avoidance

                Increased friendliness

        Activaton of the human amygdala

            Expressions that require emotional processing → amygdala response

            Emotions elicited by angry or fearful faces: Depend on gaze direction

            Names of famous people who were liked or disliked → amygdala responds

            Amygdala responds to emotional stimuli that person may not detect

            Amygdala response: Also depends on gaze direction

                Complex: Depends on need for emotional interpretation, subject's mood

                Responds even if stimulus not identified consciously

                Cortical blindness: Better-than-chance identification of emotion in pictures, via right amygdala, even though no cortical response

        Damage to the human amygdala

            Urbach-Wiethe disease (genetic disease → calcium accumulation in amygdala)

            Strokes or brain surgery

Report normal emotions, but are impaired at processing emotions when signals are subtle

Inability to judge trustworthiness

Inability to focus attention on emotional stimuli

Difficulty recognizing fear and disgust in photos

    Some difficulty with anger, surprise, arrogance, guilt, admiration and flirtation

    Focus mostly on nose and mouth—not eyes

Personality differences

    Gene interferes with serotonin uptake in amygdala → strong negative emotions

Anxiety-reducing drugs

    Hyperactive amygdala → exaggerated fears

    Transmitters in amygdala: CCK, excitatory; GABA, inhibitory

        "Intruder" rats

            CCK in prefrontal cortex → anxiety

            CCK type B antagonist → no anxiety

        CCK-stimulating drugs in amygdala → enhance startle reflex

        GABA type B antagonist → panic

Benzodiazepines

    Barbiturates: Habit forming, easy to take fatal overdose

    Common benzodiazepine tranquilizers

        Diazepam (Valium)

        Chlordiazepoxide (Librium)

        Alprazolam (Xanax)

    $GABA_A$ receptor complex

        Chloride channel → hyperpolarization

    Benzodiazepine effects

        Amygdala, hypothalamus, midbrain → decrease learned shock avoidance

        Cerebral cortex, thalamus → sleepiness, decrease epilepsy, impair memory

    Diazepam-binding inhibitor (DBI), an endozepine: Endogenous antibenzodiazepine

        Released mainly by glia cells

        Changes in genes controlling endozepines may influence probability of developing anxiety disorders

Alcohol as a tranquilizer

    Alcohol → increased flow of chloride ions through $GABA_A$ receptor complex

    Antianxiety effects: Similar to benzodiazepines

    Ro15-4313: Blocks effects of moderate amounts of alcohol on $GABA_A$ receptors and behavior

        Not marketed because of potential for misuse

3.   In closing: Doing something about emotions

    Problem: How to use new understanding

Module 12.3 Stress and Health

1.   Concepts of stress

    Behavioral medicine: Effects on health of diet, smoking, exercise, stressful experiences

    Hans Selye: Stress is nonspecific response of body to any demand made upon it

        Any threat → specific effects - generalized response to stress

General adaptation syndrome
>Three stages
>>Alarm: Increased sympathetic nervous system activity
>>Resistance: Adrenal cortex secretes cortisol → prolonged alertness, fight infections, heal wounds
>>Exhaustion: Tired, inactive, vulnerable
>Robert Sapolsky: Today's crises more prolonged → harmful
>Bruce McEwen: Stress = threatening events that elicit behavioral and physiological responses

2.   Stress and the hypothalamus-pituitary-adrenal cortex axis
>Activation of hypothalamus → anterior pituitary → adrenocorticotropic hormone (ACTH) → human adrenal cortex → cortisol (rat adrenal cortex → corticosterone) → increased blood sugar and metabolism
>>Cortisol: Useful in short term (improves attention, memory, immune system); harmful if prolonged (impairs memory and immune system)
>The immune system
>>Protects against viruses, bacteria, and other intruders
>>Autoimmune disease: Immune system attacks "self"
>>>Examples: myasthenia gravis, rheumatoid arthritis
>>Leukocytes (white blood cells)
>>>B cells
>>>>Mature in bone marrow
>>>>Plasma cells → antibodies
>>>>B memory cells
>>>T cells
>>>>Mature in thymus
>>>>Some directly attack intruder
>>>>Others stimulate other T or B cells to multiply
>>Natural killer cells: Relatively nonspecific in their targets
>>Cytokines
>>>Example: Interleukin-1 (IL-1)
>>>Attack infections
>>>Cytokines → hypothalamus → produce fever, sleepiness, lack of energy, decrease appetite and sex drive.
>>>Prostaglandins : in response to infection
>>>>Release cytokines in brain → anti-illness behaviors
>>>>Fever → fight infections
>>>>Sleepiness → conserve energy
>Effects of stress on the immune system
>>Psychoneuroimmunology
>>Inescapable, temporary stressors → response similar to illness
>>Brief stressors → brief activation of immune system
>>>Also symptoms resembling illness
>>>Depression, increased cytokines → influences symptoms
>>Long-term stressors → decreased protein synthesis, including immune system proteins
>>>High cortisol → hippocampal damage
>>>>Decreased learning and memory

Stress in rats → shrinks dendrites in hippocampus and impaired memory
Older people with higher cortisol → smaller hippocampi and impaired memory
Early stress in rats → fewer hippocampal neurons in adulthood

3. Stress control

Breathing routines, exercise, meditation, distraction, social support

Social support, reduces response of brain to stressful stimuli

4. Post-traumatic stress disorder (PTSD)

Symptoms

Flashbacks and nightmares

Avoidance of reminders

Exaggerated arousal in response to noises and other stimuli

Vulnerability

Small hippocampus (cause or effect?)

Low cortisol levels → ill-equipped to combat stress?

Small hippocampus in both twins

Only one was in war and had PTSD

Therefore, small hippocampus predisposed to PTSD

Vietnam War veterans with damage in amygdala did not suffer PTSD

5. In closing: Emotions and body reactions

Stress → adrenal cortex and immune system → reactions similar to illness

Short-Answer Questions

Module 12.1 What Is Emotion?

1. *Emotions, autonomic arousal, and the James-Lange theory*

   a. What are the roles of the sympathetic and parasympathetic nervous systems?

   b. Describe the James-Lange theory of emotions.

   c. Is physiological arousal necessary for emotions? What is the implication of the very rapid response of the prefrontal cortex to emotional stimuli?

   d. Describe the condition of pure autonomic failure.

   e. Describe the experience of panic attack.

   f. Describe the findings of the experiment in which subjects held a pencil between their teeth or with their lips.

   g. Summarize the current understanding of the importance of physiological arousal for emotions.

2. *Brain areas associated with emotion*

   a. Describe the responses of the frontal and temporal lobes to photographs, stories, or recalled personal experiences associated with particular emotions. On the basis of these data, can we localize specific emotions to particular brain areas?

   b. Describe the evidence indicating a role for the insular cortex in detecting disgust?

   c. What are the roles of the right and left hemispheres in the detection and expression of emotion?

3. *The functions of emotions*

    a. Describe the findings of the experiment in which people were shocked after either snake or spider pictures that were presented too fast for conscious identification. What can we conclude about the value of "gut feelings"?

    b. How might emotions influence moral decisions?

    c. Describe the behavior of people with damage to the prefrontal cortex.

Module 12.2 Attack and Escape Behaviors

1. *Attack behaviors*

    a. What is one explanation of a cat's "play" behavior with its prey?

    b. What are the effects of stimulation of the amygdala on aggressive behavior? Which area of the amygdala is especially important for this effect?

    c. Describe the evidence for heritability of violence in adulthood, but not in childhood.

    d. What environmental risk factor is compounded with complications during pregnancy in determining predisposition toward violence?

    e. Does genetic predisposition alone predict increased violence? What factors coupled with genetic predisposition increase antisocial behaviors?

    f. How strong is the correlation between testosterone levels and aggressive behavior? By what psychological effect may testosterone promote aggression?

    g. What transmitter abnormality appears to be associated with aggressive behavior? How can it be measured?

    h. Describe the experimental evidence in mice for the relationship between a transmitter abnormality and aggressive behavior.

    i. How was serotonin turnover related to behavior in male monkeys in a natural-environment study?

    j. What evidence implicates low serotonin turnover in humans as a factor in aggressive behavior?

    k. What dietary factors influence serotonin synthesis?

    l. Which genes have been implicated in a tendency toward aggressiveness?

    m. What other mood or behavior disorders are associated with low serotonin turnover?

    n. Describe the complication concerning the timing of serotonin release relative to aggression. What are two possible explanations for this complication?

2. *Escape, fear, and anxiety*

   a. Describe how different areas of the nucleus accumbens might influence approach or avoidance.

   b. Why should researchers be interested in the startle response?

   c. What is a key brain area for learned fears? What kinds of sensory input does it receive? Which two nuclei appear to be most important for conditioned fear responses?

   d. What are the main output connections of the amygdala? What does each control?

   e. Describe the effects of a protozoan parasite on rats. How may the behavioral change lead to the reproduction of the parasite?

   f. What are the usual effects of amygdala damage? Describe the Klüver-Bucy syndrome.

   g. Describe the responses of the human amygdala to photographs depicting various emotions. Does the amygdala respond even if the stimulus is not identified consciously?

   h. What causes Urbach-Wiethe disease? Under what conditions do people with amygdala damage have trouble processing emotional information? How do their social judgments of other people differ from those of normal people?

   i. Why may people with amygdala damage fail to identify fearful expressions in photographs?

   j. What genetic abnormality is implicated in anxiety disorders?

   k. Name one excitatory and one inhibitory transmitter in the amygdala that have been implicated in the control of anxiety.

   l. What type of drug blocked anxiety in male mice placed into a resident male's cage? What type of drug enhanced the startle reflex when injected into the amygdala?

   m. What is the most common type of drug used to reduce anxiety? What was a major problem with the use of barbiturates for anxiety?

   n. When a benzodiazepine molecule attaches to its binding site on the $GABA_A$ receptor, how is the binding of GABA affected? What effect does this have on the flow of chloride ions across the cell membrane?

   o. What are the behavioral effects of benzodiazepines on the amygdala? On the cerebral cortex and thalamus?

   p. What is one endogenous chemical that affects the benzodiazepine receptors? Why is the term endozepine confusing? Which type of cell releases it?

   q. What is the effect of alcohol on the $GABA_A$ receptor? What are the advantages and disadvantages of a drug that blocks alcohol's effects on the $GABA_A$ receptor? What is your opinion of the decision not to market the drug?

Module 12.3 Stress and Health

1. *Concepts of stress*

    a. What is the main emphasis of behavioral medicine?

    b. What was Hans Selye's definition of stress? What symptoms did Selye notice in patients with a wide variety of illnesses?

    c. What are the three stages of the General Adaptation Syndrome, and what occurs in each?

2. *Stress and the hypothalamus-pituitary-adrenal cortex axis*

    a. Describe the steps in the control of cortisol secretion from the adrenal cortex.

    b. What is the role of cortisol in the body's response to stress?

    c. Name two autoimmune diseases.

    d. What are three of the most important cells of the immune system?

    e. What are antigens?

    f. What are the roles of B cells and of T cells?

    g. What is the role of natural killer cells?

    h. What are cytokines?

    i. What are the roles of fever and fatigue in fighting illness?

    j. What evidence suggests influence by cytokines in depression?

    k. What is the effect of short-term stress on the immune system?

    l. Describe the evidence suggesting that long-term stress impairs the function of the immune system.

    m. What are cortisol's major effects on blood sugar and metabolism? How does this affect the immune system?

    n. How do high cortisol levels affect the hippocampus? How does this affect memory?

3. *Post-traumatic stress disorder (PTSD)*

    a. What are the symptoms of posttraumatic stress disorder (PTSD)?

    b. Is the hippocampus of people who suffer from PTSD likely to be larger or smaller than average? What can be inferred about cause and effect in this relationship? What may we infer about the relationship of low cortisol levels and vulnerability to PTSD?

    c. What is the prevalence of PTSD in veterans of the Vietnam War who suffered damage in their amygdala?

True/False Questions

1. Students who very briefly viewed pictures of snakes or spiders showed a physiological reaction only if they could identify the object.

   TRUE or FALSE

2. Various situations call for different amounts and combinations of sympathetic and parasympathetic nervous system activity.

   TRUE or FALSE

3. According to the James-Lange theory, our conscious identification of an emotion occurs first and instructs the autonomic nervous system to respond appropriately.

   TRUE or FALSE

4. Three cortical areas that are very responsive in emotional situations are the frontal lobe, the temporal lobe, and the insular cortex.

   TRUE or FALSE

5. The right hemisphere is more responsive to emotions, especially unpleasant emotions, than is the left.

   TRUE or FALSE

6. People with damage to their prefrontal cortex showed a lack of emotions and made stupid decisions, in spite of being able to predict the outcome of their actions.

   TRUE or FALSE

7. Testosterone may influence aggressiveness by increasing emotional arousal and decreasing emotional regulation during conflict.

   TRUE or FALSE

8. People with damage to the prefrontal cortex may be more aggressive because they have a general loss of inhibitions.

   TRUE or FALSE

9. Low serotonin turnover in people is correlated with violent crimes and suicides.

   TRUE or FALSE

10. Output from the amygdala to the hypothalamus controls skeletal responses.

    TRUE or FALSE

11. People with Urbach-Wiethe disease show an increased tendency for panic disorder.

    TRUE or FALSE

12. CCK is a major excitatory transmitter in the amygdala and tends to promote anxiety; GABA is the main inhibitory transmitter and tends to decrease anxiety.

    TRUE or FALSE

13. Benzodiazepines directly open the chloride channel in the GABA$_A$ receptor, so that GABA is no longer needed. Therefore, it is easy to take a fatal overdose.

TRUE or FALSE

14. Endozepines are powerful natural benzodiazepines and therefore inhibit fear and anxiety.

TRUE or FALSE

15. The three stages of Selye's General Adaptation Syndrome are alarm, resistance, and exhaustion.

TRUE or FALSE

16. B cells of the immune system release cytokines that directly kill invading bacteria.

TRUE or FALSE

17. T cells mature in the thymus; some directly attack intruders and others stimulate other B or T cells to multiply.

TRUE or FALSE

18. Natural killer cells release antibodies that are tailored to attack specific invaders.

TRUE or FALSE

19. Cytokines in the brain produce anti-illness behaviors.

TRUE or FALSE

20. Brief stressors inhibit the immune system, and prolonged, intense stressors inhibit it even more.

TRUE or FALSE

21. High cortisol concentrations damage the hippocampus, resulting in memory problems.

TRUE or FALSE

22. People with PTSD have very high cortisol levels, because they are so frequently under a lot of stress.

TRUE or FALSE

Fill In the Blanks

1. According to the _____ theory, autonomic arousal and skeletal actions come first; our experience of emotion is the label we give to our responses.

2. Evidence for the James-Lange theory is that people with _____ failure can report the cognitive aspects of emotions, but they do not feel emotions intensely.

3. The _____ and _____ lobes of the cortex are activated during varied emotions; the _____ cortex responds during feelings of disgust and fear.

4. The _____ hemisphere is associated with the Behavioral Activation System, which is characterized by low to moderate autonomic arousal and a tendency to approach new objects.

5. The _____ hemisphere is more responsive to emotional stimuli, both in detecting and expressing emotion.

6. People with damage to the _____ cortex or _____ showed little or no emotion and made riskier choices.

7. Stimulation of the _____ amygdala primes an animal for attack.

8. Levels of _____ are a measure of serotonin turnover. Low serotonin turnover is associated with _____.

9. Genes that have been associated with aggressiveness in humans are those that direct production of _____ and _____.

10. Damage to the _____ resulted in a lack of enhancement of the startle reflex by conditioned fear signals.

11. Monkeys with the _____ syndrome, as a result of damage to the amygdala, show little fear or avoidance.

12. In humans, the _____ disease results in degeneration of the _____ and a resultant difficulty in expressing or recognizing _____.

13. A major excitatory neurotransmitter in the amygdala is _____; the main inhibitory neurotransmitter is _____.

14. _____ bind to their own site on the GABA$_A$ receptor and enhance the binding of GABA; this tends to increase the flow of _____ ions.

15. Diazepam-binding inhibitor (DBI) is a(n) _____; it increases _____ and _____.

16. _____ defined stress as a nonspecific response of the body to any demand made upon it.

17. The _____ consists of three stages: alarm, resistance, and exhaustion.

18. Activation of the hypothalamus stimulates the anterior pituitary to produce _____, which in turn stimulates the adrenal cortex to secrete _____.

19. Leukocytes that attack tumor cells and cells infected with viruses are called _____.

20. _____, including interleukin-1, are released by leukocytes to combat infection; they also stimulate the _____ nerve, which leads to cytokine release in the brain, which in turn produces a(n) _____ and _____.

21. PTSD victims tend to have a smaller _____ and, surprisingly, also have low levels of _____.

22. Vietnam War veterans who experienced damage in their _____ did not suffer from _____.

Matching Items

1. _____ Prefrontal cortex damage
2. _____ Panic disorder
3. _____ General adaptation disorder
4. _____ B cells
5. _____ T cells
6. _____ Cytokine
7. _____ Brief stressor
8. _____ High cortisol
9. _____ Small hippocampus
10. _____ 5-HIAA
11. _____ Right hemisphere
12. _____ CCK
13. _____ GABA
14. _____ DBI

a. Alarm, resistance, exhaustion
b. Leukocytes that mature in the thymus, attack intruders, help B or T cells multiply
c. Extreme sympathetic activity interpreted as fear
d. Make stupid decisions, no moral behavior
e. Damages hippocampus
f. Leukocytes that secrete antibodies
g. Behavioral Inhibition System
h. Main inhibitory transmitter in amygdala
i. Brief activation of immune system
j. Endogenous antibenzodiazepine
k. Released by lympocytes, fight infection, inform brain
l. Metabolite of serotonin
m. A major excitatory transmitter in amygdala
n. Possible predisposition to post-traumatic stress disorder (PTSD)

Multiple-Choice Questions

1. Which of the following is true?
   a. A lack of emotions, as in people with prefrontal cortex damage, promotes rational decision making.
   b. The James-Lange theory proposed that autonomic arousal and skeletal actions precede emotions.
   c. Responses based on "gut feelings" are almost always wrong.
   d. Sympathetic nervous system activity prepares the body for digestion and relaxation.

2. Which of the following cortical areas is **not** highly activated during emotional perceptions?
   a. frontal cortex
   b. temporal cortex
   c. insular cortex
   d. occipital cortex

3. People with pure autonomic failure
   a. report the cognitive aspects of emotions, but feel emotions much less intensely.
   b. have little or no cognitive ability.
   c. express extreme panic at being unable to move.
   d. All of the above are true.

4. What is the current state of acceptance of the James-Lange theory?
   a. It is no longer thought to have any validity.
   b. It is correct in that physiological arousal is sufficient to distinguish between emotions, such as fear and anger.
   c. It is incorrect in that decreasing autonomic responses actually increases intensity of emotions.
   d. It is largely correct in that physiological arousal is both necessary and sufficient to influence the intensity of our emotions.

5. Which of the following is true?
   a. Damage to or inactivation of frontal cortex increases the perception of anger.
   b. Inactivation of the right hemisphere interferes greatly with the recall of facts but has little effect on the recall of emotion.
   c. The insular cortex is important for feelings of disgust.
   d. People with greater activity in their right hemisphere tend to be more outgoing and loving.

6. Which of the following is true?
   a. Cats that "play" with their prey are really sadistically torturing the smaller animal.
   b. Increased aggressiveness can be elicited by stimulation of the corticomedial amygdala.
   c. There is greater evidence for heritability in juvenile crimes than in adult crimes.
   d. Smoking during pregnancy primarily increases the likelihood that the offspring will be arrested for nonviolent crimes, rather than violent crimes.

7. Which of the following is true?
   a. The correlation between testosterone and aggression in humans is real, but of modest size.
   b. Both genetics and environmental factors contribute to the predisposition to commit crimes and aggressive behaviors.
   c. Many people with damage to the prefrontal cortex have a tendency toward many socially inappropriate behaviors.
   d. All of the above are true.

8. Lesions of the amygdala
   a. usually produce difficulty in interpreting social stimuli as well as decreased fear.
   b. usually cause temporal lobe epilepsy.
   c. lead to a state that resembles panic disorder.
   d. usually result in decreased serotonin turnover.

9. Which of the following is true?
   a. Mice with low levels of serotonin turnover are abnormally placid.
   b. Serotonin turnover has been found to be lower than normal in impulsive, aggressive humans.
   c. 5-HIAA is a drug that has been used successfully to treat uncontrollable violence.
   d. All of the above are true.

10. Which of the following is true?
   a. Social isolation increased aggressiveness in female mice as much as in males.
   b. Almost all monkeys with low serotonin turnover had longer lifespans, because they killed off their competitors.
   c. Low serotonin turnover in humans has been associated with depression, impulsivity, and drug craving, as well as with aggression.
   d. People who have a tendency toward aggressiveness should consume a lot of aspartame and maize (corn), in order to increase their serotonin synthesis.

11. Output from the amygdala to the hypothalamus controls
   a. the intensity of sensory input to the organism.
   b. the interpretation of potentially frightening stimuli.
   c. skeletal movements of the startle response.
   d. autonomic fear responses, such as increased blood pressure.

12. After damage, inactivation, or atrophy of the amygdala,
   a. a person has difficulty recognizing or portraying fearful expressions.
   b. a rat no longer shows any startle reflex.
   c. people with Urbach-Wiethe disease are unusually aggressive and fearful.
   d. monkeys rise to the top of the social hierarchy, because they successfully threaten others.

13. Librium, Valium, and Xanax
   a. are more habit-forming than barbiturates and more likely to lead to a fatal overdose.
   b. are benzodiazepines.
   c. act exclusively on CCK synapses.
   d. All of the above are true.

14. The benzodiazepines
   a. block $GABA_A$ synapses.
   b. decrease the membrane's permeability to chloride ions.
   c. attach to binding sites on the $GABA_A$ receptor complex, thereby facilitating GABA binding.
   d. directly open chloride channels.

15. Which of the following is true?
   a. Alcohol displaces benzodiazepines from their binding sites, thereby disrupting GABA transmission.
   b. Endozepines, including diazepam-binding inhibitor (DBI), are actually endogenous antibenzodiazepines, which inhibit GABA transmission.
   c. The most effective anti-anxiety drugs stimulate CCK receptors.
   d. Alcohol produces its antianxiety effects by blocking chloride channels.

16. Cortisol
   a. is secreted by the anterior pituitary gland.
   b. serves primarily to activate a sudden burst of "fight or flight" activity.
   c. serves primarily to decrease metabolic activity in order to save energy for later stresses.
   d. shifts energy away from synthesis of proteins, including those necessary for the immune system, and towards increasing blood sugar.

17. T cells
    a. are specialized to produce antibodies.
    b. mature in the thymus and either attack intruder cells or stimulate other B or T cells to multiply.
    c. are cells in the hypothalamus that produce cytokines.
    d. are useless until they are activated by B cells.

18. Stress
    a. is by far the major factor in the activity of nonhuman animals' immune response; however, humans are not susceptible to stress effects.
    b. impairs the immune system from the first moments of the stressor's presence.
    c. produces a brief activation of the immune system, followed by inhibition of immune response if the stressor continues for a long time and is sufficiently intense.
    d. All of the above are true.

19. Prolonged high levels of cortisol
    a. make hippocampal neurons vulnerable to damage, which results in decreased learning and memory.
    b. lead to an increase in protein synthesis, which helps the immune system during long-term stressors.
    c. are found in almost all people with PTSD.
    d. All of the above are true.

20. PTSD
    a. occurs in almost all people who are subjected to traumatic experiences.
    b. includes symptoms of flashbacks, nightmares, avoidance of reminders, and exaggerated response to noises or other stimuli.
    c. is usually accompanied by a larger than usual hippocampus, because the memory of the trauma is so firmly established.
    d. All of the above are true.

Solutions

True/False Questions

1. F	7. T	13. T	19. F
2. T	8. T	14. F	20. T
3. F	9. T	15. F	21. F
4. F	10. T	16. T	22. T
5. T	11. F	17. F	23. F
6. T	12. F	18. T	

Fill In The Blanks

1. James- Lange
2. pure autonomic
3. frontal; temporal; insular
4. left
5. right
6. prefrontal; amygdala
7. corticomedial
8. 5-HIAA; aggressiveness
9. tryptophan hydroxylase; monoamine oxidase
10. amygdala
11. Klüver-Bucy
12. Urbach-Wiethe; amygdale; fear
13. CCK; GABA
14. Benzodiazepines; chloride
15. endozepine; fearfulness; aggression
16. Hans Selye
17. general adaption syndrome
18. ACTH; cortisol.
19. natural killer cells
20. Cytokines; vagus; fever; fatigue
21. hippocampus; cortisol
22. amygdala; PTSD

Matching Items

1. d	5. b	9. n	13. h
2. c	6. k	10. l	14. j
3. a	7. i	11. g	
4. f	8. e	12. m	

Multiple Choice Questions

1. b	6. b	11. d	16. d
2. d	7. d	12. a	17. b
3. a	8. a	13. b	18. c
4. d	9. b	14. c	19. a
5. c	10. c	15. b	20. b

CHAPTER 12

CHAPTER 13

The Biology of Learning and Memory

Introduction

Learning depends upon changes within single cells, which then work together as a system to produce adaptive behavior. Different kinds of learning and memory may rely on different neural mechanisms. Classical conditioning establishes a learned association between a neutral (conditioned) stimulus (CS) and an unconditioned stimulus (UCS) that evokes a reflexive response (UCR). As a result, the previously neutral stimulus comes to evoke a conditioned response (CR), which is often, but not always, similar to the reflexive response. Operant conditioning is the increase or decrease in a behavior as a result of reinforcement or punishment. Other forms of learning, such as bird song learning, may fall outside the categories of classical or operant conditioning.

Ivan Pavlov hypothesized that all learning is based on simple neural connections formed between two brain areas active at the same time. Karl Lashley tested this hypothesis by making various cuts that disconnected brain areas from each other and by removing varying amounts of cerebral cortex after rats had learned mazes or discrimination tasks. To his surprise, he found that no particular connection or part of the cortex was critical for any task. Lashley incorrectly assumed that all learning occurred in the cortex and that all types of learning relied on the same physiological mechanism. Recent evidence suggests that certain subcortical nuclei may be important for specific types of learning and that several different neural mechanisms underlie different types of learning. For example, one simple type of conditioning, the eye-blink response, relies on the lateral interpositus nucleus of the cerebellum. The red nucleus, a midbrain motor center, is necessary for the motor expression of the eye-blink response, but not formation of the memory. Similar mechanisms appear to underlie eye-blink conditioning in rats and in humans.

Memory can be divided into several types: short-term vs. long-term, explicit vs. implicit, and declarative vs. procedural. Short-term memories have relatively low capacity and fade rapidly, unless they are rehearsed. When an item in short-term memory is forgotten, it cannot be reconstructed. Long-term memory has a vast capacity, can be recalled even years later, and can often be reconstructed if an item is forgotten. Working memory is the temporary storage of information while we are using it. Working memory lasts longer than short-term memory, but is not a station on the way to long-term memory. The prefrontal cortex seems to be especially important for working memory. A common test of working memory is the delayed response task, in which one must respond to a stimulus presented a short time earlier. Neurons in the prefrontal cortex are active during the delay. Aged monkeys have fewer neurons in the prefrontal cortex. Aging humans with declining memory have declining prefrontal activity, while aging humans with intact memory show greater activity than in young adults, perhaps because the neurons have to work harder to compensate for impairments elsewhere.

Information about memory has been obtained from studies of three major syndromes involving amnesia in humans. A main cognitive deficit in all three syndromes is the inability to form new long-term declarative or explicit memories. Declarative memory is memory that people can state in words, whereas procedural memory consists of motor or perceptual skills. Explicit memory is deliberate recall of information that one recognizes as a memory; implicit memories can be detected as indirect influences on behavior and do not require recollection of specific information. One syndrome results from hippocampal damage and is exemplified by the patient H. M., who had bilateral removal of the hippocampus to relieve incapacitating epilepsy. Following surgery, H. M. has suffered extensive anterograde amnesia (inability to form memories of events after the damage) and moderate retrograde amnesia (loss of memories of events before the damage); however, his working memory remains intact. The cases of H. M. and other patients with hippocampal damage suggest that the primary function of the hippocampus is to promote storage of declarative, explicit memory, especially episodic memory—memory for single events or episodes. Such patients are as impaired at imagining the future as at describing the past. Nonhuman animals with hippocampal damage show memory impairments on delayed matching tasks, which test abilities similar to human declarative memory. Declarative memory does seem to rely mostly on the hippocampus, whereas procedural memory relies mostly on the basal ganglia. However, both brain areas may contribute to both tasks, and most tasks require both kinds of memory. A second hypothesis is that a major function of the hippocampus is spatial memory. Hippocampal neurons are tuned to specific locations. Rats with hippocampal damage forget which arms of a radial arm maze they have already entered in search of food; they also forget the location of a platform submerged in murky water. Among related species of birds that live in different habitats, those that are most dependent on finding previously hidden food have the largest hippocampus. Humans also use their hippocampus to solve spatial problems. The hippocampus of London taxi drivers is activated while answering spatial questions, and their posterior hippocampus is larger than in other people. A third hypothesis is that the hippocampus is important for context learning, in which the meaning of a stimulus depends upon other stimuli that are paired with it. Context is especially important for episodic memories, and people with hippocampal damage have great trouble with episodic memories.

Another function of the hippocampus is to consolidate short-term memories into long-term memories. Injection of a protein synthesis inhibitor into the hippocampus blocks consolidation, but not the initial learning. Highly emotional events are easily remembered because of the effects of cortisol. Small to moderate amounts of cortisol stimulate the amygdala and hippocampus; the amygdala then further activates the hippocampus and cerebral cortex. However, prolonged or excessive stress, and its accompanying high cortisol level, impairs memory. The brain appears to work harder to remember recent items, whereas older memories are stored more firmly. There appears to be an "autobiographical memory bump," with items from ages 10 to 30 being recalled better than those either earlier or later.

Another human disorder, Korsakoff's syndrome, occurs almost exclusively in severe alcoholics and is characterized by apathy, confusion, and memory loss. It is caused by prolonged thiamine deficiency, which results in loss of neurons throughout the brain, especially in the dorsomedial thalamus, which projects to prefrontal cortex. In addition to their deficit in explicit memory, Korsakoff's patients have difficulty recalling the temporal order of events. They also confabulate, or make a guess to fill in the memory gaps.

A third human memory disorder is Alzheimer's disease, which is characterized by memory loss, confusion, depression, restlessness, hallucinations, delusions, and loss of sleep and appetite. People with Down syndrome, who have three copies of chromosome 21, almost always get Alzheimer's disease if they survive into middle age. Mutations of other genes account for a small percentage of late-onset Alzheimer's disease. However, half of all patients have no relatives with the disease. Alzheimer's disease is associated with the accumulation of amyloid deposits in the brain. Amyloid precursor protein is normally cleaved to form a smaller protein of 40 amino acids, amyloid-β 40 ($A\beta_{40}$), which probably has a useful function. In people with Alzheimer's disease, the precursor is cleaved to form a slightly larger protein consisting of 42 amino acids ($A\beta_{42}$), which accumulates and damages the membranes of axons and dendrites. Amyloid plaques, formed in the extracellular space from degenerating axons and dendrites, lead to atrophy of the cerebral cortex, hippocampus, and other areas. An abnormal form of tau protein, which forms part of the intracellular support structure of neurons, also accumulates in Alzheimer's patients, forming tangles within cell bodies. Drugs that stimulate acetylcholine receptors or prolong acetylcholine release may help to relieve symptoms. Stimulation of cannabinoid receptors can limit overstimulation of glutamate receptors, thereby protecting neurons. Antioxidants and curcumin (a component of Indian curry) may block amyloid-β formation and guard against brain degeneration. One lesson from amnesic patients is that there are somewhat independent kinds of memory that depend on different brain areas.

In addition to the hippocampus (important for storing declarative, episodic, spatial, and contextual memories), the basal ganglia (important for procedural memories) and prefrontal cortex (important for working memory and reasoning), numerous other brain areas contribute to memory. The amygdala is especially important for fear learning, and the parietal lobe helps to associate one piece of information with another. The anterior and inferior regions of the temporal lobe contribute to semantic memory; it communicates with other parts of the brain for a full concept of something. Parts of the prefrontal cortex are important for learning about rewards and punishments. The basal ganglia also learn about rewards, but more slowly. Ventromedial prefrontal cortex compares the expected reward with past experience, and the orbitofrontal cortex determines how one reward compares to others. Some cells in the anterior cingulate cortex respond when reward is greater than expected, while others respond when the reward is less than expected. People who show greater prefrontal cortex reactions to loss have been found to be more willing to gamble.

Many researchers have studied the cellular mechanisms of learning in invertebrates, which have simple, well-defined nervous systems. Studies using Aplysia have demonstrated changes in identified synapses during habituation and sensitization. Long-term potentiation (LTP) is increased synaptic responsiveness in cells of the mammalian hippocampus. LTP shows specificity, in that only the active synapses become strengthened. It also shows cooperativity, in which near simultaneous stimulation by two or more axons increases responsiveness. A third characteristic is associativity, which refers to the increased responsiveness to a weak stimulus as a result of its being paired with a strong stimulus. The opposite change, long term depression (LTD), occurs in both the hippocampus and cerebellum. It is a decrease in responsiveness to a synaptic input that has been repeatedly paired with another input at low frequency. LTP depends on stimulation of two types of glutamate receptors. Stimulation of AMPA receptors depolarizes the neuron, thereby displacing the magnesium ions that normally block the ion channels of nearby NMDA receptors. As a result, the NMDA receptors are able to respond to glutamate, allowing both sodium and calcium ions to enter the cell. The calcium, in turn, activates certain chemicals inside the postsynaptic neuron that result in either increased numbers or responsiveness of AMPA or NMDA receptors and increased dendritic branches. Finally, a retrograde neurotransmitter, such as nitric oxide, may increase the responsiveness and size of presynaptic terminals and increase the number of transmitter release sites. Drugs that enhance LTP also enhance memory. For example, caffeine increases arousal and enhances memory, and drugs that facilitate acetylcholine in people with Alzheimer's disease also result in increased memory. Finally, ginko biloba and other "natural" drugs touted to enhance memory do increase blood flow and produce small benefits, but only in those with circulatory problems. Drugs, such as propranolol, that block memories may be used to decrease post-traumatic stress disorder.

Learning Objectives

Module 13.1 Learning, Memory, Amnesia, and Brain Functioning
1. Know the differences between classical and operant conditioning and the terms used in each.
2. Be able to describe Lashley's search for the engram and his conclusions and why Richard Thompson's search arrived at a different conclusion.
3. Know the characteristics of short-term, long-term and working memory.
4. Be able to describe the theories of the function of the hippocampus in declarative memory, spatial memory, context learning, and consolidation.
5. Know the symptoms and causes of Korsakoff's syndrome and Alzheimer's disease.
6. Know the other brain areas that contribute to various aspects of memory.

Module 13.2 Storing Information in the Nervous System
1. Understand the mechanisms of habituation and sensitization in Aplysia.
2. Be able to describe the characteristics of long-term potentiation (LTP) and long-term depression (LTD).
3. Understand the roles of AMPA and NMDA receptors in LTP.

Key Terms and Concepts

Module 13.1 Learning, Memory, Amnesia, and Brain Functioning
1. Localized representations of memory
     Memory nearly synonymous with "self"
     Classical conditioning
          Ivan Pavlov
          Conditioned stimulus (CS)
          Unconditioned stimulus (UCS)
          Unconditioned response (UCR)
          Conditioned response (CR)
     Operant conditioning
          Reinforcer
          Punishment
     Neither classical nor operant
          Bird-song learning
          Food aversion
     Lashley's search for the engram
          Engram: Physical representation of what has been learned
          Amount of damage, not location, is important
               Equipotentiality: All parts of cortex contribute equally to complex behaviors
               Mass action: Cortex works as a whole
          Unnecessary assumptions:
               Cerebral cortex is the only site of the engram
               All kinds of memory are the same
     The modern search for the engram
          Richard F. Thompson
               Rabbit eye-blink response
               Lateral interpositus (LIP) nucleus of cerebellum: Site of conditioning
                    Last structure in the circuit that had to be awake during conditioning
                    Necessary for learning, retention, and extinction
               Red nucleus: Motor expression
          Classical conditioning of eye-blink in humans
               PET scans: increased activity in cerebellum, red nucleus, and other areas
               Damage to cerebellum → impaired eye-blink conditioning
2.   Types of memory
     Short-term and long-term memory
          Difference between learning research and memory research
               Learning research: Classical or operant research on animals
               Memory research: People describe events
          Donald Hebb
               Short-term memory
                    Seven unrelated items
                    Fades quickly without rehearsal
                    Once forgotten, it is lost
               Long-term memory

Vast capacity

Hints → reconstruction of memory

Weakened distinction between short-term and long-term memory

Time for consolidation varies

Familiarity helps

Working memory

Delayed response task

Prefrontal cortex

Elevated calcium: Economical storage of temporary information

Older people

Aged monkeys: Decreased number of neurons and input to prefrontal cortex

Declining activity in prefrontal cortex → impaired working memory

Those with intact memory: Greater activity than young adults

Stimulant drugs → enhanced activity in prefrontal cortex of aging monkeys → improved memory

3.   The hippocampus and amnesia

Amnesia: Memory loss

People with hippocampal damage

H. M.: Surgery for severe epilepsy

Anterograde and retrograde memory

Decreased epilepsy

Severe anterograde amnesia (loss of memory for events after surgery)

Moderate retrograde amnesia (loss of memory for events years before surgery)

Intact short-term memory

Severe impairment of episodic memories (memories of single events)

A few weak semantic (factual) memories

Improvement with repeated practice if patients devise own labels

K. C.: Motorcycle accident → diffuse brain damage, including hippocampus

Lack of episodic memories

Remembers factual information from before the injury

Describe past events, imagine future events: Same brain areas, including hippocampus

Amnesia: Similar impairment in describing past, imagining future

Better implicit than explicit memory

Explicit memory: Deliberate recall of information one recognizes as a memory

Implicit memory: Influence of recent experience on behavior, even without realizing one is using memory

Amnesia:

Normal short-term or working memory

Severe anterograde declarative memory

In many cases, severe loss of episodic memories

Better implicit than explicit memory

Theories of the function of the hippocampus

The hippocampus and declarative memory

Damage to the hippocampus in humans

Impaired declarative memory (ability to state memory in words), especially episodic memory

Intact procedural memory (development of motor skills and habits)

Damage to the hippocampus in rats

Impairs memory of when they smelled an odor

Damage to the hippocampus in monkeys

Delayed matching-to-sample test: Impaired

Delayed nonmatching-to-sample test: Impaired

Basal ganglia important for procedural memory

Most tasks: Both declarative and procedural memory

The hippocampus and spatial memory

Rats: Hippocampal neurons tuned to spatial locations or directions

"Remap" environment after a change

Young rats remap faster than old rats

London taxi drivers

Hippocampus activated by answering spatial questions

Posterior hippocampus larger than in other people

Damage to the hippocampus in rats

Radial maze: Forget which arms they already tried

Damage to areas of thalamus and cortex that send input to   hippocampus → similar impairments

Morris water maze task: Slowly learns location of platform

Disoriented if start area or platform changes location

Damage after learning → rat doesn't remember the task

Closely related species that differ in spatial memory

Clark's nutcracker: Most dependent on buried food

Largest hippocampus

Best performance on spatial tasks

Pinyon jays: Moderately dependent on buried food

Second largest hippocampus

Second best performance on spatial tasks

Scrub jay and Mexican jay: Least dependent on buried food

Smallest hippocampus

Worst performance on spatial tasks

The hippocampus and context

Hippocampus → details and context

Soon after learning: Context helps, memory better

Later: Context doesn't help, memory worse

The hippocampus and consolidation

Consolidation of long-term memories

Protein synthesis inhibitor in hippocampus → blocks consolidation, not initial learning

Emotional events easy to remember

Cortisol in small to moderate amounts:

Stimulates amygdala and hippocampus

Amygdala → hippocampus → cerebral cortex → memory storage

Excessive or prolonged → memory impairment

      Brain works harder to remember more recent events

        Events from ages 10 – 30: "Autobiographical memory bump"

4.   Other types of amnesia

  Korsakoff's syndrome and other prefrontal damage

      Wernicke-Korsakoff syndrome

      Prolonged thiamine (vitamin B_1) deficiency

        Chronic alcoholics

      Widespread loss of neurons, especially in:

        Dorsomedial thalamus (projects to prefrontal cortex)

      Apathy, confusion, memory loss

      Fencing damage to dorsomedial thalamus → severe memory loss

      Poor recall of temporal order of events

      Confabulation: Guess to fill in gaps in memory

        Study best by repetition, not reading then testing

  Alzheimer's disease

      Better procedural than declarative memory

      Memory and alertness vary day to day and within a day

      Memory loss, confusion, depression, restlessness, hallucinations, delusions, sleeplessness, loss of appetite

      Genetic and nongenetic causes

        Relationship to Down syndrome (3 copies of chromosome 21)

          Genes on chromosome 21 and others linked to early-onset Alzheimer's

          Genes → less control of late-onset Alzheimer's

          Half of all patients: No known relatives with Alzheimer's

        Amyloid precursor protein → amyloid-β protein 40 (amyloid-β, or $A\beta_{40}$)

          Alzheimer's disease: Amyloid beta protein 42 ($A\beta_{42}$, longer form, impairs function)

          Plaques (degenerating axons and dendrites in space between neurons) → atrophy of cerebral cortex, hippocampus, other areas

        Tau protein: Part of intracellular support

          Abnormal tau → tangles (degeneration within cell bodies)

        Main problem: Probably amyloid-β, though tau contributes

          Decreasing tau → improved memory in mice with similar disorder

  Prevention or alleviation

      Stimulate acetylcholine receptors or prolong acetylcholine release

      Stimulate cannabinoid receptors → limits overstimulation of glutamate receptors

      Block formation of amyloid-β

        Antioxidants: Dark fruits and vegetables

        Curcumin (component of turmeric, in Indian curry)

  What patients with amnesia teach us

      Somewhat independent kinds of memory: Dependent on different brain areas

5.   The role of other brain areas in memory

  Entire cortex and many subcortical areas

  Amygdala → fear learning

  Parietal lobe damage → episodic memories intact, could not elaborate on them

Damage to anterior and inferior regions of temporal lobe → semantic dementia
    Lose concepts of appearance of certain animals, fruits and vegetables
Parts of prefrontal cortex: Learning about rewards and punishments
    Basal ganglia also learn about rewards, but more slowly
    Ventromedial prefrontal cortex: Expected reward, based on past experience
    Orbitofrontal cortex: How reward compares to others
    Anterior cingulate cortex:
        Some cells respond when reward more than expected
        Others respond when reward less than expected
    Greater prefrontal cortex reactions to loss: More willing to gamble
6.   In closing: Different types of memory
   "Overall intelligence" as measured by IQ tests: Convenient fiction
   Different abilities: Different brain processes

Module 13.2 Storing Information in the Nervous System

1.   Blind alleys and abandoned mines
   Wilder Penfield: Each neuron stores particular memory
      "Memories" vague, not accurate
   G. A. Horridge: "Learning" in decapitated cockroaches
      Process slow, variable
   James McConnell and others: Transfer of memories by feeding or injecting "trained" RNA
      Variable results
2.   Learning and the Hebbian synapse
   Repeated stimulation of neuron B by neuron A → synapse becomes strengthened
   Hebbian synapse: Synapse that is increased in effectiveness due to simultaneous pre- and postsynaptic activity
   May mediate classical conditioning, visual system development, associative learning
3.   Single-cell mechanisms of invertebrate behavior change
   Aplysia as an experimental animal
      Touch siphon, mantle, or gill → withdrawal response
   Habituation in Aplysia
      Decreased ability of sensory neuron to activate motor neuron
      Not due to muscle fatigue
      Not due to changes in sensory neuron
   Sensitization in Aplysia
      Increase in response to mild stimuli after more intense stimuli
      Facilitating interneuron: Serotonin (5-HT) → presynaptic terminals of many sensory neurons
      5-HT → closing of potassium channels → prolonged action potential → more transmitter release
      Protein synthesis → long-term sensitization
4.   Long-term potentiation in vertebrates (LTP)
   Rat hippocampus: Brief but rapid series of stimuli → increased responsiveness for minutes, days, or weeks
   Characteristics
      Specificity: Only active synapses strengthened
      Cooperativity: Nearly simultaneous stimuli more effective than single stimuli

Associativity: Pairing weak and strong inputs → enhanced later response to weaker one

Long term depression (LTD) in hippocampus and cerebellum

LTD: Prolonged decrease in response to inputs presented at low frequencies

LTP in one synapse → decreased responsiveness in neighbors

Biochemical mechanisms

Hippocampus

GABA synapses → LTP in a few cases

Most cases: AMPA and NMDA synapses

AMPA glutamate receptors

Open sodium channels

NMDA glutamate receptors: Depends on degree of polarization across membrane

Magnesium blockade of ion channel

Removal of magnesium by depolarization

Sodium and calcium influx into postsynaptic neuron

Calcium → increase in later responsiveness to glutamate

CaMKII (α-calcium-calmodulin-dependent protein kinase II) activation →

New AMPA receptors or old ones moved to better location

New NMDA receptors

Dendrite: New branches

Some AMPA receptors: More responsive

Fewer than half of highly activated neurons show LTP

LTD: Opposite of LTP

NMDA receptors: Establish, not maintain, LTP

Presynaptic changes

Retrograde neurotransmitter → presynaptic neuron →

Decrease threshold for action potentials

Increase neurotransmitter release

Expand its axon

Release transmitter from additional sites on axon

Nitric oxide: Common retrograde transmitter

LTP and behavior

LTP: Ordinary learning, explore new environment, develop drug addiction, repetitive sensory stimulation

NMDA antagonists: Impair retention 24 hours later, not immediately

LTP → protein production → enhanced memory

Drugs that inhibit protein production → weaker memory, even if given days after training

Drugs and memory

Caffeine → arousal → memory

Alzheimer's disease: Drugs that facilitate acetylcholine → memory

Increase in dopamine or glutamate may → memory

Ginko biloba and other chemicals → increase blood flow → small benefits in those with circulatory problems

5.   In closing: The physiology of memory

Requirement of memory: Record what we need to remember, not everything

Short-Answer Questions

Module 13.1 Learning, Memory, Amnesia, and Brain Functioning

1. *Localized representations of memory*

    a. Describe the relationships among the conditioned and unconditioned stimuli and the unconditioned and conditioned responses in classical conditioning.

    b. Who discovered classical conditioning? What were the conditioned and unconditioned stimuli in his experiments? What was the unconditioned, and eventually the conditioned, response?

    c. What is the fundamental difference between classical and operant conditioning? Define reinforcement and punishment in terms of operant conditioning.

    d. Why is bird-song learning difficult to classify?

    e. What is an engram? What two principles did Lashley propose based on his search for the engram?

    f. What two assumptions did Lashley make, which later investigators rejected?

    g. What brain area was found by Richard F. Thompson to be important for classical conditioning of the eye-blink response in rabbits?

    h. What area was important for the expression of the motor response, but not for the initial conditioning?

    i. Which areas showed increased activity on PET scans during eye-blink conditioning in humans?

2. *Types of memory*

    a. Define short-term memory and long-term memory.

    b. What is working memory?

    c. What is the delayed response task? Which brain area is especially important for performance on this task?

    d. Compare activity in the prefrontal cortex in older people who have declining memory with that of young adults. Describe prefrontal activity in older people who have intact memory.

    e. What mechanism of temporary storage of information appears to be more economical than repetitive action potentials?

3. *The hippocampus and amnesia*

    a. Why was H. M.'s hippocampus removed bilaterally? How successful was this treatment at relieving epilepsy? What were the other effects of the surgery?

    b. What is the difference between retrograde and anterograde amnesia? Which is more evident in H. M.?

    c. What is episodic memory? How was that affected by H. M.'s surgery?

d. Distinguish between declarative and procedural memory. Which is impaired in H. M.? What is a test for procedural memory?

e. Distinguish between explicit memory and implicit memory. What is one test of implicit memory?

f. For what three types of memory is the hippocampus hypothesized to be important?

g. Describe the delayed matching-to-sample and delayed nonmatching-to-sample tasks. Damage to which brain area impairs performance on these tasks?

h. What type of memory is tested by the radial maze and the Morris water maze task? What two kinds of errors can rats make in the radial maze? Which type of error do rats make after damage to the hippocampus?

i. Describe the Morris water maze task. What deficits on this task are seen in hippocampally-damaged rats?

j. Describe the relationship between birds' dependence on finding previously hidden food and the size of their hippocampus.

k. What is context learning?

l. By what two chemicals do exciting experiences enhance memory consolidation? What is the effect of excessive or prolonged stress on memory?

m. Which ages are considered the "autobiographical memory bump?" Are events remembered better or worse during these ages?

4. *Other types of amnesia*

a. What is the immediate cause of Korsakoff's syndrome? What are its symptoms? In what group of people does it usually occur?

b. Which brain area shows neuronal loss in Korsakoff's syndrome? Where does this area project?

c. What is confabulation? What is the best method of study for most people when learning a list? What is the best method for those with Korsakoff's syndrome? Why?

d. Describe the symptoms of Alzheimer's disease.

e. Why are some cases of early-onset Alzheimer's disease thought to be related to a gene on chromosome 21?

f. How important are genetic factors in late-onset Alzheimer's disease?

g. What is amyloid precursor protein? What are the two forms of amyloid-β protein? Which form is implicated in the formation of amyloid deposits?

h. What other protein is implicated in Alzheimer's disease? What is its normal function? What is the relative importance of these two proteins in causing the disease?

i. What are two temporary means of alleviating Alzheimer's disease? What dietary factors may guard against Alzheimer's disease?

j. What have we learned about memory from amnesic patients?

5. *The role of other brain areas in memory*

   a. What is the brain area that is most important for fear learning?

   b. Describe the symptoms of damage to the parietal lobe.

   c. What is the result of damage to the anterior and inferior regions of the temporal lobe?

   d. What area of the brain, besides the prefrontal cortex, contributes to reward learning? How does its contribution differ from that of the prefrontal cortex?

   e. Distinguish between the roles of the ventromedial prefrontal cortex and orbitofrontal cortex in reward learning.

   f. What are the response characteristics of two types of neurons in the anterior cingulate cortex?

   g. Describe the characteristics of neurons in the prefrontal cortex in people who are more likely to gamble.

Module 13.2 Storing Information in the Nervous System

1. *Blind alleys and abandoned mines*

   a. What did Wilder Penfield conclude from his brain stimulation experiments? What are some problems with his conclusion?

   b. Describe G. A. Horridge's experiments with headless cockroaches. Why was this experimental approach abandoned?

   c. Describe the experiments in planaria and rats that seemed to show transfer of training from one individual to another via RNA or protein. Why were these experiments abandoned?

2. *Learning and the Hebbian synapse*

   a. How did Donald Hebb explain consolidation?

   b. What is a Hebbian synapse? How is it related to classical conditioning?

3. *Single-cell mechanisms of invertebrate behavior change*

   a. Why should anyone be interested in the cellular mechanisms of habituation or sensitization in the lowly Aplysia?

   b. What possible mechanisms of habituation were ruled out? What mechanism does seem to account for habituation in Aplysia?

   c. How is sensitization produced experimentally in Aplysia?

   d. Describe the cellular events that explain sensitization in Aplysia. How does a decrease in potassium outflow increase transmitter release?

   e. How does long-term sensitization differ from the short-term variety?

4. *Long-term potentiation in vertebrates*

  a. How is long-term potentiation (LTP) produced? How long does it last? In what brain area was it first discovered?

  b. What is meant by specificity? Cooperativity? Associativity?

  c. What is long term depression (LTD)? Where has it been observed? How does it differ from LTP?

  d. Which transmitter stimulates both NMDA and AMPA receptors? Why must AMPA receptors be stimulated, in addition to NMDA receptors, in order to produce LTP?

  e. Describe the sequence of events that follows the successful activation of NMDA receptors.

  f. What is CaMKII?

  g. List four changes in the postsynaptic neuron that can contribute to LTP.

  h. Are NMDA receptors important for the establishment or the maintenance of LTP?

  i. What is a retrograde neurotransmitter? What changes in the presynaptic terminal may contribute to LTP?

  j. Name several kinds of situations in which LTP might produce learning.

  k. When do drugs that block NMDA receptors affect learning or retention?

  l. What kinds of drugs can enhance learning or memory?

  m. How beneficial is ginko biloba to memory? What is its mechanism of action? In what group of people is it beneficial?

True/False Questions

1. In some classical conditioning experiments the UR resembles the UCR, and in other cases it does not.

  TRUE or FALSE

2. Lashley proposed the principles of Equipotentiality and Mass Action.

  TRUE or FALSE

3. Richard F. Thompson presented data showing that Lashley's principles were indeed true.

  TRUE or FALSE

4. Donald Hebb proposed that short-term and long-term memory used the same chemical process; we just happen to tap into them at different times.

  TRUE or FALSE

5. Working memory is the way we store information while we are working on it. It lasts longer than short-term memory but is not a station on the route to long-term memory.

TRUE or FALSE

6. Temporary storage of information, as in the delayed response task, may depend on elevated levels of calcium, which is a more economical way of storing information than repetitive action potentials.

TRUE or FALSE

7. H. M.'s major problems are severe retrograde amnesia and deficits in implicit memory.

TRUE or FALSE

8. Damage to the hippocampus disrupts declarative memory, especially episodic memory, but leaves procedural memory intact.

TRUE or FALSE

9. Patients with hippocampal damage are as impaired at imagining the future as at describing the past.

TRUE or FALSE

10. London taxi drivers have especially large amygdalas, which help them find their way around the city.

TRUE or FALSE

11. Rats with damage to the hippocampus, or to areas of the thalamus and cortex that send information to the hippocampus, seldom enter a correct arm twice, but often enter the never-correct arms of a radial maze.

TRUE or FALSE

12. Korsakoff's syndrome is characterized by widespread loss of neurons, especially in the dorsomedial thalamus, which projects to the prefrontal cortex.

TRUE or FALSE

13. Early-onset Alzheimer's disease is primarily caused by thiamine deficiency, as a result of prolonged heavy drinking.

TRUE or FALSE

14. Early-onset Alzheimer's disease is linked to genes on chromosome 21 and others; however, half of all Alzheimer's patients have no known relatives with Alzheimer's.

TRUE or FALSE

15. A long form of amyloid-β protein produces plaques made up of degenerating axons and dendrites and leads to atrophy of the cerebral cortex, hippocampus, and other areas in Alzheimer's disease.

TRUE or FALSE

16. Damage to anterior and inferior regions of temporal lobe leads to a loss of fear learning.

TRUE or FALSE

17. Several areas of prefrontal cortex are important for learning about rewards and punishments; the basal ganglia also learn about rewards, but more slowly.

TRUE or FALSE

18. Decapitated cockroaches show very impressive learning ability and are very popular subjects for current research on learning.

TRUE or FALSE

19. Aplysia show sensitization when serotonin from a facilitating interneuron closes potassium channels on presynaptic terminals of sensory neurons, thereby prolonging the action potential and releasing more neurotransmitter.

TRUE or FALSE

20. The influx of magnesium through NMDA receptors triggers many intracellular changes that result in LTP.

TRUE or FALSE

21. Activation of CaMKII sets in motion many processes, including increasing AMPA and/or NMDA receptors, growing more dendritic branches, and increasing responsiveness of some AMPA receptors.

TRUE or FALSE

22. Activation of NMDA receptors is necessary for both establishing and maintaining LTP.

TRUE or FALSE

23. In some cases LTP depends on changes in the presynaptic neuron, produced by a retrograde transmitter.

TRUE or FALSE

Fill In The Blanks

1. In _____ conditioning the individual's response determines the outcome; in _____ conditioning the CS and UCS are presented independently of the individual's behavior.

2. A(n) _____ is the physical representation of what has been learned.

3. The _____ of the cerebellum is the site of conditioning of the eye-blink response. The _____ is required for motor expression of this response.

4. The deliberate recall of information one recognizes as a memory is _____ memory.

5. HM shows severe _____ amnesia and moderate _____ amnesia.

6. Damage to the hippocampus impairs _____ memory, _____ memory, and _____ learning, as well as _____ of memory.

7. During emotional situations moderate increases in the hormone _____ activate the _____, which relays the information to the _____ and _____.

8. _____ syndrome results from thiamine deficiency, which causes widespread loss of neurons, especially in the _____ thalamus, which projects to the prefrontal cortex.

9. Alzheimer's disease is characterized by _____, formed from degenerating axons and dendrites, and _____, resulting from abnormal _____ protein, which normally forms part of the intracellular support network.

10. Some possible means of preventing or alleviating Alzheimer's disease are stimulating _____ or _____ receptors, blocking the formation of amyloid-β by including _____ or _____ in the diet.

11. The _____ is important for fear learning.

12. Damage to the _____ lobe leaves episodic memories intact, but the person is unable to elaborate on them.

13. Some cells in the _____ cortex respond when reward is more than expected, whereas others respond when reward is less than expected.

14. Greater reactions to loss in the _____ occur in people who are more willing to gamble.

15. The main difference between stimuli leading to LTP or to LTD is the _____ of stimulation of the two inputs.

16. Stimulation of AMPA receptors is needed to remove the _____ ions that normally block the ion channels of NMDA receptors.

17. LTP may increase the number of _____ and/or _____ receptors, increase _____, and increase sensitivity of some _____ receptors.

18. A(n) _____ neurotransmitter from the postsynaptic neuron to the presynaptic neuron may decrease the threshold for _____, increase _____ release, expand the size of the _____, and increase the number of sites of transmitter release.

19. A common retrograde neurotransmitter is _____.

20. _____ increases blood flow in people with circulatory problems and may thereby produce small increases in memory.

Matching Items

1. _____ Bird song learning
2. _____ Mass action
3. _____ Lateral interpositus nucleus
4. _____ Memory of single events
5. _____ Cortisol
6. _____ Economical way to store information temporarily
7. _____ Prefrontal cortex
8. _____ H. M.
9. _____ Rat hippocampal neurons
10. _____ Korsakoff syndrome
11. _____ Alzheimer's disease
12. _____ Aplysia sensitization
13. _____ NMDA receptors
14. _____ Amygdala

a. Episodic memory
b. Site of eye-blink conditioning
c. Lashley: Cortex works as a whole
d. Moderate amounts facilitate memory
e. Severe anterograde amnesia
f. Neither classical nor operant conditioning
g. Responses tuned to spatial locations
h. $A\beta_{42}$, abnormal tau, plaques, and tangles
i. Elevated levels of calcium
j. Severe thiamine deficiency
k. Site of working memory
l. Area important for fear learning
m. Serotonin from facilitating interneurons
n. Establish, not maintain, LTP

Multiple-Choice Questions

1. In classical conditioning
   a. the meat used by Pavlov was the conditioned stimulus.
   b. the learner's behavior controls the presentation of reinforcements and punishments.
   c. a stimulus comes to elicit a response that may be similar to a response elicited by another stimulus.
   d. bird-song learning can be fully explained in terms of CS and UCS.

2. Ivan Pavlov showed that
   a. after some pairings of the CS and the UCS, the individual begins to make a new, learned response to the CS.
   b. all parts of the cortex contribute equally to complex learning.
   c. the cortex works as a whole—the more cortex, the better.
   d. learning occurs when cells in the UCS center degenerate and cells in the CS center branch diffusely.

3. Lashley successfully demonstrated that
   a. the lateral interpositus nucleus is the site of all engrams.
   b. all learning takes place in the cerebral cortex.
   c. the same neural mechanisms underlie all types of learning.
   d. none of the above

4. The lateral interpositus nucleus of the cerebellum
   a. is important for the motor expression of eye-blink conditioning in rabbits, but not the actual conditioning.
   b. is important for the actual conditioning of the eye-blink response.
   c. is more important for explicit than implicit memory formation.
   d. is an area that shows a great deal of damage in Korsakoff's syndrome.

5. Hebb's distinction between short-term and long-term memory
   a. was based on observations that the two types memory differ in capacity, in how long they last, and whether a hint can help reconstruct a memory that seemed forgotten.
   b. is supported by data showing that short-term memories are stored in the amygdala and long-term memories are stored in the lateral interpositus nucleus of the cerebellum.
   c. has been rejected by researchers because short-term and long-term memory merge so gradually that they are considered to be a single type of memory.
   d. has recently been attributed to Pavlov instead of Hebb.

6. Working memory
   a. lasts longer than short-term memory and is not a way-station to long-term memory.
   b. can be tested by the delayed response task.
   c. is stored in the prefrontal cortex.
   d. all of the above

7. The delayed response task for monkeys
   a. showed that visual memories are stored in primary visual cortex.
   b. showed that high activity in prefrontal cortex during the delay was correlated with successful performance on the task, suggesting that this area does store working memory.
   c. showed that cells in the prefrontal cortex are more important for initiating movement than for storing information about the stimulus.
   d. is no longer used as a test for working memory.

8. H. M.
   a. had his hippocampus removed because of his uncontrollable violence.
   b. acquired severe epilepsy as a result of the surgery.
   c. has a terrific memory for numbers but can learn no new skills.
   d. has more severe problems with declarative than with procedural memory.

9. Which of the following statements applies to H. M.?
   a. He has more severe anterograde than retrograde amnesia.
   b. He has more trouble with implicit than with explicit memory.
   c. His deficits show that the hippocampus is the storage site for all factual memories.
   d. All of the above are true.

10. Your memory of what you had for dinner last night is an example of
    a. explicit memory.
    b. implicit memory.
    c. procedural memory.
    d. short-term memory.

11. Which of the following is true?
    a. Hippocampal damage impairs implicit memory more than explicit memory
    b. The basal ganglia are more important for declarative than procedural memory.
    c. Implicit memory is an influence of recent experience on behavior, even if one does not recognize that influence.
    d. All of the above are true.

12. Damage to the hippocampus produces impairment on tasks requiring
    a. declarative, explicit memory.
    b. context learning.
    c. spatial memory.
    d. all of the above.

13. Damage to the hippocampus results in
    a. rats going down a never-correct arm of the radial maze.
    b. rats forgetting which arms they have already explore.
    c. inability to climb onto a platform in the Morris search task because of motor impairment.
    d. monkeys that cannot choose a nonmatching stimulus under any conditions.

14. Which of the following is true?
    a. Clark's nutcracker birds are very dependent on previously hidden food and have a large hippocampus.
    b. Mexican jays are also dependent on previously hidden food, but have a small hippocampus.
    c. The use of color memory in solving problems is a better predictor of hippocampal size than is dependence on previously hidden food.
    d. Hippocampal damage impairs performance on all tasks that use spatial memory, but does not impair any other tasks.

15. Experiments on consolidation have shown that
    a. a protein synthesis inhibitor in the hippocampus affected the initial learning, so there was nothing to consolidate.
    b. more brain activity may be required to remember recent events than those that were consolidated years ago.
    c. prolonged high elevations of cortisol levels are even more effective than brief moderate elevations for promoting memory storage.
    d. all of the above are true.

16. Which of the following is true?
    a. Even moderate levels of cortisol are usually harmful to the consolidation of memories.
    b. Testing rats in the Morris water maze is difficult, because rats enjoy swimming so much that they don't try to find the hidden platform.
    c. When humans recall a recent memory (which includes details and context), the hippocampus is activated; however, when recalling an older memory, the hippocampus may or may not be activated.
    d. Recent experiments show that the hippocampus is important only for spatial memories.

17. Korsakoff's syndrome
    a. occurs because alcohol dissolves proteins in the brain, thereby shrinking presynaptic endings.
    b. is caused by prolonged thiamine deficiency.
    c. results from damage primarily to the hippocampus.
    d. all of the above

18. Patients with Korsakoff's syndrome
    a. have damage in the dorsomedial nucleus of the thalamus, which projects to prefrontal cortex.
    b. have symptoms somewhat similar to those of patients with damage to the prefrontal cortex.
    c. have better implicit memory than explicit memory.
    d. all of the above

19. Alzheimer's disease
    a. results from three copies of chromosome 21.
    b. results from a long history of excessive alcohol consumption.
    c. results in memory loss, confusion, depression, restlessness, hallucinations, delusions, sleeplessness, and loss of appetite.
    d. impairs procedural memory more than declarative memory.

20. Patients with Alzheimer's disease
    a. have plaques and tangles in damaged areas of their brains.
    b. unlike H. M. and Korsakoff's patients, have more problems with implicit than explicit memory.
    c. have a nearly 100% probability of passing the disease on to their offspring.
    d. all of the above

21. Which of the following is true concerning Alzheimer's disease?
    a. Amyloid precursor protein can be cleaved to produce amyloid-β protein 42 ($A\beta_{42}$), which accumulates in the brain and impairs the function of neurons.
    b. An abnormal form of the tau protein, which forms part of the intracellular support structure in neurons, also accumulates in Alzheimer's patients.
    c. Certain genes have been implicated in early-onset Alzheimer's disease.
    d. All of the above are true.

22. Techniques for alleviating or preventing Alzheimer's disease include
    a. totally avoiding curcumin, an ingredient in Indian curry.
    b. eating a diet rich in antioxidants.
    c. giving drugs that block acetylcholine receptors or decrease acetylcholine release.
    d. injecting large amounts of $A\beta_{42}$ into the brains of aging people.

23. Which of the following is true?
    a. The amygdala is important for fear learning.
    b. Parietal lobe damage leads to inability to elaborate on episodic memories.
    c. Damage to anterior and inferior regions of the temporal lobe result in semantic dementia (loss of concepts of appearance of certain animals, fruits and vegetables.
    d. All of the above are true.

24. Donald Hebb proposed that
    a. a cellular basis of memory is the strengthening of synapses by simultaneous activity in the pre- and postsynaptic neurons.
    b. having two different axons stimulating a given dendrite at the same time is confusing to the dendrite and leads to long-term depression.
    c. short-term and long-term memory are the same thing.
    d. Hebbian synapses can explain operant, but not classical, conditioning.

25. Aplysia are studied because
    a. they are the intellectual giants of the ocean.
    b. they have simple nervous systems with large neurons that are virtually identical among individuals.
    c. they have the most complex brains of all invertebrates.
    d. we can automatically infer the principles of learning in complex vertebrates.

26. Habituation in Aplysia is the result of
    a. a decrease in the firing rate of a facilitating interneuron.
    b. a decrease in the firing rate of the sensory neuron.
    c. decreased ability of the sensory neuron to activate the motor neuron.
    d. muscle fatigue.

27. The mechanism mediating sensitization in Aplysia includes
    a. the release of dopamine from the sensory neuron onto the facilitating interneuron.
    b. the release of serotonin by the sensory neuron onto the motor neuron.
    c. release of serotonin by the facilitating interneuron onto the presynaptic terminals of sensory neurons → decreased potassium outflow in the sensory neurons → prolongation of transmitter release.
    d. synthesis of new proteins in short-term, but not long-term sensitization.

28. Long-term potentiation (LTP)
    a. was first discovered in Aplysi.
    b. results from increased inflow of magnesium ions through AMPA receptors.
    c. requires depolarization via NMDA receptors in order to allow calcium to flow out through AMPA receptors.
    d. requires depolarization via AMPA receptors in order to dislodge magnesium ions from NMDA receptors.

29. LTP
    a. is very powerful but lasts only a few seconds.
    b. may result from increased responsiveness of AMPA receptors, increased numbers of AMPA or NMDA receptors, increased dendritic branching, and/or some AMPA receptors becoming more responsive.
    c. depends on NMDA receptors for its maintenance, but not for its establishment.
    d. may result from decreased sensitivity of the postsynaptic cell to the inhibitory transmitter glutamate.

30. Presynaptic changes in LTP
    a. are mediated by a retrograde neurotransmitter.
    b. may include a decreased threshold for action potentials and increased transmitter release.
    c. may include expansion of axons and release of transmitter from new sites on the axon.
    d. all of the above

31. Which of the following is true of LTP and behavior?
    a. Caffeine increases arousal, which enhances memory.
    b. Drugs that block memories actually make post-traumatic stress disorder worse.
    c. Drugs that decrease protein production weaken memory only if given immediately before the learning.
    d. Ginko biloba is one of the best facilitators yet discovered for memory.

Solutions

True/False Questions

1.	T	7.	F	13.	F	19.	T
2.	T	8.	T	14.	T	20.	F
3.	F	9.	T	15.	T	21.	T
4.	F	10.	F	16.	F	22.	F
5.	T	11.	F	17.	T	23.	T
6.	T	12.	T	18.	F		

Fill In The Blanks

1. operant; classical
2. engram
3. lateral interpositus nucleus; red nucleus
4. explicit
5. anterograde; retrograde
6. declarative; spatial; context; consolidation
7. cortisol; amygdale; hippocampus; cerebral cortex
8. Korsakoff's; dorsomedial
9. plaques; tangles; tau
10. acetylcholine; cannabinoid; antioxidants; curcumin
11. amygdala
12. parietal
13. anterior cingulate
14. prefrontal cortex
15. frequency
16. magnesium
17. AMPA; NMDA; dendrite branching; AMPA
18. retrograde; action potentials; neurotransmitter; axon
19. nitric oxide
20. Ginko biloba

Matching Items

1.	f	5.	d	9.	g	13.	n
2.	c	6.	i	10.	j	14.	l
3.	b	7.	k	11.	h		
4.	a	8.	e	12.	m		

Multiple Choice Questions

1.	c	9.	a	17.	b	25.	b
2.	a	10.	a	18.	d	26.	c
3.	d	11.	c	19.	c	27.	c
4.	b	12.	d	20.	a	28.	d
5.	a	13.	b	21.	d	29.	b
6.	d	14.	a	22.	b	30.	d
7.	b	15.	b	23.	d	31.	a
8.	d	16.	c	24.	a		

CHAPTER 14

Cognitive Functions

Introduction

Each hemisphere of the brain receives sensory input primarily from the opposite side of the body and controls motor output to that side as well. The hemispheres are connected by a large bundle of fibers, the corpus callosum, as well as several smaller bundles. In humans, the eyes are connected with the brain in such a way that the left half of each retina supplies input to the left hemisphere, and vice versa. Furthermore, the left half of each retina receives input from the right half of the visual field. Therefore, the right half of the visual field projects to the left hemisphere, and vice versa. The auditory system projects bilaterally, although the projection to the opposite side is stronger. This relationship has allowed researchers to test the roles of the two hemispheres in people whose corpus callosum had been severed in order to relieve epilepsy. Such studies have shown that the left hemisphere is specialized for language and details, whereas the right hemisphere is particularly adept at emotional expression and perception, complex spatial problems, and overall patterns. Split-brain people sometimes seem to have two "selves" occupying the same body. In these people each half of the brain processes information and solves problems more or less independently of the other, although cooperation can be learned, thanks to enhanced function of subcortical connections. Even in intact people, evidence for hemispheric specialization can be seen. One possible basis for the lateralization of language functions in the left hemisphere is that in 65 percent of people a portion of the left temporal lobe, the planum temporale, is larger on the left side than on the right. The size difference is apparent even shortly after birth, and is correlated with performance on language tests.

The corpus callosum matures gradually, and experience determines the survival of the axons that make the best functional connections through the corpus callosum. People born without a corpus callosum are different from those who had split-brain surgery in adulthood. They can verbally describe sensory input from either hand and from either visual field. They may rely on greater development of the anterior and hippocampal commissures to convey information from one hemisphere to the other. In addition, each hemisphere develops connections to both sides of the body. About 10% of people are either left-handed or ambidextrous; most of them have mixed hemispheric control of speech, though the left is usually dominant. Although there may be hemisphere specialization, almost all tasks require cooperation by both hemispheres.

Because new features evolve from older ones that may have served similar functions, researchers have studied the language abilities of our nearest relatives, the chimpanzees. A number of chimpanzees have been taught to communicate with their trainers, a computer, or each other using various nonspoken language systems. However, even after years of training, their linguistic abilities fall far short of those of young children. Bonobos (Pan paniscus, or pygmy chimpanzees) have shown the most impressive linguistic abilities among our primate relatives.

They have learned by imitation, have used words to describe objects (as opposed to making a request) or to refer to a past event, and have created original sentences. In addition, some have learned to understand spoken English sentences. Parrots also show some language-like abilities. Studies of nonhuman language abilities may stimulate consideration of the unique versus shared abilities of humans and of the nature of language. Language may have evolved as a by-product of larger brains and increasing intelligence. However, some people with normal brains and intelligence have severely impaired language. Conversely, people with Williams syndrome have severe mental retardation and abnormally developed brains, but nearly normal language, social, and musical abilities. On some tests they even have better than average abilities. An alternative view is that language arose as an extra brain module. This view is supported by the ease with which children develop language. Indeed, if children do not learn some language when they are young, they will always be disadvantaged. However, much of the brain is involved in language processing, and parts of the brain important for language are also important for memory, music perception and other abilities. Therefore, increasing intelligence may have occurred because of the growing importance of language for social interaction. In general, children learn new languages more easily than do adults, especially pronunciation and unfamiliar grammar. On the other hand, adults are better at memorizing vocabulary.

Paul Broca discovered that damage to an area of the left frontal lobe results in difficulties with language production and with the use of grammatical connectives and other closed-class grammatical forms. People with such damage can usually understand both written and spoken language better than they can produce it, although they do have difficulty understanding the closed class words that they have most trouble producing. Carl Wernicke, on the other hand, described a pattern of deficits almost the opposite of Broca's aphasia: poor language comprehension, anomia (difficulty finding the right word), but articulate (though frequently meaningless) speech. This syndrome results from destruction of an area in the left temporal lobe near the primary auditory cortex. Although Wernicke's area and surrounding areas are specialized for language comprehension, connections to other areas, including the motor cortex, are also important. People who are bilingual do not store different languages in different parts of the brain; the same brain areas process both languages. In these same individuals, switching between languages recruits the frontal cortex, temporal cortex, and basal ganglia, thereby priming one set of word representations and inhibiting the other. Language and music have many parallels. Broca's area responds when musician's sight-read music. Musicians and music students are able to learn a second language more readily than others might be. A final parallel is our preference for music that resembles our own language in rhythm and tone.

Dyslexia, a reading disorder in otherwise normal people, may result from having a bilaterally symmetrical cortex, microscopic abnormalities, subtle hearing deficits, or differences in attention. Four genes that produce deficits in hearing and cognition are linked to dyslexia. There are many kinds of dyslexia, which have different underlying causes. Dysphonetic dyslexics have difficulty sounding out words, whereas dyseidetic dyslexics have trouble recognizing words as a whole. Some dyslexics' reading ability may be improved by focusing on one word at a time.

Consciousness of a stimulus depends on the amount of brain activity it elicits. Also, attention given to a stimulus increases the response to that stimulus. Certain brain areas respond more strongly to their preferred stimuli when those stimuli are presented with an incongruent distracting stimulus. This suggests that the major function of attention is to enhance the processing of relevant stimuli rather than to inhibit processing of irrelevant stimuli. Damage to parts of the right hemisphere may result in spatial neglect, a tendency to ignore the left side of the body and its surroundings or the left side of objects. The deficit is in attention, not sensation. There are several ways to increase attention to the neglected stimuli. Many patients with neglect also have problems with spatial working memory and with shifting attention in non-spatial contexts.

Learning Objectives

Module 14.1 Lateralization of Function
1. Be able to describe the visual and auditory connections to the hemispheres.
2. Know why some people have had their corpus callosum cut and how that operation affected their everyday lives and their ability to do conflicting tasks with their two hands.
3. Be able to describe the functions of the right and left hemispheres.
4. Understand the relationship of handedness and language dominance to the anatomical differences between the hemispheres.

Module 14.2 Evolution and Physiology of Language
1. Be able to describe the language abilities of common chimpanzees, bonobos, and parrots.
2. Understand the problems with the hypothesis that language is a product of overall intelligence.
3. Understand the evidence for and against the development of language as a special module.
4. Know the symptoms and causes of Broca's aphasia and Wernicke's aphasia.
5. Understand differences in the brain of those who are bilingual compared with those who are not.
6. Know the parallels in the brain between language and music.
7. Be able to describe the symptoms of dyslexia and some contributing anatomical, physiological, and functional factors.

Module 14.3 Consciousness and Attention
1. Know the similarities and differences in the early processing of conscious vs. unconscious stimuli and some factors that can select certain stimuli for consciousness.
2. Be able to describe examples of brain processing of attended vs. ignored stimuli and the implications for the role of attention in this processing.
3. Be able to describe the symptoms and physical causes of sensory neglect.

Key Terms and Concepts

Module 14.1 Lateralization of Function
1.   The left and right hemispheres
   Primarily contralateral control of the body
     Exceptions: Taste and smell
   Hemispheric connections
     Corpus callosum
     Anterior commissure
     Hippocampal commissure
   Lateralization
     Left hemisphere specialized for language
     Right hemisphere: Functions difficult to summarize
2.   Visual and auditory connections to the hemispheres
   Right visual field → left half of both retinas → left hemisphere (and vice versa)
     Small vertical strip in center of retina → both hemispheres
     Optic chiasm
   Both ears → both hemispheres
     Receive different information → Opposite side stronger
3.   Cutting the corpus callosum
   Decreases frequency of epileptic seizures
   Epilepsy: Repeated episodes of excessive synchronized neural activity
     Causes
       Decreased release of GABA
       Mutation of gene for GABA receptor
       Trauma, infection, tumor, toxic substance
     Antiepileptic drugs
       Block sodium flow across membrane
       Enhance effects of GABA
     Surgical removal of focus (origin)
     Cut corpus callosum if more than one focus
       Restricts seizures to one side
       Decreases number of seizures
   Split-brain people
     Maintain intellect and motivation
     Independent control of two sides of body
     Abnormal behavior only if input is restricted to one side
     No problem with familiar tasks, new tasks difficult
     Can use two hands independently
       Conflicting tasks: Cognitive, not motor problem for intact-brain people
         Easier if clear targets direct movement
    Left hemisphere: Speech comprehension and production
     95% of right-handers
     80% of left-handers
     Some speech understanding in both hemispheres
     Canary Island shepherds: Whistle communication → mostly left hemisphere

People who don't understand the language → react as if music

Split-brain → can name and describe object if processed with left hemisphere

Bilateral control of speech → stuttering in some people

Split hemispheres: Competition and cooperation

Hands do conflicting tasks

Learning to cooperate

Use of subcortical connections

Guess with left hemisphere → if wrong, right hemisphere → frown on both sides of face → left hemisphere detects frown → changes answer

Verbal task: One word to each hemisphere

Right hand drew input to left hemisphere

Left hand drew two pictures, but not combined concept

The right hemisphere

Understands simple speech

Emotional content of speech and facial expression, humor, and sarcasm

Left hemisphere damage → better detection of lying

Left hemisphere interferes with right hemisphere emotional perception

Right hemisphere damage → monotone; can't understand emotional expression, humor, or sarcasm

Right hemisphere: Recognizes both pleasant and unpleasant emotions in others

Spatial relationships

Right hemisphere: Overall patterns

Left hemisphere: Details

Hemispheric specializations in intact brains

Small differences

Difficulty doing two things at once when both depend on same hemisphere

4. Development of lateralization and handedness

Anatomical differences between the hemispheres

Innate tendency to attend to language sounds

Planum temporale: Larger in left hemisphere

Left to right ratio

Greater in those who are strongly right-handed

Correlated with language skills

Left/right difference even in infants

Smaller, but significant, left/right differences in gorillas and chimpanzees

Chimpanzees with larger left planum temporale → preference for right hand

Less ability to acquire language after early damage to left than to right

Maturation of the corpus callosum

Maturation over first 5 to 10 years

Survival of functional connections

Matures enough between ages 3 and 5 to compare stimuli between two hands

Development without a corpus callosum

Verbally describe stimuli in either hand

Can feel and differentiate objects with two hands

Speech still in left hemisphere

Each hemisphere: Increased connections to both sides of body

Anterior commissure

Hippocampal commissure

Hemispheres, handedness, and language dominance

More than 95% of right-handed: Left hemisphere for speech

Most left-handers (including those forced to write with right hand): Left hemisphere for speech, though some mixed control

Choice of path:

Right-handers turn left, and vice versa

5. Avoiding overstatements

Complicated tasks: Both hemispheres

6. In closing: One brain, two hemispheres

Module 14.2 Evolution and Physiology of Language

1. Nonhuman precursors of language

Productivity: Ability to produce new signals to represent new ideas

Common chimpanzees

Inability to speak

Ability to use visual symbols

Few original combinations: Little productivity

Symbols used to request, not describe

Limited comprehension of others' communications

Bonobos

Pan paniscus (pygmy chimpanzees)

Social order similar to humans'

Language ability of 2- to 2½-year-old child

Understand more than they produce

Name and describe without request

Request what they do not see

Refer to past

Creative requests

Early training by observation and imitation

Nonprimates

Parrots

Speak, name, count, form concepts

2. How did humans evolve language?

Language as a product of overall intelligence

First problem: People with normal intelligence and impaired language

Genetic condition → use of posterior areas, rather than frontal cortex

Second problem: Williams syndrome

Mental retardation, skillful use of language

Genes deleted from chromosome 7

Abnormal development of brain areas for visual processing

Severe impairment in numerical and visual-spatial skills

Normal abilities:

Music

Friendliness

Interpretation of facial expressions

Large amygdala, other areas for emotional processing → low social anxiety, more anxiety about inanimate objects

Language: Variable, from near normal to spectacular

Slow development

Sometimes odd grammar

Language not product of overall intelligence

Language as a special module

Language acquisition device

Ease of language development in most children

Poverty of the stimulus argument:

Children hear few examples of some grammatical structures they acquire

Therefore, rules inborn

But: Thousands of languages; can't be born knowing all

Areas in left temporal and frontal cortices essential to human language

Similar areas in monkeys respond to monkey vocalization

Intelligence as a byproduct of language

A sensitive period for language learning

Adults: Better at memorizing vocabulary

Children: Better at pronunciation and unfamiliar grammar

No age cutoff, but earlier is better

3. Brain damage and language

Broca's aphasia (nonfluent aphasia)

Aphasia (language impairment)

Broca's area: Small part of left frontal cortex, near motor cortex

Serious deficits only with more extensive damage

Broca's aphasia or nonfluent aphasia (language impairment caused by brain damage)

Deficits in comprehension if meaning is difficult

Difficulty in language production

Articulation, writing, and gestures

Affects production of sign language

Omission of closed-class grammatical forms (prepositions, conjunctions, etc.)

Ability to speak open-class forms (nouns and verbs)

Problem with meanings, not just pronunciation

May leave out weakest elements

Problems comprehending grammatical words and devices

Problems understanding prepositions and conjunctions

Still use normal word order for their language

Comprehension resembles normal people who are distracted

Rely on inferences

Wernicke's aphasia (fluent aphasia)

Wernicke's area: Near auditory cortex

Wernicke's aphasia or fluent aphasia (poor language comprehension, impaired ability to remember names of objects)

Articulate speech

Difficulty finding the right word (anomia, difficulty recalling the names of objects)

Poor language comprehension

Listen to speech → first, the temporal lobe (including Wernicke's area) responds → frontal lobe (including Broca's area)

Connections to other brain areas

Reading a verb → activation of motor cortex that would produce the movement

Brain mechanisms for bilinguals

Speak two languages

Languages are not kept separate

Same brain areas for both languages

Learned in early childhood → thicker language areas in temporal and frontal cortex

Switching between languages → activates frontal cortex, temporal cortex, and basal ganglia

Priming one language and inhibiting the other

4. Music and language

Language and music have parallels

Broca's area is activated when musicians sight-read music

Musicians better at learning second language

Alter timing and volume

Time and space between beats

We prefer music that resembles our language

5. Dyslexia

Specific impairment of reading

Adequate vision and other academic skills

More common in boys than girls

Linked to four genes that produce deficits in hearing or cognition

More common in English readers than in more phonetic language readers

Occurs in all languages

Mild microscopic abnormalities

Brain abnormalities are different between dyslexics who speak English versus Chinese

Nature of language determines which brain areas are most important for reading

Bilaterally symmetrical cortex, especially planum temporale

Auditory problems

Small number have impaired eye movements

Dysphonetic vs. dyseidetic dyslexics

Dysphonetic → difficulty sounding out words

Dyseidetic → difficulty recognizing words as wholes

Subtle hearing impairment

Difficulty distinguishing temporal order

Spoonerisms

Tapping rhythms

Converting vision to sound, vice versa

Differences in attention

Shifting attention from one word to another

Attentional focus to right of word in visual focus

Treatment: Read one word at a time

Attend to several tasks at once

6. In closing: Language and the brain

Language neither a simple by-product of intelligence nor independent of other functions

Module 14.3 Consciousness and attention

1. Brain activity associated with consciousness

Consciousness of a stimulus → amount of brain activity it elicits

Directing attention to a stimulus → increases the brain's response to that stimulus

Binocular rivalry

Consciousness as a threshold phenomenon

Yes-no phenomenon

People rated word stimulus as fully conscious or not at all

The fate of an unattended stimulus

Familiar/meaningful stimulus captures attention faster

Unconscious activity may influence behavior

2. The timing of consciousness

Phi phenomenon (motion is perceived from alternating image moving back and forth)

Second position influences perception of first position

3. Neglect

Spatial neglect: Damage to right hemisphere

Ignore left side of body and its surroundings

Damage to inferior right parietal cortex → neglect of everything to left of body

Damage to superior right parietal cortex → neglect left side of objects, regardless of location

Deviations when estimating midpoint: pick spots in the middle of line well to the right

Problem with attention, not sensation

Problems with spatial working memory and shifting attention

4. In closing: Attending to attention and being conscious of consciousness

Attention → enhancement of one stimulus after another

Theoretical implications about the nature of consciousness

Short-Answer Questions
Module 14.1 Lateralization of Function

1. *The left and right hemispheres*

    a. What are the main connections between the hemispheres?

2. *Visual and auditory connections to the hemispheres*

    a. To which hemisphere(s) does the right visual field project? To which hemisphere(s) does the right half of both retinas project? To which hemisphere(s) does the right eye project?

    b. To which hemisphere(s) does the right ear project? What ability requires this distribution of input? When the two hemispheres receive different information, which ear does each hemisphere pay more attention to?

3. *Cutting the corpus callosum*

   a. What are the causes of epilepsy? What are several ways in which it can be treated?

   b. What is the corpus callosum? Why is it sometimes severed in cases of severe epilepsy? What are the effects of such an operation on overall intelligence, motivation, and gross motor coordination?

   c. What have we learned from split-brain humans concerning specialization of the two hemispheres? Which tasks are best accomplished by the left hemisphere?

   d. What percentage of right-handed people have left-hemisphere dominance for language? Describe the control of language in left-handed people.

   e. What is a cause of stuttering in some people?

   f. What is the basis for learned cooperation between the hemispheres in split-brain people?

   g. What did the split-brain person draw with his right hand, when two different words were flashed to his right and left visual fields? What did he sometimes draw with his left hand? Could he combine information from his right and left visual fields to form a new concept?

   h. Which functions are best performed by the right hemisphere?

   i. What is one simple task that can show hemispheric specialization in intact people? How large are the hemispheric differences in intact people?

4. *Development of lateralization and handedness*

   a. What is the planum temporale and what is its significance for language?

   b. How early is the size difference in the left vs. right planum temporale apparent?

   c. Compare the ability of 3-year-olds and of 5-year-olds to discriminate fabrics with either one hand or different hands. What can we infer from this about the development of the corpus callosum?

   d. In what ways are people who never had a corpus callosum different from split-brain people?

   e. Which other commissures between the two hemispheres may compensate for the lack of a corpus callosum in people born without one?

Module 14.2 Evolution and Physiology of Language

1. *Nonhuman precursors of language*

   a. What are some differences between the abilities of common chimpanzees and of humans to use symbols?

   b. What was unusual about the ability of some bonobos to learn language?

   c. In what ways do bonobos resemble humans more than common chimpanzees in language abilities?

2. *How did humans evolve language?*

a. Briefly discuss the proposal that our language may have developed as a by-product of overall intelligence.

b. How well do the correlations between general intelligence and language hold up? How is this a problem for the view that language evolved as a product of large brains and intelligence?

c. Describe the pattern of abilities and disabilities in the family with a genetic mutation that produces language deficits. How is this a problem for the view that language evolved as a product of large brains and intelligence?

d. Describe Williams syndrome. How does this relate to the evolution of language as a product of general intelligence?

e. What is the main argument for the hypothesis that language evolved as an extra brain module? What is a problem with that hypothesis?

f. What is an alternative hypothesis regarding the evolution of language and intelligence?

g. Is there a critical period for language learning? What are some ways of testing this idea?

3. *Brain damage and language*

   a. Where is Broca's area located?

   b. Describe the effects of damage to Broca's area. What are closed-class words?

   c. Locate Wernicke's area.

   d. Contrast the effects of damage to Wernicke's area with those of damage to Broca's area.

   e. What other brain areas contribute to language comprehension?

   f. Contrast areas of the brain in those who speak one language with those who are bilingual.

4. *Music and language*

   a. What are the parallels between language and music?

   b. How might understanding music influence your ability to learn a second language?

   c. How does the language you speak influence your preference in music?

5. *Dyslexia*

   a. What is dyslexia? How consistent are its symptoms?

   b. What are some possible biological causes of dyslexia?

   c. Describe dysphonetic and dyseidetic types of dyslexia.

   d. What other difficulties do people with dyslexia often have?

   e. What is one method of improving the ability of dyslexics to read?

Module 14.3 Consciousness and Attention

1. *Brain activity associated with consciousness*

    a. In what time frame does the processing of conscious stimuli begin to differ from that of unconscious stimuli?

    b. What factors may lead to the selection of certain stimuli to be processed consciously?

2. *Neglect*

    a. Describe spatial neglect.

    b. Damage to what part of the brain gives rise to spatial neglect?

    c. How may the attention of a person with spatial neglect be directed to objects on his or her left side?

    d. What other deficits do many patients with spatial neglect have?

True/False Questions

1. The right visual field projects to the left half of both retinas, and from there to the left hemisphere.

    TRUE or FALSE

2. As with the visual system, the right auditory field projects only to the left hemisphere, in order to be able to coordinate auditory and visual input.

    TRUE or FALSE

3. The primary causes of epilepsy are decreased release of the excitatory transmitter glutamate and mutation of a gene for a glutamate receptor.

    TRUE or FALSE

4. Split-brain people can perform familiar tasks with no problem and can use their hands independently to perform competing tasks, which is difficult for intact-brain people.

    TRUE or FALSE

5. Specialties of the right hemisphere include emotional expression and interpretation, spatial abilities, humor, and sarcasm.

    TRUE or FALSE

6. The right hemisphere is unable to understand even simple speech.

    TRUE or FALSE

7. The left-to-right ratio of the size of the planum temporale is positively correlated with language ability.

    TRUE or FALSE

8. Some aspects of the behavior of young children are similar to those of split-brain people.

    TRUE or FALSE

9. Bonobo chimpanzees develop the language ability characteristic of human teenagers.

TRUE or FALSE

10. Areas of the brain essential to human language are similar to areas in the monkey's brain that respond to vocalization of monkeys.

TRUE or FALSE

11. People with Williams syndrome are mentally retarded except in language, social, and musical abilities and ability to interpret facial expressions.

TRUE or FALSE

12. Broca's aphasia results from fairly extensive damage to Broca's area in the frontal lobe and cortical areas surrounding it.

TRUE or FALSE

13. Wernicke's aphasia results in difficulty speaking and omission of closed-class words.

TRUE or FALSE

14. People who speak two languages use separate brain areas for each language.

TRUE or FALSE

15. Switching between languages, in those who are bilinguals, activates the frontal cortex, temporal cortex, and basal ganglia.

TRUE or FALSE

16. The language you speak influences your preference in music.

TRUE or FALSE

17. Dyslexia may have a variety of types and causes, including mild microscopic abnormalities, bilaterally symmetrical cortex, and subtle hearing impairment.

TRUE or FALSE

18. Genes that produce deficits in hearing or cognition are linked to dyslexia.

TRUE or FALSE

19. Brain abnormalities are identical between dyslexics who speak English or Chinese.

TRUE or FALSE

20. Dyslexics can sometimes be helped by trying to view a whole sentence at a time, rather than focusing on one word at a time.

TRUE or FALSE

21. The amount of brain activity evoked by a stimulus does not correlate with consciousness of that stimulus.

TRUE or FALSE

22. A familiar stimulus captures faster attention.

TRUE or FALSE

23. Presenting pictures of faces with emotional expressions elicits emotional responses even in those who are not consciously aware of the stimulus.

TRUE or FALSE

24. Spatial neglect results from extensive damage to the right hemisphere, especially the right parietal cortex.

TRUE or FALSE

25. The problem in spatial neglect is due to inadequate sensory processing, rather than a deficit in attention.

TRUE or FALSE

Fill In The Blanks

1. The major connections between the hemispheres are the _____, the _____, and the _____.

2. The left visual field projects to the _____ half of both retinas, which then project to the _____ hemisphere.

3. Cutting the corpus callosum is an effective treatment for _____ when drugs and simpler surgery are ineffective.

4. The _____ hemisphere is more important for expressing and understanding emotional content of speech and facial expression, humor, and sarcasm.

5. The _____ is an area in the temporal lobe that is larger on the left than the right side in most people.

6. _____ chimpanzees can acquire the ability to use visual symbols to name and describe (even when not requesting something), to refer to the past, to request things they do not see, and to make creative requests.

7. Brain areas in the _____ temporal and _____ cortices are essential to human language.

8. _____ aphasia, also known as nonfluent aphasia, is characterized by difficulty in language _____ and in omission of _____ grammatical forms.

9. _____ aphasia, also known as fluent aphasia, is characterized by articulate speech, combined with _____ (difficulty finding the right word) and poor comprehension of nouns and verbs.

10. _____ is a specific impairment of reading, together with adequate vision and other academic skills.

11. Spatial neglect is often the result of extensive damage to the right hemisphere, especially the _____.

Matching Items

1. _____ Split-brain people or animals
2. _____ Left hemisphere
3. _____ Right hemisphere
4. _____ Corpus callosum
5. _____ Anterior commissure
6. _____ Planum temporale
7. _____ Productivity
8. _____ Bonobos
9. _____ Williams syndrome
10. _____ Broca's aphasia
11. _____ Wernicke's aphasia
12. _____ Dyslexia

a. Area larger in left than right temporal lobe
b. Major connection between hemispheres
c. Specialized for spatial, emotional abilities
d. Independent control of two sides of body
e. Specialized for language, details
f. Chimpanzees with good language skills
g. Nonfluent aphasia, difficult closed-class words
h. Minor connection between hemispheres
i. Fluent aphasia, anomia
j. Reading impairment, other skills OK
k. Produce new signals for new ideas
l. Normal language, mentally retarded in other skills

Multiple-Choice Questions

1. The left and right hemispheres are connected via the
   a. corpus callosum.
   b. anterior commissure.
   c. posterior commissure.
   d. all of the above

2. Severing the corpus callosum
   a. usually destroys language abilities.
   b. usually relieves the symptoms of epilepsy.
   c. has provided evidence that linguistic abilities reside largely in the right hemisphere.
   d. none of the above

3. People with bisected brains
   a. can use their two hands independently in a way that other people cannot.
   b. develop cooperation between the hemispheres because the corpus callosum grows back.
   c. perform very poorly on intelligence tests.
   d. all of the above

4. The only way to restrict visual input to only the right hemisphere of a split-brain person is to
   a. flash it briefly to the left eye while the right eye is closed.
   b. flash it briefly to the right eye while the left eye is closed.
   c. flash it briefly in the left visual field while the person is looking straight ahead.
   d. flash it briefly in the right visual field while the person is looking straight ahead.

5. A split-brain person who sees a picture of an object in his left visual field usually
   a. will be able both to point to the correct object with his left hand and to name it.
   b. will not be able to pick out the object or to name it.
   c. will be able to pick it out with his left hand, but will not be able to name it.
   d. will be able to name it but not pick it out.

6. People with right-hemisphere damage
   a. have trouble producing and understanding emotional facial expressions.
   b. have trouble speaking with emotional expression and understanding others' vocal emotional expression.
   c. have trouble with some complex visual and spatial tasks.
   d. all of the above

7. People with left-hemisphere damage
   a. have great difficulties with spatial relationships.
   b. perform better than chance in detecting lying.
   c. easily begin to use the right hemisphere for language function.
   d. all of the above

8. Hemispheric specialization in intact people
   a. has not been demonstrated.
   b. can be shown but is small and inconsistent.
   c. is consistent with that observed in split-brain people but is even more dramatic.
   d. is the reverse of specialization in split-brain people.

9. Which of the following is true of the planum temporale?
   a. Children with the biggest ratio of left to right planum temporale performed best on language tests.
   b. It is larger in the right than in the left hemisphere for almost everyone.
   c. It is equal in size in the two hemispheres at birth, indicating that maturation of language causes the size difference in adults.
   d. All of the above are true.

10. What did Galin et al. discover when they asked 3-year-old and 5-year-old children to discriminate two fabrics?
    a. The 3-year-olds were better than the 5-year-olds.
    b. All children made fewer errors with their right hands than with their left.
    c. All children made 90 percent more errors using different hands than when using the same hand.
    d. Three-year-olds made 90 percent more errors using different hands than using the same hand, but 5-year-olds did equally well with one hand or two.

11. People who never had a corpus callosum
    a. are just like split-brain patients.
    b. can verbally describe objects in either visual field and name objects that they touch with either hand.
    c. are especially fast at tasks requiring coordination of both hands.
    d. all of the above

12. Productivity
    a. refers to the ability to produce new language signals to represent new ideas.
    b. is a characteristic of communication systems of most mammals.
    c. refers to the ability to translate one signal into another.
    d. is only a means of increasing ones income, and has nothing to do with language.

13. Ordinary chimpanzees
    a. frequently use symbols in new, original combinations.
    b. frequently use symbols to describe scenes and events.
    c. have a social order much like that of humans.
    d. use symbols almost always to request, only rarely to describe.

14. Bonobos
    a. are unable to put symbols together in new ways to express new meanings.
    b. use symbols only to request objects.
    c. can understand some spoken English sentences.
    d. have learned to speak English fluently.

15. Which of the following is a problem with the theory that human language evolved as a product of overall intelligence and larger brains?
    a. Some people have normal overall intelligence, but have impaired language.
    b. Some people are severely retarded and have abnormal brain development, but have near normal, and sometimes spectacular, language ability.
    c. Selective pressure for social interactions may have favored the evolution of language, and overall intelligence may have developed as a by-product of language.
    d. All of the above are true.

16. People with Williams syndrome
    a. have severe difficulties with even simple grammatical rules.
    b. have good language abilities, but are retarded in nonlinguistic function.
    c. can draw beautifully, but cannot write.
    d. have almost total loss of Wernicke's area.

17. A patient has great difficulty in articulating words and a tendency to omit endings and abstract words, but less difficulty comprehending spoken and written words. The patient probably has damage in
    a. Broca's area.
    b. Wernicke's area.
    c. the corpus callosum.
    d. primary motor cortex controlling muscles of articulation.

18. A second patient has difficulty naming objects and understanding both spoken and written language; speech is fluent but not very meaningful. You suspect that the patient has damage in
    a. Broca's area.
    b. Wernicke's area.
    c. the anterior commissure and hippocampal commissure.
    d. left visual cortex and posterior corpus callosum.

19. Which of the following is true of those who speak two languages?
    a. People who are bilingual use different areas of the brain to store each language.
    b. Learning a second language in early childhood increases thickness of language areas in the brain.
    c. Brain activity does not change in bilinguals when switching between languages.
    d. all of the above

20. Which of the following is true regarding parallels between music and languages?
    a. Sight-reading music activates Broca's area in musicians.
    b. Musicians and music students tend to be better than average at learning a second language.
    c. We prefer music that resembles our own language in rhythm and tone.
    d. all of the above

21. Dyslexic people
    a. all have very similar symptoms, and all of the symptoms are limited to difficulties in visual perception.
    b. are sometimes helped by focusing on whole paragraphs at a time, rather than reading one word at a time.
    c. are more likely than normal readers to have a bilaterally symmetrical cerebral cortex, especially planum temporale.
    d. all of the above

22. Spatial neglect
    a. results from ineffective sensory input, rather than a problem with attention.
    b. results from damage to the right parietal cortex.
    c. results from damage to the left parietal cortex.
    d. is a symptom of ADHD.

Solutions

True/False Questions

1. T	8. T	15. T	22. T
2. F	9. F	16. T	23. T
3. F	10. T	17. T	24. T
4. T	11. T	18. T	25. F
5. T	12. T	19. F	
6. F	13. F	20. F	
7. T	14. F	21. F	

Fill In The Blanks

1. corpus callosum; anterior commissure; hippocampal commissure.
2. right; right
3. epilepsy
4. right
5. planum temporale
6. Bonobo
7. left; frontal
8. Broca's; production; closed-class
9. Wernicke's; anomia
10. Dyslexia
11. right parietal cortex.

Matching Items

1. d	4. b	7. k	10. g
2. e	5. h	8. f	11. i
3. c	6. a	9. l	12. j

Multiple Choice Questions

1. d	7. b	13. d	19. b
2. b	8. b	14. c	20. d
3. a	9. a	15. d	21. c
4. c	10. d	16. b	22. b
5. c	11. b	17. a	
6. d	12. a	18. b	

CHAPTER 15

Psychological Disorders

Introduction

Depression is typified by episodic sadness and helplessness, lack of energy, feelings of worthlessness, suicidal ideas, sleep disorders, and lack of pleasure. Five percent of adults in the United States have "clinically significant" depression each year, and 10 percent will have depression at some time over their lifetime. Women are at greater risk for depression than are men. While the cause of depression is not fully understood, a number of possible factors have been identified. There may be a genetic component to depression; the risk is highest in relatives of women with early-onset depression. Several genes have been found to have a link to depression, including one that controls the serotonin transporter; however, it may work by increasing sensitivity to either stressful or supportive environmental influences. Depression may occasionally be caused by exposure to a virus at some point in life. The Borna virus predisposes people to various psychiatric difficulties, including depression. Giving birth triggers a relatively brief depression in about 20% of women; in about 0.1% the depression persists, especially in women who have suffered depression previously. Abnormal hemispheric dominance is sometimes associated with mood disorders. Happiness in normal people is associated with activation of the left prefrontal cortex, whereas depressed people have lower metabolic activity in the left, and increased activity in the right prefrontal cortex. A traumatic experience may trigger the first episode of depression; however, subsequent episodes may occur spontaneously.

Most antidepressants act in one of three ways: blocking reuptake of monoamines (tricyclics), blocking reuptake of only serotonin (selective serotonin reuptake inhibitors, or SSRIs) or inhibiting monoamine oxidase (monoamine oxidase inhibitors, or MAOIs). Fluoxetine and other SSRIs have fewer side effects than do the tricyclics. Several atypical antidepressants have other mechanisms of action. Bupropion (Welbutrin) inhibits reuptake of dopamine and, to some extent, norepinephrine. St. John's wort is an herb and is not regulated by the Food and Drug Administration. Its effects are variable but similar to those of SSRIs; however, it may also contribute to more rapid breakdown of beneficial drugs. Antidepressants produce improvement in 50 – 60% of patients in a few months. Cognitive behavioral or interpersonal psychotherapy produces similar results and activates similar areas of the brain. The combination of drugs and psychotherapy results in a slight improvement over either alone. However, Freudian psychotherapy or placebos have a 30% success rate. Antidepressants are only slightly more effective than placebo for mild depression but have greater benefits with more severe depression. They are not effective in those who were abused, neglected, or traumatized in childhood. Because SSRIs affect serotonin levels and are at least somewhat effective in treating depression, one hypothesis is that depression results from a deficit in serotonin and perhaps other transmitters. However, some studies actually show an increase in serotonin turnover in depressed patients. Also, decreasing serotonin levels by decreasing intake of its precursor, tryptophan, does not lead to depression in most people, but often does produce a brief bout of depression in those with a previous history of depression. Another problem is that drugs affect transmitter levels almost immediately but exert noticeable effects on mood only after two or three weeks. A possible explanation is that brain-derived neurotrophic factor (BDNF) is released with neurotransmitters and would take a few weeks to increase proliferation of new neurons in the hippocampus. Neurons in the hippocampus and cerebral cortex shrink in depressed people. All current antidepressants increase proliferation, and blocking proliferation blocks behavioral effects of antidepressants.

In addition to treatment by drug therapy, mood disorders are sometimes treated with electroconvulsive therapy (ECT), sleep alterations, or bright lights. ECT is particularly useful for patients who are unresponsive to antidepressants or who are suicidal and need rapid relief. Memory loss that is sometimes associated with ECT is minimized by administering the ECT only to the right hemisphere. ECT alters the expression of numerous genes, including those that affect neurotrophins, arachidonic acid, generation of new neurons, and responsiveness to exercise. Repetitive transcranial magnetic stimulation is also moderately effective. It stimulates axons near the surface of the brain. Sleep-deprivation therapy is based on observations that depressed persons enter REM sleep much sooner than normal persons. A regimen of earlier bedtimes following one sleepless night usually offers relief from depression for at least a week, and a combination of sleep alteration and antidepressant drugs produces long-term benefits. Another therapy is regular exercise, which increases blood flow to the brain and decreases the effects of stress. There are also several drugs under development, including leptin, that may be beneficial.

Depression can occur as either a unipolar or a bipolar disorder. A unipolar disorder is one in which an individual varies between normal mood and depression. Bipolar disorder, or manic-depressive disorder, is characterized by cycles of depression and mania. During their manic phase, people are restless, uninhibited, excitable, impulsive, self-confident, and apparently happy. In bipolar I disorder there is a full-blown manic phase; in bipolar II disorder the manic phase is milder and is referred to as hypomania. There is evidence for a genetic influence on bipolar disorder. Monozygotic twins are more likely to share the disorder than are dizygotic twins, and biological relatives are more likely than adoptive relatives to share it. Lithium is effective in treating bipolar I disorder and, if taken regularly, prevents relapse into either mania or depression. However, it can have toxic effects, so the dose must be carefully regulated. Valproate and carbamazepine are effective treatments for bipolar II disorder. All three drugs decrease the number of AMPA type glutamate receptors in the hippocampus and also block synthesis of arachidonic acid, which is produced during brain inflammation. Bipolar patients show increased expression of genes associated with inflammation. A diet rich in polyunsaturated fatty acids, which are abundant in seafood, also blocks the effects of arachadonic acid. One additional treatment for bipolar disorder is to keep a consistent sleep schedule in a darkened, quiet room.

Seasonal affective disorder (SAD) occurs mostly in areas where nights are long in the winter. SAD patients may have phase-delayed sleep and temperature cycles, unlike other depressed people, who are phase-advanced. Exposure to bright lights for an hour or more per day is usually an effective treatment for SAD.

Schizophrenia is an illness in which emotions are "split off" from the intellect. Its positive symptoms (behaviors that are present but should be absent) include a psychotic cluster (hallucinations and delusions) and a disorganized cluster (inappropriate emotions, bizarre behaviors, incoherent speech, and thought disorder). Negative symptoms (behaviors that are absent but should be present) include deficits in social interaction, emotional expression, speech, and working memory. The main problem may be disordered thoughts, which result from abnormal connections between the cortex and the thalamus and cerebellum. Approximately 1 percent of people suffer schizophrenia at any given time. There has been a gradual decline in both the prevalence and severity of schizophrenia worldwide, for unknown reasons. Schizophrenia is much less common in the Third World than in the United States and Europe. It is more prevalent and more severe in men than in women, and men's brains release more dopamine, especially in the basal ganglia. Much evidence favors a genetic predisposition to schizophrenia. There is a higher concordance rate for schizophrenia in monozygotic than in dizygotic twins and in biological than in adoptive relatives. Genetics cannot completely explain the occurrence of schizophrenia, however, since the concordance rate for monozygotic twins is about only about 50%. Perhaps a gene may be expressed in one twin and suppressed in the other. Also, the greater similarity between dizygotic twins than siblings may be due to greater similarity of prenatal and early postnatal life. A confounding factor in genetic studies is that biological parents of schizophrenics are more likely to engage in unhealthy habits, including eating an unhealthy diet, smoking and drinking; they are also more likely to have complications during pregnancy and delivery. However, some studies have found genes with possible links to schizophrenia. A disrupted form of one gene (DISC1, disrupted in schizophrenia) has been found to control neuron generation in the hippocampus and to thereby predispose a person to schizophrenia. Natural selection should decrease the incidence of any gene that predisposes to schizophrenia, since people with schizophrenia have fewer children and die younger than others. However, genetic microdeletions and microduplications have been found to be distributed over many genes in people with schizophrenia. As soon as natural selection gets rid of the affected genes, new mutations may occur. Older fathers are more likely to have mutations in their sperm and also have a greater incidence of schizophrenia in their children. Some cases of schizophrenia probably have a genetic basis, and others may be due to environmental factors or an interaction between the two.

The neurodevelopmental hypothesis suggests that schizophrenia results from abnormal early development of the brain. Difficulties surrounding birth or during pregnancy have been linked to increased incidence of schizophrenia. These include poor nutrition during pregnancy, premature birth, Rh incompatibility, complications during delivery, low birth weight, and various infections during pregnancy or childhood. A number of minor brain abnormalities have been found in the brains of schizophrenics. Left temporal and prefrontal cortex are smaller than usual; the ventricles are larger; cell bodies in the hippocampus and prefrontal cortex are smaller; and the left hemisphere is smaller and less active. The area of most consistent abnormalities is the dorsolateral prefrontal cortex, one of the latest brain areas to mature. Because there is no evidence of neuronal loss in adulthood, it is thought that the brain abnormalities result from early developmental factors. Since the most affected brain areas are those that mature slowly, the behavioral problems may not emerge until long after the damage occurred. However, neurons may continue to shrink, rather than die, in adulthood.

Antipsychotic drugs, including phenothiazines (chlorpromazine: Thorazine) and butyrophenones (haloperidol: Haldol), block dopamine receptors. Furthermore, some symptoms of schizophrenia can be temporarily experienced by people who take large doses of drugs that stimulate dopamine synapses. On the basis of such observations it has been hypothesized that schizophrenia occurs because of excess activity at dopamine synapses. Although levels of dopamine are normal in schizophrenia, dopamine turnover is elevated, especially in the basal ganglia. There is also evidence for greater occupation of dopamine D_2 receptors in patients with schizophrenia in one study, and another study found that the greater the D_2 receptor occupation in the prefrontal cortex of schizophrenic patients, the greater the cognitive impairment. There is a problem with this hypothesis, however. Neuroleptic drugs block dopamine receptors almost immediately, but take 2 or 3 weeks to produce therapeutic benefits. A second hypothesis is that there may be a deficit in glutamate activity, especially in the prefrontal cortex. People with schizophrenia release less glutamate in prefrontal cortex and hippocampus than do other people, and glutamate has effects that are frequently opposite to those of dopamine. Therefore, any problem observed could be due to either insufficient glutamate or excess dopamine. Phencyclidine (PCP) inhibits NMDA glutamate receptors and produces both positive and negative symptoms similar to schizophrenia. It also produces little psychotic response in preadolescents but produces a long-lasting relapse in recovered schizophrenics. Although there is evidence of glutamate deficiency in schizophrenia, glutamate itself cannot be administered, because too much glutamate can kill neurons. However, drugs that stimulate certain metabotropic glutamate receptors are a promising treatment. Also, the amino acid glycine is a co-transmitter at NMDA glutamate receptors and increases the effectiveness of glutamate. It is not effective by itself, but it increases the effectiveness of antipsychotic drugs, especially for negative symptoms. In mice, extra glycine decreased behavioral responses to PCP. Both dopamine and glutamate may play roles in schizophrenia.

The decision to administer neuroleptic drugs has been complicated by their potentially severe side effects. The most troublesome effect is tardive dyskinesia, which consists of tremors and other involuntary movements. This condition develops gradually and may last long after the drug is discontinued. Recent advances in research have led to the use of new atypical antipsychotic drugs (such as clozapine, amisulpride, risperidone, olanzapine, and aripiprazole), which appear to control the negative symptoms of schizophrenia better than the older drugs and do so without causing tardive dyskinesia. These newer drugs have less effect on dopamine D_2 receptors than the older drugs but block serotonin 5-HT_2 receptors and increase the release of glutamate. However, clozapine, the most effective antipsychotic, impairs the immune system, and these drugs do not improve the overall quality of life more than the older drugs. Schizophrenia does not result from disruption of only one gene or abnormality of a single transmitter. Several genes, several transmitters, and several brain areas have been implicated, as well as environmental factors.

Learning Objectives

Module 15.1 Mood Disorders
1. Know the symptoms of depression and the evidence for a genetic contribution to depression.
2. Understand the possible roles of genetics, stress, hormones, abnormalities of hemispheric dominance, and viruses in the onset or worsening of depression.
3. Be able to describe the short-term and long-term mechanisms of action of antidepressant drugs.
4. Understand the possible mechanisms of action and the advantages and disadvantages of psychotherapy, electroconvulsive therapy, and altered sleep patterns.
5. Know the symptoms of bipolar disorder and the possible contributions of genetics.
6. Know the mechanisms of action of drugs used to treat bipolar disorder.
7. Be able to describe seasonal affective disorder and a treatment for it.

Module 15.2 Schizophrenia
1. Be able to describe the negative and positive symptoms of schizophrenia.
2. Know the conditions resembling schizophrenia, with which it may be confused, and the demographic factors related to schizophrenia.
3. Be able to describe the evidence for a genetic contribution to schizophrenia.
4. Understand the evidence for the neurodevelopmental hypothesis.
5. Understand the evidence for and against the dopamine hypothesis of schizophrenia.
6. Be able to describe the evidence for the glutamate hypothesis of schizophrenia and the potential role for glycine and for metabotropic glutamate receptors in treating it.
7. Know one undesired effect of antipsychotic drugs and the mechanisms of action of the newer drugs that minimize these effects.

Key Terms and Concepts

Module 15.1 Mood Disorders
1. Major depressive disorder
   May be caused by genetics, traumatic experiences, hormonal problems, substance abuse, head injuries, brain tumors, other illnesses
   Symptoms
      Sad and helpless for weeks
      Little energy, feel worthless, contemplate suicide
      Trouble sleeping, concentrating
      Little pleasure
      Cannot imagine being happy again
      Absence of happiness more reliable than increased sadness
   Incidence
      Twice as common in women as men
      Any time after adolescence
      5% of adults in United States each year: "Clinically significant" depression
         10% incidence over a lifetime
      Episodes of various durations

Often triggered initially by stressful event
    Later episodes not linked to stressful events
Genetics and life events
    Moderate heritability
    Relatives more likely to suffer from other psychological disorders, as well as depression
    Risk highest in relatives of women with early-onset depression
    Several genes increase risk
        Variable effects may depend on experience
    One gene controls serotonin transporter
        Two copies of "short" form: Increasing stress → increased depression
        Two copies of "long" form: Little effect of stress
        One copy of each: Intermediate effect of stress
        Short form associated with sensitivity to environmental influence
            Stressful environment → depressive symptoms
            Supportive environment → fewer symptoms
        Other genes → risk only with child abuse or neglect
Nongenetic biological influences
    Viral infections: Borna disease → Frantic activity alternating with inactivity
        Virus found in 2% of normal people, 30% of severely depressed
        May predispose to psychiatric difficulties in general
    Postpartum depression
        0.1%: serious lengthy depression
        More common in women depressed at other times
        Decrease estradiol and progesterone → depression in vulnerable women
        Older men: Decreasing testosterone increases probability of depression
    Abnormalities of hemispheric dominance
        Happy mood: Increased activity in left prefrontal cortex
        Depression: Decreased activity in left and increased in right prefrontal cortex
        Right-hemisphere dominance in depressives
2.   Antidepressant drugs
    Accidental discoveries of psychiatric drugs
        Disulfiram (Antabuse): Helps people avoid alcohol
            Originally used in manufacture of rubber
        Bromides: Treatment for epilepsy
            Originally thought to reduce sexual drive, masturbation
        Iproniazid: First antidepressant
            Originally used to treat tuberculosis
        Chlorpromazine: First antipsychotic
            Originally used as tranquilizer
        Today: Evaluate new drugs in test tubes or tissue samples
    Types of antidepressants
        Tricyclics
            Decrease reuptake of catecholamines and serotonin → longer in synapse
            Imipramine (Tofranil)

Also block histamine and acetylcholine receptors and some sodium channels
→ side effects
Selective serotonin reuptake inhibitors (SSRIs)
Similar to tricyclics, but selective for serotonin
Fluoxetine (Prozac), sertraline (Zoloft), fluvoxamine (Luvox), citalopram (Celexa) and paroxetine (Paxil or Seroxat)
Milder side effects
MAOIs
Block monoamine oxidase → monoamines broken down more slowly
Phenelzine (Nardil)
Avoid foods containing tyramine: Tyramine + MAOI → high blood pressure
Atypical antidepressants
Bupropion (Wellbutrin): Inhibits reuptake of dopamine and, to some extent, norepinephrine, but not serotonin
St. John's wort: Herb, not regulated by FDA
Effects similar to SSRIs, but variable
Increases effect of enzyme → breaks down toxins and beneficial drugs
Effectiveness of antidepressants
Variable duration of depressive episodes
Antidepressants → improvement of 50–60% of patients in a few months
Similar improvement with cognitive behavioral or interpersonal psychotherapy
Combination antidepressant and psychotherapy → slightly better results
Psychotherapy and antidepressants increase metabolism in same brain areas Placebo or Freudian therapy → improvement of 30% of patients in a few months
Mild depression: Antidepressants only slightly better than placebo
More severe depression: Antidepressants → greater benefit
Those abused, neglected, or traumatized in childhood:
Antidepressants ineffective
Psychotherapy works better
Children and adolescents:
Antidepressants ineffective, may increase suicidal thoughts
Recent decrease in use of antidepressants in children
Recent increase in teenage suicide rate: Due to lack of treatment?
Exactly how do antidepressants work?
SSRIs block reuptake of serotonin
Normal or *increased* serotonin turnover in depressed patients
Dietary decrease in serotonin levels→ temporary depression in patients with history of depression, no effect in other people
Problem of time course
Effect on synapses within hours, effect on behavior, two or more weeks
Brain-derived neurotrophic factor (BDNF)
Released with neurotransmitters
Promotes survival and growth of hippocampal neurons
Parts of hippocampus and cerebral cortex shrink during depression
BDNF → learning improvement
Block neurogenesis → block behavioral benefits

Electroconvulsive therapy (ECT)
    Initially used to treat schizophrenia
    Now used for patients who do not respond to drug therapy or who are suicidal
    Works faster than drugs
    Administered every other day for two weeks
    Used with muscle relaxants or anesthetics
    Side effect: Memory loss; minimized with shock to right hemisphere only
        Right-hemisphere activity associated with unpleasant mood
    High rate of relapse within a few months
    Increases proliferation of new neurons in hippocampus
    Alters expression of ~120 genes in hippocampus and frontal cortex
        Neurotrophins
        Arachidonic acid
        Generation of new neurons
        Responsiveness to exercise
Repetitive transcranial magnetic stimulation
    Stimulates axons near surface of brain
    Moderately effective
    Not clear how it works
Altered sleep patterns
    Depressed: REM within 45 minutes, awaken early
        Increased eye movements per minute during REM
        Relatives with similar sleep patterns: More likely to become depressed
    Therapy
        Stay awake all night → fastest improvement
        Increases new neurons in hippocampus
        Often effective only until next night's sleep
        Combine with earlier bedtime → effective for at least a week
        Sleep alteration + drug therapy → long-lasting benefits
Other therapies
    Drugs under investigation include leptin
    Regular exercise: Increases blood flow to brain, reduces effects of stress
    Can be combined with other treatments

3.   Bipolar disorder
    Definitions
        Unipolar disorder: One extreme – vary between normal and depression
        Bipolar disorder: Manic-depressive disorder
            Vary between mania and depression
            Mania: Restlessness, excitement, laughter, self-confidence, rambling speech, loss of inhibitions
            Glucose metabolism: Higher than normal in mania, lower than normal in depression
            Full-blown mania: Bipolar I disorder
            Hypomania → agitation, anxiety: Bipolar II disorder
        Also have attention deficits, poor impulse control, verbal memory problems
    Genetics

Greater similarity in monozygotic > dizygotic twins and in biological > adoptive relatives

Two genes seem to increase probability for bipolar II disorder

Treatments
Lithium salts
Stabilize mood, prevent relapse
May have toxic side effects
Effective for bipolar I disorder
Other drugs
Valproate (Depakene, Depakote), carbamazepine
How do drugs relieve bipolar disorder?
All decrease AMPA type glutamate receptors in hippocampus
Block synthesis of arachidonic acid
Produced during brain inflammation
Bipolar patients: Increased expression of genes associated with inflammation
Polyunsaturated fatty acids (abundant in seafood) also block effects of arachidonic acid
Consistent sleep schedule in dark, quiet room
4. Seasonal affective disorder (SAD)
Common where nights are long in winter
SAD: Phase-delayed sleep and temperature rhythms, unlike other depressed people, who are phase-advanced
Bright lights for an hour or more per day
As effective as drugs or psychotherapy, less expensive, faster
5. In closing: The biology of mood swings
Traumatic experience → bout of depression
Once depressed: Mood persists for months; little cheer
Bipolar manic phase: Boundless energy
Studying these states may → information about brain states and moods

Module 15.2 Schizophrenia
1. Characteristics
Deteriorating function in everyday life; some combination of hallucinations, delusions, thought disorder, movement disorder, and inappropriate emotional expressions
Acute condition: Sudden onset and good prospects for recovery
Chronic condition: Gradual onset and a long-term course
Dementia praecox: Premature mental deterioration
Not dissociative identity disorder (multiple personality)
Split between emotional and intellectual aspects
Behavioral symptoms
Negative symptoms: Behaviors that are absent, but should be present
Weak social interactions, emotional expression, speech, and working memory
More stable, less responsive to treatment
Positive symptoms: Behaviors that are present, but should be absent
Psychotic cluster: Delusions and hallucinations

Increased activity in thalamus, hippocampus, and parts of cortex, including auditory areas

Disorganized cluster: Inappropriate emotion displays, bizarre behaviors, incoherent speech, and thought disorder

Difficulty with abstract concepts, attention, working memory

IQ often a few points below average

Main problem: Disordered thinking

Abnormal connections between cortex and thalamus and cerebellum

Memory impairment may be central symptom

Differential diagnosis of schizophrenia

Conditions resembling schizophrenia

Mood disorder with psychotic features

Substance abuse

May → visual hallucinations

Brain damage

Temporal or prefrontal cortex

Undetected hearing deficits

Huntington's disease

Catatonic schizophrenia → motor and psychological abnormalities similar to Huntington's disease

Nutritional abnormalities

Deficiency of niacin, vitamin C

Allergy to milk proteins, wheat gluten, other proteins

Demographic data

Approximately 1% of people: Schizophrenia at any given time

Gradual decline in prevalence and severity

10-100 times more common in United States and Europe than in Third World

Diet high in fat and sugar aggravates schizophrenia

Diet rich in fish alleviates it

More common and more severe in men than women

Men's brains release more dopamine, especially in basal ganglia

Unexplained oddities

Type I diabetes: Schizophrenia less common

Type II diabetes: Schizophrenia more common

Schizophrenia: Increased risk of colon cancer, decreased risk of respiratory, brain cancer

Schizophrenia: Decreased risk of rheumatoid arthritis, allergies

Women with schizophrenic breakdown during pregnancy: Gave birth to girls

Women with schizophrenic breakdown soon after birth pregnancy: Gave birth to sons

Schizophrenia: Body odor due to trans-3-methhyl-2-hexenoic acid

They cannot smell it

2. Genetics

Twin studies

Greater concordance for monozygotic (50%) than dizygotic (15-20%) twins

Heredity not the only factor

Monozygotic twins: Gene can be expressed in one twin, suppressed in other

Dizygotic twins: Same genetic resemblance as siblings, but higher concordance, due to similar prenatal, neonatal environment

Adopted children who develop schizophrenia

Greater concordance with biological than adoptive relatives

Biological mother → genes + prenatal environment

Poor nutrition; smoke, drink; poor medical care; complications during pregnancy or delivery

Efforts to locate a gene

Gene for childhood-onset schizophrenia

But childhood-onset schizophrenia different from other forms, uncommon

More than a dozen genes implicated

One form of *DISC1* ("disrupted in schizophrenia 1") controls neuron proliferation in hippocampus

Natural selection should decrease responsible gene

Schizophrenics: Fewer children and die younger

Relatives: Average number of children, not more

Genetic microdeletions and microduplications distributed over many genes

Schizophrenia more common in children of older fathers

More mutations in sperm from older fathers

Some cases: Environmental influence

3. The neurodevelopmental hypothesis

Abnormalities due to genes or early difficulties: Aggravated by later environmental influences

Argument for:

Several kinds of pre- or neonatal difficulties linked to later schizophrenia

People with schizophrenia: Minor brain abnormalities originating early in life

Plausible that early brain abnormalities → adult behavioral abnormalities

Prenatal and neonatal environment

Poor nutrition, premature birth, low birth weight, delivery complications

Mother exposed to severe stress early in pregnancy

Head injuries in childhood

Rh-positive child of Rh-negative mother→ immunological rejection

Later-born boys with Rh incompatibility → schizophrenia, hearing & mental problems

Season of birth effect

Winter births → higher risk

Mostly in non-tropical climates

Viral epidemics

Influenza in fall → later schizophrenia in babies born in winter

Cytokines in mother cross placenta → impaired brain development

Fever in mother slows cell division, damages brain

Mice with influenza during pregnancy → behavioral abnormalities in offspring

Increased schizophrenia after influenza epidemic in 1967

Blood samples from pregnant women: Increased virus and immune system proteins → later risk of schizophrenic children

Rubella ("German measles"), herpes, or other infections during pregnancy → increased risk of schizophrenic children

Cat parasite in childhood → impaired brain development, memory disorder, hallucinations, delusions

Several drugs that relieve schizophrenia block replication of parasite

Infections: Alternative or supplement to genetics and other influences

Mild brain abnormalities

Smaller left temporal and frontal cortex

Most cortical areas smaller in at least one study

Thalamus also smaller

Enlarged ventricles: Less space taken by brain cells

Especially in those with complications during pregnancy or birth

Areas that mature slowly most affected: Dorsolateral prefrontal cortex

Memory and attention deficits similar to those with temporal or prefrontal cortex damage

Difficulty with Wisconsin card sorting task: Can't shift to new rule

Microscopic level

Smaller cell bodies, especially in hippocampus and prefrontal cortex

Lateralization

Right planum temporale equal to or larger than left

Lower activity in left hemisphere

More likely left-handed

Brain abnormalities not due to antipsychotic drugs

Abuse of alcohol, marijuana, and other drugs by schizophrenics may contribute to brain abnormalities

Brain damage may not be progressive

Brain abnormalities similar in older and younger patients

No glial cell proliferation or activation of genes for repair

Cells may shrink but not die

Early development and later psychopathology

Why is it diagnosed after age 20, if early brain development is the cause?

Earlier problems: Deficits in attention, memory, impulse control

Prefrontal cortex: Slow maturing

Damage to prefrontal cortex in monkeys → progressive deterioration

Neurodevelopmental hypothesis: Plausible, not firmly established

Methods 15.1 The Wisconsin card-sorting task

Measures functioning of prefrontal cortex

Deck of cards sorted first by one rule, then by a different (conflicting) rule

Schizophrenia or damage to prefrontal cortex → difficulty shifting to the new rule

4.   Treatments

Antipsychotic drugs and dopamine

The dopamine hypothesis: Excess activity at certain dopamine synapses

Antipsychotic (neuroleptic) drugs: Block dopamine receptors

Phenothiazines

Chlorpromazine (Thorazine)

Butyrophenones

Haloperidol (Haldol)

Correlation between clinically effective dose and dose needed to block dopamine receptors

Concentration of dopamine in schizophrenia: Normal, but turnover elevated

Drugs that can provoke schizophrenic symptoms

Substance-induced psychotic disorder

Hallucinations and delusions: Positive symptoms

Amphetamine, methamphetamine, cocaine → increase activity at dopamine synapses

LSD → effects at serotonin synapses; increases activity at dopamine synapses

Schizophrenia: Twice as many dopamine D_2 receptors occupied as normal

IBZM: Binds to D_2 receptors

Compare IBZM binding before and after blocking synthesis of dopamine

Difference = number of D_2 receptors occupied by dopamine

Greater D_2 activation in prefrontal cortex → greater cognitive impairment

Problem with the dopamine hypothesis: Time course of drugs

Affect synapses quickly

Effects on behavior build up over 2 to 3 weeks

Role of glutamate

The glutamate hypothesis

Deficient activity at glutamate synapses, especially in prefrontal cortex

Relationships between dopamine and glutamate: Opposing effects

Dopamine inhibits glutamate release

Glutamate excites neurons that inhibit dopamine release

Therefore, increase in dopamine similar to decrease in glutamate

Measurements of glutamate

Schizophrenia → less glutamate release in prefrontal cortex and hippocampus

Also fewer glutamate receptors

The effects of phencyclidine (PCP, "angel dust")

Inhibits NMDA glutamate receptors

Positive and negative symptoms similar to schizophrenia

PCP and ketamine → little psychotic effect in preadolescents

PCP → long-lasting relapse in people recovered from schizophrenia

LSD, amphetamine, and cocaine → only temporary symptoms

Enhancing glutamate activity

Too much glutamate → toxic effects

Stimulate certain metabotropic glutamate receptors: Promising treatment

Glycine: Co-transmitter at NMDA glutamate receptors

Increases effectiveness of glutamate

Not effective antipsychotic by itself

Increases effectiveness of antipsychotic drugs, especially for negative symptoms

Mice: Extra glycine decreases behavioral response to phencyclidine

Schizophrenia: Both dopamine and glutamate may play roles

New drugs

Antipsychotic drugs → decrease mesolimbocortical activity → beneficial effects

Decrease activity of dopamine neurons in mesostriatal system to basal ganglia →
undesired effects
Tardive dyskinesia: Tremors and other involuntary movements
May last for years after quitting drug
Second generation (or atypical) antipsychotics
Clozapine, amisulpride, resperidone, olanzapine, aripiprazole
More effective than older drugs for negative symptoms
Quality of life similar to that with older drugs
Clozapine most effective, but impairs immune system
Less intense blockade of D_2 receptors
More strongly block serotonin 5-HT_2 receptors
Increase glutamate release
Schizophrenia not a one-gene or a one-transmitter disorder
5. In closing: The fascination of schizophrenia
Search for pattern among many clues and false leads

Short-Answer Questions

Module 15.1 Mood Disorders

1. *Major depressive disorder*

   a. List the symptoms of major depression.

   b. What is the evidence for a genetic predisposition for depression?

   c. What seems to be the role of stress in the onset of episodes of depression?

   d. Are men or women more vulnerable to depression?

   e. What is Borna disease? What evidence links it to depression?

   f. What may be the role of hormones in depression?

   g. What patterns of hemispheric dominance have been associated with happy moods in normal people? What is the pattern in depressed people?

   h. Name three groups of antidepressant drugs and explain how each exerts its effects.

   i. Why are selective serotonin reuptake inhibitors (SSRIs) preferred over tricyclics and monoamine oxidase inhibitors?

   j. What is one atypical antidepressant? How does it differ from SSRIs?

   k. How effective is St. John's wort in relieving depression? Which class of antidepressants produces effects similar to those of St. John's wort? What is one potential problem with the use of St. John's wort?

   l. Explain the problem of the time course of drugs' effects on neurotransmitters and their effects on depressive symptoms.

   m. What neurotrophin is produced as a result of repeated use of antidepressants? In which brain area is it produced?

n. How is electroconvulsive therapy (ECT) applied today? How is this an improvement over practices in the 1950s?

o. For which two groups of patients is ECT most often used?

p. What are the advantages and disadvantages of ECT?

q. What are the effects of ECT on the expression of some genes? What newer treatment is similar to ECT?

r. How does the onset of REM sleep differ in depressed people, compared to nondepressed individuals?

s. What changes in sleeping schedules have been found to alleviate depression? How long do the benefits last?

2. *Bipolar disorder*

a. What is the difference between unipolar and bipolar disorder? What is another term for bipolar disorder?

b. Describe the symptoms of mania. What is hypomania? What is the difference between bipolar I and bipolar II disorder?

c. Describe the pattern of glucose metabolism in the two extreme conditions of bipolar I disorder.

d. What can we say about genetic factors in bipolar disorder?

e. What drug is effective for bipolar I disorder? Which two drugs are used to treat bipolar II disorder?

f. What are two possible mechanisms by which these drugs achieve their effects?

g. What is a possible non-drug treatment for bipolar disorder?

3. *Seasonal affective disorder (SAD)*

a. What is seasonal affective disorder? How is it treated?

b. How are the sleep and temperature rhythms of SAD patients different from those of other depressed patients?

Module 15.2 Schizophrenia

1. *Characteristics*

a. What is the origin of the term schizophrenia?

b. What are the negative symptoms of schizophrenia? How stable are they?

c. What are the two clusters of positive symptoms of schizophrenia?

d. What is the main cognitive problem in schizophrenia? What is the physiological problem that may underlie this problem?

e. What are some conditions resembling schizophrenia that may be confused with it?

f. What is the overall incidence of schizophrenia? Does this incidence vary among ethnic groups or sexes?

2. *Genetics*

   a. What evidence from twin studies suggests a genetic basis for schizophrenia? What are concordance rates?

   b. What other factor may explain the greater concordance with biological than adoptive parents?

   c. How may one form of the *DISC1* gene increase the incidence of schizophrenia?

   d. What can we conclude about the role of genetics in schizophrenia?

3. *The neurodevelopmental hypothesis*

   a. What evidence suggests that schizophrenia may result from abnormalities in the early development of the brain?

   b. What specific prenatal and neonatal conditions have been associated with increased risk for schizophrenia?

   c. In which season of birth is there a slightly greater likelihood of developing schizophrenia? What factors may account for this effect?

   d. What brain abnormalities have been linked with schizophrenia?

   e. Which brain areas have been most strongly implicated? What are some psychological functions of those areas? Do schizophrenics show impairment of those functions?

   f. Why do researchers believe that these abnormalities resulted from early developmental effects, rather than from gradual brain damage in adulthood?

   g. How might one explain the late onset of schizophrenic symptoms, if the brain damage occurred during early development?

4. *Treatments*

   a. What is the dopamine hypothesis of schizophrenia? What are the main lines of evidence favoring it?

   b. What are two chemical families of antipsychotic (neuroleptic) drugs that have been in wide use for many years? What is their major effect on receptors?

   c. Which drugs can induce a state similar to schizophrenia? What is their major mechanism of action?

   d. What is a problem with the dopamine hypothesis?

   e. What other neurotransmitter has been hypothesized to be abnormal in schizophrenia? What is the relationship between these two neurotransmitters?

   f. Why may blockade of dopamine receptors have beneficial effects, if the original problem is deficient glutamate?

   g. What is phencyclidine (PCP)? What are its effects on receptors? What are its psychological effects?

   h. What kinds of evidence suggest an abnormality in glutamate release or receptors?

   i. Why would it be unwise to administer glutamate to people with schizophrenia?

j. What is glycine? How does it affect NMDA receptors? What are the clinical findings concerning glycine?

k. What is another type of glutamatergic drug that seems promising?

l. What is tardive dyskinesia? How rapid is its onset?

m. What are five atypical antipsychotic drugs? What are their effects on receptors and neurotransmitter release?

n. What is a major advantage of atypical antipsychotic drugs?

True/False Questions

1. The most reliable symptom of depression is absence of happiness, rather than increased sadness.

    TRUE or FALSE

2. There is little evidence for a genetic predisposition to depression; environmental stressors are sufficient to account for almost all cases.

    TRUE or FALSE

3. During depression, there is decreased activity in the left hemisphere and increased activity in the right prefrontal cortex.

    TRUE or FALSE

4. Depression is more common in women than in men; decreases in estrogen and progesterone in vulnerable women may lead to depression.

    TRUE or FALSE

5. Tricyclic antidepressants work by inhibiting monoamine oxidase, which would otherwise metabolize the monoamine neurotransmitters.

    TRUE or FALSE

6. One problem with the hypothesis that depression results from a deficit of serotonin and possibly other neurotransmitters is that antidepressants produce effects on synapses within hours, but their beneficial effects on mood take two to three weeks to occur.

    TRUE or FALSE

7. St. John's wort is an especially effective antidepressant that has no bad side effects.

    TRUE or FALSE

8. Brain-derived neurotrophic factor (BDNF) is released with neurotransmitters and may mediate the effects of antidepressant drugs.

    TRUE or FALSE

9. Antidepressants are especially helpful for people who were abused, neglected, or traumatized during childhood.

    TRUE or FALSE

10. ECT increases the expression of at least 120 genes, including those regulating neurotrophins, arachidonic acid, generation of new neurons, and responsiveness to exercise.

TRUE or FALSE

11. Bipolar disorder is usually treated with the same drugs as are used for unipolar depression.

TRUE or FALSE

12. Arachidonic acid is a neurotransmitter that increases dopamine release.

TRUE or FALSE

13. The main symptom of schizophrenia is dissociative identity disorder (multiple personality).

TRUE or FALSE

14. Negative symptoms of schizophrenia include deficits in social interaction, emotional expression, speech, and working memory.

TRUE or FALSE

15. The neurodevelopmental hypothesis of schizophrenia is supported by evidence that several kinds of prenatal or neonatal difficulties are linked to later development of schizophrenia.

TRUE or FALSE

16. The hypothesis that cat parasites during development can lead to schizophrenia has now been disproven.

TRUE or FALSE

17. Two ways in which influenza during prenatal development may predispose to schizophrenia are that cytokines from the mother can cross the placenta and impair brain development, and fever in the mother slows cell division and damages the brain.

TRUE or FALSE

18. Support for the dopamine hypothesis includes the fact that the time courses of neuroleptic drugs on dopamine synapses and on clinical symptoms are similar.

TRUE or FALSE

19. There is evidence that people with schizophrenia have more of their dopamine D_2 receptors occupied, compared to normal people.

TRUE or FALSE

20. Glycine is a co-transmitter at glutamate synapses and increases the effectiveness of glutamate.

TRUE or FALSE

21. The glutamate hypothesis states that dopamine and glutamate have the same effects on postsynaptic neurons.

TRUE or FALSE

22. Drugs that stimulate certain metabotropic glutamate receptors are a promising treatment under development.

TRUE or FALSE

23. Atypical antipsychotics are more effective than earlier ones at relieving negative symptoms.

TRUE or FALSE

Fill In The Blanks

1. One gene that may increase the risk of depression controls the _____; however, it may be primarily a gene that influences sensitivity to _____ influences.

2. The three classes of typical antidepressants are _____, _____ (_____), and _____ (_____).

3. Atypical antidepressants include _____ (_____), which inhibits the reuptake of _____ and to some extent, norepinephrine, but not serotonin.

4. _____ is released with neurotransmitters and promotes survival and growth of neurons in the _____.

5. _____ works faster than drugs but may cause memory loss, which can be lessened by administration only to the _____ hemisphere.

6. _____ stimulation is similar to ECT; it stimulates axons near the surface of the brain.

7. Additional non-drug therapies for depression include altered _____ patterns and regular _____.

8. Three drugs used to treat bipolar disorder are _____, _____, and _____; they decrease the number of _____ type glutamate receptors and also block _____, which is produced during brain inflammation.

9. Other ways to treat bipolar disorder are to eat foods high in _____ (abundant in seafood) and have a consistent _____ in a dark, quiet room.

10. Seasonal affective disorder is often associated with phase-_____ sleep and temperature rhythms, unlike rhythms in other depressed people.

11. Positive symptoms of schizophrenia are grouped into a(n) _____ cluster and a(n) _____ cluster; the main problem is _____.

12. Schizophrenia is more common in _____ than in _____; _____ brains also release more dopamine, especially in the _____.

13. There is a greater _____ rate for schizophrenia between monozygotic than dizygotic twins and between biological relatives compared to adoptive relatives.

14. Researchers have found a greater rate of genetic _____ and _____, spread over many genes, in people with schizophrenia.

15. One form of the gene DISC1 decreases the proliferation of neurons in the

    _____.

16. The _____ hypothesis proposes that prenatal or neonatal difficulties produce minor brain abnormalities that do not result in behavioral abnormalities until adulthood.

17. Brain abnormalities in schizophrenia include smaller _____ and _____ cortex, especially in the _____ hemisphere, and smaller cells in the _____ and _____ cortex.

18. It is plausible that an excess of the neurotransmitter _____ may produce symptoms comparable to a deficiency in _____.

19. Tremors and other involuntary movements that result from prolonged use of neuroleptic drugs are referred to as _____.

20. Atypical antipsychotic drugs block _____ receptors less than they block serotonin _____ receptors, and they also increase _____ release.

Matching Items

1. _____ Works faster than antidepressants

2. _____ Promotes proliferation of hippocampal neurons

3. _____ May predispose to schizophrenia

4. _____ Psychotic cluster of positive symptoms

5. _____ Detects impaired prefrontal cortex function

6. _____ Less space taken by brain cells, seen in schizophrenia

7. _____ Fluoxetine (Prozac)

8. _____ Bupropion (Wellbutrin)

9. _____ Increased activity in right prefrontal cortex, decrease in left

10. _____ Bright lights for at least 1 hour per day

11. _____ Lithium salts

12. _____ Haloperidol (Haldol)

13. _____ Phencyclidine (PCP)

14. _____ Tardive dyskinesia

15. _____ Glycine

16. _____ Clozapine

a. Delusions, hallucinations
b. Wisconsin card sorting task
c. Atypical antidepressant
d. Atypical antipsychotic
e. Influenza during pregnancy
f. Tremors, involuntary movements
g. Associated with depression
h. Treatment for SAD
i. Enlarged ventricles
j. Typical antipsychotic
k. Enhances effect of glutamate
l. An SSRI antidepressant
m. Electroconvulsive therapy (ECT)
n. Treatment for bipolar I disorder
o. Brain-derived neurotrophic factor (BDNF)
p. Blocks NMDA receptors → psychotic symptoms

Multiple-Choice Questions

1. Which of the following is **not** a common symptom of major depression?
   a. sleeping soundly for at least 10 - 12 hours per night
   b. sadness and helplessness
   c. lack of energy
   d. lack of pleasure

2. Which of the following is true of depression?
   a. A gene on chromosome 11 is now known to be the cause of most cases of depression.
   b. Hormonal changes after childbirth often cause major depression, even in women without a biological predisposition to, or history of, that disorder.
   c. Since no specific genetic abnormality has been linked to depression, it is now commonly agreed that depression does not have any genetic basis.
   d. A gene that controls the serotonin transporter has been linked to depression in some people, although its effects may relate to sensitivity to environmental factors.

3. Depression is frequently associated with
   a. increased activity in the left, and decreased activity in the right prefrontal cortex.
   b. decreased activity in the left, and increased activity in the right prefrontal cortex.
   c. increased activity in the right, and decreased activity in the left temporal cortex.
   d. decreased activity in the right, and increased activity in the left temporal cortex.

4. Research on Borna disease suggests that
   a. a virus causes an autoimmune attack on the brain.
   b. any illness that causes a fever also causes major depression.
   c. a virus may be one cause of depression or bipolar disorder.
   d. the viruses that infect animals cannot infect humans.

5. Which of the following is **not** a type of antidepressant drug?
   a. monoamine oxidase inhibitors
   b. tricyclics
   c. selective serotonin reuptake inhibitors (SSRIs)
   d. dopamine receptor blockers

6. Which of the following is true?
   a. The effects of antidepressants on transmitter systems occur almost immediately, but their effects on depression are delayed for two weeks or longer.
   b. The effects of drugs on transmitter systems are delayed for two to three weeks, but their effects on depression are immediate.
   c. Depression results from having excessive activity of all the monoamine transmitters.
   d. The major effect of fluoxetine (Prozac) is to block serotonin receptors.

7. Use of antidepressant drugs
   a. results in transmitters activating other types of receptors.
   b. inhibits the release of brain-derived neurotrophic factor (BDNF) in the hippocampus.
   c. increases release of brain-derived neurotrophic factor (BDNF) in the hippocampus.
   d. none of the above

8. Electroconvulsive therapy (ECT)
   a. is effective because it confuses patients, and they forget their depressing thoughts.
   b. is rarely used anymore because of its bad reputation.
   c. increases the expression of at least 120 genes in the hippocampus and frontal cortex, including those related to neurotrophins, arachidonic acid, generation of new neurons, and responsiveness to exercise.
   d. must be administered to the left hemisphere, which produces loss of language ability.

9. Depressed people
   a. enter REM sleep more slowly than do normal people.
   b. are sometimes helped by skipping one night's sleep and then adopting an earlier bedtime.
   c. have their symptoms worsened by exposure to transcranial magnetic stimulation.
   d. all of the above

10. Bipolar disorder is characterized by
    a. cycles between depression and normal moods.
    b. cycles between depression and mania or hypomania.
    c. higher glucose metabolism in the brain during depression, and lower activity during mania.
    d. Unusually regular sleep habits.

11. Lithium
    a. is more effective than valproate and carbamazepine for bipolar I disorder.
    b. is extremely safe because it is so simple.
    c. is helpful for depression but not for mania.
    d. all of the above

12. All drugs commonly used to treat bipolar disorder
    a. decrease the number of AMPA type glutamate receptors in the hippocampus.
    b. block synthesis of arachidonic acid, which is produced during brain inflammation.
    c. both a and b
    d. none of the above

13. People with seasonal affective disorder (SAD)
    a. become more depressed during winter because of the cold.
    b. are frequently helped by sitting in hot sauna baths for an hour or more each day.
    c. show phase-advanced sleep and temperature rhythms, similar to those of other depressed people.
    d. are frequently helped by exposure to bright lights for an hour or more each day.

14. Schizophrenia
    a. is characterized by multiple personalities.
    b. refers to a split between the emotions and the intellect.
    c. is rarely misdiagnosed because its symptoms are so clearly distinctive.
    d. is typically first diagnosed in the elderly.

15. Which of the following is true of the positive symptoms of schizophrenia?
    a. They are usually associated with increased neural activity in the visual cortex, because almost all hallucinations are visual, and an especially large dorsolateral prefrontal cortex.
    b. They include deficits in social interactions, emotional expression, and speech.

c. They consist of a disorganized cluster, including inappropriate emotions, bizarre behaviors, incoherent speech, and thought disorder, and a psychotic cluster, including delusions and hallucinations.

d. They are more stable over time and more difficult to treat than are negative symptoms.

16. The prevalence of schizophrenia
   a. is declining, for unknown reasons.
   b. is higher in Third World countries than in the United States and Europe.
   c. is higher in women than in men.
   d. is fairly easy to study, since schizophrenia is one of the easiest disorders to diagnose.

17. Which of the following provides some support for a genetic basis for schizophrenia?
   a. Adopted children have a higher concordance rate with their adoptive than biological kin.
   b. The concordance rate for schizophrenia is greater for dizygotic than monozygotic twins.
   c. The concordance rate for schizophrenia is greater for monozygotic than dizygotic twins.
   d. Mutation of a gene on chromosome 7 has been shown to cause schizophrenia.

18. A problem with estimating the possibility of a genetic basis for schizophrenia is that
   a. monozygotic twins have only about a 50% concordance rate; monozygotic twins may both have the same gene, but it may be activated in one twin, but suppressed in the other.
   b. common prenatal factors, such as smoking, drinking, and other poor health habits, as well as complications during pregnancy and delivery, may at least partially explain the increased concordance rate with biological, rather than adoptive, relatives of schizophrenics.
   c. both a and b
   d. none of the above

19. Research on possible causes of schizophrenia has demonstrated that
   a. a prenatal viral infection may cause fever, which results in impaired brain development.
   b. several studies have converged on a single gene as the primary cause of schizophrenia.
   c. conflicting messages from parents are a major cause of schizophrenia.
   d. the season-of-birth effect occurs more often in the tropics, where diseases are harder to control.

20. Studies of the brains of schizophrenics have revealed that
   a. they have shrunken ventricles.
   b. their prefrontal and temporal cortical areas are smaller, especially in the left hemisphere.
   c. they have more abnormalities in rapidly maturing areas, such as the brain stem, than in slowly maturing areas, such as dorsolateral prefrontal cortex.
   d. they have evidence of proliferation of glial cells and expression of genes activated during repair, indicating that much of the damage is caused during adulthood.

21. Drug-induced psychosis
   a. causes a full-blown state of schizophrenia, with mostly negative, rather than positive, symptoms.
   b. is caused by drugs that block dopamine receptors.
   c. is caused by drugs that increase the stimulation of dopamine receptors.
   d. is caused by drugs that stimulate glutamate receptors.

22. Which of the following is **not** an effective antipsychotic (neuroleptic) drug?
    a. haloperidol
    b. chlorpromazine
    c. amphetamine
    d. clozapine

23. According to the dopamine hypothesis of schizophrenia, people with schizophrenia have
    a. excessive activity at dopamine synapses.
    b. deficient activity at dopamine synapses.
    c. glutamate in neurons that should release dopamine.
    d. dopamine in neurons that should release glutamate.

24. A problem with the dopamine hypothesis is that
    a. neuroleptic drugs improve schizophrenic symptoms before they have a significant effect on dopamine synapses.
    b. neuroleptic drugs affect dopamine synapses before they have a significant effect on schizophrenic symptoms.
    c. there was actually less occupation of dopamine D_2 receptors in schizophrenics, whereas there should have been more, if excess dopamine was the problem.
    d. amphetamine, cocaine, methamphetamine, and LSD increase activity at dopamine receptors, but are among the best treatments for schizophrenia, suggesting that excess dopamine activity cannot be a cause of that disorder.

25. Which of the following is true?
    a. Phencyclidine (PCP) is an atypical neuroleptic drug that treats schizophrenia by stimulating glutamate receptors.
    b. Since there is too much glutamate in the brains of schizophrenic people, a good way to improve their symptoms is to block glutamate receptors.
    c. Glycine interferes with the binding of glutamate to NMDA receptors, thereby worsening schizophrenic symptoms.
    d. In many brain areas, dopamine inhibits glutamate release, or glutamate stimulates neurons that inhibit dopamine release; therefore, increased dopamine would produce the same effects as decreased glutamate.

26. Tardive dyskinesia
    a. recedes completely once all traces of antipsychotic drugs have left the body.
    b. usually occurs soon after beginning antipsychotic drug treatment.
    c. is characterized by tremors or involuntary movements and may result from blocking of dopamine receptors in the basal ganglia.
    d. is caused by the newer atypical antipsychotics more than the older drugs.

27. Atypical antipsychotic drugs
    a. include clozapine, amisulpride, resperidone, olanzpine, and aripiprazole.
    b. block serotonin 5-HT$_2$ receptors.
    c. are more effective on negative symptoms than older drugs.
    d. all of the above

Solutions

True/False Questions

1. T	7. F	13. F	19. T
2. F	8. T	14. T	20. T
3. T	9. F	15. T	21. F
4. T	10. T	16. F	22. T
5. F	11. F	17. T	23. T
6. T	12. F	18. F	

Fill In The Blanks

1. serotonin transporter; environmental
2. tricyclics; SSRIs; selective serotonin reuptake inhibitors; MAOIs; monoamine oxidase inhibitors
3. bupropion; Welbutrin; dopamine
4. delayed
5. ECT; right
6. Repetitive transcranial magnetic
7. Sleep; exercise
8. lithium salts; valproate; carbamazepine; AMPA; arachidonic acid
9. polyunsaturated fatty acids; sleep schedule
10. Brain-derived neurotrophic factor; hippocampus
11. Psychotic; disorganized; disordered thinking.
12. Men; women; men's; basal ganglia
13. concordance
14. microdeletions; microduplications
15. hippocampus
16. neurodevelopmental
17. frontal; temporal; left; hippocampus; prefrontal
18. dopamine; glutamate.
19. tardive dyskinesia
20. D_2; $5HT_2$; glutamate

Matching Items

1. m	5. b	9. g	13. p
2. o	6. i	10. h	14. f
3. e	7. l	11. n	15. k
4. a	8. c	12. j	16. d

Multiple Choice Questions

1. a	8. c	15. c	22. c
2. d	9. b	16. a	23. a
3. b	10. b	17. c	24. b
4. c	11. a	18. c	25. d
5. d	12. c	19. a	26. c
6. a	13. d	20. b	27. d
7. c	14. b	21. c	

ABLATION

ABSOLUTE
REFRACTORY
PERIOD

ACETYLCHOLINE

ACETYLCHOLINESTERASE

ACROSS-FIBER
PATTERN
PRINCIPLE

ACTION
POTENTIAL

ACTIVATING
EFFECT

ACTIVATION-
SYNTHESIS
HYPOTHESIS

Time immediately after an action potential, when sodium gates close and the membrane cannot produce an action potential in response to stimulation of any intensity

Removal of a structure

Enzyme that breaks acetylcholine into acetate and choline

Chemical similar to an amino acid, except that the NH_2 group has been replaced by an $N(CH_3)_3$ group; a neurotransmitter

Rapid depolarization and slight reversal of the usual polarization caused by stimulation beyond the threshold

Notion that each receptor responds to a wide range of stimuli and contributes to the perception of every stimulus in its system

View that during dreams, parts of the cortex are activated by the input arising from the pons plus whatever stimuli are present in the room, & the cortex synthesizes a story to make sense of the activity

Temporary effect of a hormone on behavior or anatomy, occurring only while the hormone is present

ACTIVE TRANSPORT

ACUTE CONDITIONS

ADAPTATION

ADRENOCORTICOTROPIC
HORMONE (ACTH)

AEROBIC PROCESS

AFFERENT AXON

AFFINITY

2-AG (sn-2
ARACHIDONYLGLYCEROL)

Conditions having a sudden onset and a strong possibility of ending quickly

Protein-mediated process that expends energy to pump chemicals from the blood into the brain

Hormone that stimulates the human adrenal cortex to release cortisol and the rat adrenal gland to release corticosterone

Decreased response to a stimulus as a result of recent exposure to it

Neuron that brings information into a structure

One that uses oxygen during the activity

Chemical that is produced in large quantities by the brain and that attaches to cannabinoid receptors

Tendency of a drug to bind to a particular type of receptor

AGONIST

AGOUTI-RELATED PEPTIDE
(AgRP)

ALCOHOLISM (ALCOHOL
DEPENDENCE)

ALDOSTERONE

ALL-OR-NONE LAW

ALLOSTASIS

ALPHA-FETOPROTEIN

ALPHA WAVE

Inhibitory neurotransmitter found in the areas of the hypothalamus that regulate feeding

Drug that mimics or increases the effects of a neurotransmitter

Adrenal hormone that causes the kidneys to conserve sodium when excreting urine

Inability to quite drinking or to limit intake of alcohol in spite of strong intentions to do so

Adaptive way in which the body changes its set points in response to changes in its life or changes in the environment

Principle stating that the size, amplitude, and velocity of the action potential are independent of the intensity of the stimulus that initiated it

Rhythm of 8 to 12 brain waves per second, generally associated with relaxation

Protein that bind with estrogen in the bloodstream of many immature mammals

ALTRUISTIC BEHAVIOR

ALZHEIMER'S DISEASE

AMINO ACIDS

AMNESIA

AMPA RECEPTOR

AMPHETAMINE

APMPLITUDE

AMYLOID- (OR -AMYLOID)

Condition characterized by memory loss, confusion, depression, restlessness, hallucinations, delusions, sleeplessness, and loss of appetite

Behavior that benefits someone other than the individual engaging in the behavior

Memory loss

Acids containing an amine group

Stimulant drug that increases the release of dopamine

Glutamate receptor that also responds to the drug a-amino-3-hydroxy-5-methyl-4-isoxazolepropionic acid

Protein that accumulates to higher than normal levels in the brains of people with Alzheimer's disease

Intensity of a sound or other stimulus

ANTAGONIST	ANTAGONISTIC MUSCLES
ANTERIOR	ANTERIOR COMMISSURE
ANTERIOR PITUITARY	ANTEROGRADE AMNESIA
ANTIBODY	ANTIGEN

Pairs of muscles that move a limb in opposite directions (e.g., extensor and flexor)	Drug that blocks the effects of a neurotransmitter
Set of axons connecting the two cerebral hemispheres; smaller than the corpus callosum	Located toward the front end
Loss of memory for events that happened after brain damage	Portion of the pituitary gland, composed of glandular tissue
Protein on the surface of a microorganism in response to which the immune system generates antibodies	Y-shaped protein that fits onto an antigen and weakens it or marks it for destruction

ANTIPSYCHOTIC

APHASIA

APOPTSIS

ARCUATE NUCLEUS

ARTIFICIAL SELECTION

ASSOCIATIVITY

ASTIGMATISM

ASTROCYTE (ASTROGLIA)

Language Impairment	Drug that relieves schizophrenia
Hypothalamic area with one set of neurons sensitive to hunger signals and another sensitive to satiety signals	Developmental program by which a neuron kills itself at a certain age unless inhibited from doing so
Tendency for pairing a weak input with a stronger input to enhance the later effectiveness of the weaker input	Change in the frequencies of various genes in a population because of a breeder's selection of desired individuals for mating purposes
Relatively large, star-shaped glia cells	Blurring of vision for lines in one direction because of the nonspherical shape of the eye

ATOM	ATOMIC NUMBER
ATOMIC WEIGHT	ATP (ADENOSINE TRIPHOSPHATE)
ATYPICAL ANTIDEPRESSANTS	AUTONOMIC NERVOUS SYSTEM
AUTORECEPTOR	AUTOSOMAL GENE

Number of protons in the nucleus of an atom

Piece of an element that cannot be divided any further

Compound that stores energy; also used as a neuromodulator

Number indicating the weight of an atom relative to a weight of one for a proton

Set of neurons that regulates functioning of the internal organs

Miscellaneous group of drugs with antidepressant effects but only mild side effects

Gene on any of the chromosomes other than the sex chromosomes (X and Y)

Presynaptic receptor that is stimulated by the neurotransmitter released by the presynaptic cell itself, feeding back to decrease further release of the transmitter

AXON

AXON HILLOCK

BABINSKI REFLEX

BALLISTIC MOVEMENT

BASAL FOREBRAIN

BASAL GANGLIA

BASAL METABOLISM

BEHAVIORAL ACTIVATION
SYSTEM (BAS)

Swelling of the soma, the point where the axon begins

Single thin fiber of constant diameter that extends from a neuron

Motion that proceeds as a single organized unit that cannot be redirected once it begins

Reflexive flexion of the big toe when the sole of the foot is stimulated

Set of subcortical forebrain structures lateral to the hypothalamus, including the caudate nucleus, putamen, and globus pallidus

Forebrain area anterior and dorsal to the hypothalamus; includes cell clusters that promote wakefulness and other cell clusters that promote sleep

Brain system associated with low to moderate arousal and a tendency to approach

Rate of energy use while the body is at rest, used largely for maintaining a constant body temperature

BEHAVIORAL INHIBITION SYSTEM (BIS)	BEHAVIORAL MEDICINE
BELL-MAGENDIE LAW	BENZODIAZEPINES
BINDING PROBLEM	BINOCULAR INPUT
BINOCULAR RIVALRY	BIOLOGICAL PSYCHOLOGY

Field that includes the influence of eating and drinking habits, smoking, stress, exercise, and other behavioral variables on health

Brain system associated with increased attention and arousal and inhibited action

Class of widely used antianxiety drugs

Observation that the dorsal roots of the spinal cord carry sensory information and that the ventral roots carry motor information toward the muscles and glands

Stimulation from both eyes

Question of how the visual, auditory, and other areas of the brain influence one another to produce a combined perception of a single object

Study of the physiological, evolutionary, and developmental mechanisms of behavior and experience

Alternating perception of what the left eye sees with what the right eye sees, when the two are incompatible

BIPOLAR CELL

BIPOLAR DISORDER

BIPOLAR I DISORDER

BIPOLAR II DISORDER

BLINDSIGHT

BLOOD-BRAIN BARRIER

BRAIN DEATH

BRAINSTEM

Condition in which a person alternates between the two poles of mania and depression

Type of neuron in the retina that receives input directly from the receptors

Condition with only manic phases, characterized mostly by agitation or anxiety

Condition including full-blown episodes of mania

Mechanism that keeps many chemicals out of the brain

Ability to localize objects within an apparently blind visual field

Hindbrain, midbrain, and posterior central structures of the forebrain

Condition with no sign of brain activity and no response to any stimulus

CARNIVORES

CATAPLEXY

CATECHOLAMINES

CAUDATE NUCLEUS

CELL BODY (SOMA)

CENTRAL CANAL

CENTRAL NERVOUS
SYSTEM (CNS)

CENTRAL PATTERN
GENERATOR

Attack of muscle weakness while a person remains awake

Animals that eat meat

Large subcortical structure, on epart of the basal ganglia

Compounds such as dopamine, norepinephrine, and epinephrine that contain both catechol and amine (NH2)

Fluid-filled channel in the center of the spinal cord

Structure of a cell that contains the nucleus

Neural mechanism in the spinal cord or elsewhere that generates rhythmic patters of motor output

Brain and spinal cord

CENTRAL SULCUS

CEREBRAL CORTEX

CEREBELLUM

CEREBROSPINAL
FLUID (CSF)

CHLORPROMAZINE
(THORAZINE)

CHOLECYSTOKININ
(CCK)

CHROMOSOME

CHRONIC CONDITIONS

Outer covering of the cerebellum

Large groove in the surface of the primate cerebral cortex, separating frontal from parietal cortex

Liquid similar to blood serum, found in the ventricles of the brain and in the central canal of the spinal cord

Highly convoluted structure in the hindbrain

Hormone released by the duodenum in response to food distention

First drug found to relieve the positive symptoms of schizophrenia

Conditions having a gradual onset and long duration

Strand of DNA bearing the genes

CLASSICAL CONDITIONING

CLINICO-ANATOMICAL HYPOTHESIS

CLOSED HEAD INJURY

COCAINE

COCHLEA

COLLATERAL SPROUT

COLOR CONSTANCY

COLOR VISION DEFICIENCY

View that regards dreams as just thinking that takes place under unusual conditions

Type of conditioning produced by the pairing of two stimuli, one of which evokes an automatic response

Stimulant drug that increases the stimulation of dopamine synapses by blocking the reuptake of dopamine by the presynaptic neuron

Sharp blow to the head resulting from a fall, an automobile or motorcycle accident, an assault, or other sudden trauma that does not actually puncture the brain

Newly formed branch from an uninjured axon that attaches to a synapse vacated when another axon was destroyed

Structure in the inner ear containing auditory receptors

Inability to perceive color differences as most people do

Ability to recognize the color of an object despite changes in lighting

COMPLEX

COMPLEX CELL

COMPUTERIZED AXIAL
TOMOGRAPHY (CT OR CAT SCAN)

COMT (CATECHOL-
O-METHYLTRANSFERASE

CONCENTRATION GRADIENT

CONCORDANCE

CONDITIONED RESPONSE (CR)

CONDITIONED STIMULUS (CS)

Cell type of the visual cortex that responds best to a light stimulus of a particular shape anywhere in its receptive field cannot be mapped into fixed excitatory and inhibitory zones

Extended period of unconsciousness, with a steady low level of brain activity

Enzyme that converts catecholamines into synaptically inactive forms

Method of visualizing a living brain by injecting a dye into the blood and then passing x-rays through the head and recording them by detectors on the other side

Pair of twins is concordant for a trait if both of them have it or neither has it

Difference in distribution of ions across a membrane

Stimulus that evokes a particular response only after it has been paired with an unconditioned stimulus

Response evoked by a conditioned stimulus after it has been paired with an unconditioned stimulus

CONDITIONED TASTE
AVERSIONS

CONDUCTIVE DEAFNESS
(MIDDLE-EAR DEAFNESS)

CONE

CONFABULATION

CONGENITAL ADRENAL
HYPERPLASIA (CAH)

CONSCIOUS

CONSOLIDATION

COOPERATIVITY

Hearing loss that occurs if the bones of the middle ear fail to transmit sound waves properly to the cochlea

Learned avoidance of a food whose consumption is followed by illness

Making up an answer to a question and then accepting the invented information as if it were a memory

Type of retinal receptor that contributes to color perception

Capable of reporting the presence of a stimulus

Overdevelopment of the adrenal glands from birth

Tendency for nearly simultaneous stimulation by two or more axons to produce long-term potentiation much more effectively than stimulation by just one

Conversion of short-term memories into long-term memories and strengthening of those memories

CORPUS CALLOSUM

CORTICOSPINAL TRACTS

CORTISOL

CRANIAL NERVES

CROSS-ADAPTATION

CYTOKINES

Δ9–TETRAHYDROCANNABINOL
(Δ9–THC)

DEAFFERENT

Axon paths from the cerebral cortex to the spinal cord

Large set of axons that connects the two hemispheres of the cerebral cortex

Part of a set of nerves controlling sensory and motor information of the head, connecting to nuclei in the medulla, pons, midbrain, or forebrain

Hormone released by the adrenal cortex that elevates blood sugar and enhances metabolism

Chemicals released by the immune system that attack infections and communicate with the brain to elicit anti-illness behaviors

Reduced response to one stimulus because of recent exposures to some other stimulus

To remove or disable the sensory nerves from a body part

Chemical found in the leaves of marijuana plants

DECLARATIVE
MEMORY

DELAYED
MATCHING-TO-SAMPLE
TASK

DELAYED
NONMATCHING-TO-SAMPLE
TASK

DELAYED-RESPONSE
TASK

DELUSIONS

DENDRITIC SPINE

DENERVATION
SUPERSENSITIVITY

DEOXYRIBONUCLEIC ACID
(DNA)

Task in which an animal sees a sample object and then after a delay must choose an object that matches the samples

memory that a person can state in words

Assignment in which an animal must respond on the basis of a signal that it remembers but that is no longer present

Task in which an animal sees an object and then after a delay must choose an object that does not match the sample

Short outgrowth along the dendrites

Beliefs that other people regard as unfounded, such as the belief that one is being severely persecuted

Double-stranded chemical that composes the chromosomes; it serves as a template for the synthesis of RNA

Increased sensitivity by a postsynaptic cell after removal of an axon that formerly innervated it

DEPOLARIZATION

DERMATOME

DIASCHISIS

DIAZEPAM-BINDING
INHIBITOR (DBI)

DIFFERENTIAL DIAGNOSIS

DIFFERENTIATION

DISUSE
SUPERSENSITIVITY

DIZYGOTIC TWINS

Area of skin connected to a particular spinal nerve

Reduction in the level of polarization across a membrane

Brain protein that blocks the behavioral effect of diazepam and other benzodiazepines

Decreased activity of surviving neurons after other neurons are damages

Formation of the axon and dendrites that gives a neuron its distinctive shape

Identification of a condition as distinct from all similar conditions

Fraternal (nonidentical) twins

Increased sensitivity by a postsynaptic cell because of decreased input by incoming axons

DOMINANT GENE

DOPAMINE HYPOTHESIS OF
SCHIZOPHRENIA

DOPAMINE TRANSPORTER̀

DORSAL

DORSAL ROOT GANGLIA

DORSAL STREAM

DUDENUM

DYSLEXIA

Proposal that schizophrenia is due to excess activity at certain dopamine synapses

Gene that shows a strong effect in either the homozygous or heterozygous condition

Located toward the back, away from the ventral (stomach side)

Membrane protein that enables the presynaptic neuron to reabsorb dopamine after releasing it

Visual path in the parietal cortex, sometimes known as the "where" or "how" pathway

Set of sensory neuron somata on the dorsal side of the spinal cord

Specific reading difficulty in a person with adequate vision and at least average skills in other academic areas

Part of the small intestine adjoining the stomach; the first part of the digestive system that absorbs food

EDEMA

EFFERENT AXON

EFFICACY

ELECTRICAL GRADIENT

ELECTROCONVULSIVE
THERAPY (ECT)

ELECTROENCEPHALOGRAPH
(EEG)

END-STOPPED
(HYPERCOMPLEX) CELL

ENDOCRINE GLAND

Neuron that carries information away from a structure

Accumulation of fluid

Difference in positive and negative charges across a membrane

Tendency of a drug to activate a particular kind of receptor

Device that measures the brain's electrical activity through electrodes on the scalp

Electrically inducing a convulsion in an attempt to relieve depression or other disorder

Structure that releases hormones into the blood

Cell of the visual cortex that responds best to stimuli of a precisely limited type, anywhere in a large receptive field, with a strong inhibitory field at one end of its field

ENDOGENOUS CIRCADIAN
RHYTHM

ENDOGENOUS CIRCANNUAL
RHYTHM

ENDOPLASMIC RETICULUM

ENDORPHINS

ENDOZEPINE

ENGRAM

ENZYMES

EPILEPSY

Self-generated rhythm that lasts about a year

Self-generated rhythm that lasts about a day

Category of chemicals the body produces that stimulate the same receptors as do opiates

Network of thin tubes within a cell that transports newly synthesized proteins to other locations

Physical representation of what has been learned

Brain protein that counteracts the effects of benzodiazepines

Condition characterized by repeated episodes of excessive, synchronized neural activity, mainly because of decreased release of the inhibitory transmitter GABA

Any proteins that catalyze biological reactions

EPISODIC MEMORIES	EQUIPOTENTIALITY
ESTRADIOL	ESTROGEN
EVOKED POTENTIALS OR EVOKED RESPONSES	EVOLUTION
EVOLUTIONARY EXPLANATION	EVOLUTIONARY PSYCHOLOGY

Concept that all parts of the cortex contribute equally to complex behaviors such as learning; that any part of the cortex can substitute for any other

Memories of single events

Class of steroid hormones that are more abundant in females than in males for most species

One type of estrogen

Change in the frequencies of various genes in a population over generations

Electrical activity of the brain in response to a stimulus, as recorded from the scalp

Field that deals with how behaviors have evolved

Understanding in terms of the evolutionary history of a species

EXCITATORY POSTSYNAPTIC
POTENTIAL (EPSP)

EXOCYTOSIS

EXPLICIT MEMORY

EXTENSOR

FAST-TWITCH FIBERS

FEATURE DETECTOR

FETAL ALCOHOL SYDROME

FLEXOR

Excretion of neurotransmitter through the membrane of a presynaptic terminal and into the synaptic cleft between the presynaptic and postsynaptic neurons

Graded depolarization of a neuron

Muscle that extends a limb

Deliberate recall of information that one recognizes as a memory, detectable by direct testing such as asking a person to describe a past event

Neuron whose responses indicate the presence of a particular feature

Muscle fibers that produce fast contractions but fatigue rapidly

Muscle that flexes a limb

Condition resulting from prenatal exposure to alcohol and marked by decreased alertness, hyperactivity, varying degrees of mental retardation, motor problems, heart defects, and facial abnormalities

FOREBRAIN

FOVEA

FREE-RUNNING RHYTHM

FREQUENCY

FREQUENCY THEORY

FRONTAL LOBE

FUNCTIONAL EXPLANATION

FUNCTIONAL MAGNETIC
RESONANCE IMAGING (fMRI)

Area in the center of the human retina specialized for acute, detailed vision

Most anterior part of the brain, including the cerebral cortex and other structures

Number of sound waves per second

Circadian or circannual rhythm that is not being periodically reset by light or other cues

Section of cerebral cortex extending from the central sulcus to the anterior limit of the brain, containing the primary motor cortex and the prefrontal cortex

Concept that pitch perception depends on differences in frequency of action potentials by auditory neurons

Modified version of MRI that measures energies released by hemoglobin molecules in an MRI scan and then determines the brain areas receiving the greatest supply of blood and oxygen

Understanding why a structure or behavior evolved as it did

G-PROTEIN

GABAA RECEPTOR COMPLEX

GANGLION CELL

GASES

GATE THEORY

GENDER IDENTITY

GENE

GENE-KNOCKOUT APPROACH

Structure that includes a site that binds GABA, as well as sites that bind other chemicals that modify the sensitivity of the GABA site

Protein coupled to GTP (guanosine triphosphate, an energy-storing molecule)

One of the categories of neurotransmitters, including nitric oxide and possibly others

type of neuron in the retina that receives input from the bipolar cells

Sex with which a person identifies

Assumption that stimulation of certain nonpain axons in the skin or in the brain can inhibit transmission of pain messages in the spinal cord

Use of biochemical methods to direct a mutation to a particular gene that is important for certain types of cells, transmitters, or receptors

Unit of heredity that maintains its structural identity from one generation to another

GENERAL ADAPTIATION
SYNDROME

GHRELIN

GLIA

GLOBUS PALLIDUS

GLUCAGON

GLUCOSE

GLUTAMATE HYPOTHESIS OF
SCHIZOPHRENIA

GOLGI TENDON ORGAN

Chemical released by stomach during food deprivation; also released as a neurotransmitter in the brain, where it stimulates eating

Generalized response to any kind of stress

Large subcortical structure, one part of the basal ganglia

Type of cell in the nervous system that, in contrast to neurons, does not conduct impulses to other cells

A simple sugar, the main fuel of vertebrate neurons

Pancreatic hormone that stimulates the liver to convert stored glycogen to glucose

Receptor that responds to the contraction of a muscle

Proposal that schizophrenia is due to deficient activity at certain glutamate synapses

GRADED POTENTIAL

GRASP REFLEX

GRAY MATTER

HABITUATION

HAIR CELL

HALLUCINATION

HALLUCINOGENIC DRUGS

HARD PROBLEM

Reflexive grasp of an object placed firmly in the hand

Membrane potential that varies in magnitude and does not follow the all-or-none law

Decrease in response to a stimulus that is presented repeatedly and is accompanied by no change in other stimuli

Areas of the nervous system with a high density of cell bodies and dendrites, with few myelinated axons

Sensory experience that does not correspond to reality

Type of sensory receptor shaped like a hair; auditory receptors are hair cells

Philosophical question of why and how any kind of brain activity is associated with consciousness

Drugs that grossly distort perception, such as LSD

HEBBIAN SYNAPSE

HEMORRHAGE

HERBIVORES

HERITABILITY

HERMAPHRODITE

HETEROZYGOUS

HINDBRAIN

HIPPOCAMPUS

Rupture of an artery

Synapse that increases in effectiveness because of simultaneous activity in the presynaptic axon and the postsynaptic neuron

Estimate of the degree to which variance in a characteristic depends on variations in heredity for a given population

Animals that eat plants

Having two unlike genes for a given trait

Individual whose genitals do not match the usual development for his or her genetic sex

Large forebrain structure between the thalamus and cortex

Most posterior part of the brain, including the medulla, pons, and cerebellum

HOMEOSTASIS

HOMEOTHERMIC

HOMOZYGOUS

HORIZONTAL CELL

HORMONE

HPA AXIS

HUNTINGTON'S DISEASE

5-HYDROXYINDOLEACETIC
ACID (5-HIAA)

Maintaining nearly constant body temperature over a wide range of environmental temperatures

Tendency to maintain a variable, such as temperature, within a fixed range

Type of cell that receives input from receptors and delivers inhibitory input to bipolar cells

Having two identical genes for a given characteristic

Hypothalamus, pituitary gland, and adrenal cortex

Chemical secreted by glands and conveyed by the blood to other organs

A serotonin metabolite

Inherited disorder characterized initially by jerky arm movements and facial twitches and later by tremors, writhing movements, and psychological symptoms, including depression, memory impairment, hallucinations, and delusions

HYPERPOLARIZATION

HYPOTHALAMUS

HYPOVOLEMIC THIRST

IDENTITY POSITION

IMMUNE SYSTEM

IMPLICIT MEMORY

IMPOTENCE

INATTENTIONAL BLINDNESS

Forebrain structure near the base of the brain just ventral to the thalamus

Increased polarization across a membrane

View that mental processes are the same as certain kinds of brain processes but described in different terms

Thirst provoked by low blood volume

Influence of recent experience on memory, even if one does not recognize that influence or realize that one is using memory at all

Set of structures that protects the body against viruses and bacteria

Unawareness of stimuli to which a person did not direct his or her attention

Inability to have an erection

INFERIOR COLLICULUS

INFERIOR TEMPORAL
CORTEX

INHIBITORY POSTSYAPTIC
POTENTIAL (IPSP)

INSOMNIA

INSULIN

INTERNEURON

INTERSEX (OR
PSEUDOHERMAPHRODITE)

INTRINSIC NEURON

Portion of the cortex where neurons are highly sensitive to complex aspects of the shape of visual stimuli within very large receptive fields

Swelling on each side of the tectum in the midbrain

Lack of sleep, leaving the person feeling poorly rested the following day

Temporary hyperpolarization of a membrane

Neuron whose axons and dendrites are entirely contained within a given structure

Pancreatic hormone that facilitates the entry of glucose into the cells

Neuron whose axons and dendrites are all confined within a given structure

Individual whose sexual development is intermediate or ambiguous

IONOTROPIC EFFECT

ISCHEMIA

JAMES-LANGE THEORY

JET LAG

K-COMPLEX

KIN SELECTION

KLÜVER-BUCY SYNDROME

KONIOCELLULAR NEURONS

Local insufficiency of blood because a blood clot or other obstruction has closed an artery

Synaptic effect that depends on the rapid opening of some kind of gate in the membrane

Disruption of biological rhythms caused by travel across time zones

Proposal that an event first provokes autonomic and skeletal responses and that emotion is the perception of those responses

Selection for a gene because it benefits the individual's relatives

sharp, high-amplitude, negative wave followed by a smaller, slower, positive wave

Ganglion cells located throughout the retina

Condition in which monkeys with damaged temporal lobes fail to display normal fears and anxieties

KORSAKOFF'S SYNDROME

LABELED-LINE PRINCIPLE

LACTASE

LACTOSE

LAMARCKIAN EVOLUTION

LAMINA (PL: LAMINAE)

LANGUAGE ACQUISITION DEVICE

LATERAL GENICULATE NUCLEUS

Concept that each receptor responds to a limited range of stimuli and has a direct line to the brain

Type of brain damage caused by thiamine deficiency, characterized by apathy, confusion, and memory impairment

The sugar in milk

Enzyme necessary for lactose metabolism

Layer of cell bodies parallel to the surface of the cortex and separated from other laminae by layers of fibers

Discredited theory that evolution proceeds through the inheritance of acquired characteristics

Thalamic nucleus that receives incoming visual information

Built-in mechanism for acquiring language

LATERAL HYPOTHALAMUS

LATERAL INHIBITION

LATERAL INTERPOSITUS
NUCLEUS (LIP)

LATERAL PREOPTIC AREA

LATERALIZATION

LAW OF SPECIFIC NERVE
ENERGIES

L-DOPA

LEPTIN

Restraint of activity in one neuron by activity in a neighboring neuron

Area of the hypothalamus that is important for the control of eating and drinking

Portion of the hypothalamus that includes some cells that facilitate drinking and some that inhibit it, as well as passing axons that are important for osmotic thirst

Nucleus of the cerebellum that is critical for classical conditioning of the eye-blink response

Statement that each nerve always conveys the same kind of information to the brain

Statement that each nerve always conveys the same kind of information to the brain

Peptide released by fat cells; tends to decrease eating, partly by inhibiting release of neuropeptide Y in the hypothalamus

Chemical precursor of dopamine and other catecholamines

LESION	LEUKOCYTE
LIMBIC SYSTEM	LITHIUM
LOCAL ANESTHETIC	LOCAL NEURON
LOCUS COERULEUS	LONG-TERM DEPRESSION (LTD)

White blood cell; a component of the immune system

Damage to a structure

Element whose salts are often used as a therapy for bipolar disorder

Set of forebrain areas, critical for emotion, which form a border around the brainstem, including the olfactory bulb, hypothalamus, hippocampus, amygdala, cingulate gyrus of the cerebral cortex, and several other smaller structures

Small neuron with no axon or a very short one

Drug that attaches to the sodium channels of the membrane, preventing sodium ions from entering and thereby blocking action potentials

Prolonged decrease in response at a synapse where the axons have been less active than certain other axons afferent to that neuron

Small hindbrain structure whose widespread axons send bursts of norepinephrine in response to meaningful stimuli

LONG-TERM MEMORY

LONG-TERM POTENTIATION (LTP)

LOUDNESS

LUTEINIZING HORMONE (LH)

MAGNETOENCEPH-
ALOGRAPH (MEG)

MAGNOCELLULAR NEURON

MAJOR DEPRESSION

MANIA

Phenomenon that after one or more axons bombard a dendrite with a rapid series of stimuli, the synapses between those axons and the dendrite become more sensitive

Memory of an event that is not currently held in attention

Anterior pituitary hormone that stimulates the release of an ovum

Perception of the intensity of a sound

Large-celled neuron of the visual system that is sensitive to changing or moving stimuli in a relatively large visual field

Device that measures the faint magnetic fields generated by the brain's activity

Condition of restless activity, excitement, laughter, self-confidence, and few inhibitions

State of feeling sad, helpless, and lacking in energy and pleasure for weeks at a time

MAO (MONOAMINE OXIDASE)

MASS ACTION

MATERIALISM

MEDIAL CORTICOSPINAL TRACT

MEDULLA

MELANOCORTIN

MELATONIN

MEMBRANE

Theory that the cortex works as a whole, and the more cortex the better

Enzyme that converts catecholamines and serotonin into synaptically inactive forms

Set of axons from many parts of the cerebral cortex, midbrain, and medulla, descending in the medial part of the spinal cord, responsible for bilateral control of trunk muscles

View that everything that exists is material, or physical

Type of chemical that promotes satiety in the hypothalamus

Hindbrain structure located just above the spinal cord; the medulla could be regarded as an enlarged, elaborated extension of the spinal cord

Structure that separates the inside of a cell from the outside

Hormone that among other effects induces sleepiness

MENINGES

MENSTRUAL CYCLE

MENTALISM

MESOLIMBOCORTICAL
SYSTEM

METABOTROPIC EFFECT

METHADONE

METHYLPHENIDATE
(RITALIN)

MICROGLIA

In women, periodic variation in hormones and fertility over the course of approximately 1 month	Membranes surrounding the brain and spinal cord
Set of neurons that project from the midbrain tegmentum to the limbic system	View that only the mind really exists
Chemical similar to heroin and morphine but often given as a substitute because it can be taken orally, in which case its effects rise and fall more slowly	Effect at a synapse that produces a relatively slow but long-lasting effect through metabolic reactions
Very small neurons that remove waste materials and microorganisms from the central nervous system	Stimulant drug that increases the stimulation of dopamine synapses by blocking the reuptake of dopamine by the presynaptic neuron

MIDBRAIN

MIDGET GANGLION CELLS

MIGRATION

MID-BODY PROBLEM OR
MIND-BRAIN PROBLEM

MINIMALLY CONSCIOUS
STATE

MIRROR NEURONS

MITOCHONDRION (PL:
MITOCHONDRIA)

MONISM

Ganglion cells in the fovea of humans and other primates

Middle part of the brain, including superior colliculus, inferior colliculus, tectum, and tegmentum

Question of how the mind is related to the brain

Movement of neurons toward their eventual destinations in the brain

Cells that are active during a movement and while watching another perform the same movement

Condition of decreased brain activity with occasional, brief periods of purposeful actions and limited speech comprehension

Theory that only one kind of substance exists in the universe (not separate physical and mental substances)

Structure where the cell performs the metabolic activities that provide energy

MONOAMINE

MONAMINE OXIDASE
INHIBITOR (MAOI)

MONOZYGOTIC TWINS

MORRIS WATER MAZE TASK

MOTION BLINDNESS

MOTOR NEURON

MOTOR PROGRAM

MPTP, MPP

Drug that blocks the enzyme monoamine oxidase (MAO), a presynaptic terminal enzyme that metabolizes catecholamines and serotonin into inactive forms

Nonacidic neurotransmitter containing an amine group (NH2), formed by a metabolic change of certain amino acids

Procedure in which a subject must find his or her way to a slightly submerged platform that is not visible in murky water

Identical twins, derived from a single fertilized egg

Neuron that receives excitation from other neurons and conducts impulses from its soma in the spinal cord to muscle or gland cells

Impaired ability to perceive the direction or speed of movement, despite otherwise satisfactory vision

Chemicals known to be toxic to the dopamine-containing cells in the substantia nigra, capable of producing the symptoms of Parkinson's disease

Fixed sequence of movements that occur as a single unit

MST

MT (OR AREA V5)

MÜLLERIAN DUCTS

MULTIPLIER EFFECT

MUSCLE SPINDLE

MYASTHENIA GRAVIS

MYELIN

MYELIN SHEATH

Middle temporal cortex, an area activated by seeing objects in motion

Medial superior temporal cortex, an area in which neurons are sensitive to expansion, contraction, or rotation of the visual field or to the movement of an object relative to its background

Tendency for small genetic or prenatal influences to change the environment in a way that magnifies the change

Early precursors to female reproductive structures (the oviducts, uterus, and upper vagina)

Disease in which the immune system attacks the acetylcholine receptors at the nerve-muscle junctions

Receptor parallel to the muscle that responds to the stretch of a muscle

Insulating material that covers many vertebrate axons

Insulating material composed of fats and proteins

MYELINATED AXON

MYELINATION

NARCOLEPSY

NEGATIVE FEEDBACK

NEGATIVE SYMPTOM

NERVE DEAFNESS
(INNER-EAR DEAFNESS)

NERVE GROWTH FACTOR
(NGF)

NEUROANATOMY

Development of a myelin sheath that insulates an axon

Axon covered with a myelin sheath

In homeostasis, processes that reduce discrepancies from the set point

Condition characterized by unexpected periods of sleepiness during the day

Hearing loss that results from damage to the cochlea, the hair cells, or the auditory nerve

Absence of a behavior ordinarily seen in normal people (e.g., lack of emotional expression)

Anatomy of the nervous system

Protein that promotes the survival and growth of axons in the sympathetic nervous system and certain axons in the brain

NEURODEVELOPMENTAL HYPOTHESIS	NEUROMUSCULAR JUNCTION
NEURON	NEUROPEPTIDE
NEUROPEPTIDE Y (NPY)	NEUROTRANSMITTER
NEUROTROPHIN	NICOTINE

Synapse where a motor neuron's axon meets a muscle fiber

Proposal that schizophrenia is based on abnormalities in the prenatal or neonatal development of the nervous system, which lead to subtle but important abnormalities of brain anatomy and major abnormalities in behavior

Chemical formed of a chain of amino acids; released by a neuron to diff use widely, aff ecting many other neurons

Cell that receives information and transmits it to other cells by conducting electrochemical impulses

Chemical released by neurons that affects other neurons

Peptide found in the brain, especially the hypothalamus; it inhibits activity of the paraventricular nucleus and thereby increases meal size

Drug found in tobacco that, among other effects, stimulates certain acetylcholine receptors

Chemical that promotes the survival and activity of neurons

NIGHT TERROR

NITRIC OXIDE

MNDA RECEPTOR

NODE OF RANVIER

NON-REM (NREM) SLEEP

NUCLEI OF THE
CEREBELLUM

NUCLEUS

NUCLEUS BASALIS

Gas released by many small neurons; alters blood flow as well as neuronal activity

Experience of intense anxiety during sleep from which a person awakens screaming in terror

Short unmyelinated section of axon between segments of myelin

Glutamate receptor that also responds to the drug N-methyl-D-aspartate

Clusters of neurons in the interior of the cerebellum that send axons to motor-controlling areas outside the cerebellum

Sleep stages other than REM sleep

Area on the dorsal surface of the forebrain; a major source of axons that release acetylcholine to widespread areas in the cerebral cortex

Structure within a cell that contains the chromosomes; also a cluster of neuron cell bodies within the CNS

NUCLEUS OF THE TRACTUS
SOLITARIUS (NTS)

OCCIPITAL LOBE

OLFACTION

OLFACTORY CELLS

OLIGODENDROCYTES

OMNIVORES

ONTOGENETIC
EXPLANATION

OPERANT CONDITIONING

Posterior (caudal) section of the cerebral cortex	Area in the medulla that receives input from taste receptors
Neurons responsible for the sense of smell, located on the olfactory epithelium in the rear of the nasal air passages	Sense of smell
Animals that eat both meat and plants	Glia cells that surround and insulate certain axons in the vertebrate brain and spinal cord
Type of conditioning in which reinforcement or punishment changes the future probabilities of a given behavior	Understanding in terms of how a structure or a behavior develops

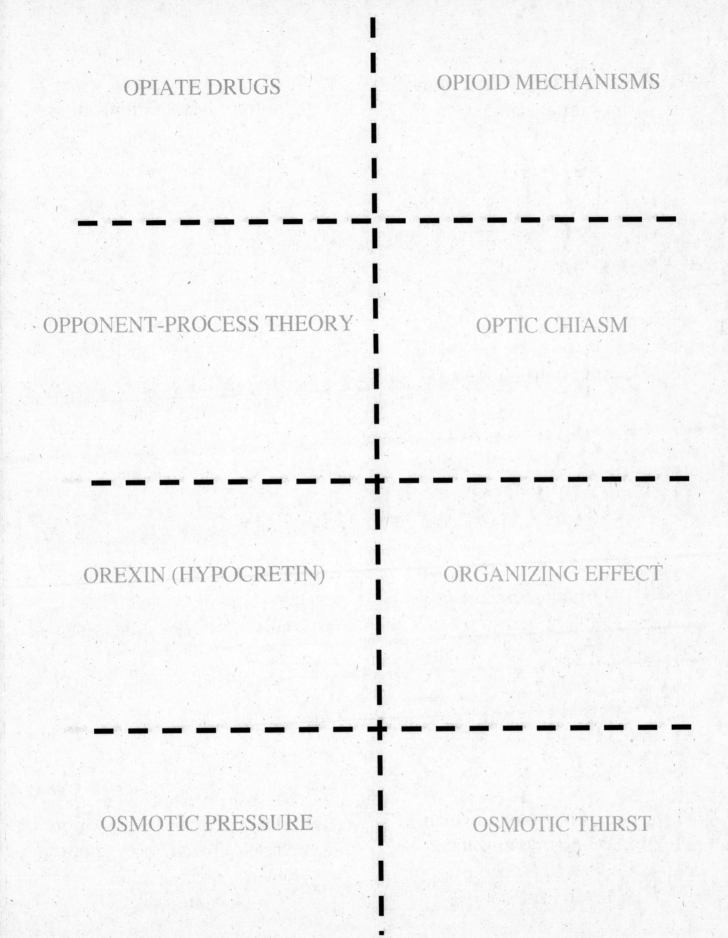

OPIATE DRUGS

OPIOID MECHANISMS

OPPONENT-PROCESS THEORY

OPTIC CHIASM

OREXIN (HYPOCRETIN)

ORGANIZING EFFECT

OSMOTIC PRESSURE

OSMOTIC THIRST

Systems responsive to opiate drugs and similar chemicals

Class of drugs derived from, or similar to those derived from, opium poppies

Point at which parts of the optic nerves cross from one side of the brain to the other

Theory that we perceive color in terms of paired opposites: white versus black, red versus green, and blue versus yellow

Long-lasting effect of a hormone that is present during a sensitive period early in development

Neurotransmitter that stimulates acetylcholine-releasing cells and thereby increases wakefulness and arousal

Thirst that results from an increase in the concentration of solutes in the body

Tendency of water to flow across a semipermeable membrane from the area of low solute concentration to the area of high solute concentration

OVAL WINDOW

OVARIES

OVLT (ORGANUM
VASCULOSUM LAMINAE
TERMINALIS)

OXYTOCIN

PACINIAN CORPUSCLE

PANIC ATTACK

PAPILLA (PL: PAPILLAE)

PARADOXICAL SLEEP

Female gonads that produce eggs

Membrane of the inner ear,
adjacent to the stirrup

Hormone released by the posterior
pituitary; also a neurotransmitter;
important for sexual and parental
behaviors

Brain structure on the border of the
third ventricle, highly sensitive to
the osmotic pressure of the blood

Period marked by extreme
sympathetic nervous system
arousal

Receptor that responds to a sudden
displacement of the skin or high
frequency vibration on the skin

Sleep that is deep in some ways
and light in others

Structure on the surface of the
tongue containing taste buds

PARALLEL FIBERS	PARASYMPATHETIC NERVOUS SYSTEM
PARAVENTRICULAR NUCLEUS (PVN)	PARIETAL LOBE
PARKINSON'S DISEASE	PARVOCELLULAR NEURON
PENUMBRA	PEPTIDE HORMONE

System of nerves that facilitate vegetative, nonemergency responses by the body's organs

Axons that run parallel to one another but perpendicular to the planes of the Purkinje cells in the cerebellum

Section of the cerebral cortex between the occipital lobe and the central sulcus

Area of the hypothalamus in which activity tends to limit meal size and damage leads to excessively large meals

Small-celled neuron of the visual system that is sensitive to color differences and visual details in its small visual field

Malady caused by damage to a dopamine pathway, resulting in slow movements, difficulty initiating movements, rigidity of the muscles, and tremors

Hormone composed of a short chain of amino acids

Area of endangered cells surrounding an area of primary damage

PERIAQUEDUCTAL GRAY
AREA

PERIODIC LIMB MOVEMENT
DISORDER

PERIOVULATORY PERIOD

PERIPHERAL NERVOUS SYSTEM

PGO WAVE

PHANTOM LIMB

PHENCYCLIDINE (PCP)

PHENOTHIAZINES

Repeated involuntary movement of the legs and sometimes arms during sleep

Area of the brainstem that is rich in enkephalin synapses

Nerves outside the brain and spinal cord

Time just before and after the release of the ovum, when fertility is highest

Continuing sensation of an amputated body part

Pattern of high-amplitude electrical potentials that occurs first in the pons, then in the lateral geniculate, and finally in the occipital cortex

Class of antipsychotic drugs that includes chlorpromazine

Drug that inhibits type NMDA glutamate receptors; at low doses, produces intoxication and slurred speech, and at higher doses, produces both positive and negative symptoms of schizophrenia

PHENYLKETONURIA (PKU)

PHEROMONE

PHI PHENOMENON

PHOTOPIGMENT

PHRENOLOGY

PHYSIOLOGICAL EXPLANATION

PINEAL GLAND

PINNA

Chemical released by one animal that affects the behavior of other members of the same species

Inherited inability to metabolize phenylalanine, leading to mental retardation unless the afflicted person stays on a strict low-phenylalanine diet throughout childhood

Chemical that releases energy when struck by light

Tendency to see something as moving back and forth between positions, when in fact it is alternately blinking on and off in those positions

Understanding in terms of the activity of the brain and other organs

Pseudoscience that claimed a relationship between skull anatomy and behavioral capacities

Outer-ear structure of flesh and cartilage that sticks out from each side of the head

Small unpaired gland in the brain, just posterior to the thalamus, that releases the hormone melatonin

PITCH

PITUITARY GLAND

PLACE THEORY

PLACEBO

PLANUM TEMPORALE

POIKILOTHERMIC

POLARIZATION

POLYSOMNOGRAPH

Endocrine gland attached to the base of the hypothalamus

Experience that corresponds to the frequency of a sound

drug or other procedure with no pharmacological effects

Concept that pitch perception depends on which part of the inner ear has cells with the greatest activity level

Maintaining the body at the same temperature as the environment

Area of the temporal cortex that for most people is larger in the left hemisphere than in the right hemisphere

Combination of EEG and eyemovement records, and sometimes other data, for a sleeping person

Electrical gradient across a membrane

PONS

PONTOMESENCEPHALON

POSITIVE SYMPTOM

POSITRON-EMISSION
TOMOGRAPHY (PET)

POSTCENTRAL GYRUS

POSTERIOR PARIETAL CORTEX

POSTERIOR PITUITARY

POSTPARTUM DEPRESSION

Part of the reticular formation that contributes to cortical arousal by axons that release acetylcholine and glutamate in the basal forebrain and thalamus

Hindbrain structure, anterior and ventral to the medulla

Method of mapping activity in a living brain by recording the emission of radioactivity from injected chemicals

Presence of a behavior not seen in normal people

Area with a mixture of visual, somatosensory, and movement functions, particularly in monitoring the position of the body relative to objects in the world

Gyrus of the cerebral cortex just posterior to the central gyrus; a primary projection site for touch and other body sensations

Depression after giving birth

Portion of the pituitary gland, which releases hormones synthesized by the hypothalamus

POSTSYNAPTIC NEURON

POVERTY OF THE STIMULUS ARGUMENT

PREFRONTAL CORTEX

PREFRONTAL LOBOTOMY

PREMOTOR CORTEX

PREOPTIC AREA/ANTERIOR HYPOTHALAMUS (POA/AH)

PRESYNAPTIC NEURON

PRESYNAPTIC TERMINAL

Claim that children do not hear many examples of some of the grammatical structures they acquire and therefore that they could not learn them

Neuron on the receiving end of a synapse

Surgical disconnection of the prefrontal cortex from the rest of the brain

Anterior portion of the frontal lobe of the cortex, which responds mostly to the sensory stimuli that signal the need for a movement

Brain area important for temperature control

Area of the frontal cortex, just anterior to the primary motor cortex, active during the planning of a movement

Tip of an axon, the point from which the axon releases chemicals

Neuron on the releasing end of a synapse

PRIMARY AUDITORY
CORTEX (AREA A1)

PRIMARY MOTOR CORTEX

PRIMARY VISIUAL CORTEX
(AREA V1)

PRIMATE

PROBLEM OF OTHER MINDS

PROCEDURAL MEMORY

PRODUCTIVITY

PROGESTERONE

Area of the frontal cortex just anterior to the central sulcus; a primary point of origin for axons conveying messages to the spinal cord

Area in the temporal lobes in which cells respond best to tones of a particular frequency

Order of mammals that includes humans, chimpanzees, gorillas, and others

Area of the cortex responsible for the first stage of visual processing

Memory of motor skills

Difficulty of knowing whether other people or animals have conscious experiences

Steroid hormone which, among other functions, prepares the uterus for the implantation of a fertilized ovum and promotes the maintenance of pregnancy

Ability of language to produce new signals to represent new ideas

PROLIFERATION

PROPOGATION OF THE
ACTION POTENTIAL

PROPRIOCEPTOR

PROSOPAGNOSIA

PROTEIN HORMONE

PSYCHONEURO-
IMMUNOLOGY

PUNISHMENT

PUPIL

Transmission of an action potential down an axon	Production of new cells
Impaired ability to recognize or identify faces	Receptor that is sensitive to the position and movement of a part of the body
Study of the ways in which experiences, especially stressful ones, alter the immune system and how the immune system in turn influences the central nervous system	Hormone composed of a long chain of amino acids
Opening in the center of the iris through which light enters	Event that suppresses the frequency of the preceding response

PURE AUTONOMIC FAILURE

PURINE

PRUKINJE CELL

PUTAMEN

RADIAL GLIA

RADIAL MAZE

RAPHE SYSTEM

READINESS POTENTIAL

Category of chemicals including adenosine

Condition in which output from the autonomic nervous system to the body fails

Large subcortical structure, one part of the basal ganglia

Neuron type in the cerebellum; a very flat cell in a plane perpendicular to that of other Purkinje cells

Apparatus with many arms radiating from a central point; reinforcement is put at the ends of some or all of the arms

Type of glia cells that guides the migration of neurons and the growth of their axons and dendrites during embryological development

Recordable activity in the motor cortex prior to voluntary movement

Group of neurons in the pons and medulla whose axons extend throughout much of the forebrain

RECEPTIVE FIELD	RECESSIVE GENE
RECIPROCAL ALTRUISM	RED NUCLEUS
REFLEX	REFLEX ARC
REFRACTORY PERIOD	REINFORCER

Gene that shows its effects only in the homozygous condition	Part of the visual field to which any one neuron responds
Nucleus midbrain structure whose axons join the lateral corticospinal tract; mainly responsible for control of arm muscles	Helping individuals who may later be helpful in return
Circuit of neurons from the sensory neurons to muscle responses that produces a reflex	Consistent, automatic response to a stimulus
Event that increases the future probability of the preceding response	Brief period following an action potential, when the cell resists the production of further action potentials

RELATIVE REFRACTORY PERIOD	RELEASING HORMONE
REM BEHAVIOR DISORDER	RESTING POTENTIAL
RETICULAR FORMATION	RETINA
RETINAL DISPARITY	RETINEX THEORY

Hormone released by the hypothalamus that flows through the blood to the anterior pituitary

Time after the absolute refractory period, when potassium gates remain open wider than usual, requiring a stronger than usual stimulus to initiate an action potential

---

Electrical potential across a membrane when a neuron is not being stimulated

Condition in which people move around vigorously during REM sleep

---

Rear surface of the eye, lined with visual receptors

Network of neurons in the medulla and other parts of the brainstem; the descending portion controls motor areas of the spinal cord; the ascending portion selectively increases arousal and attention in various forebrain areas

---

Concept that when information from various parts of the retina reaches the cortex, the cortex compares each of the inputs to determine the color perception in each area

Discrepancy between what the left eye sees and what the right eye sees

RETROGRADE AMNESIA	RETROGRADE TRANSMITTER
REUPTAKE	RIBONUCLEIC ACID (RNA)
RIBOSOME	ROD
ROOTING REFLEX	SACCADE

Transmitter, released by a postsynaptic cell under extensive stimulation, that travels back to the presynaptic cell to modify it

Loss of memory for events that occurred before brain damage

Single strand chemical; one type of an RNA molecule serves as a template for the synthesis of protein molecules

Reabsorption of a neurotransmitter by the presynaptic terminal

Type of retinal receptor that does not contribute to color perception

Site at which the cell synthesizes new protein molecules

Ballistic movement of the eyes from one fixation point to another

Reflexive head turning and sucking after a touch on the cheek

SALTATORY CONDUCTION

SCHIZOPHRENIA

SCHWANN CELL

SEASON-OF-BIRTH EFFECT

SEASONAL AFFECTIVE
DISORDER (SAD)

SECOND MESSENGER

SECOND-GENERATION
ANTIPSYCHOTICS

SECONDARY VISUAL
CORTEX (AREA V2)

Disorder including deteriorating ability to function in everyday life and some combination of hallucinations, delusions, thought disorder, movement disorder, and inappropriate emotional expressions

Jumping of action potentials from one node to another by the flow of positive ions

- -

Tendency for people born in winter to have a greater probability of developing schizophrenia than people born in other seasons

Glia cell that surrounds and insulates certain axons in the periphery of the vertebrate body

- -

Chemical within a neuron that, when activated by a neurotransmitter, initiates processes that carry messages to several areas within the neuron

Period of depression that recurs seasonally, such as in winter

- -

Area of the visual cortex responsible for the second stage of visual processing

Drugs that alleviate schizophrenia without serious risk of producing movement disorders

SELECTIVE PERMEABILITY

SELECTIVE SEROTONIN
REUPTAKE INHIBITOR (SSRI)

SELF-STIMULATION OF THE
BRAIN

SEMANTIC DEMENTIA

SEMICIRCULAR CANAL

SENSITIVE PERIOD

SENSITIZATION

SENSORY NEURON

Drug that blocks the reuptake of serotonin into the presynaptic terminal

Ability of certain chemicals to pass more freely than others through a membrane

Loss of semantic memory (factual knowledge)

Behavior that is reinforced by direct electrical stimulation of a brain area

Time early in development during which some event (e.g., an experience or the presence of a hormone) has a strong and long-lasting effect

Canal lined with hair cells and oriented in three planes, sensitive to the direction of tilt of the head

Neuron specialized to be highly sensitive to a specific type of stimulation

Increase in the response to mild stimuli as a result of previous exposure to more intense stimuli

SET POINT	SEX-LIMITED GENE
SEX-LINKED GENE	SEXUALLY DIMORPHIC NUCLEUS (SDN)
SHAM-FEEDING	SHAM LESION
SHAPE CONSTANCY	SHORT TERM MEMORY

Gene that exerts its effects primarily in one sex because of activation by androgens or estrogens, although members of both sexes may have the gene

Level at which homeostatic processes maintain a variable

Part of the medial preoptic nucleus of the hypothalamus, larger in males than in females and linked to male sexual behavior

Gene on either the X or the Y chromosome

Control procedure for an experiment, in which an investigator inserts an electrode into a brain but does not pass a current

Procedure in which everything that an animal swallows leaks out a tube connected to the esophagus or stomach

Memory of an event that just happened

Ability to perceive the shape of an object despite the movement or rotation of the object

SIMPLE CELL

SKELETAL (STRIATED)
MUSCLES

SLEEP APNEA

SLEEP SPINDLE

SLOW-TWITCH FIBERS

SMOOTH MUSCLES

SODIUM-POTASSIUM PUMP

SODIUM-SPECIFIC HUNGER

Muscles that control the movement of the body in relation to the environment (e.g., arm and leg muscles)

Type of visual cortex cell that has fixed excitatory and inhibitory zones in its receptive field

12- to 14-Hz brain waves in bursts that last at least half a second

Inability to breathe while sleeping

Muscles that control the movements of internal organs

Muscle fibers that produce less vigorous contractions without fatiguing

Enhanced preference for salty tastes during a period of sodium deficiency

Mechanism that actively transports three sodium ions out of the cell while simultaneously drawing in two potassium ions

SOLIPSISM

SOMATIC NERVOUS SYSTEM

SOMATOSENSORY SYSTEM

SPATIAL NEGLECT

SPATIAL SUMMATION

SPECIFICITY

SPINAL CORD

SPLIT-BRAIN PEOPLE

Nerves that convey messages from the sense organs to the CNS and from the CNS to muscles and glands

Philosophical position that I alone exist or I alone am conscious

Tendency to ignore the left side of the body or its surroundings

Sensory network that monitors the surface of the body and its movements

Property (found in long-term potentiation) that highly active synapses become strengthened but less active synapses do not

Combination of effects of activity from two or more synapses onto a single neuron

Those who have undergone damage to the corpus callosum

Part of the CNS found within the spinal column; it communicates with the sense organs and muscles below the level of the head

SPONTANEOUS FIRING RATE

SRY GENE

STARTLE REFLEX

STEM CELLS

STEREOTAXIC INSTRUMENT

STEROID HORMONE

STIMULANT DRUGS

STRABISMUS

Sex-region Y gene, which causes the primitive gonads to develop into testes

Periodic production of action potentials by a neuron in the absence of synaptic input

Undifferentiated cells that can divide and produce daughter cells that develop more specialized properties

Response that one makes after a sudden, unexpected loud noise or similar sudden stimulus

Hormone that contains four carbon rings

Device for the precise placement of electrodes in the head

Condition in which the two eyes point in different directions

Drugs that tend to produce excitement, alertness, elevated mood, decreased fatigue, and sometimes increased motor activity

STRESS

STRETCH REFLEX

STROKE
(CEREBROVASCULAR
ACCIDENT)

SUBFORNICAL ORGAN (SFO)

SUBSTANCE-INDUCED
PSYCHOTIC DISORDER

SUBSTANCE P

SUBSTANTIA NIGRA

SUPERIOR COLLICULUS

Reflexive contraction of a muscle in response to a stretch of that muscle

Nonspecific response of the body to any demand made upon it

Brain structure adjoining the third ventricle of the brain, where its cells monitor blood volume and relay information to the preoptic area of the hypothalamus

Temporary loss of normal blood flow to a brain area

Neurotransmitter released by nerves that are sensitive to pain

Condition that includes hallucinations and delusions, provoked by large, repeated doses of a drug

Swelling on either side of the tectum, responsible for certain aspects of vision, including eye movements

Midbrain area that gives rise to a dopamine-containing pathway

SUPERTASTERS

SUPPLEMENTARY MOTOR
CORTEX

SUPRACHIASMATIC NUCLEUS
(SCN)

SUPRAOPTIC NUCLEUS

SYMPATHETIC NERVOUS SYSTEM

SYNAPSE

SYNAPTOGENESIS

SYNESTHESIA

Area of the frontal cortex, active during preparation for a rapid sequence of movements

People with heightened sensitivity to taste

One of two areas of the hypothalamus that controls secretion of vasopressin

Area of the hypothalamus, located just above the optic chiasm, that constitutes the biological clock

Point of communication at the gap between two neurons or between a neuron and a muscle

Network of nerves that prepare the body's organs for vigorous activity

Experience of one sense in response to stimulation of another sense

Formation of synapses

TARDIVE DYSKINESIA

TASTE BUDS

TAU PROTEIN

TECTUM

TEGMENTUM

TEMPORAL LOBE

TEMPORAL SUMMATION

TESTIS

Structures on the tongue that contain taste receptors	Side effect of neuroleptic drugs characterized by tremors and other involuntary movements
Roof of the midbrain	Part of the intracellular support structure of a neuron
Lateral portion of each hemisphere, near the temples	Intermediate level of the midbrain
Male gonad that produces testosterone and sperm	Cumulative effect as a result of repeated synaptic stimulation within a brief time

THIAMINE (VITAMIN B1)

THRESHOLD OF EXCITATION

TINNITUS

TISSUE PLASMINOGEN
ACTIVATOR (tPA)

TRANSCRANIAL MAGNETIC
STIMULATION

TRANSMITTER-GATED CHANNEL

TRANSPORTER

TRICHROMATIC THEORY (OR
YOUNG-HELMHOLTZ THEORY)

Level of depolarization at which a brief stimulation triggers a rapid, massive electrical change by the membrane

Chemical necessary for the metabolism of glucose

Drug that breaks up blood clots

Frequent or constant ringing in the ears

Ion channel that opens temporarily when a neurotransmitter binds to it

Application of an intense magnetic field to a portion of the scalp to influence the neurons below the magnet

Theory that we perceive color through the relative rates of response by three kinds of cones, with each kind maximally sensitive to a different set of wavelengths

Membrane protein responsible for the reuptake of a neurotransmitter after its release

TRICYCLIC

TURNOVER

TYPE I (TYPE A) ALCOHOLISM

TYPE II (TYPE B) ALCOHOLISM

UNCONDITIONED RESPONSE
(UCR)

UNCONDITIONED STIMULUS
(UCS)

UNIPOLAR DEPRESSION

VAGUS NERVE

Release and resynthesis of a neurotransmitter

Drug that prevents the presynaptic neuron that releases serotonin or catecholamine molecules from reabsorbing them

Severe alcohol abuse with a strong genetic basis and rapid onset early in life; much more common in men

Generally less severe type of alcohol abuse with a gradual onset and only a weak genetic predisposition; occurs about equally in men and women

Stimulus that automatically evokes an unconditioned response

Response automatically evoked by an unconditioned stimulus

Tenth cranial nerve, which has branches to and from the stomach and several other organs; it conveys information about the stretching of the stomach walls

Mood disorder with only one extreme (or pole), generally depression

VASOPRESSIN
(ANTIDIURETIC HORMONE)

VEGETATIVE STATE

VENTRAL

VENTRAL STREAM

VENTRICLE

VENTROMEDIAL
HYPOTHALAMUS (VMH)

VESICLES

VESTIBULAR NUCLEUS

Condition in which someone has decreased brain activity and alternates between wakefulness and sleep but shows only limited responsiveness, such as increased heart rate in response to a painful stimulus

Pituitary hormone that raises blood pressure and enables the kidneys to reabsorb water and therefore to secrete highly concentrated urine

Visual paths in the temporal cortex, sometimes known as the "what" pathway

Located toward the stomach, away from the back (dorsal) side

Region of the hypothalamus in which damage leads to faster stomach emptying and increased secretion of insulin

Any of the four fluid-filled cavities in the brain

Cluster of neurons in the brainstem, primarily responsible for motor responses to vestibular sensation

Tiny, nearly spherical packets near the axon terminals filled with the neurotransmitter

VISUAL AGNOSIA

VISUAL FIELD

VOLLEY PRINCIPLE

VOLTAGE-GATED CHANNEL

VOMERONASAL ORGAN
(VNO)

WERNICKE'S APHASIA
(FLUENT APHASIA)

WERNICKE'S AREA

WHITE MATTER

Area of the world that an individual can see at any time

Impaired ability to identify visual objects despite otherwise satisfactory vision

Membrane channel whose permeability to sodium (or some other ion) depends on the voltage difference across the membrane

Tenet that a sound wave of a moderately high pitch may produce a volley of impulses by various fibers even if no individual fiber can produce impulses in synchrony with the sound waves

Condition marked by poor language comprehension and great difficulty remembering the names of objects

Set of receptors located near, but separate from, the olfactory receptors

Area of the nervous system consisting mostly of myelinated axons

Portion of the human left temporal lobe associated with language comprehension

WILLIAMS SYNDROME

WOLFFIAN DUCTS

WORKING MEMORY

X CHROMOSOME

Y CHROMOSOME

ZEITGEBER

Early precursors to male reproductive structures

Type of mental retardation in which the person has relatively good language skills in spite of extremely limited abilities in other regards

Chromosome of which female mammals have two and males have one

Temporary storage of memories while we are working with them or attending to them

Stimulus that resets a biological clock

Chromosome of which female mammals have none and males have one